Learn You a Haskell for Great Good!

A Beginner's Guide

Miran Lipovača

no starch
press

San Francisco

LEARN YOU A HASKELL FOR GREAT GOOD! Copyright © 2011 Miran Lipovača

Fifth printing

16 15 14   5 6 7 8 9

ISBN-10: 1-59327-283-9
ISBN-13: 978-1-59327-283-8

Publisher: William Pollock
Production Editors: Ansel Staton and Serena Yang
Cover and Interior Design: Octopod Studios
Developmental Editor: Keith Fancher
Technical Reviewer: Samuel Hughes
Copyeditor: Marilyn Smith
Compositor: Alison Law
Proofreader: Ellen Brink
Indexer: Valerie Haynes Perry

For information on distribution, translations, or bulk sales, please contact No Starch Press, Inc. directly:

No Starch Press, Inc.
245 8th Street, San Francisco, CA 94103
phone: 415.863.9900; info@nostarch.com; www.nostarch.com

Library of Congress Cataloging-in-Publication Data
Lipovaca, Miran.
 Learn you a Haskell for great good! : a beginner's guide / by Miran Lipovaca.
     p. cm.
 ISBN-13: 978-1-59327-283-8
 ISBN-10: 1-59327-283-9
 1. Haskell (Computer program language) I. Title.
QA76.73.H37L69 2012
005.1'3-dc22
                                    2011000790

ᵔing & Li
a Ilvfrᵹ

PRAISE FOR *LEARN YOU A HASKELL FOR GREAT GOOD!*

"The thing that's most impressive about *Learn You a Haskell for Great Good!* is how well written it is. This book is just fantastic."
—GREGORY COLLINS, GOOGLE SWITZERLAND

"Managed to walk me through all important Haskell concepts without ever making any of the material sound complicated. A good introduction to functional programming."
—MARIJN HAVERBEKE, AUTHOR OF *ELOQUENT JAVASCRIPT*

"This is a fantastic book and I highly recommend it as the first book on Haskell—and possibly even the second."
—MICHAEL FOGUS, AUTHOR OF *THE JOY OF CLOJURE*

"A fantastic, fun, thorough introduction to Haskell, spiced up by Miran's great sense of humor and zany illustrations."
—BRENT YORGEY, THE MATH LESS TRAVELED

"Miran Lipovača has done a fantastic job of writing a book aimed at beginning Haskell programmers. I like his very straightforward writing style of introducing each topic with the minimum of complexity."
—BRYAN BELL, MATH AND MORE

"This is a remarkable book and may be just what this beautiful language was missing."
—MICHAEL KOHL, CITIZEN428

"The best way I know to obtain the Haskell foundation you need for fluency."
—JEREMY BOWERS, JERF.ORG

"A terrific book. It takes what might otherwise seem impenetrable mathy-code and makes it fun and approachable."
—SIMON REYNOLDS

BRIEF CONTENTS

CONTENTS IN DETAIL

6
MODULES
87

7
MAKING OUR OWN TYPES AND TYPE CLASSES
109

8
INPUT AND OUTPUT

9
MORE INPUT AND MORE OUTPUT

10
FUNCTIONALLY SOLVING PROBLEMS

203

11
APPLICATIVE FUNCTORS

217

INTRODUCTION

Haskell is fun, and that's what it's all about!

This book is aimed at people who have experience programming in imperative languages—such as C++, Java, and Python—and now want to try out Haskell. But even if you don't have any significant programming experience, I'll bet a smart person like you will be able to follow along and learn Haskell.

My first reaction to Haskell was that the language was just too weird. But after getting over that initial hurdle, it was smooth sailing. Even if Haskell seems strange to you at first, don't give up. Learning Haskell is almost like learning to program for the first time all over again. It's fun, and it forces you to think differently.

NOTE *If you ever get really stuck, the IRC channel #haskell on the freenode network is a great place to ask questions. The people there tend to be nice, patient, and understanding. They're a great resource for Haskell newbies.*

So, What's Haskell?

Haskell is a *purely functional* programming language.

In *imperative* programming languages, you give the computer a sequence of tasks, which it then executes. While executing them, the computer can change state. For instance, you can set the variable a to 5 and then do some stuff that might change the value of a. There are also flow-control structures for executing instructions several times, such as for and while loops.

Purely functional programming is different. You don't tell the computer what to do—you tell it *what stuff is*. For instance, you can tell the computer that the factorial of a number is the product of every integer from 1 to that number or that the sum of a list of numbers is the first number plus the sum of the remaining numbers. You can express both of these operations as *functions*.

In functional programming, you *can't* set a variable to one value and then set it to something else later on. If you say a is 5, you can't just change your mind and say it's something else. After all, you said it was 5. (What are you, some kind of liar?)

In purely functional languages, a function has no *side effects*. The only thing a function can do is calculate something and return the result. At first, this seems limiting, but it actually has some very nice consequences. If a function is called twice with the same parameters, it's guaranteed to return the same result both times. This property is called *referential transparency*. It lets the programmer easily deduce (and even prove) that a function is correct. You can then build more complex functions by gluing these simple functions together.

Haskell is *lazy*. This means that unless specifically told otherwise, Haskell won't execute functions until it needs to show you a result. This is made possible by referential transparency. If you know that the result of a function depends only on the parameters that function is given, it doesn't matter when you actually calculate the result of the function. Haskell, being a lazy language, takes advantage of this fact and defers actually computing results for as long as possible. Once you want your results to be displayed, Haskell will do just the bare minimum computation required to display them. Laziness also allows you to make seemingly infinite data structures, because only the parts of the data structures that you choose to display will actually be computed.

Let's look at an example of Haskell's laziness. Say you have a list of numbers, xs = [1,2,3,4,5,6,7,8], and a function called doubleMe that doubles every element and returns the result as a new list. If you want to multiply your list by 8, your code might look something like this:

```
doubleMe(doubleMe(doubleMe(xs)))
```

An imperative language would probably pass through the list once, make a copy, and then return it. It would then pass through the list another two times, making copies each time, and return the result.

In a lazy language, calling doubleMe on a list without forcing it to show you the result just makes the program tell you, "Yeah yeah, I'll do it later!" Once you want to see the result, the first doubleMe calls the second one and says it wants the result immediately. Then the second one says the same thing to the third one, and the third one reluctantly gives back a doubled 1, which is 2. The second doubleMe receives that and returns 4 to the first one. The first doubleMe then doubles this result and tells you that the first element in the final resulting list is 8. Because of Haskell's laziness, the doubleMe calls pass through the list just once, and only when you really need that to happen.

Haskell is *statically typed*. This means that when you compile your program, the compiler knows which piece of code is a number, which is a string, and so on. Static typing means that a lot of possible errors can be caught at compile time. If you try to add together a number and a string, for example, the compiler will whine at you.

Haskell uses a very good type system that has *type inference*. This means that you don't need to explicitly label every piece of code with a type, because Haskell's type system can intelligently figure it out. For example, if you say a = 5 + 4, you don't need to tell Haskell that a is a number—it can figure that out by itself. Type inference makes it easier for you to write code that's more general. If you write a function that takes two parameters and adds them together, but you don't explicitly state their type, the function will work on any two parameters that act like numbers.

Haskell is *elegant and concise*. Because it uses a lot of high-level concepts, Haskell programs are usually shorter than their imperative equivalents. Shorter programs are easier to maintain and have fewer bugs.

Haskell was made by some really smart guys (with PhDs). Work on Haskell began in 1987 when a committee of researchers got together to design a kick-ass language. The Haskell Report, which defines a stable version of the language, was published in 1999.

What You Need to Dive In

In short, to get started with Haskell, you need a text editor and a Haskell compiler. You probably already have your favorite text editor installed, so we won't waste time on that. The most popular Haskell compiler is the Glasgow Haskell Compiler (GHC), which we will be using throughout this book.

The best way to get what you need is to download the *Haskell Platform*. The Haskell Platform includes not only the GHC compiler but also a bunch of useful Haskell libraries! To get the Haskell Platform for your system, go to *http://hackage.haskell.org/platform/* and follow the instructions for your operating system.

GHC can compile Haskell scripts (usually with an *.hs* extension), and it also has an interactive mode. From there, you can load functions from scripts and then call them directly to see immediate results. Especially when you're learning, it's much easier to use the interactive mode than it is to compile and run your code every time you make a change.

Once you've installed the Haskell Platform, open a new terminal window, assuming you're on a Linux or Mac OS X system. If your operating system of choice is Windows, go to the command prompt. Once there, type `ghci` and press ENTER to start the interactive mode. (If your system fails to find the GHCi program, you can try rebooting your computer.)

If you've defined some functions in a script—for example, *myfunctions.hs*—you can load these functions into GHCi by typing :l myfunctions. (Make sure that *myfunctions.hs* is in the same folder from which you started GHCi.)

If you change the *.hs* script, run :l myfunctions to load the file again or run :r, which reloads the current script. My usual workflow is to define some functions in an *.hs* file, load it into GHCi, mess around with it, change the file, and repeat. This is what we'll be doing in this book.

Acknowledgments

Thanks to everyone who sent in corrections, suggestions, and words of encouragement. Also thanks to Keith, Sam, and Marilyn for making me look like a real writer.

1

STARTING OUT

If you're the horrible sort of person who doesn't read introductions, you might want to go back and read the last section anyway—it explains how to use this book, as well as how to load functions with GHC.

First, let's start GHC's interactive mode and call some functions, so we can get a very basic feel for Haskell. Open a terminal and type `ghci`. You will be greeted with something like this:

```
GHCi, version 6.12.3: http://www.haskell.org/ghc/   :? for help
Loading package ghc-prim ... linking ... done.
Loading package integer-gmp ... linking ... done.
Loading package base ... linking ... done.
Loading package ffi-1.0 ... linking ... done.
```

NOTE   *GHCi's default prompt is* Prelude>, *but we'll be using* ghci> *as our prompt for the examples in this book. To make your prompt match the book's, enter* :set prompt "ghci> " *into GHCi. If you don't want to do this every time you run GHCi, create a file called* .ghci *in your home folder and set its contents to* :set prompt "ghci> ".

Congratulations, you're in GHCi! Now let's try some simple arithmetic:

```
ghci> 2 + 15
17
ghci> 49 * 100
4900
ghci> 1892 - 1472
420
ghci> 5 / 2
2.5
```

If we use several operators in one expression, Haskell will execute them in an order that takes into account the precedence of the operators. For instance, * has higher precedence than -, so 50 * 100 - 4999 is treated as (50 * 100) - 4999.

We can also use parentheses to explicitly specify the order of operations, like this:

```
ghci> (50 * 100) - 4999
1
ghci> 50 * 100 - 4999
1
ghci> 50 * (100 - 4999)
-244950
```

Pretty cool, huh? (Yeah, I know it's not, yet, but bear with me.)

One pitfall to watch out for is negative number constants. It's always best to surround these with parentheses wherever they occur in an arithmetic expression. For example, entering 5 * -3 will make GHCi yell at you, but entering 5 * (-3) will work just fine.

Boolean algebra is also straightforward in Haskell. Like many other programming languages, Haskell has the Boolean values True and False, and uses the && operator for conjunction (Boolean *and*), the || operator for disjunction (Boolean *or*), and the not operator to negate a True or False value:

```
ghci> True && False
False
ghci> True && True
True
ghci> False || True
True
ghci> not False
True
ghci> not (True && True)
False
```

We can test two values for equality or inequality with the == and /= operators, like this:

```
ghci> 5 == 5
True
ghci> 1 == 0
False
ghci> 5 /= 5
False
ghci> 5 /= 4
True
ghci> "hello" == "hello"
True
```

Watch out when mixing and matching values, however! If we enter something like 5 + "llama", we get the following error message:

```
No instance for (Num [Char])
arising from a use of `+' at <interactive>:1:0-9
Possible fix: add an instance declaration for (Num [Char])
In the expression: 5 + "llama"
In the definition of `it': it = 5 + "llama"
```

What GHCi is telling us here is that "llama" is not a number, so it does not know how to add it to 5. The + operator expects both of its inputs to be numbers.

On the other hand, the == operator works on any two items that can be compared, with one catch: they both have to be of the same type. For instance, if we tried entering True == 5, GHCi would complain.

NOTE   *5 + 4.0 is a valid expression, because although 4.0 isn't an integer, 5 is sneaky and can act like either an integer or a floating-point number. In this case, 5 adapts to match the type of the floating-point value 4.0.*

We'll take a closer look at types a bit later.

Calling Functions

You may not have realized it, but we've actually been using functions this whole time. For instance, * is a function that takes two numbers and multiplies them. As you've seen, we apply (or *call*) it by sandwiching it between the two numbers we want to multiply. This is called an *infix* function.

Most functions, however, are *prefix* functions. When calling prefix functions in Haskell, the function name comes first, then a space, then its parameters (also separated by spaces). As an example, we'll try calling one of the most boring functions in Haskell, succ:

```
ghci> succ 8
9
```

The succ function takes one parameter that can be anything that has a well-defined successor, and returns that value. The successor of an integer value is just the next higher number.

Now let's call two prefix functions that take multiple parameters, min and max:

```
ghci> min 9 10
9
ghci> min 3.4 3.2
3.2
ghci> max 100 101
101
```

The min and max functions each take two parameters that can be put in some order (like numbers!), and they return the one that's smaller or larger, respectively.

Function application has the highest precedence of all the operations in Haskell. In other words, these two statements are equivalent.

```
ghci> succ 9 + max 5 4 + 1
16
ghci> (succ 9) + (max 5 4) + 1
16
```

This means that if we want to get the successor of $9 * 10$, we couldn't simply write

```
ghci> succ 9 * 10
```

Because of the precedence of operations, this would evaluate as the successor of 9 (which is 10) multiplied by 10, yielding 100. To get the result we want, we need to instead enter

```
ghci> succ (9 * 10)
```

This returns 91.

If a function takes two parameters, we can also call it as an infix function by surrounding its name with backticks (`). For instance, the div function takes two integers and executes an integral division, as follows:

```
ghci> div 92 10
9
```

However, when we call it like that, there may be some confusion as to which number is being divided by which. By using backticks, we can call it as an infix function, and suddenly it seems much clearer:

```
ghci> 92 `div` 10
9
```

Many programmers who are used to imperative languages tend to stick to the notion that parentheses should denote function application, and they have trouble adjusting to the Haskell way of doing things. Just remember, if you see something like bar (bar 3), it means that we're first calling the bar function with 3 as the parameter, then passing that result to the bar function again. The equivalent expression in C would be something like bar(bar(3)).

Baby's First Functions

The syntax of a function definition is similar to that of a function call: the function name is followed by parameters, which are separated by spaces. But then the parameter list is followed by the = operator, and the code that makes up the body of the function follows that.

As an example, we'll write a simple function that takes a number and multiplies it by two. Open up your favorite text editor and type in the following:

```
doubleMe x = x + x
```

Save this file as *baby.hs*. Now run ghci, making sure that *baby.hs* is in your current directory. Once in GHCi, enter **:l baby** to load the file. Now we can play with our new function:

```
ghci> :l baby
[1 of 1] Compiling Main             ( baby.hs, interpreted )
Ok, modules loaded: Main.
ghci> doubleMe 9
18
ghci> doubleMe 8.3
16.6
```

Because + works on integers as well as on floating point numbers (indeed, on anything that can be considered a number), our function also works with any of these types.

Now let's make a function that takes two numbers, multiplies each by two, then adds them together. Append the following code to *baby.hs*:

```
doubleUs x y = x * 2 + y * 2
```

NOTE *Functions in Haskell don't have to be defined in any particular order, so it doesn't matter which function comes first in the* baby.hs *file.*

Now save the file, and enter **:l baby** in GHCi to load your new function. Testing this function yields predictable results:

```
ghci> doubleUs 4 9
26
ghci> doubleUs 2.3 34.2
73.0
ghci> doubleUs 28 88 + doubleMe 123
478
```

Functions that you define can also call each other. With that in mind, we could redefine doubleUs in the following way:

```
doubleUs x y = doubleMe x + doubleMe y
```

This is a very simple example of a common pattern you will see when using Haskell: Basic, obviously correct functions can be combined to form more complex functions. This is a great way to avoid code repetition. For example, what if one day mathematicians figure out that 2 and 3 are actually the same, and you have to change your program? You could just redefine doubleMe to be x + x + x, and since doubleUs calls doubleMe, it would now also automatically work correctly in this strange new world where 2 is equal to 3.

Now let's write a function that multiplies a number by 2, but only if that number is less than or equal to 100 (because numbers bigger than 100 are big enough as it is!).

```
doubleSmallNumber x = if x > 100
                        then x
                        else x*2
```

This example introduces Haskell's if statement. You're probably already familiar with if statements from other languages, but what makes Haskell's unique is that the else part is mandatory.

Programs in imperative languages are essentially a series of steps that the computer executes when the program is run. When there is an if statement that doesn't have a corresponding else, and the condition isn't met, then the steps that fall under the if statement don't get executed. Thus, in imperative languages, an if statement can just do nothing.

On the other hand, a Haskell program is a collection of functions. Functions are used to transform data values into result values, and every function should return some value, which can in turn be used by another function. Since every function has to return something, this implies that every if has to have a corresponding else. Otherwise, you could write a function that has a return value when a certain condition is met but doesn't have one when that condition isn't met! Briefly: Haskell's if is an *expression* that must return a value, and not a statement.

Let's say we want a function that adds one to every number that would be produced by our previous doubleSmallNumber function. The body of this new function would look like this:

```
doubleSmallNumber' x = (if x > 100 then x else x*2) + 1
```

Note the placement of the parentheses. If we had omitted them, the function would only add one if x is less than or equal to 100. Also note the apostrophe (') at the end of the function's name. The apostrophe doesn't have any special meaning in Haskell's syntax, which means it's a valid character to use in a function name. We usually use ' to denote either a *strict* version of a function (i.e., one that isn't lazy), or a slightly modified version of a function or variable with a similar name.

Since ' is a valid character for function names, we can write a function that looks like this:

```
conanO'Brien = "It's a-me, Conan O'Brien!"
```

There are two things to note here. The first is that we didn't capitalize *Conan* in the name of the function. In Haskell, functions can't begin with capital letters. (We'll see why a bit later.) The second thing to note is that conanO'Brien doesn't take any parameters. This means that it's not a function but a *definition* or a *name*. Because we cannot change what names (or functions) mean once we have defined them, *conanO'Brien* and the string "It's a-me, Conan O'Brien!" can be used interchangeably.

An Intro to Lists

Lists in Haskell are *homogeneous* data structures, which means they store several elements of the same type. We can have a list of integers or a list of characters, for example, but we can't have a list made up of both integers and characters.

Lists are surrounded by square brackets, and the list values are separated by commas:

```
ghci> let lostNumbers = [4,8,15,16,23,42]
ghci> lostNumbers
[4,8,15,16,23,42]
```

NOTE *Use the let keyword to define a name in GHCi. Entering* let a = 1 *in GHCi is equivalent to writing* a = 1 *in a script, then loading it with* :l.

Concatenation

One of the most common operations when working with lists is concatenation. In Haskell, this is done using the ++ operator:

```
ghci> [1,2,3,4] ++ [9,10,11,12]
[1,2,3,4,9,10,11,12]
ghci> "hello" ++ " " ++ "world"
"hello world"
ghci> ['w','o'] ++ ['o','t']
"woot"
```

NOTE *In Haskell, strings are really just lists of characters. For example, the string* "hello" *is actually the same as the list* ['h','e','l','l','o']. *Because of this, we can use list functions on strings, which is really handy.*

Be careful when repeatedly using the ++ operator on long strings. When you put together two lists, Haskell has to walk through the entire first list (the one on the left side of ++). That's not a problem when dealing with smaller lists, but appending something to the end of a list with fifty million entries is going to take a while.

However, adding something to the beginning of a list is a nearly instantaneous operation. We do this with the : operator (also called the *cons* operator):

```
ghci> 'A':" SMALL CAT"
"A SMALL CAT"
ghci> 5:[1,2,3,4,5]
[5,1,2,3,4,5]
```

Notice how in the first example, : takes a character and a list of characters (a string) as its arguments. Similarly, in the second example, : takes a number and a list of numbers. The first argument to the : operator always needs to be a single item of the same type as the values in the list it's being added to.

The ++ operator, on the other hand, always takes two lists as arguments. Even if you're only adding a single element to the end of a list with ++, you still have to surround that item with square brackets, so Haskell will treat it like a list:

```
ghci> [1,2,3,4] ++ [5]
[1,2,3,4,5]
```

Writing [1,2,3,4] ++ 5 is wrong, because both parameters to ++ should be lists, and 5 isn't a list; it's a number.

Interestingly, in Haskell, [1,2,3] is just syntactic sugar for 1:2:3:[]. [] is an empty list. If we prepend 3 to that, it becomes [3]. Then if we prepend 2 to that, it becomes [2,3], and so on.

[], [[]] and [[],[],[]] are all different things. The first is an empty list, the second is a list that contains one empty list, and the third is a list that contains three empty lists.

Accessing List Elements

If you want to get an element of a list by index, use the !! operator. As with most programming languages, the indices start at 0:

```
ghci> "Steve Buscemi" !! 6
'B'
ghci> [9.4,33.2,96.2,11.2,23.25] !! 1
33.2
```

However, if you try (say) to get the sixth element from a list that only has four elements, you'll get an error, so be careful!

Lists Inside Lists

Lists can contain lists as elements, and lists can contain lists that contain lists, and so on. . . .

```
ghci> let b = [[1,2,3,4],[5,3,3,3],[1,2,2,3,4],[1,2,3]]
ghci> b
[[1,2,3,4],[5,3,3,3],[1,2,2,3,4],[1,2,3]]
ghci> b ++ [[1,1,1,1]]
[[1,2,3,4],[5,3,3,3],[1,2,2,3,4],[1,2,3],[1,1,1,1]]
ghci> [6,6,6]:b
[[6,6,6],[1,2,3,4],[5,3,3,3],[1,2,2,3,4],[1,2,3]]
ghci> b !! 2
[1,2,2,3,4]
```

Lists within a list can be of different lengths, but they can't be of different types. Just like you can't have a list that has some characters and some numbers as elements, you also can't have a list that contains some lists of characters and some lists of numbers.

Comparing Lists

Lists can be compared if the items they contain can be compared. When using <, <=, >= and > to compare two lists, they are compared in lexicographical order. This means that first the two list heads are compared, and if they're equal, the second elements are compared. If the second elements are also equal, the third elements are compared, and so on, until differing elements are found. The order of the two lists is determined by the order of the first pair of differing elements.

For example, when we evaluate [3,4,2] < [3,4,3], Haskell sees that 3 and 3 are equal, so it compares 4 and 4. Those two are also equal, so it compares 2 and 3. 2 is smaller than 3, so it comes to the conclusion that the first list is smaller than the second one. The same goes for <=, >=, and >.

```
ghci> [3,2,1] > [2,1,0]
True
ghci> [3,2,1] > [2,10,100]
True
ghci> [3,4,2] < [3,4,3]
True
ghci> [3,4,2] > [2,4]
True
ghci> [3,4,2] == [3,4,2]
True
```

Also, a nonempty list is always considered to be greater than an empty one. This makes the ordering of two lists well defined in all cases, including when one is a proper initial segment of the other.

More List Operations

Here are some more basic list functions, followed by examples of their usage.

The head function takes a list and returns its head, or first element:

```
ghci> head [5,4,3,2,1]
5
```

The tail function takes a list and returns its tail. In other words, it chops off a list's head:

```
ghci> tail [5,4,3,2,1]
[4,3,2,1]
```

The last function returns a list's last element:

```
ghci> last [5,4,3,2,1]
1
```

The init function takes a list and returns everything except its last element:

```
ghci> init [5,4,3,2,1]
[5,4,3,2]
```

To help us visualize these functions, we can think of a list as a monster, like this:

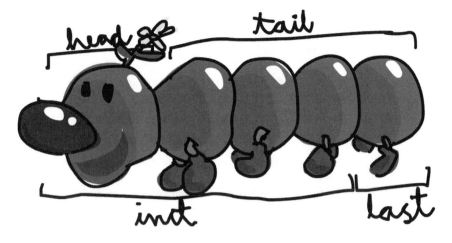

But what happens if we try to get the head of an empty list?

```
ghci> head []
*** Exception: Prelude.head: empty list
```

Oh my—it blows up in our face! If there's no monster, it doesn't have a head. When using head, tail, last, and init, be careful not to use them on empty lists. This error cannot be caught at compile time, so it's always good practice to take precautions against accidentally telling Haskell to give you elements from an empty list.

The length function takes a list and returns its length:

```
ghci> length [5,4,3,2,1]
5
```

The null function checks if a list is empty. If it is, it returns True, otherwise it returns False.

```
ghci> null [1,2,3]
False
ghci> null []
True
```

The reverse function reverses a list:

```
ghci> reverse [5,4,3,2,1]
[1,2,3,4,5]
```

The take function takes a number and a list. It extracts the specified number elements from the beginning of the list, like this:

```
ghci> take 3 [5,4,3,2,1]
[5,4,3]
ghci> take 1 [3,9,3]
[3]
ghci> take 5 [1,2]
[1,2]
ghci> take 0 [6,6,6]
[]
```

If we try to take more elements than there are in the list, Haskell just returns the entire list. If we take 0 elements, we get an empty list.

The drop function works in a similar way, only it drops (at most) the specified number of elements from the beginning of a list:

```
ghci> drop 3 [8,4,2,1,5,6]
[1,5,6]
ghci> drop 0 [1,2,3,4]
[1,2,3,4]
ghci> drop 100 [1,2,3,4]
[]
```

The maximum function takes a list of items that can be put in some kind of order and returns the largest element. The minimum function is similar, but it returns the smallest item:

```
ghci> maximum [1,9,2,3,4]
9
ghci> minimum [8,4,2,1,5,6]
1
```

The sum function takes a list of numbers and returns their sum. The product function takes a list of numbers and returns their product:

```
ghci> sum [5,2,1,6,3,2,5,7]
31
ghci> product [6,2,1,2]
24
ghci> product [1,2,5,6,7,9,2,0]
0
```

The elem function takes an item and a list of items and tells us if that item is an element of the list. It's usually called as an infix function because it's easier to read that way.

```
ghci> 4 `elem` [3,4,5,6]
True
ghci> 10 `elem` [3,4,5,6]
False
```

Texas Ranges

What if we need a list made up of the numbers between 1 and 20? Sure, we could just type them all out, but that's not a solution for gentlemen who demand excellence from their programming languages. Instead, we'll use *ranges*. Ranges are used to make lists composed of elements that can be *enumerated*, or counted off in order.

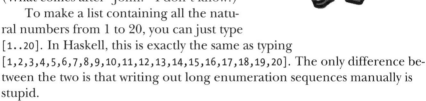

For example, numbers can be enumerated: 1, 2, 3, 4, and so on. Characters can also be enumerated: the alphabet is an enumeration of characters from A to Z. Names, however, can't be enumerated. (What comes after "John?" I don't know!)

To make a list containing all the natural numbers from 1 to 20, you can just type [1..20]. In Haskell, this is exactly the same as typing [1,2,3,4,5,6,7,8,9,10,11,12,13,14,15,16,17,18,19,20]. The only difference between the two is that writing out long enumeration sequences manually is stupid.

Here are a few more examples:

```
ghci> [1..20]
[1,2,3,4,5,6,7,8,9,10,11,12,13,14,15,16,17,18,19,20]
ghci> ['a'..'z']
"abcdefghijklmnopqrstuvwxyz"
ghci> ['K'..'Z']
"KLMNOPQRSTUVWXYZ"
```

You can also specify a *step* between items in your range. What if we want a list of every even number between 1 and 20? Or every third number between 1 and 20? It's simply a matter of separating the first two elements with a comma and specifying the upper limit:

```
ghci> [2,4..20]
[2,4,6,8,10,12,14,16,18,20]
ghci> [3,6..20]
[3,6,9,12,15,18]
```

While they are pretty convenient, ranges with steps aren't always as smart as people expect them to be. For example, you can't enter [1,2,4,8,16..100] and expect to get all the powers of 2 that are no greater than 100. For one thing, you can only specify a single step size. Also, some sequences that aren't arithmetic can't be specified unambiguously by giving only their first few terms.

NOTE *To make a list with all the numbers from 20 down to 1, you can't just type [20..1], you have to type [20,19..1]. When you use a range without steps (like [20..1]), Haskell will start with an empty list and then keep increasing the starting element by one until it reaches or surpasses the end element in the range. Because 20 is already greater than 1, the result will just be an empty list.*

You can also use ranges to make infinite lists by not specifying an upper limit. For example, let's create a list containing the first 24 multiples of 13. Here's one way to do it:

```
ghci> [13,26..24*13]
[13,26,39,52,65,78,91,104,117,130,143,156,169,182,195,208,221,234,247,260,273,286,299,312]
```

But there's actually a better way—using an infinite list:

```
ghci> take 24 [13,26..]
[13,26,39,52,65,78,91,104,117,130,143,156,169,182,195,208,221,234,247,260,273,286,299,312]
```

Because Haskell is *lazy*, it won't try to evaluate the entire infinite list immediately (which is good because it would never finish anyway). Instead, it will wait to see which elements you need to get from that infinite list. In the above example, it sees that you just want the first 24 elements, and it gladly obliges.

Here are a few functions that can be used to produce long or infinite lists:

- cycle takes a list and replicates its elements indefinitely to form an infinite list. If you try to display the result, it will go on forever, so make sure to slice it off somewhere:

  ```
  ghci> take 10 (cycle [1,2,3])
  [1,2,3,1,2,3,1,2,3,1]
  ghci> take 12 (cycle "LOL ")
  "LOL LOL LOL "
  ```

- repeat takes an element and produces an infinite list of just that element. It's like cycling a list with only one element:

  ```
  ghci> take 10 (repeat 5)
  [5,5,5,5,5,5,5,5,5,5]
  ```

- replicate is an easier way to create a list composed of a single item. It takes the length of the list and the item to replicate, as follows:

```
ghci> replicate 3 10
[10,10,10]
```

One final note about ranges: watch out when using them with floating-point numbers! Because floating-point numbers, by their nature, only have finite precision, using them in ranges can yield some pretty funky results, as you can see here:

```
ghci> [0.1, 0.3 .. 1]
[0.1,0.3,0.5,0.7,0.8999999999999999,1.0999999999999999]
```

I'm a List Comprehension

List comprehensions are a way to filter, transform, and combine lists.

They're very similar to the mathematical concept of *set comprehensions*. Set comprehensions are normally used for building sets out of other sets. An example of a simple set comprehension is: $\{2 \cdot x \mid x \in \mathbf{N}, x \leq 10\}$. The exact syntax used here isn't crucial—what's important is that this statement says, "take all the natural numbers less than or equal to 10, multiply each one by 2, and use these results to create a new set."

If we wanted to write the same thing in Haskell, we could do something like this with list operations: take 10 [2,4..]. However, we could also do the same thing using list comprehensions, like this:

```
ghci> [x*2 | x <- [1..10]]
[2,4,6,8,10,12,14,16,18,20]
```

Let's take a closer look at the list comprehension in this example to better understand list comprehension syntax.

In [x*2 | x <- [1..10]], we say that we *draw* our elements from the list [1..10]. [x <- [1..10]] means that x takes on the value of each element that is drawn from [1..10]. In other words, we *bind* each element from [1..10] to x. The part before the vertical pipe (|) is the *output* of the list comprehension. The output is the part where we specify how we want the elements that we've drawn to be reflected in the resulting list. In this example, we say that we want each element that is drawn from the list [1..10] to be doubled.

This may seem longer and more complicated than the first example, but what if we want to do something more complex than just doubling these numbers? This is where list comprehensions really come in handy.

For example, let's add a condition (also called a *predicate*) to our comprehension. Predicates go at the end of the list comprehension and are separated from the rest of the comprehension by a comma. Let's say we want only the elements which, after being doubled, are greater than or equal to 12:

```
ghci> [x*2 | x <- [1..10], x*2 >= 12]
[12,14,16,18,20]
```

What if we want all numbers from 50 to 100 whose remainder when divided by 7 is 3? Easy:

```
ghci> [ x | x <- [50..100], x `mod` 7 == 3]
[52,59,66,73,80,87,94]
```

NOTE   *Weeding out parts of lists using predicates is also called* filtering.

Now for another example. Let's say we want a comprehension that replaces every odd number greater than 10 with "BANG!", and every odd number less than 10 with "BOOM!". If a number isn't odd, we throw it out of our list. For convenience, we'll put that comprehension inside a function so we can easily reuse it:

```
boomBangs xs = [ if x < 10 then "BOOM!" else "BANG!" | x <- xs, odd x]
```

NOTE   *Remember, if you're trying to define this function inside GHCi, you have to include a* let *before the function name. However, if you're defining this function inside a script and then loading that script into GHCi, you don't have to mess around with* let.

The odd function returns True when passed an odd number, otherwise it returns False. The element is included in the list only if all the predicates evaluate to True.

```
ghci> boomBangs [7..13]
["BOOM!","BOOM!","BANG!","BANG!"]
```

We can include as many predicates as we want, all separated by commas. For instance, if we wanted all numbers from 10 to 20 that are not 13, 15 or 19, we'd do:

```
ghci> [ x | x <- [10..20], x /= 13, x /= 15, x /= 19]
[10,11,12,14,16,17,18,20]
```

Not only can we have multiple predicates in list comprehensions, we can also draw values from several lists. When drawing values from several lists, every combination of elements from these lists is reflected in the resulting list:

```
ghci> [x+y | x <- [1,2,3], y <- [10,100,1000]]
[11,101,1001,12,102,1002,13,103,1003]
```

Here, x is drawn from [1,2,3] and y is drawn from [10,100,1000]. These two lists are combined in the following way. First, x becomes 1, and while x is 1, y takes on every value from [10,100,1000]. Because the output of the list comprehension is x+y, the values 11, 101, and 1001 are added to the beginning of the resulting list (1 is added to 10, 100, and 1000). After that, x becomes 2 and the same thing happens, resulting in the elements 12, 102, and 1002 being added to the resulting list. The same goes when x draws the value 3.

In this manner, each element x from [1,2,3] is combined with each element y from [10,100,1000] in all possible ways, and x+y is used to make the resulting list from those combinations.

Here's another example: if we have two lists, [2,5,10] and [8,10,11], and we want to get the products of all possible combinations of numbers in those lists, we could use the following comprehension:

```
ghci> [ x*y | x <- [2,5,10], y <- [8,10,11]]
[16,20,22,40,50,55,80,100,110]
```

As expected, the length of the new list is 9. Now, what if we wanted all possible products that are more than 50? We can just add another predicate:

```
ghci> [ x*y | x <- [2,5,10], y <- [8,10,11], x*y > 50]
[55,80,100,110]
```

For epic hilarity, let's make a list comprehension that combines a list of adjectives and a list of nouns.

```
ghci> let nouns = ["hobo","frog","pope"]
ghci> let adjectives = ["lazy","grouchy","scheming"]
ghci> [adjective ++ " " ++ noun | adjective <- adjectives, noun <- nouns]
["lazy hobo","lazy frog","lazy pope","grouchy hobo","grouchy frog",
"grouchy pope","scheming hobo","scheming frog","scheming pope"]
```

We can even use list comprehensions to write our own version of the length function! We'll call it length'. This function will replace every element in a list with 1, then add them all up with sum, yielding the length of the list.

```
length' xs = sum [1 | _ <- xs]
```

Here we use underscore (_) as a temporary variable to store the items as we draw them from the input list, since we don't actually care about the values.

Remember, strings are lists too, so we can use list comprehensions to process and produce strings. Here's an example of a function that takes a string and removes all the lowercase letters from it:

```
removeNonUppercase st = [ c | c <- st, c `elem` ['A'..'Z']]
```

The predicate here does all the work. It says that the character will be included in the new list only if it's an element of the list ['A'..'Z']. We can load the function in GHCi and test it out:

```
ghci> removeNonUppercase "Hahaha! Ahahaha!"
"HA"
ghci> removeNonUppercase "IdontLIKEFROGS"
"ILIKEFROGS"
```

You can also create nested list comprehensions if you're operating on lists that contain lists. For example, let's take a list that contains several lists of numbers and remove all the odd numbers without flattening the list:

```
ghci> let xxs = [[1,3,5,2,3,1,2,4,5],[1,2,3,4,5,6,7,8,9],[1,2,4,2,1,6,3,1,3,2,3,6]]
ghci> [ [ x | x <- xs, even x ] | xs <- xxs]
[[2,2,4],[2,4,6,8],[2,4,2,6,2,6]]
```

Here the output of the outer list comprehension is another list comprehension. A list comprehension always results in a list of something, so we know that the result here will be a list of lists of numbers.

NOTE *You can split list comprehensions across several lines to improve their readability. If you're not in GHCi, this can be a great help, especially when dealing with nested comprehensions.*

Tuples

Tuples are used to store several heterogeneous elements as a single value.

In some ways, tuples are a lot like lists. However, there are some fundamental differences. First, as mentioned, tuples are heterogeneous. This means that a single tuple can store elements of several different types. Second, tuples have a fixed size—you need to know how many elements you'll be storing ahead of time.

Tuples are surrounded by parentheses, and their components are separated by commas:

```
ghci> (1, 3)
(1,3)
ghci> (3, 'a', "hello")
(3,'a',"hello")
ghci> (50, 50.4, "hello", 'b')
(50,50.4,"hello",'b')
```

Using Tuples

As an example of when tuples would be useful, let's think about how we'd represent a two-dimensional vector in Haskell. One way would be to use a two item list, in the form of [x,y]. But suppose we wanted to make a list of vectors, to represent the corners of a two-dimensional shape in a coordinate plane. We could just create a list of lists, like this: [[1,2],[8,11],[4,5]].

The problem with this method, however, is that we could also make a list like [[1,2],[8,11,5],[4,5]] and try to use it in the place of a list of vectors. Even though it doesn't make sense as a list of vectors, Haskell has no problem with this list appearing wherever the previous list can, since both are of the same type (a list of lists of numbers). This could make it more complicated to write functions to manipulate vectors and shapes.

In contrast, a tuple of size two (also called a *pair*) and a tuple of size three (also called a *triple*) are treated as two distinct types, which means a list can't be composed of both pairs and triples. This makes tuples much more useful for representing vectors.

We can change our vectors to tuples by surrounding them with parentheses instead of square brackets, like this: [(1,2),(8,11),(4,5)]. Now, if we try to mix pairs and triples, we get an error, like this:

```
ghci> [(1,2),(8,11,5),(4,5)]
Couldn't match expected type `(t, t1)'
against inferred type `(t2, t3, t4)'
In the expression: (8, 11, 5)
In the expression: [(1, 2), (8, 11, 5), (4, 5)]
In the definition of `it': it = [(1, 2), (8, 11, 5), (4, 5)]
```

Haskell also considers tuples that have the same length but contain different types of data to be distinct types of tuples. For example, you can't make a list of tuples like [(1,2),("One",2)], because the first is a pair of numbers, and the second is a pair containing a string followed by a number.

Tuples can be used to easily represent a wide variety of data. For instance, if we wanted to represent someone's name and age in Haskell, we could use a triple: ("Christopher", "Walken", 55).

Remember, tuples are of a fixed size—you should only use them when you know in advance how many elements you'll need. The reason tuples are so rigid in this way is that, as mentioned, the size of a tuple is treated as part of its type. Unfortunately, this means that you can't write a general function to append an element to a tuple—you'd have to write a function for appending to a pair (to produce a triple), another one for appending to a triple (to produce a 4-tuple), another one for appending to a 4-tuple, and so on.

Like lists, tuples can be compared with each other if their components can be compared. However, unlike lists, you can't compare two tuples of different sizes.

Although there are singleton lists, there's no such thing as a singleton tuple. It makes sense when you think about it: a singleton tuple's properties would simply be those of the value it contains, so distinguishing a new type wouldn't give us any benefit.

Using Pairs

Storing data in pairs is very common in Haskell, and there are some useful functions in place to manipulate them. Here are two functions that operate on pairs:

- fst takes a pair and returns its first component:

```
ghci> fst (8, 11)
8
ghci> fst ("Wow", False)
"Wow"
```

- snd takes a pair and—surprise!—returns its second component:

```
ghci> snd (8, 11)
11
ghci> snd ("Wow", False)
False
```

NOTE   *These functions only operate on pairs. They won't work on triples, 4-tuples, 5-tuples, etc. We'll go over extracting data from tuples in different ways a bit later.*

The zip function is a cool way to produce a list of pairs. It takes two lists, then "zips" them together into one list by joining the matching elements into pairs. It's a really simple function, but it can be very useful when you want to combine two lists in a particular way or traverse two lists simultaneously. Here's a demonstration:

```
ghci> zip [1,2,3,4,5] [5,5,5,5,5]
[(1,5),(2,5),(3,5),(4,5),(5,5)]
ghci> zip [1..5] ["one", "two", "three", "four", "five"]
[(1,"one"),(2,"two"),(3,"three"),(4,"four"),(5,"five")]
```

Notice that because pairs can have different types in them, zip can take two lists that contain elements of different types. But what happens if the lengths of the lists don't match?

```ghci
ghci> zip [5,3,2,6,2,7,2,5,4,6,6] ["im","a","turtle"]
[(5,"im"),(3,"a"),(2,"turtle")]
```

As you can see in the above example, only as much of the longer list is used as needed—the rest is simply ignored. And because Haskell uses lazy evaluation, we can even zip finite lists with infinite lists:

```ghci
ghci> zip [1..] ["apple", "orange", "cherry", "mango"]
[(1,"apple"),(2,"orange"),(3,"cherry"),(4,"mango")]
```

Finding the Right Triangle

Let's wrap things up with a problem that combines tuples and list comprehensions. We'll use Haskell to find a right triangle that fits all of these conditions:

- The lengths of the three sides are all integers.
- The length of each side is less than or equal to 10.
- The triangle's perimeter (the sum of the side lengths) is equal to 24.

A triangle is a right triangle if one of its angles is a right angle (a 90-degree angle). Right triangles have the useful property that if you square the lengths of the sides forming the right angle and then add those squares, that sum is equal to the square of the length of the side that's opposite the right angle. In the picture, the sides that lie next to the right angle are labeled a and b, and the side opposite the right angle is labeled c. We call that side the *hypotenuse*.

As a first step, let's generate all possible triples with elements that are less than or equal to 10:

```ghci
ghci> let triples = [ (a,b,c) | c <- [1..10], a <- [1..10], b <- [1..10] ]
```

We're drawing from three lists on the right-hand side of the comprehension, and the output expression on the left combines them into a list of triples. If you evaluate triples in GHCi, you'll get a list that is 1,000 entries long, so we won't show it here.

Next, we'll filter out triples that don't represent right triangles by adding a predicate that checks to see if the Pythagorean theorem (a^2 + b^2 == c^2) holds. We'll also modify the function to ensure that side a isn't larger than the hypotenuse c, and that side b isn't larger than side a:

```
ghci> let rightTriangles = [ (a,b,c) | c <- [1..10], a <- [1..c], b <- [1..a],
a^2 + b^2 == c^2]
```

Notice how we changed the ranges in the lists that we draw values from. This ensures that we don't check unnecessary triples, such as ones where side b is larger than the hypotenuse (in a right triangle, the hypotenuse is always the longest side). We also assumed that side b is never larger than side a. This doesn't harm anything, because for every triple (a,b,c) with a^2 + b^2 == c^2 and b > a that is left out of consideration, the triple (b,a,c) is included—and is the same triangle, just with the legs reversed. (Otherwise, our list of results would contain pairs of triangles that are essentially the same.)

NOTE   *In GHCi, you can't break up definitions and expressions across multiple lines. In this book, however, we occasionally need to break up a single line so the code can all fit on the page. (Otherwise the book would have to be really wide, and it wouldn't fit on any normal shelf—and then you'd have to buy bigger shelves!)*

We're almost done. Now, we just need to modify the function to only output the triangles whose perimeter equals 24:

```
ghci> let rightTriangles' = [ (a,b,c) | c <- [1..10], a <- [1..c], b <- [1..a],
a^2 + b^2 == c^2, a+b+c == 24]
ghci> rightTriangles'
[(6,8,10)]
```

And there's our answer! This is a common pattern in functional programming: you start with a certain set of candidate solutions, and successively apply transformations and filters to them until you've narrowed the possibilities down to the one solution (or several solutions) that you're after.

2

BELIEVE THE TYPE

One of Haskell's greatest strengths is its powerful type system.

In Haskell, every expression's type is known at compile time, which leads to safer code. If you write a program that tries to divide a Boolean type with a number, it won't compile. This is good because it's better to catch those kinds of errors at compile time, rather than having your program crash later on. Everything in Haskell has a type, so the compiler can reason quite a lot about your program before compiling it.

Unlike Java or Pascal, Haskell has type inference. If we write a number, for example, we don't need to tell Haskell it's a number, because it can infer that on its own.

So far, we've covered some of the basics of Haskell with only a very superficial glance at types, but understanding the type system is a very important part of learning Haskell.

Explicit Type Declaration

We can use GHCi to examine the types of some expressions. We'll do that by using the :t command which, followed by any valid expression, tells us its type. Let's give it a whirl:

```
ghci> :t 'a'
'a' :: Char
ghci> :t True
True :: Bool
ghci> :t "HELLO!"
"HELLO!" :: [Char]
ghci> :t (True, 'a')
(True, 'a') :: (Bool, Char)
ghci> :t 4 == 5
4 == 5 :: Bool
```

The :: operator here is read as "has type of." Explicit types are always denoted with the first letter in uppercase. 'a' has a type of Char, which stands for *character*. True is a Bool, or a Boolean type. "HELLO!", which is a string, shows its type as [Char]. The square brackets denote a list, so we read that as it being a list of characters. Unlike lists, each tuple length has its own type. So the tuple (True, 'a') has a type of (Bool, Char), and ('a','b','c') has a type of (Char, Char, Char). 4 == 5 will always return False, so its type is Bool.

Functions also have types. When writing our own functions, we can choose to give them an explicit type declaration. This is generally considered to be good practice (except when writing very short functions). From here on, we'll give all the functions that we make type declarations.

Remember the list comprehension we made in Chapter 1—the one that filters out a string's lowercase letters? Here's how it looks with a type declaration:

```
removeNonUppercase :: [Char] -> [Char]
removeNonUppercase st = [ c | c <- st, c `elem` ['A'..'Z']]
```

The removeNonUppercase function has a type of [Char] -> [Char], meaning that it takes one string as a parameter and returns another as a result.

But how do we specify the type of a function that takes several parameters? Here's a simple function that takes three integers and adds them together:

```
addThree :: Int -> Int -> Int -> Int
addThree x y z = x + y + z
```

The parameters and the return type are separated by -> characters, with the return type always coming last in the declaration. (In Chapter 5, you'll see why they're all separated with ->, instead of having a more explicit distinction.)

If you want to give your function a type declaration, but are unsure as to what it should be, you can always just write the function without it, and then check it with :t. Since functions are expressions, :t works on them in the same way as you saw at the beginning of this section.

Common Haskell Types

Let's take a look at some common Haskell types, which are used for representing basic things like numbers, characters, and Boolean values. Here's an overview:

- Int stands for integer. It's used for whole numbers. 7 can be an Int, but 7.2 cannot. Int is *bounded*, which means that it has a minimum value and a maximum value.

NOTE *We're using the GHC compiler, where the range of Int is determined by the size of a machine word on your computer. So if you have a 64-bit CPU, it's likely that the lowest Int on your system is -2^{63}, and the highest is $2^{63} - 1$.*

- Integer is also used to store integers, but it's not bounded, so it can be used to represent really big numbers. (And I mean *really* big!) However, Int is more efficient. As an example, try saving the following function to a file:

```
factorial :: Integer -> Integer
factorial n = product [1..n]
```

Then load it into GHCi with :l and test it:

```
ghci> factorial 50
30414093201713378043612608166064768844377641568960512000000000000
```

- Float is a real floating-point number with single precision. Add the following function to the file you've been working in:

```
circumference :: Float -> Float
circumference r = 2 * pi * r
```

Then load and test it:

```
ghci> circumference 4.0
25.132742
```

- Double is a real floating-point number with double the precision. Double-precision numeric types use twice as many bits to represent numbers. The extra bits increase their precision at the cost of hogging more memory. Here's another function to add to your file:

```
circumference' :: Double -> Double
circumference' r = 2 * pi * r
```

Now load and test it. Pay particular attention to the difference in precision between circumference and circumference'.

```
ghci> circumference' 4.0
25.132741228718345
```

- Bool is a Boolean type. It can have only two values: True and False.
- Char represents a Unicode character. It's denoted by single quotes. A list of characters is a string.
- Tuples are types, but their definition depends on their length as well as the types of their components. So, theoretically, there is an infinite number of tuple types. (In practice, tuples can have at most 62 elements—far more than you'll ever need.) Note that the empty tuple () is also a type, which can have only a single value: ().

Type Variables

It makes sense for some functions to be able to operate on various types. For instance, the head function takes a list and returns the head element of that list. It doesn't really matter if the list contains numbers, characters, or even more lists! The function should be able to work with lists that contain just about anything.

What do you think the type of the head function is? Let's check with the :t function:

```
ghci> :t head
head :: [a] -> a
```

What is this a? Remember that type names start with capital letters, so it can't be a type. This is actually an example of a *type variable*, which means that a can be of any type.

Type variables allow functions to operate on values of various types in a type-safe manner. This is a lot like *generics* in other programming languages. However, Haskell's version is much more powerful, since it allows us to easily write very general functions.

Functions that use type variables are called *polymorphic functions*. The type declaration of head states that it takes a list of any type and returns one element of that type.

Remember fst? It returns the first item in a pair. Let's examine its type:

```
ghci> :t fst
fst :: (a, b) -> a
```

You can see that fst takes a tuple and returns an element that is of the same type as its first item. That's why we can use fst on a pair that contains items of any two types. Note that even though a and b are different type variables, they don't necessarily need to be different types. This just means that the first item's type and the return value's type will be the same.

Type Classes 101

A *type class* is an interface that defines some behavior. If a type is an *instance* of a type class, then it supports and implements the behavior the type class describes.

More specifically, a type class specifies a bunch of functions, and when we decide to make a type an instance of a type class, we define what those functions mean for that type.

A type class that defines equality is a good example. The values of many types can be compared for equality by using the == operator. Let's check the type signature of this operator:

```
ghci> :t (==)
(==) :: (Eq a) => a -> a -> Bool
```

Note that the equality operator (==) is actually a function. So are +, *, -, /, and almost every other operator. If a function is composed of only special characters, it's considered an infix function by default. If we want to examine its type, pass it to another function, or call it as a prefix function, we need to surround it in parentheses, as in the preceding example.

This example shows something new: the => symbol. Everything before this symbol is called a *class constraint*. We can read this type declaration like this: The equality function takes any two values that are of the same type and returns a Bool. The type of those two values must be an instance of the Eq class.

The Eq type class provides an interface for testing for equality. If it makes sense for two items of a particular type to be compared for equality, then that type can be an instance of the Eq type class. All standard Haskell types (except for input/output types and functions) are instances of Eq.

NOTE   *It's important to note that type classes are* not *the same as classes in object-oriented programming languages.*

Let's look at some of the most common Haskell type classes, which enable our types to be easily compared for equality and order, printed as strings, and so on.

The Eq Type Class

As we've discussed, Eq is used for types that support equality testing. The functions its instances implement are == and /=. This means that if there's an Eq class constraint for a type variable in a function, it uses == or /= somewhere inside its definition. When a type implements a function, that means it defines what the function does when used with that particular type. Here are some examples of performing these operations on various instances of Eq:

```
ghci> 5 == 5
True
ghci> 5 /= 5
False
ghci> 'a' == 'a'
True
ghci> "Ho Ho" == "Ho Ho"
True
ghci> 3.432 == 3.432
True
```

The Ord Type Class

Ord is a type class for types whose values can be put in some order. For example, let's look at the type of the greater-than (>) operator:

```
ghci> :t (>)
(>) :: (Ord a) => a -> a -> Bool
```

The type of > is similar to the type of ==. It takes two items as parameters and returns a Bool, which tells us if some relation between those two things holds or not.

All the types we've covered so far (again, except for functions) are instances of Ord. Ord covers all the standard comparison functions such as >, <, >=, and <=.

The compare function takes two values whose type is an Ord instance and returns an Ordering. Ordering is a type that can be GT, LT, or EQ, which represent greater than, lesser than, or equal, respectively.

```
ghci> "Abrakadabra" < "Zebra"
True
ghci> "Abrakadabra" `compare` "Zebra"
LT
ghci> 5 >= 2
True
ghci> 5 `compare` 3
GT
ghci> 'b' > 'a'
True
```

The Show Type Class

Values whose types are instances of the Show type class can be represented as strings. All the types we've covered so far (except for functions) are instances of Show. The most commonly used function that operates on instances of this type class is show, which prints the given value as a string:

```
ghci> show 3
"3"
ghci> show 5.334
"5.334"
ghci> show True
"True"
```

The Read Type Class

Read can be considered the opposite type class of Show. Again, all the types we've covered so far are instances of this type class. The read function takes a string and returns a value whose type is an instance of Read:

```
ghci> read "True" || False
True
ghci> read "8.2" + 3.8
12.0
ghci> read "5" - 2
3
```

```
ghci> read "[1,2,3,4]" ++ [3]
[1,2,3,4,3]
```

So far so good. But what happens if we try entering read "4"?

```
ghci> read "4"
<interactive>:1:0:
    Ambiguous type variable 'a' in the constraint:
      'Read a' arising from a use of 'read' at <interactive>:1:0-7
    Probable fix: add a type signature that fixes these type variable(s)
```

GHCi is telling us that it doesn't know what we want in return. Notice that in the previous uses of read, we did something with the result afterward, which let GHCi infer the kind of result we wanted. If we used it as a Boolean, for example, it knew it had to return a Bool. But now it knows we want some type that is part of the Read class, but it doesn't know which one. Let's take a look at the type signature of read:

```
ghci> :t read
read :: (Read a) => String -> a
```

NOTE *String is just another name for [Char]. String and [Char] can be used interchangeably, but we'll mostly be sticking to String from now on because it's easier to write and more readable.*

We can see that the read function returns a value whose type is an instance of Read, but if we use that result in some way, it has no way of knowing which type. To solve this problem, we can use *type annotations.*

Type annotations are a way to explicitly tell Haskell what the type of an expression should be. We do this by adding :: to the end of the expression and then specifying a type:

```
ghci> read "5" :: Int
5
ghci> read "5" :: Float
5.0
ghci> (read "5" :: Float) * 4
20.0
ghci> read "[1,2,3,4]" :: [Int]
[1,2,3,4]
ghci> read "(3, 'a')" :: (Int, Char)
(3, 'a')
```

The compiler can infer the type of most expressions by itself. However, sometimes the compiler doesn't know whether to return a value of type Int or Float for an expression like read "5". To see what the type is, Haskell would need to actually evaluate read "5". But since Haskell is a statically typed language, it needs to know all the types before the code is compiled (or in the case of GHCi, evaluated). So we need to tell Haskell, "Hey, this expression should have this type, in case you didn't know!"

We can give Haskell only the minimum amount of information it needs to figure out which type of value read should return. For instance, if we're using read and then cramming its result into a list, Haskell can use the list to figure out which type we want by looking at the other elements of the list:

```
ghci> [read "True", False, True, False]
[True, False, True, False]
```

Since we used read "True" as an element in a list of Bool values, Haskell sees that the type of read "True" must also be Bool.

The Enum Type Class

Enum instances are sequentially ordered types—their values can be enumerated. The main advantage of the Enum type class is that we can use its values in list ranges. They also have defined successors and predecessors, which we can get with the succ and pred functions. Some examples of types in this class are (), Bool, Char, Ordering, Int, Integer, Float, and Double.

```
ghci> ['a'..'e']
"abcde"
ghci> [LT .. GT]
[LT,EQ,GT]
ghci> [3 .. 5]
[3,4,5]
ghci> succ 'B'
'C'
```

The Bounded Type Class

Instances of the Bounded type class have an upper bound and a lower bound, which can be checked by using the minBound and maxBound functions:

```
ghci> minBound :: Int
-2147483648
ghci> maxBound :: Char
'\1114111'
ghci> maxBound :: Bool
True
ghci> minBound :: Bool
False
```

The minBound and maxBound functions are interesting because they have a type of (Bounded a) => a. In a sense, they are polymorphic constants.

Note that tuples whose components are all instances of Bounded are also considered to be instances of Bounded themselves:

```
ghci> maxBound :: (Bool, Int, Char)
(True,2147483647,'\1114111')
```

The Num Type Class

Num is a numeric type class. Its instances can act like numbers. Let's examine the type of a number:

```
ghci> :t 20
20 :: (Num t) => t
```

It appears that whole numbers are also polymorphic constants. They can act like any type that's an instance of the Num type class (Int, Integer, Float, or Double):

```
ghci> 20 :: Int
20
ghci> 20 :: Integer
20
ghci> 20 :: Float
20.0
ghci> 20 :: Double
20.0
```

For example, we can examine the type of the * operator:

```
ghci> :t (*)
(*) :: (Num a) => a -> a -> a
```

This shows that * accepts two numbers and returns a number of the same type. Because of this type constraint, (5 :: Int) * (6 :: Integer) will result in a type error, while 5 * (6 :: Integer) will work just fine. 5 can act like either an Integer or an Int, but not both at the same time.

To be an instance of Num, a type must already be in Show and Eq.

The Floating Type Class

The Floating type class includes the Float and Double types, which are used to store floating-point numbers.

Functions that take and return values that are instances of the Floating type class need their results to be represented with floating-point numbers in order to do meaningful computations. Some examples are sin, cos, and sqrt.

The Integral Type Class

Integral is another numeric type class. While Num includes all numbers, including real number integers, the Integral class includes *only* integral (whole) numbers. This type class includes the Int and Integer types.

One particularly useful function for dealing with numbers is fromIntegral. It has the following type declaration:

```
fromIntegral :: (Integral a, Num b) => a -> b
```

From its type signature, we can see that fromIntegral takes an integral number and turns it into a more general number. This is very useful when you want integral and floating-point types to work together nicely. For instance, the length function has this type declaration:

```
length :: [a] -> Int
```

This means that if we try to get the length of a list and add it to 3.2, we'll get an error (because we tried to add an Int to a floating-point number). To get around this, we can use fromIntegral, like this:

```
ghci> fromIntegral (length [1,2,3,4]) + 3.2
7.2
```

Some Final Notes on Type Classes

Because a type class defines an abstract interface, one type can be an instance of many type classes, and one type class can have many types as instances. For example, the Char type is an instance of many type classes, two of them being Eq and Ord, because we can check if two characters are equal as well as compare them in alphabetical order.

Sometimes a type must first be an instance of one type class to be allowed to become an instance of another. For example, to be an instance of Ord, a type must first be an instance of Eq. In other words, being an instance of Eq is a *prerequisite* for being an instance of Ord. This makes sense if you think about it, because if you can compare two things for ordering, you should also be able to tell if those things are equal.

3

SYNTAX IN FUNCTIONS

In this chapter, we'll take a look at the syntax that enables you to write Haskell functions in a readable and sensible manner. We'll look at how to quickly deconstruct values, avoid big `if else` chains, and store the results of intermediate computations so that you can reuse them multiple times.

Pattern Matching

Pattern matching is used to specify patterns to which some data should conform and to deconstruct the data according to those patterns.

When defining functions in Haskell, you can create separate function bodies for different patterns. This leads to simple, readable code. You can pattern match on pretty much any data type—

numbers, characters, lists, tuples, and so on. For example, let's write a simple function that checks if the number we pass to it is a 7:

```
lucky :: Int -> String
lucky 7 = "LUCKY NUMBER SEVEN!"
lucky x = "Sorry, you're out of luck, pal!"
```

When you call lucky, the patterns will be checked from top to bottom. When the passed argument conforms to a specified pattern, the corresponding function body will be used. The only way a number can conform to the first pattern here is if it is a 7. In that case, the function body "LUCKY NUMBER SEVEN!" is used. If it's not a 7, it falls through to the second pattern, which matches anything and binds it to x.

When we use a name that starts with a lowercase letter (like x, y, or myNumber) in our pattern instead of an actual value (like 7), it will act as a catchall pattern. That pattern will always match the supplied value, and we will be able to refer to that value by the name that we used for the pattern.

The sample function could have also been easily implemented by using an if expression. However, what if we wanted to write a function that takes a number and prints it out as a word if it's between 1 and 5; otherwise, it prints "Not between 1 and 5"? Without pattern matching, we would need to make a pretty convoluted if/then/else tree. However, pattern matching makes this a simple function to write:

```
sayMe :: Int -> String
sayMe 1 = "One!"
sayMe 2 = "Two!"
sayMe 3 = "Three!"
sayMe 4 = "Four!"
sayMe 5 = "Five!"
sayMe x = "Not between 1 and 5"
```

Note that if we moved the last pattern (sayMe x) to the top, the function would always print "Not between 1 and 5", because the numbers wouldn't have a chance to fall through and be checked for any other patterns.

Remember the factorial function we implemented in the previous chapter? We defined the factorial of a number n as product [1..n]. We can also define a factorial function *recursively*. A function is defined recursively if it calls itself inside its own definition. The factorial function is usually defined this way in mathematics. We start by saying that the factorial of 0 is 1. Then we state that the factorial of any positive integer is that integer multiplied by the factorial of its predecessor. Here's how that looks translated into Haskell terms:

```
factorial :: Int -> Int
factorial 0 = 1
factorial n = n * factorial (n - 1)
```

This is the first time we've defined a function recursively. Recursion is important in Haskell, and we'll take a closer look at it in Chapter 4.

Pattern matching can also fail. For instance, we can define a function like this:

```
charName :: Char -> String
charName 'a' = "Albert"
charName 'b' = "Broseph"
charName 'c' = "Cecil"
```

This function seems to work fine at first. However, if we try to call it with an input that it didn't expect, we get an error:

```
ghci> charName 'a'
"Albert"
ghci> charName 'b'
"Broseph"
ghci> charName 'h'
"*** Exception: tut.hs:(53,0)-(55,21): Non-exhaustive patterns in function charName
```

It complains that we have "non-exhaustive patterns," and rightfully so. When making patterns, we should always include a catchall pattern at the end so our program doesn't crash if we get some unexpected input.

Pattern Matching with Tuples

Pattern matching can also be used on tuples. What if we wanted to write a function that takes two vectors in 2D space (represented as pairs) and adds them together? (To add two vectors, we add their x components separately and their y components separately.) Here's how we might have done this if we didn't know about pattern matching:

```
addVectors :: (Double, Double) -> (Double, Double) -> (Double, Double)
addVectors a b = (fst a + fst b, snd a + snd b)
```

Well, that works, but there's a better way to do it. Let's modify the function so that it uses pattern matching:

```
addVectors :: (Double, Double) -> (Double, Double) -> (Double, Double)
addVectors (x1, y1) (x2, y2) = (x1 + x2, y1 + y2)
```

This is much better. It makes it clear that the parameters are tuples, and increases readability by giving names to the tuple components right away. Note that this is already a catchall pattern. The type of addVectors is the same in both cases, so we are guaranteed to get two pairs as parameters:

```
ghci> :t addVectors
addVectors :: (Double, Double) -> (Double, Double) -> (Double, Double)
```

fst and snd extract the components of pairs. But what about triples? Well, there are no provided functions to extract the third component in a triple, but we can make our own:

```
first :: (a, b, c) -> a
first (x, _, _) = x

second :: (a, b, c) -> b
second (_, y, _) = y

third :: (a, b, c) -> c
third (_, _, z) = z
```

The _ character means the same thing it does in list comprehensions. We really don't care about that part, so we just use a _ to represent a generic variable.

Pattern Matching with Lists and List Comprehensions

You can also use pattern matching in list comprehensions, like this:

```
ghci> let xs = [(1,3),(4,3),(2,4),(5,3),(5,6),(3,1)]
ghci> [a+b | (a, b) <- xs]
[4,7,6,8,11,4]
```

If a pattern match fails, the list comprehension will just move on to the next element, and the element that failed won't be included in the resulting list.

Regular lists can also be used in pattern matching. You can match with the empty list [] or any pattern that involves : and the empty list. (Remember that [1,2,3] is just syntactic sugar for 1:2:3:[].) A pattern like x:xs will bind the head of the list to x and the rest of it to xs. If the list has only a single element, then xs will simply be the empty list.

NOTE *Haskell programmers use the x:xs pattern often, especially with recursive functions. However, patterns that include the : character will match only against lists of length one or more.*

Now that we've looked at how to pattern match against lists, let's make our own implementation of the head function:

```
head' :: [a] -> a
head' [] = error "Can't call head on an empty list, dummy!"
head' (x:_) = x
```

After loading the function, we can test it, like this:

```
ghci> head' [4,5,6]
4
ghci> head' "Hello"
'H'
```

Notice that if we want to bind something to several variables (even if one of them is just _), we must surround them in parentheses so Haskell can properly parse them.

Also notice the use of the error function. This function takes a string as an argument and generates a runtime error using that string. It essentially crashes your program, so it's not good to use it too much. (But calling head on an empty list just doesn't make sense!)

As another example, let's write a simple function that takes a list and prints its elements out in a wordy, inconvenient format:

```
tell :: (Show a) => [a] -> String
tell [] = "The list is empty"
tell (x:[]) = "The list has one element: " ++ show x
tell (x:y:[]) = "The list has two elements: " ++ show x ++ " and " ++ show y
tell (x:y:_) = "This list is long. The first two elements are: " ++ show x
                ++ " and " ++ show y
```

Note that (x:[]) and (x:y:[]) could be rewritten as [x] and [x,y]. However, we can't rewrite (x:y:_) using square brackets, because it matches any list of length 2 or more.

Here are some examples of using this function:

```
ghci> tell [1]
"The list has one element: 1"
ghci> tell [True,False]
"The list has two elements: True and False"
ghci> tell [1,2,3,4]
"This list is long. The first two elements are: 1 and 2"
ghci> tell []
"The list is empty"
```

The tell function is safe to use because it can match to the empty list, a singleton list, a list with two elements, and a list with more than two elements. It knows how to handle lists of any length, and so it will always return a useful value.

How about if instead we defined a function that only knows how to handle lists with three elements? Here's an example of such a function:

```
badAdd :: (Num a) => [a] -> a
badAdd (x:y:z:[]) = x + y + z
```

Here's what happens when we give it a list that it doesn't expect:

```
ghci> badAdd [100,20]
*** Exception: examples.hs:8:0-25: Non-exhaustive patterns in function badAdd
```

Yikes! Not cool! If this happened inside a compiled program instead of in GHCi, the program would crash.

One final thing to note about pattern matching with lists: You can't use the ++ operator in pattern matches. (Remember that the ++ operator joins two lists into one.) For instance, if you tried to pattern match against (xs ++ ys), Haskell wouldn't be able to tell what would be in the xs list and what would be in the ys list. Though it seems logical to match stuff against (xs ++ [x,y,z]), or even just (xs ++ [x]), because of the nature of lists, you can't.

As-patterns

There's also a special type of pattern called an *as-pattern*. As-patterns allow you to break up an item according to a pattern, while still keeping a reference to the entire original item. To create an as-pattern, precede a regular pattern with a name and an @ character.

For instance, we can create the following as-pattern: xs@(x:y:ys). This pattern will match exactly the same lists that x:y:ys would, but you can easily access the entire original list using xs, instead of needing to type out x:y:ys every time. Here's an example of a simple function that uses an as-pattern:

```
firstLetter :: String -> String
firstLetter "" = "Empty string, whoops!"
firstLetter all@(x:xs) = "The first letter of " ++ all ++ " is " ++ [x]
```

After loading the function, we can test it as follows:

```
ghci> firstLetter "Dracula"
"The first letter of Dracula is D"
```

Guards, Guards!

We use patterns to check if the values passed to our functions are constructed in a certain way. We use *guards* when we want our function to check if some property of those passed values is true or false. That sounds a lot like an if expression, and it is very similar. However, guards are a lot more readable when you have several conditions, and they play nicely with patterns.

Let's dive in and write a function that uses guards. This function will tell you different things depending on your body mass index (BMI). Your BMI is calculated by dividing your weight (in kilograms) by your height (in meters) squared. If your BMI is less than 18.5, you're considered underweight. If it's anywhere from 18.5 to 25, you're considered normal. A BMI of 25 to 30 is overweight, and more than 30 is obese. (Note that this function won't actually calculate your BMI; it just takes it as an argument and then tells you something.) Here's the function:

```haskell
bmiTell :: Double -> String
bmiTell bmi
    | bmi <= 18.5 = "You're underweight, eat more!"
    | bmi <= 25.0 = "Looking good!"
    | bmi <= 30.0 = "You're overweight. Let's work out together!"
    | otherwise   = "You're obese. Go see a doctor."
```

A guard is indicated by a pipe character (|), followed by a Boolean expression, followed by the function body that will be used if that expression evaluates to True. If the expression evaluates to False, the function drops through to the next guard, and the process repeats. Guards must be indented by at least one space. (I like to indent them by four spaces so that the code is more readable.)

For instance, if we call this function with a BMI of 24.3, it will first check if that's less than or equal to 18.5. Because it isn't, it falls through to the next guard. The check is carried out with the second guard, and because 24.3 is less than 25.0, the second string is returned.

Guards are very reminiscent of a big if/else tree in imperative languages, though they're far more readable. While big if/else trees are usually frowned upon, sometimes a problem is defined in such a discrete way that you can't get around them. Guards are a very nice alternative in these cases.

Many times, the last guard in a function is otherwise, which catches everything. If all the guards in a function evaluate to False, and we haven't provided an otherwise catchall guard, evaluation falls through to the next pattern. (This is how patterns and guards play nicely together.) If no suitable guards or patterns are found, an error is thrown.

Of course, we can also use guards with functions that take multiple parameters. Let's modify bmiTell so that it takes a height and weight, and calculates the BMI for us:

```haskell
bmiTell :: Double -> Double -> String
bmiTell weight height
    | weight / height ^ 2 <= 18.5 = "You're underweight, eat more!"
    | weight / height ^ 2 <= 25.0 = "Looking good!"
```

```
| weight / height ^ 2 <= 30.0 = "You're overweight. Let's work out together!"
| otherwise = "You're obese. Go see a doctor."
```

Now, let's try it out:

```
ghci> bmiTell 85 1.90
"Looking good!"
```

Nice, Haskell says I look good.

NOTE   *A common newbie mistake is to put an equal sign (=) after the function name and parameters, before the first guard. This will cause a syntax error.*

As another simple example, let's implement our own max function to compare two items and return the larger one:

```
max' :: (Ord a) => a -> a -> a
max' a b
    | a <= b    = b
    | otherwise = a
```

We can also implement our own compare function using guards:

```
myCompare :: (Ord a) => a -> a -> Ordering
a `myCompare` b
    | a == b    = EQ
    | a <= b    = LT
    | otherwise = GT
```

```
ghci> 3 `myCompare` 2
GT
```

NOTE   *Not only can we call functions as infix with backticks, we can also define them using backticks. Sometimes this makes them easier to read.*

where?!

When programming, we usually want to avoid calculating the same value over and over again. It's much easier to calculate something only once and store the result. In imperative programming languages, you would solve this problem by storing the result of a computation in a variable. In this section, you'll learn how to use Haskell's where keyword to store the results of intermediate computations, which provides similar functionality.

In the previous section, we defined a BMI calculator function like this:

```
bmiTell :: Double -> Double -> String
bmiTell weight height
    | weight / height ^ 2 <= 18.5 = "You're underweight, eat more!"
    | weight / height ^ 2 <= 25.0 = "Looking good!"
    | weight / height ^ 2 <= 30.0 = "You're overweight. Let's work out together!"
    | otherwise = "You're obese. Go see a doctor."
```

Notice that we repeat the BMI calculation three times in this code. We can avoid this by using the where keyword to bind that value to a variable and then using that variable in place of the BMI calculation, like this:

```
bmiTell :: Double -> Double -> String
bmiTell weight height
    | bmi <= 18.5 = "You're underweight, eat more!"
    | bmi <= 25.0 = "Looking good!"
    | bmi <= 30.0 = "You're overweight. Let's work out together!"
    | otherwise = "You're obese. Go see a doctor."
    where bmi = weight / height ^ 2
```

We put the where keyword after the guards and then use it to define one or more variables or functions. These names are visible across all the guards. If we decide that we want to calculate BMI a bit differently, we need to change it only once. This technique also improves readability by giving names to things, and it can even make our programs faster, since our values are calculated just once.

If we wanted to, we could even go a bit overboard and write our function like this:

```
bmiTell :: Double -> Double -> String
bmiTell weight height
    | bmi <= skinny = "You're underweight, eat more!"
    | bmi <= normal = "Looking good!"
    | bmi <= overweight = "You're overweight. Let's work out together!"
    | otherwise = "You're obese. Go see a doctor."
    where bmi = weight / height ^ 2
          skinny = 18.5
          normal = 25.0
          overweight = 30.0
```

NOTE   *Notice that all the variable names are aligned in a single column. If you don't align them like this, Haskell will get confused, and it won't know that they're all part of the same block.*

where's Scope

The variables we define in the where section of a function are visible only to that function, so we don't need to worry about them polluting the namespace of other functions. If we want to use a variable like this in several different functions, we must define it globally.

Also, where bindings are *not* shared across function bodies of different patterns. For instance, suppose we want to write a function that takes a name and greets the person nicely if it recognizes that name, but not so nicely if it doesn't. We might define it like this:

```
greet :: String -> String
greet "Juan" = niceGreeting ++ " Juan!"
greet "Fernando" = niceGreeting ++ " Fernando!"
greet name = badGreeting ++ " " ++ name
    where niceGreeting = "Hello! So very nice to see you,"
          badGreeting = "Oh! Pfft. It's you."
```

This function won't work as written. Because where bindings aren't shared across function bodies of different patterns, only the last function body sees the greetings defined by the where binding. To make this function work correctly, badGreeting and niceGreeting must be defined globally, like this:

```
badGreeting :: String
badGreeting = "Oh! Pfft. It's you."

niceGreeting :: String
niceGreeting = "Hello! So very nice to see you,"

greet :: String -> String
greet "Juan" = niceGreeting ++ " Juan!"
greet "Fernando" = niceGreeting ++ " Fernando!"
greet name = badGreeting ++ " " ++ name
```

Pattern Matching with where

You can also use where bindings to pattern match. We could have written the where section of our BMI function like this:

```
    ...
    where bmi = weight / height ^ 2
          (skinny, normal, fat) = (18.5, 25.0, 30.0)
```

As an example of this technique, let's write a function that gets a first name and last name, and returns the initials:

```
initials :: String -> String -> String
initials firstname lastname = [f] ++ ". " ++ [l] ++ "."
```

```
where (f:_) = firstname
      (l:_) = lastname
```

We could have also done this pattern matching directly in the function's parameters (it would have been shorter and more readable), but this example shows that it's possible to do it in the where bindings as well.

Functions in where Blocks

Just as we've defined constants in where blocks, we can also define functions. Staying true to our healthy programming theme, let's make a function that takes a list of weight/height pairs and returns a list of BMIs:

```
calcBmis :: [(Double, Double)] -> [Double]
calcBmis xs = [bmi w h | (w, h) <- xs]
    where bmi weight height = weight / height ^ 2
```

And that's all there is to it! The reason we needed to introduce bmi as a function in this example is that we can't just calculate one BMI from the function's parameters. We need to examine the list passed to the function, and there's a different BMI for every pair in there.

let It Be

let expressions are very similar to where bindings. where allows you bind to variables at the end of a function, and those variables are visible to the entire function, including all its guards. let expressions, on the other hand, allow you to bind to variables anywhere and are expressions themselves. However, they're very local, and they don't span across guards. Just like any Haskell construct that's used to bind values to names, let expressions can be used in pattern matching.

Now let's see let in action. The following function returns a cylinder's surface area, based on its height and radius:

```
cylinder :: Double -> Double -> Double
cylinder r h =
    let sideArea = 2 * pi * r * h
        topArea = pi * r ^ 2
    in  sideArea + 2 * topArea
```

let expressions take the form of let <bindings> in <expression>. The variables that you define with let are visible within the entire let expression.

Yes, we could have also defined this with a where binding. So what's the difference between the two? At first, it seems that the only difference is that let puts the bindings first and the expression later, whereas it's the other way around with where.

Really, the main difference between the two is that let expressions are . . . well . . . expressions, whereas where bindings aren't. If something is an expression, then it has a value. "boo!" is an expression, as are 3 + 5 and head [1,2,3]. This means that you can use let expressions almost anywhere in your code, like this:

```
ghci> 4 * (let a = 9 in a + 1) + 2
42
```

Here are a few other useful ways to use let expressions:

- They can be used to introduce functions in a local scope:

```
ghci> [let square x = x * x in (square 5, square 3, square 2)]
[(25,9,4)]
```

- They can be separated with semicolons, which is helpful when you want to bind several variables inline and can't align them in columns:

```
ghci> (let a = 100; b = 200; c = 300 in a*b*c, let foo="Hey "; bar = "there!" in foo ++ bar)
(6000000,"Hey there!")
```

- Pattern matching with let expressions can be very useful for quickly dismantling a tuple into components and binding those components to names, like this:

```
ghci> (let (a, b, c) = (1, 2, 3) in a+b+c) * 100
600
```

Here, we use a let expression with a pattern match to deconstruct the triple (1,2,3). We call its first component a, its second component b, and its third component c. The in a+b+c part says that the whole let expression will have the value of a+b+c. Finally, we multiply that value by 100.

- You can use let expressions inside list comprehensions. We'll take a closer look at this next.

If let expressions are so cool, why not use them all the time? Well, since let expressions are expressions, and are fairly local in their scope, they can't be used across guards. Also, some people prefer where bindings because their variables are defined *after* the function they're being used in, rather than before. This allows the function body to be closer to its name and type declaration, which can make for more readable code.

let in List Comprehensions

Let's rewrite our previous example of calculating lists of weight/height pairs, but we'll use a let expression inside a list comprehension instead of defining an auxiliary function with where:

```
calcBmis :: [(Double, Double)] -> [Double]
calcBmis xs = [bmi | (w, h) <- xs, let bmi = w / h ^ 2]
```

Each time the list comprehension takes a tuple from the original list and binds its components to w and h, the let expression binds w / h ^ 2 to the name bmi. Then we just present bmi as the output of the list comprehension.

We include a let inside a list comprehension much as we would use a predicate, but instead of filtering the list, it only binds values to names. The names defined in this let are visible to the output (the part before the |) and everything in the list comprehension that comes after the let. So, using this technique, we could make our function return only the BMIs of fat people, like this:

```
calcBmis :: [(Double, Double)] -> [Double]
calcBmis xs = [bmi | (w, h) <- xs, let bmi = w / h ^ 2, bmi > 25.0]
```

The (w, h) <- xs part of the list comprehension is called the *generator*. We can't refer to the bmi variable in the generator, because that is defined prior to the let binding.

let in GHCi

The in part of the binding can also be omitted when defining functions and constants directly in GHCi. If we do that, then the names will be visible throughout the entire interactive session:

```
ghci> let zoot x y z = x * y + z
ghci> zoot 3 9 2
29
ghci> let boot x y z = x * y + z in boot 3 4 2
14
ghci> boot
<interactive>:1:0: Not in scope: `boot'
```

Because we omitted the in part in our first line, GHCi knows that we're not using zoot in that line, so it remembers it for the rest of the session. However, in the second let expression, we included the in part and called boot immediately with some parameters. A let expression that doesn't leave out the in part is an expression in itself and represents a value, so GHCi just printed that value.

case Expressions

case expressions allow you to execute blocks of code for specific values of a particular variable. Essentially, they are a way to use pattern matching almost anywhere in your code. Many languages (like C, C++, and Java) have some kind of case statement, so you may already be familiar with the concept.

Haskell takes that concept and one-ups it. As the name implies, case expressions are expressions, much like if else expressions and let expressions. Not only can we evaluate expressions based on the possible cases of the value of a variable, we can also do pattern matching.

This is very similar to performing pattern matching on parameters in function definitions, where you take a value, pattern match it, and evaluate pieces of code based on that value. In fact, that kind of pattern matching is just syntactic sugar for case expressions. For example, the following two pieces of code do the same thing and are interchangeable:

```
head' :: [a] -> a
head' [] = error "No head for empty lists!"
head' (x:_) = x
```

```
head' :: [a] -> a
head' xs = case xs of [] -> error "No head for empty lists!"
                      (x:_) -> x
```

Here's the syntax for a case expression:

```
case expression of pattern -> result
                   pattern -> result
                   pattern -> result
                   ...
```

This is pretty simple. The first pattern that matches the expression is used. If it falls through the whole case expression and no suitable pattern is found, a runtime error occurs.

Pattern matching on function parameters can be done only when defining functions, but case expressions can be used anywhere. For instance, you can use them to perform pattern matching in the middle of an expression, like this:

```
describeList :: [a] -> String
describeList ls = "The list is " ++ case ls of [] -> "empty."
                                               [x] -> "a singleton list."
                                               xs -> "a longer list."
```

Here, the case expression works like this: ls is first checked against the pattern of an empty list. If ls is empty, the whole case expression then assumes the value of "empty". If ls is not an empty list, then it's checked against the pattern of a list with a single element. If the pattern match succeeds, the case expression then has the value of "a singleton list". If neither of those two patterns match, then the catchall pattern, xs, applies. Finally, the result of the case expression is joined together with the string "The list is". Each case expression represents a value. That's why we were able to use ++ between the string "The list is" and our case expression.

Because pattern matching in function definitions is the same as using case expressions, we could have also defined the describeList function like this:

```
describeList :: [a] -> String
describeList ls = "The list is " ++ what ls
    where what [] = "empty."
          what [x] = "a singleton list."
          what xs = "a longer list."
```

This function acts just like the one in the previous example, although we used a different syntactic construct to define it. The function what gets called with ls, and then the usual pattern-matching action takes place. Once this function returns a string, it's joined with "The list is".

4

HELLO RECURSION!

In this chapter, we'll take a look at recursion. We'll learn why it's important in Haskell programming and how we can find very concise and elegant solutions to problems by thinking recursively.

Recursion is a way of defining functions in which a function is applied inside its own definition. In other words, the function calls itself. If you still don't know what recursion is, read this sentence. (Haha! Just kidding!)

Kidding aside, the strategy of a recursively defined function is to break down the problem at hand into smaller problems of the same kind and then try to solve those subproblems, breaking them down further if necessary. Eventually we reach the *base case* (or base cases) of the problem, which can't be broken down any more and whose solutions need to be explicitly (nonrecursively) defined by the programmer.

Definitions in mathematics are often recursive. For instance, we can specify the *Fibonacci sequence* recursively as follows: We define the first two Fibonacci numbers directly by saying that $F(0) = 0$ and $F(1) = 1$, meaning that the zeroth and first Fibonacci numbers are 0 and 1, respectively. These are our base cases.

Then we specify that for any natural number other than 0 or 1, the corresponding Fibonacci number is the sum of the previous two Fibonacci numbers. In other words, $F(n) = F(n - 1) + F(n - 2)$. For example, $F(3)$ is $F(2) + F(1)$, which in turn breaks down as $(F(1) + F(0)) + F(1)$. Because we've now come down to nothing but nonrecursively defined Fibonacci numbers, we can safely say that the value of $F(3)$ is 2.

Recursion is important in Haskell because, unlike with imperative languages, you do computations in Haskell by declaring *what* something is rather than specifying *how* you compute it. That's why Haskell isn't about issuing your computer a sequence of steps to execute, but rather about directly defining what the desired result is, often in a recursive manner.

Maximum Awesome

Let's take a look at an existing Haskell function and see how we can write the function ourselves if we shift our brains into the "R" gear (for "recursion").

The maximum function takes a list of things that can be put in order (i.e., instances of the Ord type class) and returns the largest of them. It can be expressed very elegantly using recursion.

Before we discuss a recursive solution, think about how you might implement the maximum function imperatively. You'd probably set up a variable to hold the current maximum value, then you'd loop through every element of the list. If the current element is bigger than the current maximum value, you'd replace the maximum value with that element. The maximum value that remains at the end of the loop would be the final result.

Now let's see how we'd define it recursively. First, we need to define a base case: We say that the maximum of a singleton list is equal to the only element in it. But what if the list has more than one element? Well, then we check which is bigger: the first element (the head) or the maximum of the rest of the list (the tail). Here's the code for our recursive maximum' function:

```
maximum' :: (Ord a) => [a] -> a
maximum' [] = error "maximum of empty list!"
maximum' [x] = x
maximum' (x:xs) = max x (maximum' xs)
```

As you can see here, pattern matching is really useful for defining recursive functions. Being able to match and deconstruct values makes it easy to break down the maximum-finding problem into the relevant cases and recursive subproblems.

The first pattern says that if the list is empty, the program should crash. This makes sense, because we just can't say what the maximum of an empty list is. The second pattern says that if maximum' is passed a singleton list, it should just return that list's only element.

Our third pattern represents the meat of the recursion. The list is split into a head and a tail. We call the head x and the tail xs. Then, we make use of our old friend, the max function. The max function takes two things and returns whichever of them is larger. If x is larger than the largest element in xs, our function will return x, otherwise it will return the largest element in xs. But how does our maximum' find the largest element in xs? Simple—by calling itself, recursively!

$$\text{maximum' } [2,5,1] = \\ \text{max } 2 \left(\text{maximum' } [5,1] = \\ \text{max } 5 \left(\text{maximum' } [1] = \\ 1 \right) \right)$$

Let's work through this code with a specific example, just in case you're having trouble visualizing how maximum' works. If we call maximum' on [2,5,1], the first two patterns don't match the function call. However, the third pattern does, so the list value is split into 2 and [5,1], and maximum' is called with [5,1].

For this new call to maximum', [5,1] matches the third pattern, and once again the input list is split—this time into 5 and [1]—and maximum' is recursively called on [1]. This is a singleton list, so the newest call now matches one of our base cases and returns 1 as a result.

Now, we go up a level, comparing 5 to 1 with the use of the max function. 1 was the result of our last recursive call. Since 5 is larger, we now know that the maximum of [5,1] is 5.

Finally, comparing 2 to the maximum of [5,1], which we now know is 5, we obtain the answer to the original problem. Since 5 is greater than 2, we can now say that 5 is the maximum of [2,5,1].

A Few More Recursive Functions

Now that we've seen how to think recursively, let's implement a few more functions this way. Like maximum, these functions already exist in Haskell, but we're going to write our own versions to exercise the recursive muscle fibers in the recursive muscles of our recursive muscle groups. Let's get buff!

replicate

First off, we'll implement replicate. Remember that replicate takes an Int and a value, and returns a list that has several repetitions of that value (namely, however many the Int specifies). For instance, replicate 3 5 returns a list of three fives: [5,5,5].

Let's think about the base cases. We immediately know what to return if we're asked to replicate something zero or fewer times. If we try to replicate something zero times, we should get an empty list. And we declare that the result should be the same for negative numbers, because replicating an item fewer than zero times doesn't make sense.

In general, a list with n repetitions of x is a list with x as its head and a tail consisting of x replicated n-1 times. We get the following code:

```
replicate' :: Int -> a -> [a]
replicate' n x
    | n <= 0    = []
    | otherwise = x : replicate' (n-1) x
```

We used guards here instead of patterns because we're testing for a Boolean condition.

take

Next up, we'll implement take. This function returns a specified number of elements from a specified list. For instance, take 3 [5,4,3,2,1] will return [5,4,3]. If we try to take zero or fewer elements from a list, we should get an empty list, and if we try to take anything at all from an empty list, we should get an empty list. Notice that those are our two base cases. Now let's write the function:

```
take' :: (Num i, Ord i) => i -> [a] -> [a]
take' n _
    | n <= 0    = []
take' _ []      = []
take' n (x:xs) = x : take' (n-1) xs
```

Notice that in the first pattern, which specifies that we get an empty list if we try to take zero or fewer elements from a list, we use the _ placeholder to match the list value, because we don't really care what it is in this case. Also notice that we use a guard, but without an otherwise part. That means that if n turns out to be more than 0, the matching will fall through to the next pattern.

The second pattern indicates that if we try to take any number of things at all from an empty list, we get an empty list.

The third pattern breaks the list into a head and a tail. We call the head x and the tail xs. Then we state that taking n elements from a list is the same as creating a list that has x as its first element and n-1 elements from xs as its remaining elements.

reverse

The reverse function takes a list and returns a list with the same elements, but in the reverse order. Once again, the empty list is the base case, since trying to reverse an empty list just results in the empty list. What about the rest of the function? Well, if we split the original list into its head and tail, the reversed list that we want is the reverse of the tail, with the head stuck at the end:

```
reverse' :: [a] -> [a]
reverse' [] = []
reverse' (x:xs) = reverse' xs ++ [x]
```

repeat

The repeat function takes an element and returns an infinite list composed of that element. A recursive implementation of repeat is really easy:

```
repeat' :: a -> [a]
repeat' x = x:repeat' x
```

Calling repeat 3 will give us a list that starts with 3 as the head and has an infinite amount of 3s as the tail. So calling repeat 3 evaluates to 3:repeat 3, which evaluates to 3:(3:repeat 3), which evaluates to 3:(3:(3:repeat 3)), and so on. repeat 3 will never finish evaluating. However, take 5 (repeat 3) will give us a list of five 3s. Essentially, it's like calling replicate 5 3.

This is a nice example of how we can successfully use recursion that doesn't have a base case to make infinite lists—we just have to be sure to chop them off somewhere along the way.

zip

zip is another function for working with lists that we've met in Chapter 1. It takes two lists and zips them together. For instance, calling zip [1,2,3] [7,8] returns [(1,7),(2,8)] (the function truncates the longer list to match the length of the shorter one).

Zipping something with an empty list just returns an empty list, which gives us our base case. However, zip takes two lists as parameters, so there are actually two base cases:

```
zip' :: [a] -> [b] -> [(a,b)]
zip' _ [] = []
zip' [] _ = []
zip' (x:xs) (y:ys) = (x,y):zip' xs ys
```

The first two patterns are our base cases: If the first or second list is empty, we return an empty list. The third pattern says that zipping two lists together is equivalent to pairing up their heads, then appending their zipped tails to that.

For example, if we call zip' with [1,2,3] and ['a','b'], the function will form (1,'a') as the first element of the result, then zip together [2,3] and [b] to obtain the rest of the result. After one more recursive call, the function will try to zip [3] with [], which matches one of the base case patterns. The final result is then computed directly as (1,'a'):((2,'b'):[]), which is just [(1,'a'),(2,'b')].

elem

Let's implement one more standard library function: elem. This function takes a value and a list, and checks whether the value is a member of the list. Once again, the empty list is a base case—an empty list contains no values, so it certainly can't have the one we're looking for. In general, the value we're looking for might be at the head of the list if we're lucky; otherwise, we have to check whether it's in the tail. Here's the code:

```
elem' :: (Eq a) => a -> [a] -> Bool
elem' a [] = False
elem' a (x:xs)
    | a == x    = True
    | otherwise = a `elem'` xs
```

Quick, Sort!

The problem of sorting a list containing elements that can be put in order (like numbers) naturally lends itself to a recursive solution. There are many approaches to recursively sorting lists, but we'll look at one of the coolest ones: *quicksort*. First we'll go over how the algorithm works, and then we'll implement it in Haskell.

The Algorithm

The quicksort algorithm works like this. You have a list that you want to sort, say [5,1,9,4,6,7,3]. You select the first element, which is 5, and put all the other list elements that are less than or equal to 5 on its left side. Then you take the ones that are greater than 5 and put them on its right side. If you did this, you'd have a list that looks like this: [1,4,3,5,9,6,7]. In this example, 5 is called the *pivot*, because we chose to compare the other elements to it and move them to its left and right sides. The only reason we chose the first element as the pivot is because it will be easy to snag using pattern matching. But really, any element can be the pivot.

Now, we recursively sort all the elements that are on the left and right sides of the pivot by calling the same function on them. The final result is a completely sorted list!

The above diagram illustrates how quicksort works on our example. When we want to sort [5,1,9,4,6,7,3], we decide that the first element is our pivot. Then we sandwich it in between [1,4,3] and [9,6,7]. Once we've done that, we sort [1,4,3] and [9,6,7] by using the same approach.

To sort [1,4,3], we choose the first element, 1, as the pivot and we make a list of elements that are less than or equal to 1. That turns out to be the empty list, [], because 1 is the smallest element in [1,4,3]. The elements larger than 1 go to its right, so that's [4,3]. Again, [4,3] is sorted in the same way. It too will eventually be broken up into empty lists and put back together.

The algorithm then returns to the right side of 1, which has the empty list on its left side. Suddenly, we have [1,3,4], which is sorted. This is kept on the left side of the 5.

Once the elements on the right side of the 5 are sorted in the same way, we will have a completely sorted list: [1,3,4,5,6,7,9].

The Code

Now that we're familiar with the quicksort algorithm, let's dive into its implementation in Haskell:

```
quicksort :: (Ord a) => [a] -> [a]
quicksort [] = []
quicksort (x:xs) =
    let smallerOrEqual = [a | a <- xs, a <= x]
        larger = [a | a <- xs, a > x]
    in  quicksort smallerOrEqual ++ [x] ++ quicksort larger
```

The type signature of our function is `quicksort :: (Ord a) => [a] -> [a]`, and the empty list is the base case, as we just saw.

Remember, we'll put all the elements less than or equal to x (our pivot) to its left. To retrieve those elements, we use the list comprehension `[a | a <- xs, a <= x]`. This list comprehension will draw from xs (all the elements that aren't our pivot) and keep only those that satisfy the condition `a <= x`, meaning those elements that are less than or equal to x. We then get the list of elements larger than x in a similar fashion.

We use let bindings to give the two lists handy names: `smallerOrEqual` and `larger`. Finally, we use the list concatenation operator (++) and a recursive application of our `quicksort` function to express that we want our final list to be made of a sorted `smallerOrEqual` list, followed by our pivot, followed by a sorted `larger` list.

Let's give our function a test drive to see if it behaves correctly:

```
ghci> quicksort [10,2,5,3,1,6,7,4,2,3,4,8,9]
[1,2,2,3,3,4,4,5,6,7,8,9,10]
ghci> quicksort "the quick brown fox jumps over the lazy dog"
"        abcdeeefghhijklmnoooopqrrsttuuvwxyz"
```

Now that's what I'm talking about!

Thinking Recursively

We've used recursion quite a bit in this chapter, and as you've probably noticed, there's a pattern to it. You start by defining a base case: simple, nonrecursive solution that holds when the input is trivial. For example, the result of sorting an empty list is the empty list, because—well, what else could it be?

Then, you break your problem down into one or many subproblems and recursively solve those by applying the same function to them. You then build up your final solution from those solved subproblems. For instance, when sorting, we broke our list into two lists, plus a pivot. We sorted each of those lists separately by applying the same function to them. When we got the results, we joined them into one big sorted list.

The best way to approach recursion is to identify base cases and think about how you can break the problem at hand into something similar, but smaller. If you've correctly chosen the base cases and subproblems, you don't even have to think about the details of how everything will happen. You can just trust that the solutions of the subproblems are correct, and then you can just build up your final solutions from those smaller solutions.

5

HIGHER-ORDER FUNCTIONS

Haskell functions can take functions as parameters and return functions as return values. A function that does either of these things is called a *higher-order function.* Higher-order functions are a really powerful way of solving problems and thinking about programs, and they're indispensable when using a functional programming language like Haskell.

Curried Functions

Every function in Haskell officially takes only one parameter. But we have defined and used several functions that take more than one parameter so far—how is that possible?

Well, it's a clever trick! All the functions we've used so far that accepted multiple parameters have been *curried functions.* A curried function is a function that, instead of taking several parameters, always takes exactly one parameter.

Then when it's called with that parameter, it returns a function that takes the next parameter, and so on.

This is best explained with an example. Let's take our good friend, the max function. It looks as if it takes two parameters and returns the one that's bigger. For instance, consider the expression max 4 5. We call the function max with two parameters: 4 and 5. First, max is applied to the value 4. When we apply max to 4, the value that is returned is actually another function, which is then applied to the value 5. The act of applying this function to 5 finally returns a number value. As a consequence, the following two calls are equivalent:

```
ghci> max 4 5
5
ghci> (max 4) 5
5
```

To understand how this works, let's examine the type of the max function:

```
ghci> :t max
max :: (Ord a) => a -> a -> a
```

This can also be written as follows:

```
max :: (Ord a) => a -> (a -> a)
```

Whenever we have a type signature that features the arrow ->, that means it's a function that takes whatever is on the left side of the arrow and returns a value whose type is indicated on the right side of the arrow. When we have something like a -> (a -> a), we're dealing with a function that takes a value of type a, and it returns a function that also takes a value of type a and returns a value of type a.

So how is that beneficial to us? Simply speaking, if we call a function with too few parameters, we get back a *partially applied* function, which is a function that takes as many parameters as we left out. For example, when we did max 4, we got back a function that takes one parameter. Using partial application (calling functions with too few parameters, if you will) is a neat way to create functions on the fly, so we can pass them to other functions.

Take a look at this simple little function:

```
multThree :: Int -> Int -> Int -> Int
multThree x y z = x * y * z
```

What really happens when we call `multThree 3 5 9`, or `((multThree 3) 5) 9`? First, `multThree` is applied to 3, because they're separated by a space. That creates a function that takes one parameter and returns a function. Then that function is applied to 5, which creates a function that will take one parameter, multiply 3 and 5 together, and then multiply that by the parameter. That function is applied to 9, and the result is 135.

You can think of functions as tiny factories that take some materials and produce something. Using that analogy, we feed our `multThree` factory the number 3, but instead of producing a number, it churns out a slightly smaller factory. That factory receives the number 5 and also spits out a factory. The third factory receives the number 9, and then produces our resulting number, 135.

Remember that this function's type can also be written as follows:

```
multThree :: Int -> (Int -> (Int -> Int))
```

The type (or type variable) before the `->` is the type of the values that a function takes, and the type after it is the type of the values it returns. So our function takes a value of type `Int` and returns a function of type `(Int -> (Int -> Int)`. Similarly, *this* function takes a value of type `Int` and returns a function of type `Int -> Int`. And finally, *this* function just takes a value of type `Int` and returns another value of type `Int`.

Let's look at an example of how we can create a new function by calling a function with too few parameters:

```
ghci> let multTwoWithNine = multThree 9
ghci> multTwoWithNine 2 3
54
```

In this example, the expression `multThree 9` results in a function that takes two parameters. We name that function `multTwoWithNine`, because `multThree 9` is a function that takes two parameters. If both parameters are supplied, it will multiply the two parameters between them, and then multiply that by 9, because we got the `multTwoWithNine` function by applying `multThree` to 9.

What if we wanted to create a function that takes an `Int` and compares it to 100? We could do something like this:

```
compareWithHundred :: Int -> Ordering
compareWithHundred x = compare 100 x
```

As an example, let's try calling the function with 99:

```
ghci> compareWithHundred 99
GT
```

100 is greater than 99, so the function returns GT, or greater than.

Now let's think about what compare 100 would return: a function that takes a number and compares it with 100, which is exactly what we were trying to get in our example. In other words, the following definition and the previous one are equivalent:

```
compareWithHundred :: Int -> Ordering
compareWithHundred = compare 100
```

The type declaration stays the same, because compare 100 returns a function. compare has a type of (Ord a) => a -> (a -> Ordering). When we apply it to 100, we get a function that takes a number and returns an Ordering.

Sections

Infix functions can also be partially applied by using *sections*. To section an infix function, simply surround it with parentheses and supply a parameter on only one side. That creates a function that takes one parameter and then applies it to the side that's missing an operand. Here's an insultingly trivial example:

```
divideByTen :: (Floating a) => a -> a
divideByTen = (/10)
```

As you can see in the following code, calling divideByTen 200 is equivalent to calling 200 / 10 or (/10) 200:

```
ghci> divideByTen 200
20.0
ghci> 200 / 10
20.0
ghci> (/10) 200
20.0
```

Let's look at another example. This function checks if a character supplied to it is an uppercase letter:

```
isUpperAlphanum :: Char -> Bool
isUpperAlphanum = (`elem` ['A'..'Z'])
```

The only thing to watch out for with sections is when you're using the - (negative or minus) operator. From the definition of sections, (-4) would result in a function that takes a number and subtracts 4 from it. However, for convenience, (-4) means negative four. So if you want to make a function that subtracts 4 from the number it gets as a parameter, you can partially apply the subtract function like so: (subtract 4).

Printing Functions

So far, we've bound our partially applied functions to names and then supplied the remaining parameters to view the results. However, we never tried to print the functions themselves to the terminal. Let's give that a go then, shall we? What happens if we try entering multThree 3 4 into GHCi, instead of binding it to a name with a let or passing it to another function?

```
ghci> multThree 3 4
<interactive>:1:0:
    No instance for (Show (a -> a))
      arising from a use of `print' at <interactive>:1:0-12
    Possible fix: add an instance declaration for (Show (a -> a))
    In the expression: print it
    In a 'do' expression: print it
```

GHCi is telling us that the expression produced a function of type a -> a, but it doesn't know how to print it to the screen. Functions aren't instances of the Show type class, so we can't get a neat string representation of a function. This is different, for example, than when we enter 1 + 1 at the GHCi prompt. In that case, GHCi calculates 2 as the result, and then calls show on 2 to get a textual representation of that number. The textual representation of 2 is just the string "2", which is then printed to the screen.

NOTE   *Make sure you thoroughly understand how curried functions and partial application work, because they're really important!*

Some Higher-Orderism Is in Order

In Haskell, functions can take other functions as parameters, and as you've seen, they can also return functions as return values. To demonstrate this concept, let's write a function that takes a function, and then applies it twice to some value:

```
applyTwice :: (a -> a) -> a -> a
applyTwice f x = f (f x)
```

Notice the type declaration. For our earlier examples, we didn't need parentheses when declaring function types, because -> is naturally right-associative. However, here parentheses are mandatory. They indicate that the first parameter is a function that takes one parameter and returns a value of the same type (a -> a). The second parameter is something of type a, and the return value's type is also a. Notice that it doesn't matter what type a is—it can be Int, String, or whatever—but all the values must be the same type.

You now know that under the hood, functions that seem to take multiple parameters are actually taking a single parameter and returning a partially applied function. However, to keep things simple, I'll continue to say that a given function takes multiple parameters.

The body of the applyTwice function is very simple. We just use the parameter f as a function, applying x to it by separating the f and x with a space. We then apply the result to f again. Here are some examples of the function in action:

```
ghci> applyTwice (+3) 10
16
ghci> applyTwice (++ " HAHA") "HEY"
"HEY HAHA HAHA"
ghci> applyTwice ("HAHA " ++) "HEY"
"HAHA HAHA HEY"
ghci> applyTwice (multThree 2 2) 9
144
ghci> applyTwice (3:) [1]
[3,3,1]
```

The awesomeness and usefulness of partial application is evident. If our function requires us to pass it a function that takes only one parameter, we can just partially apply a function to the point where it takes only one parameter and then pass it. For instance, the + function takes two parameters, and in this example, we partially applied it so that it takes only one parameter by using sections.

Implementing zipWith

Now we're going to use higher-order programming to implement a really useful function in the standard library called zipWith. It takes a function and two lists as parameters, and then joins the two lists by applying the function between corresponding elements. Here's how we'll implement it:

```
zipWith' :: (a -> b -> c) -> [a] -> [b] -> [c]
zipWith' _ [] _ = []
zipWith' _ _ [] = []
zipWith' f (x:xs) (y:ys) = f x y : zipWith' f xs ys
```

First let's look at the type declaration. The first parameter is a function that takes two arguments and returns one value. They don't have to be of the same type, but they can be. The second and third parameters are lists, and the final return value is also a list.

The first list must be a list of type a values, because the joining function takes a types as its first argument. The second must be a list of b types, because the second parameter of the joining function is of type b. The result is a list of type c elements.

NOTE *Remember that if you're writing a function (especially a higher-order function), and you're unsure of the type, you can try omitting the type declaration and checking what Haskell infers it to be by using :t.*

This function is similar to the normal zip function. The base cases are the same, although there's an extra argument (the joining function). However, that argument doesn't matter in the base cases, so we can just use the _ character for it. The function body in the last pattern is also similar to zip, though instead of doing (x, y), it does f x y.

Here's a little demonstration of all the different things our zipWith' function can do:

```
ghci> zipWith' (+) [4,2,5,6] [2,6,2,3]
[6,8,7,9]
ghci> zipWith' max [6,3,2,1] [7,3,1,5]
[7,3,2,5]
ghci> zipWith' (++) ["foo ", "bar ", "baz "] ["fighters", "hoppers", "aldrin"]
["foo fighters","bar hoppers","baz aldrin"]
ghci> zipWith' (*) (replicate 5 2) [1..]
[2,4,6,8,10]
ghci> zipWith' (zipWith' (*)) [[1,2,3],[3,5,6],[2,3,4]] [[3,2,2],[3,4,5],[5,4,3]]
[[3,4,6],[9,20,30],[10,12,12]]
```

As you can see, a single higher-order function can be used in very versatile ways.

Implementing flip

Now we'll implement another function in the standard library, called flip. The flip function takes a function and returns a function that is like our original function, but with the first two arguments flipped. We can implement it like this:

```
flip' :: (a -> b -> c) -> (b -> a -> c)
flip' f = g
    where g x y = f y x
```

You can see from the type declaration that flip' takes a function that takes a and b types, and returns a function that takes b and a types. But because functions are curried by default, the second pair of parentheses actually is not necessary. The arrow -> is right-associative by default, so (a -> b -> c) -> (b -> a -> c) is the same as (a -> b -> c) -> (b -> (a -> c)), which is the same as (a -> b -> c) -> b -> a -> c. We wrote that g x y = f y x. If that's true, then f y x = g x y must also hold, right? Keeping that in mind, we can define this function in an even simpler manner:

```
flip' :: (a -> b -> c) -> b -> a -> c
flip' f y x = f x y
```

In this new version of flip', we take advantage of the fact that functions are curried. When we call flip' f without the parameters y and x, it will return an f that takes those two parameters but calls them flipped.

Even though flipped functions are usually passed to other functions, we can take advantage of currying when making higher-order functions by thinking ahead and writing what their end result would be if they were fully applied.

```
ghci> zip [1,2,3,4,5] "hello"
[(1,'h'),(2,'e'),(3,'l'),(4,'l'),(5,'o')]
ghci> flip' zip [1,2,3,4,5] "hello"
[('h',1),('e',2),('l',3),('l',4),('o',5)]
ghci> zipWith div [2,2..] [10,8,6,4,2]
[0,0,0,0,1]
ghci> zipWith (flip' div) [2,2..] [10,8,6,4,2]
[5,4,3,2,1]
```

If we flip' the zip function, we get a function that is like zip, except that the items from the first list are placed into the second components of the tuples and vice versa. The flip' div function takes its second parameter and divides that by its first, so when the numbers 2 and 10 are passed to flip' div, the result is the same as using div 10 2.

The Functional Programmer's Toolbox

As functional programmers, we seldom want to operate on just one value. We usually want to take a bunch of numbers, letters, or some other type of data, and transform the set to produce our results. In this section, we'll look at some useful functions that can help us work with multiple values.

The map Function

The map function takes a function and a list, and applies that function to every element in the list, producing a new list. Here is its definition:

```
map :: (a -> b) -> [a] -> [b]
map _ [] = []
map f (x:xs) = f x : map f xs
```

The type signature says that map takes a function from a to b and a list of a values, and returns a list of b values.

map is a versatile higher-order function that can be used in many different ways. Here it is in action:

```
ghci> map (+3) [1,5,3,1,6]
[4,8,6,4,9]
ghci> map (++ "!") ["BIFF", "BANG", "POW"]
["BIFF!","BANG!","POW!"]
```

```
ghci> map (replicate 3) [3..6]
[[3,3,3],[4,4,4],[5,5,5],[6,6,6]]
ghci> map (map (^2)) [[1,2],[3,4,5,6],[7,8]]
[[1,4],[9,16,25,36],[49,64]]
ghci> map fst [(1,2),(3,5),(6,3),(2,6),(2,5)]
[1,3,6,2,2]
```

You've probably noticed that each of these examples could also be achieved with a list comprehension. For instance, map (+3) [1,5,3,1,6] is technically the same as [x+3 | x <- [1,5,3,1,6]]. However, using the map function tends to make your code much more readable, especially once you start dealing with maps of maps.

The filter Function

The filter function takes a predicate and a list, and returns the list of elements that satisfy that predicate. (Remember that a *predicate* is a function that tells whether something is true or false; that is, a function that returns a Boolean value.) The type signature and implementation look like this:

```
filter :: (a -> Bool) -> [a] -> [a]
filter _ [] = []
filter p (x:xs)
    | p x       = x : filter p xs
    | otherwise = filter p xs
```

If p x evaluates to True, the element is included in the new list. If it doesn't evaluate to True, it isn't included in the new list.

Here are some filter examples:

```
ghci> filter (>3) [1,5,3,2,1,6,4,3,2,1]
[5,6,4]
ghci> filter (==3) [1,2,3,4,5]
[3]
ghci> filter even [1..10]
[2,4,6,8,10]
ghci> let notNull x = not (null x) in filter notNull [[1,2,3],[],[3,4,5],[2,2],[],[],[]]
[[1,2,3],[3,4,5],[2,2]]
ghci> filter (`elem` ['a'..'z']) "u LaUgH aT mE BeCaUsE I aM diFfeRent"
"uagameasadifeent"
ghci> filter (`elem` ['A'..'Z']) "i LAuGh at you bEcause u R all the same"
"LAGER"
```

As with the map function, all of these examples could also be achieved by using comprehensions and predicates. There's no set rule for when to use map and filter versus using list comprehensions. You just need to decide what's more readable depending on the code and the context.

The filter equivalent of applying several predicates in a list comprehension is either filtering something several times or joining the predicates with the logical && function. Here's an example:

```
ghci> filter (<15) (filter even [1..20])
[2,4,6,8,10,12,14]
```

In this example, we take the list [1..20] and filter it so that only even numbers remain. Then we pass that list to filter (<15) to get rid of numbers 15 and up. Here's the list comprehension version:

```
ghci> [x | x <- [1..20], x < 15, even x]
[2,4,6,8,10,12,14]
```

We use a list comprehension where we draw from the list [1..20], and then say what conditions need to hold for a number to be in the resulting list.

Remember our quicksort function from Chapter 4? We used list comprehensions to filter out the list elements that were less than (or equal to) or greater than the pivot. We can achieve the same functionality in a more readable way by using filter:

```
quicksort :: (Ord a) => [a] -> [a]
quicksort [] = []
quicksort (x:xs) =
    let smallerOrEqual = filter (<= x) xs
        larger = filter (> x) xs
    in  quicksort smallerOrEqual ++ [x] ++ quicksort larger
```

More Examples of map and filter

As another example, let's find the largest number under 100,000 that's divisible by 3,829. To do that, we'll just filter a set of possibilities in which we know the solution lies:

```
largestDivisible :: Integer
largestDivisible = head (filter p [99999,99998..])
    where p x = x `mod` 3829 == 0
```

First, we make a descending list of all numbers less than 100,000. Then we filter it by our predicate. Because the numbers are sorted in a descending manner, the largest number that satisfies our predicate will be the first element of the filtered list. And because we end up using only the head of the filtered list, it doesn't matter if the filtered list is finite or infinite. Haskell's laziness causes the evaluation to stop when the first adequate solution is found.

As our next example, we'll find the sum of all odd squares that are smaller than 10,000. In our solution, we'll use the takeWhile function. This function takes a predicate and a list. Starting at the beginning of the list, it returns the list's elements as long as the predicate holds true. Once an element is found for which the predicate doesn't hold true, the function stops and returns the resulting list. For example, to get the first word of a string, we can do the following:

```
ghci> takeWhile (/=' ') "elephants know how to party"
"elephants"
```

To find the sum of all odd squares that are less than 10,000, we begin by mapping the (^2) function over the infinite list [1..]. Then we filter this list so we get only the odd elements. Next, using takeWhile, we take elements from that list only while they are smaller than 10,000. Finally, we get the sum of that list (using the sum function). We don't even need to define a function for this example, because we can do it all in one line in GHCi:

```
ghci> sum (takeWhile (<10000) (filter odd (map (^2) [1..])))
166650
```

Awesome! We start with some initial data (the infinite list of all natural numbers), and then we map over it, filter it, and cut it until it suits our needs. Finally, we just sum it up!

We could have also written this example using list comprehensions, like this:

```
ghci> sum (takeWhile (<10000) [m | m <- [n^2 | n <- [1..]], odd m])
166650
```

For our next problem, we'll be dealing with Collatz sequences. A *Collatz sequence* (also known as a *Collatz chain*) is defined as follows:

- Start with any natural number.
- If the number is 1, stop.
- If the number is even, divide it by 2.
- If the number is odd, multiply it by 3 and add 1.
- Repeat the algorithm with the resulting number.

In essence, this gives us a chain of numbers. Mathematicians theorize that for all starting numbers, the chain will finish at the number 1. For example, if we start with the number 13, we get this sequence: 13, 40, 20, 10, 5, 16, 8, 4, 2, 1. ($13 \times 3 + 1$ equals 40. 40 divided by 2 equals 20, and so on.) We can see that the chain that starts with 13 has 10 terms.

Here is the problem we want to solve: For all starting numbers between 1 and 100, how many Collatz chains have a length greater than 15? Our first step will be to write a function that produces a chain:

```
chain :: Integer -> [Integer]
chain 1 = [1]
chain n
    | even n =  n:chain (n `div` 2)
    | odd n  =  n:chain (n*3 + 1)
```

This is a pretty standard recursive function. The base case is one, because all our chains will end at one. We can test the function to see if it's working correctly:

```
ghci> chain 10
[10,5,16,8,4,2,1]
ghci> chain 1
[1]
ghci> chain 30
[30,15,46,23,70,35,106,53,160,80,40,20,10,5,16,8,4,2,1]
```

Now we can write the numLongChains function, which actually answers our question:

```
numLongChains :: Int
numLongChains = length (filter isLong (map chain [1..100]))
    where isLong xs = length xs > 15
```

We map the chain function to [1..100] to get a list of chains, which are themselves represented as lists. Then we filter them by a predicate that checks whether a list's length is longer than 15. Once we've done the filtering, we see how many chains are left in the resulting list.

NOTE   *This function has a type of numLongChains :: Int because length returns an Int instead of a Num a. If we wanted to return a more general Num a, we could have used fromIntegral on the resulting length.*

Mapping Functions with Multiple Parameters

So far, we've mapped functions that take only one parameter (like map (*2) [0..]). However, we can also map functions that take multiple parameters. For example, we could do something like map (*) [0..]. In this case, the function *, which has a type of (Num a) => a -> a -> a, is applied to each number in the list.

As you've seen, giving only one parameter to a function that takes two parameters will cause it to return a function that takes one parameter. So if we map * to the list [0..], we will get back a list of functions that take only one parameter.

Here's an example:

```
ghci> let listOfFuns = map (*) [0..]
ghci> (listOfFuns !! 4) 5
20
```

Getting the element with the index 4 from our list returns a function that's equivalent to (4*). Then we just apply 5 to that function, which is the same as (4*) 5, or just 4 * 5.

Lambdas

Lambdas are anonymous functions that we use when we need a function only once.

Normally, we make a lambda with the sole purpose of passing it to a higher-order function. To declare a lambda, we write a \ (because it kind of looks like the Greek letter lambda (λ) if you squint hard enough), and then we write the function's parameters, separated by spaces. After that comes a ->, and then the function body. We usually surround lambdas with parentheses.

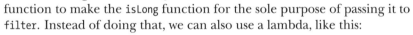

In the previous section, we used a where binding in our numLongChains function to make the isLong function for the sole purpose of passing it to filter. Instead of doing that, we can also use a lambda, like this:

```
numLongChains :: Int
numLongChains = length (filter (\xs -> length xs > 15) (map chain [1..100]))
```

Lambdas are expressions, which is why we can just pass them to functions like this. The expression (\xs -> length xs > 15) returns a function that tells us whether the length of the list passed to it is greater than 15.

People who don't understand how currying and partial application work often use lambdas where they are not necessary. For instance, the following expressions are equivalent:

```
ghci> map (+3) [1,6,3,2]
[4,9,6,5]
ghci> map (\x -> x + 3) [1,6,3,2]
[4,9,6,5]
```

Both (+3) and (\x -> x + 3) are functions that take a number and add 3 to it, so these expressions yield the same results. However, we don't want to make a lambda in this case, because using partial application is much more readable.

Like normal functions, lambdas can take any number of parameters:

```
ghci> zipWith (\a b -> (a * 30 + 3) / b) [5,4,3,2,1] [1,2,3,4,5]
[153.0,61.5,31.0,15.75,6.6]
```

And like normal functions, you can pattern match in lambdas. The only difference is that you can't define several patterns for one parameter (like making a [] and a (x:xs) pattern for the same parameter and then having values fall through).

```
ghci> map (\(a,b) -> a + b) [(1,2),(3,5),(6,3),(2,6),(2,5)]
[3,8,9,8,7]
```

NOTE *If a pattern match fails in a lambda, a runtime error occurs, so be careful!*

Let's look at another interesting example:

```
addThree :: Int -> Int -> Int -> Int
addThree x y z = x + y + z

addThree' :: Int -> Int -> Int -> Int
addThree' = \x -> \y -> \z -> x + y + z
```

Due to the way functions are curried by default, these two functions are equivalent. Yet the first addThree function is far more readable. The second one is little more than a gimmick to illustrate currying.

NOTE *Notice that in the second example, the lambdas are not surrounded with parentheses. When you write a lambda without parentheses, it assumes that everything to the right of the arrow -> belongs to it. So in this case, omitting the parentheses saves some typing. Of course, you can include the parentheses if you prefer them.*

However, there are times when using the currying notation instead is useful. I think that the flip function is the most readable when it's defined like this:

```
flip' :: (a -> b -> c) -> b -> a -> c
flip' f = \x y -> f y x
```

Even though this is the same as writing flip' f x y = f y x, our new notation makes it obvious that this will often be used for producing a new function. The most common use case with flip is calling it with just the function parameter, or the function parameter and one extra parameter, and then passing the resulting function on to a map or a zipWith:

```
ghci> zipWith (flip (++)) ["love you", "love me"] ["i ", "you "]
["i love you","you love me"]
ghci> map (flip subtract 20) [1,2,3,4]
[19,18,17,16]
```

You can use lambdas this way in your own functions when you want to make it explicit that your functions are meant to be partially applied and then passed on to other functions as a parameter.

I Fold You So

Back when we were dealing with recursion in Chapter 4, many of the recursive functions that operated on lists followed the same pattern. We had a base case for the empty list, we introduced the x:xs pattern, and then we performed some action involving a single element and the rest of the list. It turns out this is a very common pattern, so the creators of Haskell introduced some useful functions, called *folds*, to encapsulate it. Folds allow you to reduce a data structure (like a list) to a single value.

Folds can be used to implement any function where you traverse a list once, element by element, and then return something based on that. Whenever you want to traverse a list to return something, chances are you want a fold.

A fold takes a *binary function* (one that takes two parameters, such as + or div), a starting value (often called the *accumulator*), and a list to fold up.

Lists can be folded up from the left or from the right. The fold function calls the given binary function, using the accumulator and the first (or last) element of the list as parameters. The resulting value is the new accumulator. Then the fold function calls the binary function again with the new accumulator and the new first (or last) element of the list, resulting in another new accumulator. This repeats until the function has traversed the entire list and reduced it down to a single accumulator value.

Left Folds with foldl

First, let's look at the `foldl` function. This is called a *left fold*, since it folds the list up from the left side. In this case, the binary function is applied between the starting accumulator and the head of the list. That produces a new accumulator value, and the binary function is called with that value and the next element, and so on.

Let's implement the `sum` function again, this time using a fold instead of explicit recursion:

```
sum' :: (Num a) => [a] -> a
sum' xs = foldl (\acc x -> acc + x) 0 xs
```

Now we can test it:

```
ghci> sum' [3,5,2,1]
11
```

0 + 3
[3, 5, 2, 1]

3 + 5
[5, 2, 1]

8 + 2
[2, 1]

10 + 1
[1]

11

Let's take an in-depth look at how this fold happens. `\acc x -> acc + x` is the binary function. 0 is the starting value, and xs is the list to be folded up. First, 0 and 3 are passed to the binary function as the acc and x parameters, respectively. In this case, the binary function is simply an addition, so the two values are added, which produces 3 as the new accumulator value. Next, 3 and the next list value (5) are passed to the binary function, and they are added together to produce 8 as the new accumulator value. In the same way, 8 and 2 are added together to produce 10, and then 10 and 1 are added together to produce the final value of 11. Congratulations, you've folded your first list!

The diagram on the left illustrates how a fold happens, step by step. The number that's on the left side of the + is the accumulator value. You can see how the list is consumed up from the left side by the accumulator. (Om nom nom nom!) If we take into account that functions are curried, we can write this implementation even more succinctly, like so:

```
sum' :: (Num a) => [a] -> a
sum' = foldl (+) 0
```

The lambda function (\acc x -> acc + x) is the same as (+). We can omit the xs as the parameter because calling `foldl (+) 0` will return a function that takes a list. Generally, if you have a function like foo a = bar b a, you can rewrite it as foo = bar b because of currying.

Right Folds with foldr

The right fold function, `foldr`, is similar to the left fold, except the accumulator eats up the values from the right. Also, the order of the parameters in the right fold's binary function is reversed: The current list value is the first parameter, and the accumulator is the second. (It makes sense that the right fold has the accumulator on the right, since it folds from the right side.)

The accumulator value (and hence, the result) of a fold can be of any type. It can be a number, a Boolean, or even a new list. As an example, let's implement the `map` function with a right fold. The accumulator will be a list, and we'll be accumulating the mapped list element by element. Of course, our starting element will need to be an empty list:

```
map' :: (a -> b) -> [a] -> [b]
map' f xs = foldr (\x acc -> f x : acc) [] xs
```

If we're mapping (+3) to [1,2,3], we approach the list from the right side. We take the last element, which is 3, and apply the function to it, which gives 6. Then we prepend it to the accumulator, which was []. 6:[] is [6], so that's now the accumulator. We then apply (+3) to 2, yielding 5, and prepend (:) that to the accumulator. Our new accumulator value is now [5,6]. We then apply (+3) to 1 and prepend the result to the accumulator again, giving a final result of [4,5,6].

Of course, we could have implemented this function with a left fold instead, like this:

```
map' :: (a -> b) -> [a] -> [b]
map' f xs = foldl (\acc x -> acc ++ [f x]) [] xs
```

However, the `++` function is much slower than `:`, so we usually use right folds when we're building up new lists from a list.

One big difference between the two types of folds is that right folds work on infinite lists, whereas left ones don't!

Let's implement one more function with a right fold. As you know, the elem function checks whether a value is part of a list. Here's how we can use `foldr` to implement it:

```
elem' :: (Eq a) => a -> [a] -> Bool
elem' y ys = foldr (\x acc -> if x == y then True else acc) False ys
```

Here, the accumulator is a Boolean value. (Remember that the type of the accumulator value and the type of the end result are always the same when dealing with folds.) We start with a value of `False`, since we're assuming the value isn't in the list to begin with. This also gives us the correct value if we call it on the empty list, since calling a fold on an empty list just returns the starting value.

Next, we check if the current element is the element we want. If it is, we set the accumulator to True. If it's not, we just leave the accumulator unchanged. If it was False before, it stays that way because this current element is not the one we're seeking. If it was True, it stays that way as the rest of the list is folded up.

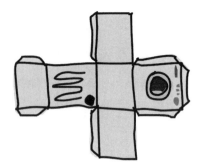

The foldl and foldr1 Functions

The foldl1 and foldr1 functions work much like foldl and foldr, except that you don't need to provide them with an explicit starting accumulator. They assume the first (or last) element of the list to be the starting accumulator, and then start the fold with the element next to it. With that in mind, the maximum function can be implemented like so:

```
maximum' :: (Ord a) => [a] -> a
maximum' = foldl1 max
```

We implemented maximum by using a foldl1. Instead of providing a starting accumulator, foldl1 just assumes the first element as the starting accumulator and moves on to the second one. So all foldl1 needs is a binary function and a list to fold up! We start at the beginning of the list and then compare each element with the accumulator. If it's greater than our accumulator, we keep it as the new accumulator; otherwise, we keep the old one. We passed max to foldl1 as the binary function because it does exactly that: takes two values and returns the one that's larger. By the time we've finished folding our list, only the largest element remains.

Because they depend on the lists they're called with having at least one element, these functions cause runtime errors if called with empty lists. foldl and foldr, on the other hand, work fine with empty lists.

NOTE *When making a fold, think about how it acts on an empty list. If the function doesn't make sense when given an empty list, you can probably use a foldl1 or foldr1 to implement it.*

Some Fold Examples

To demonstrate how powerful folds are, let's implement some standard library functions using folds. First, we'll write our own version of reverse:

```
reverse' :: [a] -> [a]
reverse' = foldl (\acc x -> x : acc) []
```

Here, we reverse a list by using the empty list as a starting accumulator and then approaching our original list from the left and placing the current element at the start of the accumulator.

The function \acc x -> x : acc is just like the : function, except that the parameters are flipped. That's why we could have also written reverse' like so:

```
reverse' :: [a] -> [a]
reverse' = foldl (flip (:)) []
```

Next, we'll implement product:

```
product' :: (Num a) => [a] -> a
product' = foldl (*) 1
```

To calculate the product of all the numbers in the list, we start with 1 as the accumulator. Then we fold left with the * function, multiplying each element with the accumulator.

Now we'll implement filter:

```
filter' :: (a -> Bool) -> [a] -> [a]
filter' p = foldr (\x acc -> if p x then x : acc else acc) []
```

Here, we use an empty list as the starting accumulator. Then we fold from the right and inspect each element. p is our predicate. If p x is True—meaning that if the predicate holds for the current element—we put it at the beginning of the accumulator. Otherwise, we just reuse our old accumulator.

Finally, we'll implement last:

```
last' :: [a] -> a
last' = foldl1 (\_ x -> x)
```

To get the last element of a list, we use a foldl1. We start at the first element of the list, and then use a binary function that disregards the accumulator and always sets the current element as the new accumulator. Once we've reached the end, the accumulator—that is, the last element—will be returned.

Another Way to Look at Folds

Another way to picture right and left folds is as successive applications of some function to elements in a list. Say we have a right fold, with a binary function f and a starting accumulator z. When we right fold over the list [3,4,5,6], we're essentially doing this:

```
f 3 (f 4 (f 5 (f 6 z)))
```

f is called with the last element in the list and the accumulator, then that value is given as the accumulator to the next-to-last value, and so on.

If we take f to be + and the starting accumulator value to be 0, we're doing this:

```
3 + (4 + (5 + (6 + 0)))
```

Or if we write + as a prefix function, we're doing this:

```
(+) 3 ((+) 4 ((+) 5 ((+) 6 0)))
```

Similarly, doing a left fold over that list with g as the binary function and z as the accumulator is the equivalent of this:

```
g (g (g (g z 3) 4) 5) 6
```

If we use flip (:) as the binary function and [] as the accumulator (so we're reversing the list), that's the equivalent of the following:

```
flip (:) (flip (:) (flip (:) (flip (:) [] 3) 4) 5) 6
```

And sure enough, if you evaluate that expression, you get [6,5,4,3].

Folding Infinite Lists

Viewing folds as successive function applications on values of a list can give you insight as to why foldr sometimes works perfectly fine on infinite lists. Let's implement the and function with a foldr, and then write it out as a series of successive function applications, as we did with our previous examples. You'll see how foldr works with Haskell's laziness to operate on lists that have infinite length.

The and function takes a list of Bool values and returns False if one or more elements are False; otherwise, it returns True. We'll approach the list from the right and use True as the starting accumulator. We'll use && as the binary function, because we want to end up with True only if all the elements are True. The && function returns False if either of its parameters is False, so if we come across an element in the list that is False, the accumulator will be set as False and the final result will also be False, even if all the remaining elements are True:

```
and' :: [Bool] -> Bool
and' xs = foldr (&&) True xs
```

Knowing how foldr works, we see that the expression and' [True,False,True] will be evaluated like this:

```
True && (False && (True && True))
```

The last True represents our starting accumulator, whereas the first three Bool values are from the list [True,False,True]. If we try to evaluate the previous expression, we will get False.

Now what if we try this with an infinite list, say repeat False, which has an infinite number of elements, all of which are False? If we write that out, we get something like this:

```
False && (False && (False && (False ...
```

Haskell is lazy, so it will compute only what it really must. And the && function works in such a way that if its first parameter is False, it disregards its second parameter, because the && function returns True only if both of its parameters are True:

```
(&&) :: Bool -> Bool -> Bool
True && x = x
False && _ = False
```

In the case of the endless list of False values, the second pattern matches, and False is returned without Haskell needing to evaluate the rest of the infinite list:

```
ghci> and' (repeat False)
False
```

foldr will work on infinite lists when the binary function that we're passing to it doesn't always need to evaluate its second parameter to give us some sort of answer. For instance, && doesn't care what its second parameter is if its first parameter is False.

Scans

The scanl and scanr functions are like foldl and foldr, except they report all the intermediate accumulator states in the form of a list. The scanl1 and scanr1 functions are analogous to foldl1 and foldr1. Here are some examples of these functions in action:

```
ghci> scanl (+) 0 [3,5,2,1]
[0,3,8,10,11]
ghci> scanr (+) 0 [3,5,2,1]
[11,8,3,1,0]
ghci> scanl1 (\acc x -> if x > acc then x else acc) [3,4,5,3,7,9,2,1]
[3,4,5,5,7,9,9,9]
ghci> scanl (flip (:)) [] [3,2,1]
[[],[3],[2,3],[1,2,3]]
```

When using a scanl, the final result will be in the last element of the resulting list. scanr will place the result in the head of the list.

Scans are used to monitor the progress of a function that can be implemented as a fold. As an exercise in using scans, let's try answering this question: How many elements does it take for the sum of the square roots of all natural numbers to exceed 1,000?

To get the square roots of all natural numbers, we just call map sqrt [1..]. To get the sum, we could use a fold. However, because we're interested in how the sum progresses, we'll use a scan instead. Once we've done the scan, we can check how many sums are under 1,000.

```
sqrtSums :: Int
sqrtSums = length (takeWhile (<1000) (scanl1 (+) (map sqrt [1..]))) + 1
```

We use takeWhile here instead of filter because filter wouldn't cut off the resulting list once a number that's equal to or over 1,000 is found; it would keep searching. Even though we know the list is ascending, filter doesn't, so we use takeWhile to cut off the scan list at the first occurrence of a sum greater than 1,000.

The first sum in the scan list will be 1. The second will be 1 plus the square root of 2. The third will be that plus the square root of 3. If there are x sums under 1,000, then it takes $x+1$ elements for the sum to exceed 1,000:

```
ghci> sqrtSums
131
ghci> sum (map sqrt [1..131])
1005.0942035344083
ghci> sum (map sqrt [1..130])
993.6486803921487
```

And behold, our answer is correct! If we sum the first 130 square roots, the result is just below 1,000, but if we add another one to that, we go over our threshold.

Function Application with $

Now we'll look at the $ function, also called the *function application operator*. First, let's see how it's defined:

```
($) :: (a -> b) -> a -> b
f $ x = f x
```

What the heck? What is this useless function? It's just function application! Well, that's almost true, but not quite. Whereas normal function application (putting a space between two things) has a really high precedence, the $ function has the lowest precedence. Function application with a space is left-associative (so f a b c is the same as ((f a) b) c), while function application with $ is right-associative.

So how does this help us? Most of the time, it's a convenience function that lets us write fewer parentheses. For example, consider the expression sum (map sqrt [1..130]). Because $ has such a low precedence, we can rewrite that expression as sum $ map sqrt [1..130]. When a $ is encountered, the expression on its right is applied as the parameter to the function on its left.

How about sqrt 3 + 4 + 9? This adds together 9, 4, and the square root of 3. However, if we wanted the square root of 3 + 4 + 9, we would need to write sqrt (3 + 4 + 9). With $, we can also write this as sqrt $ 3 + 4 + 9. You can imagine $ as almost being the equivalent of writing an opening parenthesis and then writing a closing parenthesis on the far right side of the expression.

Let's look at another example:

```
ghci> sum (filter (> 10) (map (*2) [2..10]))
80
```

Whoa, that's a lot of parentheses! It looks kind of ugly. Here, (*2) is mapped onto [2..10], then we filter the resulting list to keep only those numbers that are larger than 10, and finally those numbers are added together.

We can use the $ function to rewrite our previous example and make it a little easier on the eyes:

```
ghci> sum $ filter (> 10) (map (*2) [2..10])
80
```

The $ function is right-associative, meaning that something like f $ g $ x is equivalent to f $ (g $ x). With that in mind, the preceding example can once again be rewritten as follows:

```
ghci> sum $ filter (> 10) $ map (*2) [2..10]
80
```

Apart from getting rid of parentheses, $ lets us treat function application like just another function. This allows us to, for instance, map function application over a list of functions, like this:

```
ghci> map ($ 3) [(4+), (10*), (^2), sqrt]
[7.0,30.0,9.0,1.7320508075688772]
```

Here, the function ($ 3) gets mapped over the list. If you think about what the ($ 3) function does, you'll see that it takes a function and then applies that function to 3. So every function in the list gets applied to 3, which is evident in the result.

Function Composition

In mathematics, *function composition* is defined like this: $(f \circ g)(x) = f(g(x))$. This means that composing two functions is the equivalent of calling one function with some value and then calling another function with the result of the first function.

In Haskell, function composition is pretty much the same thing. We do function composition with the . function, which is defined like this:

```
(.) :: (b -> c) -> (a -> b) -> a -> c
f . g = \x -> f (g x)
```

Notice the type declaration. f must take as its parameter a value that has the same type as g's return value. So the resulting function takes a parameter of the same type that g takes and returns a value of the same type that f returns. For example, the expression negate . (* 3) returns a function that takes a number, multiplies it by 3, and then negates it.

One use for function composition is making functions on the fly to pass to other functions. Sure, we can use lambdas for that, but many times, function composition is clearer and more concise.

For example, say we have a list of numbers and we want to turn them all into negative numbers. One way to do that would be to get each number's absolute value and then negate it, like so:

```
ghci> map (\x -> negate (abs x)) [5,-3,-6,7,-3,2,-19,24]
[-5,-3,-6,-7,-3,-2,-19,-24]
```

Notice the lambda and how it looks like the result of function composition. Using function composition, we can rewrite that as follows:

```
ghci> map (negate . abs) [5,-3,-6,7,-3,2,-19,24]
[-5,-3,-6,-7,-3,-2,-19,-24]
```

Fabulous! Function composition is right-associative, so we can compose many functions at a time. The expression f (g (z x)) is equivalent to (f . g . z) x. With that in mind, we can turn something messy, like this:

```
ghci> map (\xs -> negate (sum (tail xs))) [[1..5],[3..6],[1..7]]
[-14,-15,-27]
```

into something much cleaner, like this:

```
ghci> map (negate . sum . tail) [[1..5],[3..6],[1..7]]
[-14,-15,-27]
```

negate . sum . tail is a function that takes a list, applies the tail function to it, then applies the sum function to the result of that, and finally applies negate to the previous result. So it's equivalent to the preceding lambda.

Function Composition with Multiple Parameters

But what about functions that take several parameters? Well, if we want to use them in function composition, we usually must partially apply them so that each function takes just one parameter. Consider this expression:

```
sum (replicate 5 (max 6.7 8.9))
```

This expression can be rewritten as follows:

```
(sum . replicate 5) (max 6.7 8.9)
```

which is equivalent to this:

```
sum . replicate 5 $ max 6.7 8.9
```

The function replicate 5 is applied to the result of max 6.7 8.9, and then sum is applied to that result. Notice that we partially applied the replicate function to the point where it takes only one parameter, so that when the result of max 6.7 8.9 gets passed to replicate 5, the result is a list of numbers, which is then passed to sum.

If we want to rewrite an expression with a lot of parentheses using function composition, we can start by first writing out the innermost function and its parameters. Then we put a $ before it and compose all the functions that came before by writing them without their last parameter and putting dots between them. Say we have this expression:

```
replicate 2 (product (map (*3) (zipWith max [1,2] [4,5])))
```

We can write this as follows:

```
replicate 2 . product . map (*3) $ zipWith max [1,2] [4,5]
```

How did we turn the first example into the second one? Well, first we look at the function on the far right and its parameters, just before the bunch of closing parentheses. That function is zipWith max [1,2] [4,5]. We're going to keep that as it is, so now we have this:

```
zipWith max [1,2] [4,5]
```

Then we look at which function was applied to zipWith max [1,2] [4,5] and see that it was map (*3). So we put a $ between it and what we had before:

```
map (*3) $ zipWith max [1,2] [4,5]
```

Now we start the compositions. We check which function was applied to all this, and we see that it was product, so we compose it with map (*3):

```
product . map (*3) $ zipWith max [1,2] [4,5]
```

And finally, we see that the function replicate 2 was applied to all this, and we can write the expression as follows:

```
replicate 2 . product . map (*3) $ zipWith max [1,2] [4,5]
```

If the expression ends with three parentheses, chances are that if you translate it into function composition by following this procedure, it will have two composition operators.

Point-Free Style

Another common use of function composition is defining functions in the *point-free style*. For example, consider a function we wrote earlier:

```
sum' :: (Num a) => [a] -> a
sum' xs = foldl (+) 0 xs
```

The xs is on the far right on both sides of the equal sign. Because of currying, we can omit the xs on both sides, since calling foldl (+) 0 creates a function that takes a list. In this way, we are writing the function in point-free style:

```
sum' :: (Num a) => [a] -> a
sum' = foldl (+) 0
```

As another example, let's try writing the following function in point-free style:

```
fn x = ceiling (negate (tan (cos (max 50 x))))
```

We can't just get rid of the x on both right sides, since the x in the function body is surrounded by parentheses. cos (max 50) wouldn't make sense—

you can't get the cosine of a function. What we *can* do is express fn as a composition of functions, like this:

```
fn = ceiling . negate . tan . cos . max 50
```

Excellent! Many times, a point-free style is more readable and concise, because it makes you think about functions and what kinds of functions composing them results in, instead of thinking about data and how it's shuffled around. You can take simple functions and use composition as glue to form more complex functions.

However, if a function is too complex, writing it in point-free style can actually be less readable. For this reason, making long chains of function composition is discouraged. The preferred style is to use let bindings to give labels to intermediary results or to split the problem into subproblems that are easier for someone reading the code to understand.

Earlier in the chapter, we solved the problem of finding the sum of all odd squares that are smaller than 10,000. Here's what the solution looks like when put into a function:

```
oddSquareSum :: Integer
oddSquareSum = sum (takeWhile (<10000) (filter odd (map (^2) [1..])))
```

With our knowledge of function composition, we can also write the function like this:

```
oddSquareSum :: Integer
oddSquareSum = sum . takeWhile (<10000) . filter odd $ map (^2) [1..]
```

It may seem a bit weird at first, but you will get used to this style quickly. There's less visual noise because we removed the parentheses. When reading this, you can just say that filter odd is applied to the result of map (^2) [1..], then takeWhile (<10000) is applied to the result of that, and finally sum is applied to that result.

6

MODULES

A Haskell *module* is essentially a file that defines some functions, types, and type classes. A Haskell *program* is a collection of modules.

A module can have many functions and types defined inside it, and it *exports* some of them. This means that it makes them available for the outside world to see and use.

Having code split up into several modules has many advantages. If a module is generic enough, the functions it exports can be used in a multitude of different programs. If your own code is separated into self-contained modules that don't rely on each other too much (we also say they are *loosely coupled*), you can reuse them later. Your code is more manageable when you split it into several parts.

The Haskell standard library is split into modules, and each of them contains functions and types that are somehow related and serve some common purpose. There are modules for manipulating lists, concurrent programming, dealing with complex numbers, and so on. All the functions, types, and type classes that we've dealt with so far are part of the Prelude module, which is imported by default.

In this chapter, we're going to examine a few useful modules and their functions. But first, you need to know how to import modules.

Importing Modules

The syntax for importing modules in a Haskell script is import ModuleName. This must be done before defining any functions, so imports are usually at the top of the file. One script can import several modules—just put each import statement on a separate line.

An example of a useful module is Data.List, which has a bunch of functions for working with lists. Let's import that module and use one of its functions to create our own function that tells us how many unique elements a list has.

```
import Data.List

numUniques :: (Eq a) => [a] -> Int
numUniques = length . nub
```

When you import Data.List, all the functions that Data.List exports become available; you can call them from anywhere in the script. One of those functions is nub, which takes a list and weeds out duplicate elements. Composing length and nub with length . nub produces a function that's the equivalent of \xs -> length (nub xs).

NOTE   *To search for functions or to find out where they're located, use Hoogle, which can be found at* http://www.haskell.org/hoogle/. *It's a really awesome Haskell search engine that allows you to search by function name, module name, or even type signature.*

You can also get access to functions of modules when using GHCi. If you're in GHCi and you want to be able to call the functions exported by Data.List, enter this:

```
ghci> :m + Data.List
```

If you want to access several modules from GHCi, you don't need to enter :m + several times. You can load several modules at once, as in this example:

```
ghci> :m + Data.List Data.Map Data.Set
```

However, if you've loaded a script that already imports a module, you don't need to use :m + to access that module. If you need only a couple of functions from a module, you can selectively import just those functions. For example, here's how you could import only the nub and sort functions from Data.List:

```
import Data.List (nub, sort)
```

You can also choose to import all of the functions of a module except a few select ones. That's often useful when several modules export functions with the same name and you want to get rid of the offending ones. Say you already have your own function called nub and you want to import all the functions from Data.List except the nub function. Here's how to do that:

```
import Data.List hiding (nub)
```

Another way of dealing with name clashes is to do *qualified imports*. Consider the Data.Map module, which offers a data structure for looking up values by key. This module exports a lot of functions with the same name as Prelude functions, such as filter and null. So if we imported Data.Map and then called filter, Haskell wouldn't know which function to use. Here's how we solve this:

```
import qualified Data.Map
```

Now if we want to reference Data.Map's filter function, we must use Data.Map.filter. Entering just filter still refers to the normal filter we all know and love. But typing Data.Map in front of every function from that module is kind of tedious. That's why we can rename the qualified import to something shorter:

```
import qualified Data.Map as M
```

Now to reference Data.Map's filter function, we just use M.filter.

As you've seen, the . symbol is used to reference functions from modules that have been imported as qualified, such as M.filter. We also use it to perform function composition. So how does Haskell know what we mean when we use it? Well, if we place it between a qualified module name and a function, without whitespace, it's regarded as just referring to the imported function; otherwise, it's treated as function composition.

NOTE *A great way to pick up new Haskell knowledge is to just click through the standard library documentation and explore the modules and their functions. You can also view the Haskell source code for each module. Reading the source code of some modules will give you a solid feel for Haskell.*

Solving Problems with Module Functions

The modules in the standard libraries provide many functions that can make our lives easier when coding in Haskell. Let's look at some examples of how to use functions from various Haskell modules to solve problems.

Counting Words

Suppose we have a string that contains a bunch of words, and we want to know how many times each word appears in the string. The first module function we'll use is words from Data.List. The words function converts a string into a list of strings where each string is one word. Here's a quick demonstration:

```
ghci> words "hey these are the words in this sentence"
["hey","these","are","the","words","in","this","sentence"]
ghci> words "hey these        are    the words in this sentence"
["hey","these","are","the","words","in","this","sentence"]
```

Then we'll use the group function, which also lives in Data.List, to group together words that are identical. This function takes a list and groups adjacent elements into sublists if they are equal:

```
ghci> group [1,1,1,1,2,2,2,2,3,3,2,2,2,5,6,7]
[[1,1,1,1],[2,2,2,2],[3,3],[2,2,2],[5],[6],[7]]
```

But what happens if the elements that are equal aren't adjacent in our list?

```
ghci> group ["boom","bip","bip","boom","boom"]
[["boom"],["bip","bip"],["boom","boom"]]
```

We get two lists that contain the string "boom", even though we want all occurrences of some word to end up in the same list. What are we to do? Well, we could sort our list of words beforehand! For that, we'll use the sort function, which hangs its hat in Data.List. It takes a list of things that can be ordered and returns a new list that is like the old one, but ordered from smallest to largest:

```
ghci> sort [5,4,3,7,2,1]
[1,2,3,4,5,7]
ghci> sort ["boom","bip","bip","boom","boom"]
["bip","bip","boom","boom","boom"]
```

Notice that the strings are put in an alphabetical order.

We have all the ingredients for our recipe. Now we just need to write it down. We'll take a string, break it down into a list of words, sort those words, and then group them. Finally, we'll use some mapping magic to get tuples like ("boom", 3), meaning that the word "boom" occurs three times.

```
import Data.List

wordNums :: String -> [(String,Int)]
wordNums = map (\ws -> (head ws, length ws)) . group . sort . words
```

We used function composition to make our final function. It takes a string, such as "wa wa wee wa", and then applies words to that string, resulting in ["wa","wa","wee","wa"]. Then sort is applied to that, and we get ["wa","wa","wa","wee"]. Applying group to this result groups adjacent words that are equal, so we get a list of lists of strings: [["wa","wa","wa"],["wee"]]. Then we map a function that takes a list and returns a tuple, where the first component is the head of the list and the second component is its length, over the grouped words. Our final result is [("wa",3),("wee",1)].

Here's how we could write this function without function composition:

```
wordNums xs = map (\ws -> (head ws,length ws)) (group (sort (words xs)))
```

Wow, parentheses overload! I think it's easy to see how function composition makes this function more readable.

Needle in the Haystack

For our next mission, should we choose to accept it, we will make a function that takes two lists and tells us if the first list is wholly contained anywhere in the second list. For instance, the list [3,4] is contained in [1,2,3,4,5], whereas [2,5] isn't. We'll refer to the list that's being searched as the *haystack* and the list that we're searching for as the *needle.*

For this escapade, we'll use the tails function, which dwells in Data.List. tails takes a list and successively applies the tail function to that list. Here's an example:

```
ghci> tails "party"
["party","arty","rty","ty","y",""]
ghci> tails [1,2,3]
[[1,2,3],[2,3],[3],[]]
```

At this point, it may not be obvious why we need tails at all. Another example will clarify this.

Let's say that we're searching for the string "art" inside the string "party". First, we use tails to get all the tails of the list. Then we examine each tail, and if any one starts with the string "art", we've found the needle in our haystack! If we were looking for "boo" inside "party", no tail would start with the string "boo".

To see if one string starts with another, we'll use the isPrefixOf function, which is also found in Data.List. It takes two lists and tells us if the second one starts with the first one.

```
ghci> "hawaii" `isPrefixOf` "hawaii joe"
True
ghci> "haha" `isPrefixOf` "ha"
False
ghci> "ha" `isPrefixOf` "ha"
True
```

Now we just need to check if any tail of our haystack starts with our needle. For that, we can use the any function from Data.List. It takes a predicate and a list, and it tells us if any element from the list satisfies the predicate. Behold:

```
ghci> any (> 4) [1,2,3]
False
ghci> any (=='F') "Frank Sobotka"
True
ghci> any (\x -> x > 5 && x < 10) [1,4,11]
False
```

Let's put these functions together:

```
import Data.List

isIn :: (Eq a) => [a] -> [a] -> Bool
needle `isIn` haystack = any (needle `isPrefixOf`) (tails haystack)
```

That's all there is to it! We use tails to generate a list of tails of our haystack and then see if any of them starts with our needle. Let's give it a test run:

```
ghci> "art" `isIn` "party"
True
ghci> [1,2] `isIn` [1,3,5]
False
```

Oh, wait a minute! It turns out that the function that we just made is already in Data.List! Curses! It's called isInfixOf, and it does the same work as our isIn function.

Caesar Cipher Salad

Gaius Julius Caesar has entrusted upon us an important task. We must transport a top-secret message to Mark Antony in Gaul. Just in case we get captured, we're going to use some functions from `Data.Char` to be a bit sneaky and encode messages by using the *Caesar cipher.*

The Caesar cipher is a primitive method of encoding messages by shifting each character by a fixed number of positions in the alphabet. We can easily create a sort of Caesar cipher of our own, and we won't constrict ourselves to the alphabet—we'll use the whole range of Unicode characters.

To shift characters forward and backward in the alphabet, we're going to use the `Data.Char` module's `ord` and `chr` functions, which convert characters to their corresponding numbers and vice versa:

```
ghci> ord 'a'
97
ghci> chr 97
'a'
ghci> map ord "abcdefgh"
[97,98,99,100,101,102,103,104]
```

`ord 'a'` returns 97 because 'a' is the ninety-seventh character in the Unicode table of characters.

The difference between the `ord` values of two characters is equal to how far apart they are in the Unicode table.

Let's write a function that takes a number of positions to shift and a string, and returns that string where every character is shifted forward in the alphabet by that many positions.

```
import Data.Char

encode :: Int -> String -> String
encode offset msg = map (\c -> chr $ ord c + offset) msg
```

Encoding a string is as simple as taking our message and mapping over it a function that takes a character, converts it to its corresponding number, adds an offset, and then converts it back to a character. A composition cowboy would write this function as (`chr . (+ offset) . ord`).

```
ghci> encode 3 "hey mark"
"kh|#pdun"
ghci> encode 5 "please instruct your men"
"uqjfxj%nsxywzhy%~tzw%rjs"
ghci> encode 1 "to party hard"
"up!qbsuz!ibse"
```

That's definitely encoded!

Decoding a message is basically just shifting it back by the number of places it was shifted by in the first place.

```
decode :: Int -> String -> String
decode shift msg = encode (negate shift) msg
```

Now we can test it by decoding Caesar's message:

```
ghci> decode 3 "kh|#pdun"
"hey mark"
ghci> decode 5 "uqjfxj%nsxywzhy%~tzw%rjs"
"please instruct your men"
ghci> decode 1 "up!qbsuz!ibse"
"to party hard"
```

On Strict Left Folds

In the previous chapter, you saw how foldl works and how you can use it to implement all sorts of cool functions. However, there's a catch to foldl that we haven't yet explored: Using foldl can sometimes lead to so-called stack overflow errors, which occur when your program uses too much space in a specific part of your computer's memory. To demonstrate, let's use foldl with the + function to sum a list that consists of a hundred 1s:

```
ghci> foldl (+) 0 (replicate 100 1)
100
```

This seems to work. What if we want to use foldl to sum a list that has, as Dr. Evil would put it, *one million* 1s?

```
ghci> foldl (+) 0 (replicate 1000000 1)
*** Exception: stack overflow
```

Ooh, that is truly evil! Now why does this happen? Haskell is lazy, and so it defers actual computation of values for as long as possible. When we use foldl, Haskell doesn't compute (that is, evaluate) the actual accumulator on every step. Instead, it defers its evaluation. In the next step, it again doesn't evaluate the accumulator, but defers the evaluation. It also keeps the old deferred computation in memory, because the new one often refers to its result. So as the fold merrily goes along its way, it builds up a bunch of deferred computations, each taking a not insignificant amount of memory. Eventually, this can cause a stack overflow error.

Here's how Haskell evaluates the expression `foldl (+) 0 [1,2,3]`:

```
foldl (+) 0 [1,2,3] =
foldl (+) (0 + 1) [2,3] =
foldl (+) ((0 + 1) + 2) [3] =
foldl (+) (((0 + 1) + 2) + 3) [] =
((0 + 1) + 2) + 3 =
(1 + 2) + 3 =
3 + 3 =
6
```

As you can see, it first builds up a big stack of deferred computations. Then, once it reaches the empty list, it goes about actually evaluating those deferred computations. This isn't a problem for small lists, but for large lists that contain upward of a million elements, you get a stack overflow, because evaluating all these deferred computations is done recursively. Wouldn't it be nice if there was a function named, say, `foldl'`, that didn't defer computations? It would work like this:

```
foldl' (+) 0 [1,2,3] =
foldl' (+) 1 [2,3] =
foldl' (+) 3 [3] =
foldl' (+) 6 [] =
6
```

Computations wouldn't be deferred between steps of `foldl`, but would get evaluated immediately. Well, we're in luck, because `Data.List` offers this stricter version of `foldl`, and it is indeed called `foldl'`. Let's try to compute the sum of a million 1s with `foldl'`:

```
ghci> foldl' (+) 0 (replicate 1000000 1)
1000000
```

Great success! So, if you get stack overflow errors when using `foldl`, try switching to `foldl'`. There's also a stricter version of `foldl1`, named `foldl1'`.

Let's Find Some Cool Numbers

You're walking along the street, and an old lady comes up to you and says, "Excuse me, what's the first natural number such that the sum of its digits equals 40?"

Well, what now, hotshot? Let's use some Haskell magic to find such a number. For instance, if we sum the digits of the number 123, we get 6, because $1 + 2 + 3$ equals 6. So, what is the first number that has such a property that its digits add up to 40?

First, let's make a function that takes a number and tells us the sum of its digits. We're going to use a cool trick here. First, we'll convert our number to a string by using the show function. Once we have a string, we'll turn each character in that string into a number and then just sum that list of numbers. To turn a character into a number, we'll use a handy function from Data.Char called digitToInt. It takes a Char and returns an Int:

```
ghci> digitToInt '2'
2
ghci> digitToInt 'F'
15
ghci> digitToInt 'z'
*** Exception: Char.digitToInt: not a digit 'z'
```

It works on the characters in the range from '0' to '9' and from 'A' to 'F' (they can also be in lowercase).

Here's our function that takes a number and returns the sum of its digits:

```
import Data.Char
import Data.List

digitSum :: Int -> Int
digitSum = sum . map digitToInt . show
```

We convert it to a string, map digitToInt over that string, and then sum the resulting list of numbers.

Now we need to find the first natural number such that when we apply digitSum to it, we get 40 as the result. To do that, we'll use the find function, which resides in Data.List. It takes a predicate and a list and returns the first element of the list that matches the predicate. However, it has a rather peculiar type declaration:

```
ghci> :t find
find :: (a -> Bool) -> [a] -> Maybe a
```

The first parameter is a predicate, and the second parameter is a list—no big deal here. But what about the return value? It says Maybe a. That's a type you haven't met before. A value with a type of Maybe a is sort of like a list of type [a]. Whereas a list can have zero, one, or many elements, a Maybe a typed value can have either zero elements or just one element. We use it when we want to represent possible failure. To make a value that holds nothing, we just use Nothing. This is analogous to the empty

list. To construct a value that holds something, say the string "hey", we write
Just "hey". Here's a quick demonstration:

```
ghci> Nothing
Nothing
ghci> Just "hey"
Just "hey"
ghci> Just 3
Just 3
ghci> :t Just "hey"
Just "hey" :: Maybe [Char]
ghci> :t Just True
Just True :: Maybe Bool
```

As you can see, a value of Just True has a type of Maybe Bool, kind of like
how a list that holds Booleans would have a type of [Bool].

If find finds an element that satisfies the predicate, it will return that
element wrapped in a Just. If it doesn't, it will return a Nothing:

```
ghci> find (> 4) [3,4,5,6,7]
Just 5
ghci> find odd [2,4,6,8,9]
Just 9
ghci> find (=='z') "mjolnir"
Nothing
```

Now let's get back to making our function. We have our digitSum function and know how find works, so all that's left to do is put these two together. Remember that we want to find the first number whose digits add
up to 40.

```
firstTo40 :: Maybe Int
firstTo40 = find (\x -> digitSum x == 40) [1..]
```

We just take the infinite list [1..], and then find the first number whose
digitSum is 40.

```
ghci> firstTo40
Just 49999
```

There's our answer! If we want to make a more general function that is
not fixed on 40 but takes our desired sum as the parameter, we can change
it like so:

```
firstTo :: Int -> Maybe Int
firstTo n = find (\x -> digitSum x == n) [1..]
```

Here's a quick test:

```
ghci> firstTo 27
Just 999
ghci> firstTo 1
Just 1
ghci> firstTo 13
Just 49
```

Mapping Keys to Values

When dealing with data in some sort of collection, we often don't care if it's in some kind of order; we just want to be able to access it by a certain key. For example, if we want to know who lives at a certain address, we want to look up the name based on the address. When doing such things, we say that we looked up our desired value (someone's name) by some sort of key (that person's address).

Almost As Good: Association Lists

There are many ways to achieve key/value mappings. One of them is the *association list*. Association lists (also called *dictionaries*) are lists that are used to store key/value pairs where ordering doesn't matter. For instance, we might use an association list to store phone numbers, where phone numbers would be the values and people's names would be the keys. We don't care in which order they're stored; we just want to get the right phone number for the right person.

The most obvious way to represent association lists in Haskell would be by having a list of pairs. The first component in the pair would be the key, and the second component would be the value. Here's an example of an association list with phone numbers:

```
phoneBook =
    [("betty", "555-2938")
    ,("bonnie", "452-2928")
    ,("patsy", "493-2928")
    ,("lucille", "205-2928")
    ,("wendy", "939-8282")
    ,("penny", "853-2492")
    ]
```

Despite this seemingly odd indentation, this is just a list of pairs of strings.

The most common task when dealing with association lists is looking up some value by key. Let's make a function that looks up some value given a key.

```
findKey :: (Eq k) => k -> [(k, v)] -> v
findKey key xs = snd . head . filter (\(k, v) -> key == k) $ xs
```

This is pretty simple. The function takes a key and a list, filters the list so that only matching keys remain, gets the first key/value pair that matches, and returns the value.

But what happens if the key we're looking for isn't in the association list? Hmm. Here, if a key isn't in the association list, we'll end up trying to get the head of an empty list, which throws a runtime error. We should avoid making our programs so easy to crash, so let's use the Maybe data type. If we don't find the key, we'll return a Nothing. If we find it, we'll return Just *something*, where *something* is the value corresponding to that key.

```
findKey :: (Eq k) => k -> [(k, v)] -> Maybe v
findKey key [] = Nothing
findKey key ((k,v):xs)
    | key == k  = Just v
    | otherwise = findKey key xs
```

Look at the type declaration. It takes a key that can be equated and an association list, and then it maybe produces a value. Sounds about right.

This is a textbook recursive function that operates on a list. Base case, splitting a list into a head and a tail, recursive calls—they're all there. This is the classic fold pattern, so let's see how this would be implemented as a fold.

```
findKey :: (Eq k) => k -> [(k, v)] -> Maybe v
findKey key xs = foldr (\(k, v) acc -> if key == k then Just v else acc) Nothing xs
```

NOTE   *It's usually better to use folds for this standard list recursion pattern, rather than explicitly writing the recursion, because they're easier to read and identify. Everyone knows it's a fold when they see the foldr call, but it takes some more thinking to read explicit recursion.*

```
ghci> findKey "penny" phoneBook
Just "853-2492"
ghci> findKey "betty" phoneBook
Just "555-2938"
ghci> findKey "wilma" phoneBook
Nothing
```

This works like a charm! If we have the girl's phone number, we Just get the number; otherwise, we get Nothing.

Enter Data.Map

We just implemented the lookup function from Data.List. If we want the value that corresponds to a key, we need to traverse all the elements of the list until we find it.

It turns out that the Data.Map module offers association lists that are much faster, and it also provides a lot of utility functions. From now on, we'll say we're working with *maps* instead of association lists.

Because Data.Map exports functions that clash with the Prelude and Data.List ones, we'll do a qualified import.

```
import qualified Data.Map as Map
```

Put this import statement into a script, and then load the script via GHCi.

We're going to turn an association list into a map by using the fromList function from Data.Map. fromList takes an association list (in the form of a list) and returns a map with the same associations. Let's play around a bit with fromList first:

```
ghci> Map.fromList [(3,"shoes"),(4,"trees"),(9,"bees")]
fromList [(3,"shoes"),(4,"trees"),(9,"bees")]
ghci> Map.fromList [("kima","greggs"),("jimmy","mcnulty"),("jay","landsman")]
fromList [("jay","landsman"),("jimmy","mcnulty"),("kima","greggs")]
```

When a map from Data.Map is displayed on the terminal, it's shown as fromList and then an association list that represents the map, even though it's not a list anymore.

If there are duplicate keys in the original association list, the duplicates are just discarded:

```
ghci> Map.fromList [("MS",1),("MS",2),("MS",3)]
fromList [("MS",3)]
```

This is the type signature of fromList:

```
Map.fromList :: (Ord k) => [(k, v)] -> Map.Map k v
```

It says that it takes a list of pairs of type k and v, and returns a map that maps from keys of type k to values of type v. Notice that when we were doing association lists with normal lists, the keys only needed to be equatable (their type belonging to the Eq type class), but now they must be orderable. That's an essential constraint in the Data.Map module. It needs the keys to be orderable so it can arrange and access them more efficiently.

Now we can modify our original phoneBook association list to be a map. We'll also add a type declaration, just because we can:

```
import qualified Data.Map as Map

phoneBook :: Map.Map String String
phoneBook = Map.fromList $
    [("betty", "555-2938")
    ,("bonnie", "452-2928")
    ,("patsy", "493-2928")
    ,("lucille", "205-2928")
    ,("wendy", "939-8282")
    ,("penny", "853-2492")
    ]
```

Cool! Let's load this script into GHCi and play around with our phoneBook. First, we'll use lookup to search for some phone numbers. lookup takes a key and a map, and tries to find the corresponding value in the map. If it succeeds, it returns the value wrapped in a Just; otherwise, it returns a Nothing:

```
ghci> :t Map.lookup
Map.lookup :: (Ord k) => k -> Map.Map k a -> Maybe a
ghci> Map.lookup "betty" phoneBook
Just "555-2938"
ghci> Map.lookup "wendy" phoneBook
Just "939-8282"
ghci> Map.lookup "grace" phoneBook
Nothing
```

For our next trick, we'll make a new map from phoneBook by inserting a number. insert takes a key, a value, and a map, and returns a new map that's just like the old one, but with the key and value inserted:

```
ghci> :t Map.insert
Map.insert :: (Ord k) => k -> a -> Map.Map k a -> Map.Map k a
ghci> Map.lookup "grace" phoneBook
Nothing
ghci> let newBook = Map.insert "grace" "341-9021" phoneBook
ghci> Map.lookup "grace" newBook
Just "341-9021"
```

Let's check how many numbers we have. We'll use the size function from Data.Map, which takes a map and returns its size. This is pretty straightforward:

```
ghci> :t Map.size
Map.size :: Map.Map k a -> Int
```

```
ghci> Map.size phoneBook
6
ghci> Map.size newBook
7
```

The numbers in our phone book are represented as strings. Suppose we would rather use lists of Ints to represent phone numbers. So, instead of having a number like "939-8282", we want to have [9,3,9,8,2,8,2]. First, we're going to make a function that converts a phone number string to a list of Ints. We can try to map digitToInt from Data.Char over our string, but it won't know what to do with the dash! That's why we need to get rid of anything in that string that isn't a number. To do this, we'll seek help from the isDigit function from Data.Char, which takes a character and tells us if it represents a digit. Once we've filtered our string, we'll just map digitToInt over it.

```
string2digits :: String -> [Int]
string2digits = map digitToInt . filter isDigit
```

Oh, be sure to import Data.Char, if you haven't already.
Let's try this out:

```
ghci> string2digits "948-9282"
[9,4,8,9,2,8,2]
```

Very cool! Now, let's use the map function from Data.Map to map string2digits over our phoneBook:

```
ghci> let intBook = Map.map string2digits phoneBook
ghci> :t intBook
intBook :: Map.Map String [Int]
ghci> Map.lookup "betty" intBook
Just [5,5,5,2,9,3,8]
```

The map from Data.Map takes a function and a map, and applies that function to each value in the map.

Let's extend our phone book. Say that a person can have several numbers, and we have an association list set up like this:

```
phoneBook =
    [("betty", "555-2938")
    ,("betty", "342-2492")
    ,("bonnie", "452-2928")
```

```
,("patsy", "493-2928")
,("patsy", "943-2929")
,("patsy", "827-9162")
,("lucille", "205-2928")
,("wendy", "939-8282")
,("penny", "853-2492")
,("penny", "555-2111")
]
```

If we just use fromList to put that into a map, we'll lose a few numbers! Instead, we'll use another function found in Data.Map: fromListWith. This function acts like fromList, but instead of discarding duplicate keys, it uses a function supplied to it to decide what to do with them.

```
phoneBookToMap :: (Ord k) => [(k, String)] -> Map.Map k String
phoneBookToMap xs = Map.fromListWith add xs
    where add number1 number2 = number1 ++ ", " ++ number2
```

If fromListWith finds that the key is already there, it uses the function supplied to it to join those two values into one and replaces the old value with the one it got by passing the conflicting values to the function:

```
ghci> Map.lookup "patsy" $ phoneBookToMap phoneBook
Just "827-9162, 943-2929, 493-2928"
ghci> Map.lookup "wendy" $ phoneBookToMap phoneBook
Just "939-8282"
ghci> Map.lookup "betty" $ phoneBookToMap phoneBook
Just "342-2492, 555-2938"
```

We could also first make all the values in the association list singleton lists and then use ++ to combine the numbers:

```
phoneBookToMap :: (Ord k) => [(k, a)] -> Map.Map k [a]
phoneBookToMap xs = Map.fromListWith (++) $ map (\(k, v) -> (k, [v])) xs
```

Let's test this in GHCi:

```
ghci> Map.lookup "patsy" $ phoneBookToMap phoneBook
Just ["827-9162","943-2929","493-2928"]
```

Pretty neat!

Now suppose we're making a map from an association list of numbers, and when a duplicate key is found, we want the biggest value for the key to be kept. We can do that like so:

```
ghci> Map.fromListWith max [(2,3),(2,5),(2,100),(3,29),(3,22),(3,11),(4,22),(4,15)]
fromList [(2,100),(3,29),(4,22)]
```

Or we could choose to add together values that share keys:

```
ghci> Map.fromListWith (+) [(2,3),(2,5),(2,100),(3,29),(3,22),(3,11),(4,22),(4,15)]
fromList [(2,108),(3,62),(4,37)]
```

So, you've seen that Data.Map and the other modules provided by Haskell are pretty cool. Next, we'll look at how to make your own module.

Making Our Own Modules

As I said at the beginning of this chapter, when you're writing programs, it's good practice to take functions and types that work toward a similar purpose and put them in a separate module. That way, you can easily reuse those functions in other programs by just importing your module.

We say that a module *exports* functions. When you import a module, you can use the functions that it exports. A module can also define functions that it uses internally, but we can see and use only the ones that it exports.

A Geometry Module

To demonstrate, we'll create a little module that provides some functions for calculating the volume and area of a few geometrical objects. We'll start by creating a file called *Geometry.hs*.

At the beginning of a module, we specify the module name. If we have a file called *Geometry.hs*, then we should name our module Geometry. We specify the functions that it exports, and then we can add the functions. So we'll start with this:

```
module Geometry
( sphereVolume
, sphereArea
, cubeVolume
, cubeArea
, cuboidArea
, cuboidVolume
) where
```

As you can see, we'll be doing areas and volumes for spheres, cubes, and cuboids. A sphere is a round thing like a grapefruit, a cube is like a game die, and a (rectangular) cuboid is like a box of cigarettes. (Kids, don't smoke!)

Now let's define our functions:

```
module Geometry
( sphereVolume
, sphereArea
, cubeVolume
, cubeArea
, cuboidArea
, cuboidVolume
) where

sphereVolume :: Float -> Float
sphereVolume radius = (4.0 / 3.0) * pi * (radius ^ 3)

sphereArea :: Float -> Float
sphereArea radius = 4 * pi * (radius ^ 2)

cubeVolume :: Float -> Float
cubeVolume side = cuboidVolume side side side

cubeArea :: Float -> Float
cubeArea side = cuboidArea side side side

cuboidVolume :: Float -> Float -> Float -> Float
cuboidVolume a b c = rectArea a b * c

cuboidArea :: Float -> Float -> Float -> Float
cuboidArea a b c = rectArea a b * 2 + rectArea a c * 2 +
rectArea c b * 2

rectArea :: Float -> Float -> Float
rectArea a b = a * b
```

This is pretty standard geometry, but there are a few items to note. One is that because a cube is only a special case of a cuboid, we define its area and volume by treating it as a cuboid whose sides are all of the same length. We also define a helper function called rectArea, which calculates a rectangle's area based on the lengths of its sides. It's rather trivial because it's just multiplication. Notice that we used it in our functions in the module (in cuboidArea and cuboidVolume), but we didn't export it! This is because we want our module to present just functions for dealing with three-dimensional objects.

When making a module, we usually export only those functions that act as a sort of interface to our module so that the implementation is hidden. People who use our Geometry module don't need to concern themselves with functions that we don't export. We can decide to change those functions completely or delete them in a newer version (we could delete rectArea and just use * instead), and no one will mind, because we didn't export them in the first place.

To use our module, we just do this:

```
import Geometry
```

However, *Geometry.hs* must be in the same folder as the module that's importing it.

Hierarchical Modules

Modules can also be given a hierarchical structure. Each module can have a number of submodules, which can have submodules of their own. Let's section our geometry functions so that Geometry is a module that has three submodules: one for each type of object.

First, we'll make a folder called *Geometry*. In it, we'll place three files: *Sphere.hs*, *Cuboid.hs*, and *Cube.hs*. Let's look at what each of the files contains.

Here are the contents of *Sphere.hs*:

```
module Geometry.Sphere
( volume
, area
) where

volume :: Float -> Float
volume radius = (4.0 / 3.0) * pi * (radius ^ 3)

area :: Float -> Float
area radius = 4 * pi * (radius ^ 2)
```

The *Cuboid.hs* file looks like this:

```
module Geometry.Cuboid
( volume
, area
) where

volume :: Float -> Float -> Float -> Float
volume a b c = rectArea a b * c

area :: Float -> Float -> Float -> Float
area a b c = rectArea a b * 2 + rectArea a c * 2 + rectArea c b * 2

rectArea :: Float -> Float -> Float
rectArea a b = a * b
```

And our last file, *Cube.hs*, has these contents:

```
module Geometry.Cube
( volume
, area
) where

import qualified Geometry.Cuboid as Cuboid

volume :: Float -> Float
volume side = Cuboid.volume side side side

area :: Float -> Float
area side = Cuboid.area side side side
```

Notice how we placed *Sphere.hs* in a folder called *Geometry*, and then defined the module name as Geometry.Sphere. We did the same for the cube and cuboid objects. Also notice how in all three submodules, we defined functions with the same names. We can do this because they're in separate modules.

So, now we can do this:

```
import Geometry.Sphere
```

And then we can call area and volume, and they'll give us the area and volume for a sphere.

If we want to juggle two or more of these modules, we need to do qualified imports because they export functions with the same names. Here's an example:

```
import qualified Geometry.Sphere as Sphere
import qualified Geometry.Cuboid as Cuboid
import qualified Geometry.Cube as Cube
```

And then we can call Sphere.area, Sphere.volume, Cuboid.area, and so on, and each will calculate the area or volume for its corresponding object.

The next time you find yourself writing a file that's really big and has a lot of functions, look for functions that serve some common purpose and consider putting them in their own module. Then you'll be able to just import your module the next time you're writing a program that requires some of the same functionality.

7

MAKING OUR OWN TYPES AND TYPE CLASSES

So far, we've run into a lot of data types: Bool, Int, Char, Maybe, and so on. But how do we make our own? In this chapter, you'll learn how to create custom types and put them to work!

Defining a New Data Type

One way to make our own type is to use the data keyword. Let's see how the Bool type is defined in the standard library.

```
data Bool = False | True
```

Using the data keyword like this means that a new data type is being defined. The part before the equal sign denotes the type, which in this case is Bool. The parts after the equal sign are value constructors. They specify the different values that this type can have. The | is read as *or*. So we can read this as saying that the Bool type can have a value of True or False. Note that both the type name and the value constructors must start with an uppercase letter.

In a similar fashion, we can think of the Int type as being defined like this:

```
data Int = -2147483648 | -2147483647 | ... | -1 | 0 | 1 | 2 | ... | 2147483647
```

The first and last value constructors are the minimum and maximum possible values of Int. It's not actually defined like this—you can see I've omitted a bunch of numbers—but this is useful for illustrative purposes.

Now let's think about how we would represent a shape in Haskell. One way would be to use tuples. A circle could be denoted as (43.1, 55.0, 10.4), where the first and second fields are the coordinates of the circle's center and the third field is the radius. The problem is that those could also represent a 3D vector or anything else that could be identified by three numbers. A better solution would be to make our own type to represent a shape.

Shaping Up

Let's say that a shape can be a circle or a rectangle. Here's one possible definition:

```
data Shape = Circle Float Float Float | Rectangle Float Float Float Float
```

What does it mean? Think of it like this: The Circle value constructor has three fields, which take floats. So when we write a value constructor, we can optionally add some types after it, and those types define the types of values it will contain. Here, the first two fields are the coordinates of its center, and the third one is its radius. The Rectangle value constructor has four fields that accept floats. The first two act as the coordinates to its upper-left corner, and the second two act as coordinates to its lower-right corner.

Value constructors are actually functions that ultimately return a value of a data type. Let's take a look at the type signatures for these two value constructors.

```
ghci> :t Circle
Circle :: Float -> Float -> Float -> Shape
ghci> :t Rectangle
Rectangle :: Float -> Float -> Float -> Float -> Shape
```

So value constructors are functions like everything else. Who would have thought? The fields that are in the data type act as parameters to its value constructors.

Now let's make a function that takes a Shape and returns its area.

```
area :: Shape -> Float
area (Circle _ _ r) = pi * r ^ 2
area (Rectangle x1 y1 x2 y2) = (abs $ x2 - x1) * (abs $ y2 - y1)
```

First, note the type declaration. It says that the function takes a Shape and returns a Float. We couldn't write a type declaration of Circle -> Float, because Circle is not a type, while Shape is (just as we can't write a function with a type declaration of True -> Int, for example).

Next, notice that we can pattern match against constructors. We've already done this against values like [], False, and 5, but those values didn't have any fields. In this case, we just write a constructor and then bind its fields to names. Because we're interested in only the radius, we don't actually care about the first two fields, which tell us where the circle is.

```
ghci> area $ Circle 10 20 10
314.15927
ghci> area $ Rectangle 0 0 100 100
10000.0
```

Yay, it works! But if we try to just print out Circle 10 20 5 from the prompt, we'll get an error. That's because Haskell doesn't know how to display our data type as a string (yet). Remember that when we try to print a value out from the prompt, Haskell first applies the show function to it to get the string representation of our value, and then it prints that to the terminal.

To make our Shape type part of the Show type class, we modify it like this:

```
data Shape = Circle Float Float Float | Rectangle Float Float Float Float
    deriving (Show)
```

We won't concern ourselves with deriving too much for now. Let's just say that if we add deriving (Show) at the end of a data declaration (it can go on the same line or the next one—it doesn't matter), Haskell automatically makes that type part of the Show type class. We'll be taking a closer look at deriving in "Derived Instances" on page 122.

So now we can do this:

```
ghci> Circle 10 20 5
Circle 10.0 20.0 5.0
ghci> Rectangle 50 230 60 90
Rectangle 50.0 230.0 60.0 90.0
```

Value constructors are functions, so we can map them, partially apply them, and so on. If we want a list of concentric circles with different radii, we can do this:

```
ghci> map (Circle 10 20) [4,5,6,6]
[Circle 10.0 20.0 4.0,Circle 10.0 20.0 5.0,Circle 10.0 20.0 6.0,Circle 10.0
20.0 6.0]
```

Improving Shape with the Point Data Type

Our data type is good, but it could be better. Let's make an intermediate data type that defines a point in two-dimensional space. Then we can use that to make our shapes more understandable.

```
data Point = Point Float Float deriving (Show)
data Shape = Circle Point Float | Rectangle Point Point deriving (Show)
```

Notice that when defining a point, we used the same name for the data type and the value constructor. This has no special meaning, although it's common if there's only one value constructor. So now the Circle has two fields: One is of type Point and the other of type Float. This makes it easier to understand what's what. The same goes for Rectangle. Now we need to adjust our area function to reflect these changes.

```
area :: Shape -> Float
area (Circle _ r) = pi * r ^ 2
area (Rectangle (Point x1 y1) (Point x2 y2)) = (abs $ x2 - x1) * (abs $ y2 - y1)
```

The only thing we needed to change were the patterns. We disregarded the whole point in the Circle pattern. In the Rectangle pattern, we just used nested pattern matching to get the fields of the points. If we wanted to reference the points themselves for some reason, we could have used as-patterns.

Now we can test our improved version:

```
ghci> area (Rectangle (Point 0 0) (Point 100 100))
10000.0
ghci> area (Circle (Point 0 0) 24)
1809.5574
```

How about a function that nudges a shape? It takes a shape, the amount to move it on the x axis, and the amount to move it on the y axis. It returns a new shape that has the same dimensions but is located somewhere else.

```
nudge :: Shape -> Float -> Float -> Shape
nudge (Circle (Point x y) r) a b = Circle (Point (x+a) (y+b)) r
nudge (Rectangle (Point x1 y1) (Point x2 y2)) a b
    = Rectangle (Point (x1+a) (y1+b)) (Point (x2+a) (y2+b))
```

This is pretty straightforward. We add the nudge amounts to the points that denote the position of the shape. Let's test it:

```
ghci> nudge (Circle (Point 34 34) 10) 5 10
Circle (Point 39.0 44.0) 10.0
```

If we don't want to deal with points directly, we can make some auxiliary functions that create shapes of some size at the zero coordinates and then nudge those.

First, let's make a function that takes a radius and makes a circle that is located at the origin of the coordinate system, with the radius we supplied:

```
baseCircle :: Float -> Shape
baseCircle r = Circle (Point 0 0) r
```

Now let's make a function that takes a width and a height and makes a rectangle with those dimensions and its bottom-left corner located at the origin:

```
baseRect :: Float -> Float -> Shape
baseRect width height = Rectangle (Point 0 0) (Point width height)
```

Now we can use these functions to make shapes that are located at the origin of the coordinate system and then nudge them to where we want them to be, which makes it easier to create shapes:

```
ghci> nudge (baseRect 40 100) 60 23
Rectangle (Point 60.0 23.0) (Point 100.0 123.0)
```

Exporting Our Shapes in a Module

You can also export your data types in your custom modules. To do that, just write your type along with the functions you are exporting, and then add some parentheses that specify the value constructors that you want to export, separated by commas. If you want to export all the value constructors for a given type, just write two dots (..).

Suppose we want to export our shape functions and types in a module. We start off like this:

```
module Shapes
( Point(..)
, Shape(..)
, area
, nudge
, baseCircle
, baseRect
) where
```

By using Shape(..), we export all the value constructors for Shape. This means that people who import our module can make shapes by using the Rectangle and Circle value constructors. It's the same as writing Shape (Rectangle, Circle), but shorter.

Also, if we decide to add some value constructors to our type later on, we don't need to modify the exports. That's because using .. automatically exports all value constructors for a given type.

Alternatively, we could opt to not export any value constructors for Shape by just writing Shape in the export statement, without the parentheses. That way, people who import our module could make shapes only by using the auxiliary functions baseCircle and baseRect.

Remember that value constructors are just functions that take the fields as parameters and return a value of some type (like Shape). So when we choose not to export them, we prevent the person importing our module from using those value constructors directly. Not exporting the value constructors of our data types makes them more abstract, since we're hiding their implementation. Also, whoever uses our module can't pattern match against the value constructors. This is good if we want people who import our module to be able to interact with our type only via the auxiliary functions that we supply in our module. That way, they don't need to know about the internal details of our module, and we can change those details whenever we want, as long as the functions that we export act the same.

Data.Map uses this approach. You can't create a map by directly using its value constructor, whatever it may be, because it's not exported. However, you can make a map by using one of the auxiliary functions like Map.fromList. The people in charge of Data.Map can change the way that maps are internally represented without breaking existing programs.

But for simpler data types, exporting the value constructors is perfectly fine, too.

Record Syntax

Now let's look at how we can create another kind of data type. Say we've been tasked with creating a data type that describes a person. The information that we want to store about that person is first name, last name, age, height, phone number, and favorite ice cream flavor. (I don't know about you, but that's all I ever want to know about a person.) Let's give it a go!

```
data Person = Person String String Int Float String String deriving (Show)
```

The first field is the first name, the second is the last name, the third is the age, and so on. Now let's make a person.

```
ghci> let guy = Person "Buddy" "Finklestein" 43 184.2 "526-2928" "Chocolate"
ghci> guy
Person "Buddy" "Finklestein" 43 184.2 "526-2928" "Chocolate"
```

That's kind of cool, although slightly unreadable.

Now what if we want to create functions to get specific pieces of information about a person? We need a function that gets some person's first name, a function that gets some person's last name, and so on. Well, we would need to define them like this:

```
firstName :: Person -> String
firstName (Person firstname _ _ _ _ _) = firstname

lastName :: Person -> String
lastName (Person _ lastname _ _ _ _) = lastname

age :: Person -> Int
age (Person _ _ age _ _ _) = age

height :: Person -> Float
height (Person _ _ _ height _ _) = height

phoneNumber :: Person -> String
phoneNumber (Person _ _ _ _ number _) = number

flavor :: Person -> String
flavor (Person _ _ _ _ _ flavor) = flavor
```

Whew! I certainly did not enjoy writing that! But despite being very cumbersome and *boring* to write, this method works.

```
ghci> let guy = Person "Buddy" "Finklestein" 43 184.2 "526-2928" "Chocolate"
ghci> firstName guy
"Buddy"
ghci> height guy
184.2
ghci> flavor guy
"Chocolate"
```

"Still, there must be a better way!" you say. Well, no, there isn't, sorry. Just kidding—there is. Hahaha!

Haskell gives us an alternative way to write data types. Here's how we could achieve the same functionality with *record syntax*:

```
data Person = Person { firstName :: String
                     , lastName :: String
                     , age :: Int
                     , height :: Float
                     , phoneNumber :: String
                     , flavor :: String } deriving (Show)
```

So instead of just naming the field types one after another and separating them with spaces, we use curly brackets. First, we write the name of the field (for instance, firstName), followed by a double colon (::), and then the type. The resulting data type is exactly the same. The main benefit of using this syntax is that it creates functions that look up fields in the data type. By using record syntax to create this data type, Haskell automatically makes these functions: firstName, lastName, age, height, phoneNumber, and flavor. Take a look:

```
ghci> :t flavor
flavor :: Person -> String
ghci> :t firstName
firstName :: Person -> String
```

There's another benefit to using record syntax. When we derive Show for the type, it displays it differently if we use record syntax to define and instantiate the type.

Say we have a type that represents a car. We want to keep track of the company that made it, the model name, and its year of production. We can define this type without using record syntax, like so:

```
data Car = Car String String Int deriving (Show)
```

A car is displayed like this:

```
ghci> Car "Ford" "Mustang" 1967
Car "Ford" "Mustang" 1967
```

Now let's see what happens when we define it using record syntax:

```
data Car = Car { company :: String
               , model :: String
               , year :: Int
               } deriving (Show)
```

We can make a car like this:

```
ghci> Car {company="Ford", model="Mustang", year=1967}
Car {company = "Ford", model = "Mustang", year = 1967}
```

When making a new car, we don't need to put the fields in the proper order, as long as we list all of them. But if we don't use record syntax, we must specify them in order.

Use record syntax when a constructor has several fields and it's not obvious which field is which. If we make a 3D vector data type by doing `data Vector = Vector Int Int Int`, it's pretty obvious that the fields are the components of a vector. However, in our `Person` and `Car` types, the fields are not so obvious, and we greatly benefit from using record syntax.

Type Parameters

A value constructor can take some parameters and then produce a new value. For instance, the `Car` constructor takes three values and produces a car value. In a similar manner, type constructors can take types as parameters to produce new types. This might sound a bit too meta at first, but it's not that complicated. (If you're familiar with templates in C++, you'll see some parallels.) To get a clear picture of how type parameters work in action, let's take a look at how a type we've already met is implemented.

```
data Maybe a = Nothing | Just a
```

The `a` here is the type parameter. And because there's a type parameter involved, we call `Maybe` a *type constructor*. Depending on what we want this data type to hold when it's not `Nothing`, this type constructor can end up producing a type of `Maybe Int`, `Maybe Car`, `Maybe String`, and so on. No value can have a type of just `Maybe`, because that's not a type—it's a type constructor. In order for this to be a real type that a value can be part of, it must have all its type parameters filled up.

So if we pass `Char` as the type parameter to `Maybe`, we get a type of `Maybe Char`. The value `Just 'a'` has a type of `Maybe Char`, for example.

Most of the time, we don't pass types as parameters to type constructors explicitly. That's because Haskell has type inference. So when we make a value `Just 'a'`, for example, Haskell figures out that it's a `Maybe Char`.

If we want to explicitly pass a type as a type parameter, we must do it in the type part of Haskell, which is usually after the :: symbol. This can come in handy if, for example, we want a value of Just 3 to have the type Maybe Int. By default, Haskell will infer the type (Num a) => Maybe a for that value. We can use an explicit type annotation to restrict the type a bit:

```
ghci> Just 3 :: Maybe Int
Just 3
```

You might not know it, but we used a type that has a type parameter before we used Maybe: the list type. Although there's some syntactic sugar in play, the list type takes a parameter to produce a concrete type. Values can have an [Int] type, a [Char] type, or a [[String]] type, but you can't have a value that just has a type of [].

NOTE   *We say that a type is* concrete *if it doesn't take any type parameters at all (like* Int *or* Bool*), or if it takes type parameters and they're all filled up (like* Maybe Char*). If you have some value, its type is always a concrete type.*

Let's play around with the Maybe type:

```
ghci> Just "Haha"
Just "Haha"
ghci> Just 84
Just 84
ghci> :t Just "Haha"
Just "Haha" :: Maybe [Char]
ghci> :t Just 84
Just 84 :: (Num a) => Maybe a
ghci> :t Nothing
Nothing :: Maybe a
ghci> Just 10 :: Maybe Double
Just 10.0
```

Type parameters are useful because they allow us to make data types that can hold different things. For instance, we could make a separate Maybe-like data type for every type that it could contain, like so:

```
data IntMaybe = INothing | IJust Int

data StringMaybe = SNothing | SJust String

data ShapeMaybe = ShNothing | ShJust Shape
```

But even better, we could use type parameters to make a generic Maybe that can contain values of any type at all!

Notice that the type of Nothing is Maybe a. Its type is *polymorphic*, which means that it features type variables, namely the a in Maybe a. If some function requires a Maybe Int as a parameter, we can give it a Nothing, because a Nothing doesn't contain a value anyway, so it doesn't matter. The Maybe a type can act like a Maybe Int if it must, just as 5 can act like an Int or a Double. Similarly, the type of the empty list is [a]. An empty list can act like a list of anything. That's why we can do [1,2,3] ++ [] and ["ha","ha","ha"] ++ [].

Should We Parameterize Our Car?

When does using type parameters make sense? Usually, we use them when our data type would work regardless of the type of the value it then holds, as with our Maybe a type. If our type acts as some kind of box, it's good to use parameters.

Consider our Car data type:

```
data Car = Car { company :: String
               , model :: String
               , year :: Int
               } deriving (Show)
```

We could change it to this:

```
data Car a b c = Car { company :: a
                     , model :: b
                     , year :: c
                     } deriving (Show)
```

But would we really benefit? Probably not, because we would just end up defining functions that work on only the Car String String Int type. For instance, given our first definition of Car, we could make a function that displays the car's properties in an easy-to-read format.

```
tellCar :: Car -> String
tellCar (Car {company = c, model = m, year = y}) =
    "This " ++ c ++ " " ++ m ++ " was made in " ++ show y
```

We could test it like this:

```
ghci> let stang = Car {company="Ford", model="Mustang", year=1967}
ghci> tellCar stang
"This Ford Mustang was made in 1967"
```

It's a good little function! The type declaration is cute, and it works nicely.

Now what if Car was Car a b c?

```
tellCar :: (Show a) => Car String String a -> String
tellCar (Car {company = c, model = m, year = y}) =
    "This " ++ c ++ " " ++ m ++ " was made in " ++ show y
```

We would need to force this function to take a Car type of (Show a) => Car String String a. You can see that the type signature is more complicated, and the only actual benefit would be that we could use any type that's an instance of the Show type class as the type for c:

```
ghci> tellCar (Car "Ford" "Mustang" 1967)
"This Ford Mustang was made in 1967"
ghci> tellCar (Car "Ford" "Mustang" "nineteen sixty seven")
"This Ford Mustang was made in \"nineteen sixty seven\""
ghci> :t Car "Ford" "Mustang" 1967
Car "Ford" "Mustang" 1967 :: (Num t) => Car [Char] [Char] t
ghci> :t Car "Ford" "Mustang" "nineteen sixty seven"
Car "Ford" "Mustang" "nineteen sixty seven" :: Car [Char] [Char] [Char]
```

In real life though, we would end up using Car String String Int most of the time. So, parameterizing the Car type isn't worth it.

We usually use type parameters when the type that's contained inside the data type's various value constructors isn't really that important for the type to work. A list of stuff is a list of stuff, and it doesn't matter what the type of that stuff is. If we need to sum a list of numbers, we can specify later in the summing function that we specifically want a list of numbers. The same goes for Maybe, which represents an option of either having nothing or having one of something. It doesn't matter what the type of that something is.

Another example of a parameterized type that you've already met is Map k v from Data.Map. The k is the type of the keys in a map, and v is the type of the values. This is a good example of where type parameters are very useful. Having maps parameterized enables us to have mappings from any type to any other type, as long as the type of the key is part of the Ord type class. If we were defining a mapping type, we could add a type class constraint in the data declaration:

```
data (Ord k) => Map k v = ...
```

However, it's a very strong convention in Haskell to never add type class constraints in data declarations. Why? Well, because it doesn't provide much benefit, and we end up writing more class constraints, even when we don't need them. If we put the Ord k constraint in the data declaration for Map k v, we still need to put the constraint into functions that assume the keys in a map can be ordered. If we don't put the constraint in the data declaration, then we don't need to put (Ord k) => in the type declarations of functions that don't care whether the keys can be ordered. An example of such a function is toList, which just takes a mapping and converts it to an associative list.

Its type signature is toList :: Map k a -> [(k, a)]. If Map k v had a type constraint in its data declaration, the type for toList would need to be toList :: (Ord k) => Map k a -> [(k, a)], even though the function doesn't compare keys by order.

So don't put type constraints into data declarations, even if it seems to make sense. You'll need to put them into the function type declarations either way.

Vector von Doom

Let's implement a 3D vector type and add some operations for it. We'll make it a parameterized type, because even though it will usually contain numeric types, it will still support several of them, like Int, Integer, and Double, to name a few.

```
data Vector a = Vector a a a deriving (Show)

vplus :: (Num a) => Vector a -> Vector a -> Vector a
(Vector i j k) `vplus` (Vector l m n) = Vector (i+l) (j+m) (k+n)

dotProd :: (Num a) => Vector a -> Vector a -> a
(Vector i j k) `dotProd` (Vector l m n) = i*l + j*m + k*n

vmult :: (Num a) => Vector a -> a -> Vector a
(Vector i j k) `vmult` m = Vector (i*m) (j*m) (k*m)
```

Imagine a vector as an arrow in space—a line that points somewhere. The vector Vector 3 4 5 would be a line that starts at the coordinates (0,0,0) in 3D space and ends at (and points to) the coordinates (3,4,5).

The vector functions work as follows:

- The vplus function adds two vectors together. This is done just by adding their corresponding components. When you add two vectors, you get a vector that's the same as putting the second vector at the end of the first one and then drawing a vector from the beginning of the first one to the end of the second one. So adding two vectors together results in a third vector.

- The dotProd function gets the dot product of two vectors. The result of a dot product is a number, and we get it by multiplying the components of a vector pairwise and then adding all that together. The dot product of two vectors is useful when we want to figure out the angle between two vectors.

- The vmult function multiplies a vector with a number. If we multiply a vector with a number, we multiply every component of the vector with that number, effectively elongating (or shortening it), but it keeps on pointing in the same general direction.

These functions can operate on any type in the form of Vector a, as long as the a is an instance of the Num type class. For instance, they can operate on values of type Vector Int, Vector Integer, Vector Float, and so on, because Int, Integer, and Float are all instances of the Num type class. However, they won't work on values of type Vector Char or Vector Bool.

Also, if you examine the type declaration for these functions, you'll see that they can operate only on vectors of the same type, and the numbers involved must also be of the type that is contained in the vectors. We can't add together a Vector Int and a Vector Double.

Notice that we didn't put a Num class constraint in the data declaration. As explained in the previous section, even if we put it there, we would still need to repeat it in the functions.

Once again, it's very important to distinguish between the type constructor and the value constructor. When declaring a data type, the part before the = is the type constructor, and the constructors after it (possibly separated by | characters) are value constructors. For instance, giving a function the following type would be wrong:

```
Vector a a a -> Vector a a a -> a
```

This doesn't work because the type of our vector is Vector a, and not Vector a a a. It takes only one type parameter, even though its value constructor has three fields.

Now, let's play around with our vectors.

```
ghci> Vector 3 5 8 `vplus` Vector 9 2 8
Vector 12 7 16
ghci> Vector 3 5 8 `vplus` Vector 9 2 8 `vplus` Vector 0 2 3
Vector 12 9 19
ghci> Vector 3 9 7 `vmult` 10
Vector 30 90 70
ghci> Vector 4 9 5 `dotProd` Vector 9.0 2.0 4.0
74.0
ghci> Vector 2 9 3 `vmult` (Vector 4 9 5 `dotProd` Vector 9 2 4)
Vector 148 666 222
```

Derived Instances

In "Type Classes 101" on page 27, you learned that a type class is a sort of an interface that defines some behavior, and that a type can be made an instance of a type class if it supports that behavior. For example, the Int type is an instance of the Eq type class because the Eq type class defines behavior for stuff that can be equated. And because integers can be equated, Int was made a part of the Eq type class. The real usefulness comes with the functions that act as the interface for Eq, namely == and /=. If a type is a part of the Eq type class, we can use the

== functions with values of that type. That's why expressions like 4 == 4 and "foo" == "bar" type check.

Haskell type classes are often confused with classes in languages like Java, Python, C++ and the like, which trips up a lot of programmers. In those languages, classes are a blueprint from which we create objects that can do some actions. But we don't make data from Haskell type classes. Instead, we first make our data type, and then we think about how it can act. If it can act like something that can be equated, we make it an instance of the Eq type class. If it can act like something that can be ordered, we make it an instance of the Ord type class.

Let's see how Haskell can automatically make our type an instance of any of the following type classes: Eq, Ord, Enum, Bounded, Show, and Read. Haskell can derive the behavior of our types in these contexts if we use the deriving keyword when making our data type.

Equating People

Consider this data type:

```
data Person = Person { firstName :: String
                     , lastName :: String
                     , age :: Int
                     }
```

It describes a person. Let's assume that no two people have the same combination of first name, last name, and age. If we have records for two people, does it make sense to see if they represent the same person? Sure it does. We can try to equate them to see if they are equal. That's why it would make sense for this type to be part of the Eq type class. We'll derive the instance.

```
data Person = Person { firstName :: String
                     , lastName :: String
                     , age :: Int
                     } deriving (Eq)
```

When we derive the Eq instance for a type and then try to compare two values of that type with == or /=, Haskell will see if the value constructors match (there's only one value constructor here though), and then it will check if all the data contained inside matches by testing each pair of fields with ==. However, there's a catch: The types of all the fields also must be part of the Eq type class. But since that's the case with both String and Int, we're okay.

First, let's make a few people. Put the following in a script:

```
mikeD = Person {firstName = "Michael", lastName = "Diamond", age = 43}
adRock = Person {firstName = "Adam", lastName = "Horovitz", age = 41}
mca = Person {firstName = "Adam", lastName = "Yauch", age = 44}
```

Now let's test our Eq instance:

```
ghci> mca == adRock
False
ghci> mikeD == adRock
False
ghci> mikeD == mikeD
True
ghci> mikeD == Person {firstName = "Michael", lastName = "Diamond", age = 43}
True
```

Of course, since Person is now in Eq, we can use it as the a for all functions that have a class constraint of Eq a in their type signature, such as elem.

```
ghci> let beastieBoys = [mca, adRock, mikeD]
ghci> mikeD `elem` beastieBoys
True
```

Show Me How to Read

The Show and Read type classes are for things that can be converted to or from strings, respectively. As with Eq, if a type's constructors have fields, their type must be a part of Show or Read if we want to make our type an instance of them.

Let's make our Person data type a part of Show and Read as well.

```
data Person = Person { firstName :: String
                     , lastName :: String
                     , age :: Int
                     } deriving (Eq, Show, Read)
```

Now we can print a person out to the terminal.

```
ghci> mikeD
Person {firstName = "Michael", lastName = "Diamond", age = 43}
ghci> "mikeD is: " ++ show mikeD
"mikeD is: Person {firstName = \"Michael\", lastName = \"Diamond\", age = 43}"
```

If we had tried to print a person on the terminal before making the Person data type part of Show, Haskell would have complained, claiming it didn't know how to represent a person as a string. But since we first derived a Show instance for the data type, we didn't get any complaints.

Read is pretty much the inverse type class of Show. It's for converting strings to values of our type. Remember though, that when we use the read function, we might need to use an explicit type annotation to tell Haskell which type we want to get as a result. To demonstrate this, let's put a string that represents a person in a script and then load that script in GHCi:

```
mysteryDude = "Person { firstName =\"Michael\"" ++
                     ", lastName =\"Diamond\"" ++
                     ", age = 43}"
```

We wrote our string across several lines like this for increased readability. If we want to read that string, we need to tell Haskell which type we expect in return:

```
ghci> read mysteryDude :: Person
Person {firstName = "Michael", lastName = "Diamond", age = 43}
```

If we use the result of our read later in a way that Haskell can infer that it should read it as a person, we don't need to use type annotation.

```
ghci> read mysteryDude == mikeD
True
```

We can also read parameterized types, but we must give Haskell enough information so that it can figure out which type we want. If we try the following, we'll get an error:

```
ghci> read "Just 3" :: Maybe a
```

In this case, Haskell doesn't know which type to use for the type parameter a. But if we tell it that we want it to be an Int, it works just fine:

```
ghci> read "Just 3" :: Maybe Int
Just 3
```

Order in the Court!

We can derive instances for the Ord type class, which is for types that have values that can be ordered. If we compare two values of the same type that were made using different constructors, the value that was defined first is considered smaller. For instance, consider the Bool type, which can have a value of either False or True. For the purpose of seeing how it behaves when compared, we can think of it as being implemented like this:

```
data Bool = False | True deriving (Ord)
```

Because the False value constructor is specified first and the True value constructor is specified after it, we can consider True as greater than False.

```
ghci> True `compare` False
GT
ghci> True > False
True
ghci> True < False
False
```

If two values were made using the same constructor, they are considered
to be equal, unless they have fields. If they have fields, the fields are compared to see which is greater. (Note that in this case, the types of the fields
also must be part of the Ord type class.)

In the Maybe a data type, the Nothing value constructor is specified before
the Just value constructor, so the value of Nothing is always smaller than the
value of Just something, even if that something is minus one billion trillion.
But if we specify two Just values, then it will compare what's inside them.

```
ghci> Nothing < Just 100
True
ghci> Nothing > Just (-49999)
False
ghci> Just 3 `compare` Just 2
GT
ghci> Just 100 > Just 50
True
```

However, we can't do something like Just (*3) > Just (*2), because (*3)
and (*2) are functions, which are not instances of Ord.

Any Day of the Week

We can easily use algebraic data types to make enumerations, and the Enum
and Bounded type classes help us with that. Consider the following data type:

```
data Day = Monday | Tuesday | Wednesday | Thursday | Friday | Saturday | Sunday
```

Because all the type's value constructors are nullary (that is, they don't
have any fields), we can make it part of the Enum type class. The Enum type
class is for things that have predecessors and successors. We can also make
it part of the Bounded type class, which is for things that have a lowest possible
value and highest possible value. And while we're at it, let's also make it an
instance of all the other derivable type classes.

```
data Day = Monday | Tuesday | Wednesday | Thursday | Friday | Saturday | Sunday
           deriving (Eq, Ord, Show, Read, Bounded, Enum)
```

Now let's see what we can do with our new Day type. Because it's part of the Show and Read type classes, we can convert values of this type to and from strings.

```
ghci> Wednesday
Wednesday
ghci> show Wednesday
"Wednesday"
ghci> read "Saturday" :: Day
Saturday
```

Because it's part of the Eq and Ord type classes, we can compare or equate days.

```
ghci> Saturday == Sunday
False
ghci> Saturday == Saturday
True
ghci> Saturday > Friday
True
ghci> Monday `compare` Wednesday
LT
```

It's also part of Bounded, so we can get the lowest and highest day.

```
ghci> minBound :: Day
Monday
ghci> maxBound :: Day
Sunday
```

As it's an instance of Enum, we can get predecessors and successors of days and make list ranges from them!

```
ghci> succ Monday
Tuesday
ghci> pred Saturday
Friday
ghci> [Thursday .. Sunday]
[Thursday,Friday,Saturday,Sunday]
ghci> [minBound .. maxBound] :: [Day]
[Monday,Tuesday,Wednesday,Thursday,Friday,Saturday,Sunday]
```

Type Synonyms

As mentioned earlier, when writing types, the [Char] and String types are equivalent and interchangeable. That's implemented with *type synonyms.*

 Type synonyms don't really do anything per se—they're just about giving some types different names so that they make more sense to someone reading our code and documentation. Here's how the standard library defines String as a synonym for [Char]:

```
type String = [Char]
```

The type keyword here might be misleading, because a new type is not being created (that's done with the data keyword). Rather, this defines a synonym for an existing type.

If we make a function that converts a string to uppercase and call it toUpperString, we can give it a type declaration of this:

```
toUpperString :: [Char] -> [Char]
```

Alternatively, we can use this type declaration:

```
toUpperString :: String -> String
```

The two are essentially the same, but the latter is nicer to read.

Making Our Phonebook Prettier

When we were dealing with the Data.Map module, we first represented a phonebook with an association list (a list of key/value pairs) before converting it into a map. Here's that version:

```
phoneBook :: [(String, String)]
phoneBook =
    [("betty", "555-2938")
    ,("bonnie", "452-2928")
    ,("patsy", "493-2928")
    ,("lucille", "205-2928")
    ,("wendy", "939-8282")
    ,("penny", "853-2492")
    ]
```

The type of phoneBook is [(String, String)]. That tells us that it's an association list that maps from strings to strings, but not much else. Let's make a type synonym to convey some more information in the type declaration.

```
type PhoneBook = [(String,String)]
```

Now the type declaration for our phonebook can be phoneBook :: PhoneBook. Let's make a type synonym for String as well.

```
type PhoneNumber = String
type Name = String
type PhoneBook = [(Name, PhoneNumber)]
```

Haskell programmers give type synonyms to the String type when they want to convey more information about the strings in their functions—what they actually represent.

So now, when we implement a function that takes a name and a number and checks if that name and number combination is in our phonebook, we can give it a very pretty and descriptive type declaration.

```
inPhoneBook :: Name -> PhoneNumber -> PhoneBook -> Bool
inPhoneBook name pnumber pbook = (name, pnumber) `elem` pbook
```

If we decided not to use type synonyms, our function would have this type:

```
inPhoneBook :: String -> String -> [(String, String)] -> Bool
```

In this case, the type declaration that takes advantage of type synonyms is easier to understand. However, you shouldn't go overboard with these synonyms. We introduce type synonyms either to describe what some existing type represents in our functions (and thus our type declarations become better documentation) or when something has a longish type that's repeated a lot (like [(String, String)]) but represents something more specific in the context of our functions.

Parameterizing Type Synonyms

Type synonyms can also be parameterized. If we want a type that represents an association list type, but still want it to be general so it can use any type as the keys and values, we can do this:

```
type AssocList k v = [(k, v)]
```

Now a function that gets the value by a key in an association list can have a type of (Eq k) => k -> AssocList k v -> Maybe v. AssocList is a type constructor that takes two types and produces a concrete type—for instance, AssocList Int String.

Just as we can partially apply functions to get new functions, we can partially apply type parameters and get new type constructors from them. When we call a function with too few parameters, we get back a new function. In the same way, we can specify a type constructor with too few type parameters and get back a partially applied type constructor. If we wanted a type that represents a map (from `Data.Map`) from integers to something, we could do this:

```
type IntMap v = Map Int v
```

Or we could do it like this:

```
type IntMap = Map Int
```

Either way, the `IntMap` type constructor takes one parameter, and that is the type of what the integers will point to.

If you're going to try to implement this, you probably will want to do a qualified import of `Data.Map`. When you do a qualified import, type constructors also need to be preceded with a module name.

```
type IntMap = Map.Map Int
```

Make sure that you really understand the distinction between type constructors and value constructors. Just because we made a type synonym called `IntMap` or `AssocList` doesn't mean that we can do stuff like `AssocList [(1,2), (4,5),(7,9)]`. All it means is that we can refer to its type by using different names. We can do `[(1,2),(3,5),(8,9)] :: AssocList Int Int`, which will make the numbers inside assume a type of `Int`. However, we can still use that list in the same way that we would use any normal list that has pairs of integers.

Type synonyms (and types generally) can be used only in the type portion of Haskell. Haskell's type portion includes data and type declarations, as well as after a :: in type declarations or type annotations.

Go Left, Then Right

Another cool data type that takes two types as its parameters is the `Either a b` type. This is roughly how it's defined:

```
data Either a b = Left a | Right b deriving (Eq, Ord, Read, Show)
```

It has two value constructors. If `Left` is used, then its contents are of type a; if `Right` is used, its contents are of type b. So we can use this type to encapsulate a value of one type or another. Then when we get a value of type `Either a b`, we usually pattern match on both `Left` and `Right`, and we do different stuff based on which one matches.

```
ghci> Right 20
Right 20
ghci> Left "w00t"
Left "w00t"
ghci> :t Right 'a'
Right 'a' :: Either a Char
```

```
ghci> :t Left True
Left True :: Either Bool b
```

In this code, when we examine the type of Left True, we see that the type is Either Bool b. The first type parameter is Bool, because we made our value with the Left value constructor, whereas the second type parameter remains polymorphic. This is similar to how a Nothing value has the type Maybe a.

So far, you've seen Maybe a mostly used to represent the results of computations that could have failed. But sometimes, Maybe a isn't good enough, because Nothing doesn't convey much information other than that something has failed. That's fine for functions that can fail in only one way, or if we're not interested in how or why they failed. For instance, a Data.Map lookup fails only if the key wasn't in the map, so we know exactly what happened.

However, when we're interested in how or why some function failed, we usually use the result type of Either a b, where a is a type that can tell us something about the possible failure, and b is the type of a successful computation. Hence, errors use the Left value constructor, and results use Right.

As an example, suppose that a high school has lockers so that students have some place to put their Guns N' Roses posters. Each locker has a code combination. When students need to be assigned a locker, they tell the locker supervisor which locker number they want, and he gives them the code. However, if someone is already using that locker, the student needs to pick a different one. We'll use a map from Data.Map to represent the lockers. It will map from locker numbers to a pair that indicates whether the locker is in use and the locker code.

```
import qualified Data.Map as Map

data LockerState = Taken | Free deriving (Show, Eq)

type Code = String

type LockerMap = Map.Map Int (LockerState, Code)
```

We introduce a new data type to represent whether a locker is taken or free, and we make a type synonym for the locker code. We also make a type synonym for the type that maps from integers to pairs of locker state and code.

Next, we'll make a function that searches for the code in a locker map. We'll use an Either String Code type to represent our result, because our lookup can fail in two ways: The locker can be taken, in which case we can't tell the code, or the locker number might not exist. If the lookup fails, we're just going to use a String to indicate what happened.

```
lockerLookup :: Int -> LockerMap -> Either String Code
lockerLookup lockerNumber map = case Map.lookup lockerNumber map of
    Nothing -> Left $ "Locker " ++ show lockerNumber ++ " doesn't exist!"
    Just (state, code) -> if state /= Taken
```

```
then Right code
else Left $ "Locker " ++ show lockerNumber
                ++ " is already taken!"
```

We do a normal lookup in the map. If we get a Nothing, we return a
value of type Left String, saying that the locker doesn't exist. If we do find
it, then we do an additional check to see if the locker is in use. If it is, we
return a Left saying that it's already taken. If it isn't, we return a value
of type Right Code, in which we give the student the correct code for the
locker. It's actually a Right String (which is a Right [Char]), but we added
that type synonym to introduce some additional documentation into the
type declaration.

Here's an example map:

```
lockers :: LockerMap
lockers = Map.fromList
    [(100,(Taken, "ZD39I"))
    ,(101,(Free, "JAH3I"))
    ,(103,(Free, "IQSA9"))
    ,(105,(Free, "QOTSA"))
    ,(109,(Taken, "893JJ"))
    ,(110,(Taken, "99292"))
    ]
```

Now let's try looking up some locker codes.

```
ghci> lockerLookup 101 lockers
Right "JAH3I"
ghci> lockerLookup 100 lockers
Left "Locker 100 is already taken!"
ghci> lockerLookup 102 lockers
Left "Locker number 102 doesn't exist!"
ghci> lockerLookup 110 lockers
Left "Locker 110 is already taken!"
ghci> lockerLookup 105 lockers
Right "QOTSA"
```

We could have used a Maybe a to represent the result, but then we
wouldn't know why we couldn't get the code. But now we have information about the failure in our result type.

Recursive Data Structures

As you've seen, a constructor in an algebraic data type can have several fields
(or none at all), and each field must be of some concrete type. So we can
make types that have themselves as types in their fields! And that means we

can create recursive data types, where one value of some type contains values of that type, which in turn contain more values of the same type, and so on.

Think about this list: [5]. That's just syntactic sugar for 5:[]. On the left side of the :, there's a value; on the right side, there's a list. In this case, it's an empty list. Now how about the list [4,5]? Well, that desugars to 4:(5:[]). Looking at the first :, we see that it also has an element on its left side and a list, (5:[]), on its right side. The same goes for a list like 3:(4:(5:6:[])), which could be written either like that or like 3:4:5:6:[] (because : is right-associative) or [3,4,5,6].

A list can be an empty list, or it can be an element joined together with a : with another list (that might be an empty list).

Let's use algebraic data types to implement our own list!

```
data List a = Empty | Cons a (List a) deriving (Show, Read, Eq, Ord)
```

This follows our definition of lists. It's either an empty list or a combination of a head with some value and a list. If you're confused about this, you might find it easier to understand in record syntax.

```
data List a = Empty | Cons { listHead :: a, listTail :: List a}
    deriving (Show, Read, Eq, Ord)
```

You might also be confused about the Cons constructor here. Informally speaking, Cons is another word for :. In lists, : is actually a constructor that takes a value and another list and returns a list. In other words, it has two fields: One field is of the type of a, and the other is of the type List a.

```
ghci> Empty
Empty
ghci> 5 `Cons` Empty
Cons 5 Empty
ghci> 4 `Cons` (5 `Cons` Empty)
Cons 4 (Cons 5 Empty)
ghci> 3 `Cons` (4 `Cons` (5 `Cons` Empty))
Cons 3 (Cons 4 (Cons 5 Empty))
```

We called our Cons constructor in an infix manner so you can see how it's just like :. Empty is like [], and 4 `Cons` (5 `Cons` Empty) is like 4:(5:[]).

Improving Our List

We can define functions to be automatically infix by naming them using only special characters. We can also do the same with constructors, since they're just functions that return a data type. There is one restriction however: Infix constructors must begin with a colon. So check this out:

```
infixr 5 :-:
data List a = Empty | a :-: (List a) deriving (Show, Read, Eq, Ord)
```

First, notice a new syntactic construct: the fixity declaration, which is the line above our data declaration. When we define functions as operators, we can use that to give them a *fixity* (but we don't have to). A fixity states how tightly the operator binds and whether it's left-associative or right-associative. For instance, the * operator's fixity is infixl 7 *, and the + operator's fixity is infixl 6. That means that they're both left-associative (in other words, 4 * 3 * 2 is the same as (4 * 3) * 2), but * binds tighter than +, because it has a greater fixity. So 5 * 4 + 3 is equivalent to (5 * 4) + 3.

Otherwise, we just wrote a :-: (List a) instead of Cons a (List a). Now, we can write out lists in our list type like so:

```
ghci> 3 :-: 4 :-: 5 :-: Empty
3 :-: (4 :-: (5 :-: Empty))
ghci> let a = 3 :-: 4 :-: 5 :-: Empty
ghci> 100 :-: a
100 :-: (3 :-: (4 :-: (5 :-: Empty)))
```

Let's make a function that adds two of our lists together. This is how ++ is defined for normal lists:

```
infixr 5  ++
(++) :: [a] -> [a] -> [a]
[]     ++ ys = ys
(x:xs) ++ ys = x : (xs ++ ys)
```

We'll just steal that for our own list. We'll name the function ^++.

```
infixr 5  ^++
(^++) :: List a -> List a -> List a
Empty ^++ ys = ys
(x :-: xs) ^++ ys = x :-: (xs ^++ ys)
```

Now let's try it:

```
ghci> let a = 3 :-: 4 :-: 5 :-: Empty
ghci> let b = 6 :-: 7 :-: Empty
ghci> a ^++ b
3 :-: (4 :-: (5 :-: (6 :-: (7 :-: Empty))))
```

If we wanted, we could implement all of the functions that operate on lists on our own list type.

Notice how we pattern matched on (x :-: xs). That works because pattern matching is actually about matching constructors. We can match on :-: because it is a constructor for our own list type, and we can also match on : because it is a constructor for the built-in list type. The same goes for [ ]. Because pattern matching works (only) on constructors, we can match for normal prefix constructors or stuff like 8 or 'a', which are basically constructors for the numeric and character types, respectively.

Let's Plant a Tree

To get a better feel for recursive data structures in Haskell, we're going to implement a binary search tree.

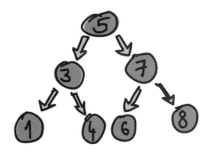

In a binary search tree, an element points to two elements—one on its left and one on its right. The element to the left is smaller; the element to the right is bigger. Each of those elements can also point to two elements (or one or none). In effect, each element has up to two subtrees.

A cool thing about binary search trees is that we know that all the elements at the left subtree of, say, 5, will be smaller than 5. Elements in the right subtree will be bigger. So if we need to find if 8 is in our tree, we start at 5, and then because 8 is greater than 5, we go right. We're now at 7, and because 8 is greater than 7, we go right again. And we've found our element in three hops! If this were a normal list (or a tree, but really unbalanced), it would take us seven hops to see if 8 is in there.

NOTE   *Sets and maps from* Data.Set *and* Data.Map *are implemented using trees, but instead of normal binary search trees, they use* balanced *binary search trees. A tree is balanced if its left and right subtrees are of approximately the same height. This makes searching through the tree faster. But for our examples, we'll just be implementing normal binary search trees.*

Here's what we're going to say: A tree is either an empty tree or it's an element that contains some value and two trees. Sounds like a perfect fit for an algebraic data type!

```
data Tree a = EmptyTree | Node a (Tree a) (Tree a) deriving (Show)
```

Instead of manually building a tree, we'll make a function that takes a tree and an element and inserts an element. We do this by comparing the new value to the tree's root node. If it's smaller than the root, we go left; if it's larger, we go right. We then do the same for every subsequent node until we reach an empty tree. Once we've reached an empty tree, we insert a node with our new value.

In languages like C, we would do this by modifying the pointers and values inside the tree. In Haskell, we can't modify our tree directly, so we need to make a new subtree each time we decide to go left or right. In the end, the insertion function returns a completely new tree, because Haskell doesn't have a concept of pointers, just values. Hence, the type for our insertion function will be something like a -> Tree a - > Tree a. It takes an element and a tree and returns a new tree that has that element inside. This might seem like it's inefficient, but Haskell makes it possible to share most of the subtrees between the old tree and the new tree.

Here are two functions for building the tree:

```
singleton :: a -> Tree a
singleton x = Node x EmptyTree EmptyTree

treeInsert :: (Ord a) => a -> Tree a -> Tree a
treeInsert x EmptyTree = singleton x
treeInsert x (Node a left right)
    | x == a = Node x left right
    | x < a  = Node a (treeInsert x left) right
    | x > a  = Node a left (treeInsert x right)
```

singleton is a utility function for making a singleton tree (a tree with just one node). It's just a shortcut for creating a node that has something set as its root, and two empty subtrees.

The treeInsert function is to insert an element into a tree. Here, we first have the base case as a pattern. If we've reached an empty subtree, that means we're where we want to go, and we insert a singleton tree with our element. If we're not inserting into an empty tree, then we need to do some checking. First, if the element we're inserting is equal to the root element, we just return a tree that's the same. If it's smaller, we return a tree that has the same root value and the same right subtree, but instead of its left subtree, we put a tree that has our value inserted into it. We do the same if our value is bigger than the root element, but the other way around.

Next up, we're going to make a function that checks if some element is in the tree:

```
treeElem :: (Ord a) => a -> Tree a -> Bool
treeElem x EmptyTree = False
treeElem x (Node a left right)
    | x == a = True
    | x < a  = treeElem x left
    | x > a  = treeElem x right
```

First, we define the base case. If we're looking for an element in an empty tree, then it's certainly not there. Notice how this is the same as the base case when searching for elements in lists. If we're not looking for an element in an empty tree, then we check some things. If the element in the root node is what we're looking for, great! If it's not, what then? Well, we can take advantage of knowing that all the left elements are smaller than the root node. If the element we're looking for is smaller than the root node, we check to see if it's in the left subtree. If it's bigger, we check to see if it's in the right subtree.

Now let's have some fun with our trees! Instead of manually creating one (although we could), we'll use a fold to build a tree from a list. Remember that pretty much everything that traverses a list one item at a time and returns a value can be implemented with a fold! We're going to start with the empty tree and then approach a list from the right and insert element after element into our accumulator tree.

```
ghci> let nums = [8,6,4,1,7,3,5]
ghci> let numsTree = foldr treeInsert EmptyTree nums
ghci> numsTree
Node 5
    (Node 3
        (Node 1 EmptyTree EmptyTree)
        (Node 4 EmptyTree EmptyTree)
    )
    (Node 7
        (Node 6 EmptyTree EmptyTree)
        (Node 8 EmptyTree EmptyTree)
    )
```

NOTE   *If you run this in GHCi, the result from* numsTree *will be printed in one long line. Here, it's broken up into many lines; otherwise, it would run off the page!*

In this foldr, treeInsert is the folding binary function (it takes a tree and a list element and produces a new tree), and EmptyTree is the starting accumulator. nums, of course, is the list we're folding over.

When we print our tree to the console, it's not very readable, but we can still make out its structure. We see that the root node is 5 and that it has two subtrees: one with a root node of 3 and the other with a root node of 7.

We can also check if certain values are contained in the tree, like this:

```
ghci> 8 `treeElem` numsTree
True
ghci> 100 `treeElem` numsTree
False
ghci> 1 `treeElem` numsTree
True
ghci> 10 `treeElem` numsTree
False
```

As you can see, algebraic data structures are a really cool and powerful concept in Haskell. We can use them to make anything from Boolean values and weekday enumerations to binary search trees, and more!

Type Classes 102

So far, you've learned about some of the standard Haskell type classes and seen which types they contain. You've also learned how to automatically make your own type instances of the standard type classes by asking Haskell to derive the instances. This section explains how to make your own type classes and how to make type instances of them by hand.

A quick type class recap: Type classes are sort of like interfaces. A type class defines some behavior (such as comparing for equality, comparing for ordering, and enumeration). Types that can behave in that way are made instances of that type class. The behavior of type classes is achieved by defining functions or just type declarations that we then implement. So when we say that a type is an instance of a type class, we mean that we can use the functions that the type class defines with that type.

Inside the Eq Type Class

As an example, let's look at the Eq type class. Remember that Eq is for values that can be equated. It defines the functions == and /=. If we have the type Car and comparing two cars with the equality function == makes sense, then it makes sense for Car to be an instance of Eq.

This is how the Eq class is defined in the standard library:

```
class Eq a where
    (==) :: a -> a -> Bool
    (/=) :: a -> a -> Bool
    x == y = not (x /= y)
    x /= y = not (x == y)
```

Whoa! Some strange syntax and keywords here!

class Eq a where means a new type class called Eq is being defined. The a is the type variable, so a will play the role of the type that will soon be made an instance of Eq. (It doesn't need to be called a, and it doesn't even need to be one letter—it just must be in all lowercase.)

Next, several functions are defined. Note that it's not mandatory to implement the function bodies themselves; just their type declarations are required. Here, the function bodies for the functions that Eq defines are implemented—defined in terms of mutual recursion. It says that two values whose types are instances of Eq are equal if they are not different, and they are different if they are not equal. You'll see how this helps us soon.

The final type of the functions that we define in a type class is also worth noting. If we have, say, class Eq a where, and then define a type declaration within that class like (==) :: a -> a -> Bool, when we examine the type of that function later, it will have the type of (Eq a) => a -> a -> Bool.

A Traffic Light Data Type

So once we have a class, what can we do with it? We can make type instances of that class and get some nice functionality. Check out this type, for instance:

```
data TrafficLight = Red | Yellow | Green
```

It defines the states of a traffic light. Notice how we didn't derive any class instances for it. That's because we're going to write some instances by hand. Here's how we make it an instance of Eq:

```
instance Eq TrafficLight where
    Red == Red = True
    Green == Green = True
    Yellow == Yellow = True
    _ == _ = False
```

We did it by using the instance keyword. So class is for defining new type classes, and instance is for making our types instances of type classes. When we were defining Eq, we wrote class Eq a where, and we said that a plays the role of whichever type will be made an instance later. We can see that clearly here, because when we're making an instance, we write instance Eq TrafficLight where. We replace the a with the actual type.

Because == was defined in terms of /= and vice versa in the class declaration, we needed to overwrite only one of them in the instance declaration. That's called the *minimal complete definition* for the type class—the minimum of functions that we must implement so that our type can behave as the class advertises. To fulfill the minimal complete definition for Eq, we need to overwrite either == or /=. If Eq were defined simply like this:

```
class Eq a where
    (==) :: a -> a -> Bool
    (/=) :: a -> a -> Bool
```

we would need to implement both of these functions when making a type an instance of Eq, because Haskell wouldn't know how these two functions are related. The minimal complete definition would then be both == and /=.

You can see that we implemented == simply by doing pattern matching. Since there are many more cases where two lights aren't equal, we specified the ones that *are* equal, and then just did a catchall pattern saying that if it's none of the previous combinations, then two lights aren't equal.

Let's make this an instance of Show by hand, too. To satisfy the minimal complete definition for Show, we just need to implement its show function, which takes a value and turns it into a string:

```
instance Show TrafficLight where
    show Red = "Red light"
    show Yellow = "Yellow light"
    show Green = "Green light"
```

Once again, we used pattern matching to achieve our goals. Let's see how it works in action:

```
ghci> Red == Red
True
ghci> Red == Yellow
False
ghci> Red `elem` [Red, Yellow, Green]
True
ghci> [Red, Yellow, Green]
[Red light,Yellow light,Green light]
```

We could have just derived Eq, and it would have had the same effect (but we didn't for educational purposes). However, deriving Show would have just directly translated the value constructors to strings. If we want our lights to appear as Red light, we need to make the instance declaration by hand.

Subclassing

You can also make type classes that are subclasses of other type classes. The class declaration for Num is a bit long, but here's the first part:

```
class (Eq a) => Ord a where
    ...
```

As mentioned previously, there are a lot of places where we can cram in class constraints. So this is just like writing class Ord a where, but we state that our type must be an instance of Eq. We're essentially saying that we need to make a type an instance of Eq before we can make it an instance of Num. Before some type can be considered orderable, it makes sense that we can determine whether values of that type can be equated.

That's all there is to subclassing—it's just a class constraint on a class declaration! When defining function bodies in the class declaration or in instance declarations, we can assume that a is a part of Eq, so we can use == on values of that type.

Parameterized Types As Instances of Type Classes

But how are the Maybe or list types made as instances of type classes? What makes Maybe different from, say, TrafficLight is that Maybe in itself isn't a concrete type—it's a type constructor that takes one type parameter (like Char) to produce a concrete type (like Maybe Char). Let's take a look at the Eq type class again:

```
class Eq a where
    (==) :: a -> a -> Bool
    (/=) :: a -> a -> Bool
    x == y = not (x /= y)
    x /= y = not (x == y)
```

From the type declarations, we see that a is used as a concrete type because all the types in functions must be concrete. Remember that you can't have a function of the type a -> Maybe, but you *can* have a function of the type a -> Maybe a or Maybe Int -> Maybe String. That's why we can't do something like this:

```
instance Eq Maybe where
    ...
```

The a must be a concrete type, and Maybe is not; it's a type constructor that takes one parameter and then *produces* a concrete type.

It would also be tedious if we needed to make a separate instance for every possible type that Maybe's type parameter could take on. If we needed to write instance Eq (Maybe Int) where, instance Eq (Maybe Char) where, and so on for every type, we would get nowhere. That's why we can just leave the parameter as a type variable, like so:

```
instance Eq (Maybe m) where
    Just x == Just y = x == y
    Nothing == Nothing = True
    _ == _ = False
```

This is like saying that we want to make all types of the form Maybe something an instance of Eq. We actually could have written (Maybe something), but using single letters conforms to the Haskell style.

The (Maybe m) here plays the role of the a from class Eq a where. While Maybe isn't a concrete type, Maybe m is. By specifying a type parameter as a type variable (m, which is in lowercase), we said that we want all types that are in the form of Maybe m, where m is any type, to be an instance of Eq.

There's one problem with this though. Can you spot it? We use == on the contents of the Maybe, but we have no assurance that what the Maybe contains can be used with Eq! That's why we modify our instance declaration like this:

```
instance (Eq m) => Eq (Maybe m) where
    Just x == Just y = x == y
    Nothing == Nothing = True
    _ == _ = False
```

We needed to add a class constraint! With this instance declaration, we say that we want all types of the form Maybe m to be part of the Eq type class, but only those types where the m (what's contained inside the Maybe) is also a part of Eq. This is actually how Haskell would derive the instance.

Most of the time, class constraints in class declarations are used for making a type class a subclass of another type class, and class constraints in instance declarations are used to express requirements about the contents of some type. For instance, here we required the contents of the Maybe to also be part of the Eq type class.

When making instances, if you see that a type is used as a concrete type in the type declarations (like the a in a -> a -> Bool), you need to supply type parameters and add parentheses so that you end up with a concrete type.

Take into account that the type you're trying to make an instance of will replace the parameter in the class declaration. The a from class Eq a where will be replaced with a real type when you make an instance, so try to mentally put your type into the function type declarations as well. The following type declaration really doesn't make much sense:

```
(==) :: Maybe -> Maybe -> Bool
```

But this does:

```
(==) :: (Eq m) => Maybe m -> Maybe m -> Bool
```

This is just something to think about, because == will always have a type of (==) :: (Eq a) => a -> a -> Bool, no matter what instances we make.

Oh, and one more thing: If you want to see what the instances of a type class are, just type :info YourTypeClass in GHCi. For instance, typing :info Num will show which functions the type class defines, and it will give you a list of the types in the type class. :info works for types and type constructors, too. If you do :info Maybe, it will show you all the type classes that Maybe is an instance of. Here's an example:

```
ghci> :info Maybe
data Maybe a = Nothing | Just a -- Defined in Data.Maybe
instance (Eq a) => Eq (Maybe a) -- Defined in Data.Maybe
instance Monad Maybe -- Defined in Data.Maybe
instance Functor Maybe -- Defined in Data.Maybe
```

```
instance (Ord a) => Ord (Maybe a) -- Defined in Data.Maybe
instance (Read a) => Read (Maybe a) -- Defined in GHC.Read
instance (Show a) => Show (Maybe a) -- Defined in GHC.Show
```

A Yes-No Type Class

In JavaScript and some other weakly typed languages, you can put almost anything inside an if expression. For example, in JavaScript, you can do something like this:

```
if (0) alert("YEAH!") else alert("NO!")
```

Or like this:

```
if ("") alert ("YEAH!") else alert("NO!")
```

Or like this:

```
if (false) alert("YEAH!") else alert("NO!")
```

All of these will throw an alert of NO!.

However, the following code will give an alert of YEAH!, since JavaScript considers any nonempty string to be a true value:

```
if ("WHAT") alert ("YEAH!") else alert("NO!")
```

Even though strictly using Bool for Boolean semantics works better in Haskell, let's try to implement this JavaScript-like behavior, just for fun! We'll start out with a class declaration:

```
class YesNo a where
    yesno :: a -> Bool
```

This is pretty simple. The YesNo type class defines one function. That function takes one value of a type that can be considered to hold some concept of trueness and tells us for sure if it's true or not. Notice that from the way we use a in the function that a must be a concrete type.

Next up, let's define some instances. For numbers, we'll assume that (as in JavaScript) any number that isn't 0 is true in a Boolean context and 0 is false.

```
instance YesNo Int where
    yesno 0 = False
    yesno _ = True
```

Empty lists (and by extension, strings) are a no-ish value, while nonempty lists are a yes-ish value.

```
instance YesNo [a] where
    yesno [] = False
    yesno _ = True
```

Notice how we just put a type parameter a in there to make the list a concrete type, even though we don't make any assumptions about the type that's contained in the list.

Bool itself also holds trueness and falseness, and it's pretty obvious which is which:

```
instance YesNo Bool where
    yesno = id
```

But what's id? It's just a standard library function that takes a parameter and returns the same thing, which is what we would be writing here anyway.

Let's make Maybe a an instance, too:

```
instance YesNo (Maybe a) where
    yesno (Just _) = True
    yesno Nothing = False
```

We didn't need a class constraint, because we made no assumptions about the contents of the Maybe. We just said that it's true-ish if it's a Just value and false-ish if it's a Nothing. We still need to write out (Maybe a) instead of just Maybe. If you think about it, a Maybe -> Bool function can't exist (because Maybe isn't a concrete type), whereas a Maybe a -> Bool is fine and dandy. Still, this is really cool, because now any type of the form Maybe something is part of YesNo, and it doesn't matter what that something is.

Previously, we defined a Tree a type that represented a binary search tree. We can say an empty tree is false-ish, and anything that's not an empty tree is true-ish:

```
instance YesNo (Tree a) where
    yesno EmptyTree = False
    yesno _ = True
```

Can a traffic light be a yes or no value? Sure. If it's red, you stop. If it's green, you go. (If it's yellow? Eh, I usually run the yellows because I live for adrenaline.)

```
instance YesNo TrafficLight where
    yesno Red = False
    yesno _ = True
```

Now that we have some instances, let's go play!

```
ghci> yesno $ length []
False
ghci> yesno "haha"
True
ghci> yesno ""
False
ghci> yesno $ Just 0
True
ghci> yesno True
True
ghci> yesno EmptyTree
False
ghci> yesno []
False
ghci> yesno [0,0,0]
True
ghci> :t yesno
yesno :: (YesNo a) => a -> Bool
```

It works!

Now let's make a function that mimics the if statement, but that works with YesNo values.

```
yesnoIf :: (YesNo y) => y -> a -> a -> a
yesnoIf yesnoVal yesResult noResult =
    if yesno yesnoVal
        then yesResult
        else noResult
```

This takes a YesNo value and two values of any type. If the yes-no–ish value is more of a yes, it returns the first of the two values; otherwise, it returns the second of them. Let's try it:

```
ghci> yesnoIf [] "YEAH!" "NO!"
"NO!"
ghci> yesnoIf [2,3,4] "YEAH!" "NO!"
"YEAH!"
ghci> yesnoIf True "YEAH!" "NO!"
"YEAH!"
ghci> yesnoIf (Just 500) "YEAH!" "NO!"
"YEAH!"
```

```
ghci> yesnoIf Nothing "YEAH!" "NO!"
"NO!"
```

The Functor Type Class

So far, we've encountered a lot of the type classes in the standard library. We've played with Ord, which is for stuff that can be ordered. We've palled around with Eq, which is for things that can be equated. We've seen Show, which presents an interface for types whose values can be displayed as strings. Our good friend Read is there whenever we need to convert a string to a value of some type. And now, we're going to take a look at the Functor type class, which is for things that can be mapped over.

You're probably thinking about lists now, since mapping over lists is such a dominant idiom in Haskell. And you're right, the list type is part of the Functor type class.

What better way to get to know the Functor type class than to see how it's implemented? Let's take a peek.

```
class Functor f where
    fmap :: (a -> b) -> f a -> f b
```

We see that it defines one function, fmap, and doesn't provide any default implementation for that function. The type of fmap is interesting. In the definitions of type classes so far, the type variable that played the role of the type in the type class was a concrete type, like the a in (==) :: (Eq a) => a -> a -> Bool. But now, the f is not a concrete type (a type that a value can hold, like Int, Bool, or Maybe String), but a type constructor that takes one type parameter. (A quick refresher example: Maybe Int is a concrete type, but Maybe is a type constructor that takes one type as the parameter.)

We see that fmap takes a function from one type to another and a functor value applied with one type and returns a functor value applied with another type. If this sounds a bit confusing, don't worry—all will be revealed soon when we check out a few examples.

Hmm . . . the type declaration for fmap reminds me of something. Let's look at the type signature of the map function:

```
map :: (a -> b) -> [a] -> [b]
```

Ah, interesting! It takes a function from one type to another and a list of one type and returns a list of another type. My friends, I think we have ourselves a functor! In fact, `map` is just an `fmap` that works only on lists. Here's how the list is an instance of the `Functor` type class:

```
instance Functor [] where
    fmap = map
```

That's it! Notice how we didn't write `instance Functor [a] where`. This is because f must be a type constructor that takes one type, which we can see in the following type declaration:

```
fmap :: (a -> b) -> f a -> f b
```

[a] is already a concrete type (of a list with any type inside it), while [] is a type constructor that takes one type and can produce types such as [Int], [String], or even [[String]].

Since for lists, `fmap` is just `map`, we get the same results when using these functions on lists:

```
ghci> fmap (*2) [1..3]
[2,4,6]
ghci> map (*2) [1..3]
[2,4,6]
```

What happens when we `map` or `fmap` over an empty list? Well, of course, we get an empty list. It turns an empty list of type [a] into an empty list of type [b].

Maybe As a Functor

Types that can act like a box can be functors. You can think of a list as a box that can be empty or have something inside it, including another box. That box can also be empty or contain something and another box, and so on. So, what else has the properties of being like a box? For one, the `Maybe a` type. In a way, it's like a box that can hold nothing (in which case it has the value of `Nothing`), or it can contain one item (like `"HAHA"`, in which case it has a value of `Just "HAHA"`).

Here's how `Maybe` is a functor:

```
instance Functor Maybe where
    fmap f (Just x) = Just (f x)
    fmap f Nothing = Nothing
```

Again, notice how we wrote `instance Functor Maybe where` instead of `instance Functor (Maybe m) where`, as we did when we were dealing with `YesNo`. `Functor` wants a type constructor that takes one type, and not a concrete type. If you mentally replace the fs with `Maybe`s, `fmap` acts like a `(a -> b) -> Maybe a -> Maybe b` for this particular type, which looks okay. But if you replace f with (`Maybe m`), then it would seem to act like a (a -> b) -> Maybe m a -> Maybe m b, which doesn't make sense, because Maybe takes just one type parameter.

The fmap implementation is pretty simple. If it's an empty value of Nothing, then just return a Nothing. If we map over an empty box, we get an empty box. If we map over an empty list, we get an empty list. If it's not an empty value, but rather a single value packed in a Just, then we apply the function on the contents of the Just:

```
ghci> fmap (++ " HEY GUYS IM INSIDE THE JUST") (Just "Something serious.")
Just "Something serious. HEY GUYS IM INSIDE THE JUST"
ghci> fmap (++ " HEY GUYS IM INSIDE THE JUST") Nothing
Nothing
ghci> fmap (*2) (Just 200)
Just 400
ghci> fmap (*2) Nothing
Nothing
```

Trees Are Functors, Too

Another thing that can be mapped over and made an instance of Functor is our Tree a type. It can be thought of as a box (it holds several or no values), and the Tree type constructor takes exactly one type parameter. If you look at fmap as if it were a function made only for Tree, its type signature would look like this: (a -> b) -> Tree a -> Tree b.

We're going to use recursion on this one. Mapping over an empty tree will produce an empty tree. Mapping over a nonempty tree will produce a tree consisting of our function applied to the root value, and its left and right subtrees will be the previous subtrees, but with our function mapped over them. Here's the code:

```
instance Functor Tree where
    fmap f EmptyTree = EmptyTree
    fmap f (Node x left right) = Node (f x) (fmap f left) (fmap f right)
```

Now let's test it:

```
ghci> fmap (*2) EmptyTree
EmptyTree
ghci> fmap (*4) (foldr treeInsert EmptyTree [5,7,3])
Node 12 EmptyTree (Node 28 (Node 20 EmptyTree EmptyTree) EmptyTree)
```

Be careful though! If you use the Tree a type to represent a binary search tree, there is no guarantee that it will remain a binary search tree after mapping a function over it. For something to be considered a binary search tree, all the elements to the left of some node must be smaller than the element in the node, and all the elements to the right must be greater. But if you map a function like negate over a binary search tree, the elements to the left of the node suddenly become greater than its element, and your binary search tree becomes just a normal binary tree.

Either a As a Functor

How about `Either a b`? Can this be made a functor? The `Functor` type class wants a type constructor that takes only one type parameter, but `Either` takes two. Hmmm . . . I know, we'll partially apply `Either` by feeding it only one parameter, so that it has one free parameter.

Here's how `Either a` is a functor in the standard libraries, more specifically in the `Control.Monad.Instances` module:

```
instance Functor (Either a) where
    fmap f (Right x) = Right (f x)
    fmap f (Left x) = Left x
```

Well well, what do we have here? You can see how `Either a` was made an instance instead of just `Either`. That's because `Either a` is a type constructor that takes one parameter, whereas `Either` takes two. If `fmap` were specifically for `Either a`, the type signature would be this:

```
(b -> c) -> Either a b -> Either a c
```

Because that's the same as the following:

```
(b -> c) -> (Either a) b -> (Either a) c
```

The function is mapped in the case of a `Right` value constructor, but it isn't mapped in the case of a `Left`. Why is that? Well, looking back at how the `Either a b` type is defined, we see this:

```
data Either a b = Left a | Right b
```

If we wanted to map one function over both of them, `a` and `b` would need to be the same type. Think about it: If we try to map a function that takes a string and returns a string, and `b` is a string but `a` is a number, it won't really work out. Also, considering what `fmap`'s type would be if it operated only on `Either a b` values, we can see that the first parameter must remain the same, while the second one can change, and the first parameter is actualized by the `Left` value constructor.

This also goes nicely with our box analogy if we think of the `Left` part as sort of an empty box with an error message written on the side telling us why it's empty.

Maps from `Data.Map` can also be made into functor values, because they hold values (or not!). In the case of `Map k v`, `fmap` will map a function `v -> v'` over a map of type `Map k v` and return a map of type `Map k v'`.

The ' character has no special meaning in types, just as it has no special meaning when naming values. It's just used to denote things that are similar, but slightly changed.

As an exercise, you can try to figure out how `Map k` is made an instance of `Functor` by yourself!

As you've seen from the examples, with `Functor`, type classes can represent pretty cool higher-order concepts. You've also had some more practice with partially applying types and making instances. In Chapter 11, we'll take a look at some laws that apply for functors.

Kinds and Some Type-Foo

Type constructors take other types as parameters to eventually produce concrete types. This behavior is similar to that of functions, which take values as parameters to produce values. Also like functions, type constructors can be partially applied. For example, `Either String` is a type constructor that takes one type and produces a concrete type, like `Either String Int`.

In this section, we'll take a look at formally defining how types are applied to type constructors. You don't really need to read this section to continue on your magical Haskell quest, but it may help you to see how Haskell's type system works. And if you don't quite understand everything right now, that's okay, too.

Values like 3, `"YEAH"`, or `takeWhile` (functions are also values—we can pass them around and such) each has their own types. Types are little labels that values carry so that we can reason about the values. But types have their own little labels called *kinds*. A kind is more or less the type of a type. This may sound a bit weird and confusing, but it's actually a really cool concept.

What are kinds, and what are they good for? Well, let's examine the kind of a type by using the :k command in GHCi:

```
ghci> :k Int
Int :: *
```

What does that * mean? It indicates that the type is a concrete type. A concrete type is a type that doesn't take any type parameters. Values can have only types that are concrete types. If I had to read * out loud (I haven't had to do that yet), I would say "star," or just "type."

Okay, now let's see what the kind of Maybe is:

```
ghci> :k Maybe
Maybe :: * -> *
```

This kind tells us that the Maybe type constructor takes one concrete type (like Int) and returns a concrete type (like Maybe Int). Just as Int -> Int means that a function takes an Int and returns an Int, * -> * means that the type constructor takes one concrete type and returns a concrete type. Let's apply the type parameter to Maybe and see what the kind of that type is:

```
ghci> :k Maybe Int
Maybe Int :: *
```

Just as you might have expected, we applied the type parameter to Maybe and got back a concrete type (that's what * -> * means). A parallel (although not equivalent—types and kinds are two different things) to this is if we call :t isUpper and :t isUpper 'A'. The isUpper function has a type of Char -> Bool, and isUpper 'A' has a type of Bool, because its value is basically True. Both those types, however, have a kind of *.

We used :k on a type to get its kind, in the same way as we can use :t on a value to get its type. Again, types are the labels of values, and kinds are the labels of types, and there are parallels between the two.

Now let's look at the kind of Either:

```
ghci> :k Either
Either :: * -> * -> *
```

This tells us that Either takes two concrete types as type parameters to produce a concrete type. It also looks somewhat like the type declaration of a function that takes two values and returns something. Type constructors are curried (just like functions), so we can partially apply them, as you can see here:

```
ghci> :k Either String
Either String :: * -> *
ghci> :k Either String Int
Either String Int :: *
```

When we wanted to make Either a part of the Functor type class, we needed to partially apply it, because Functor wants types that take only one parameter, while Either takes two. In other words, Functor wants types of kind * -> *, so we needed to partially apply Either to get this instead of its original kind, * -> * -> *.

Looking at the definition of Functor again, we can see that the f type variable is used as a type that takes one concrete type to produce a concrete type:

```
class Functor f where
    fmap :: (a -> b) -> f a -> f b
```

We know it must produce a concrete type, because it's used as the type of a value in a function. And from that, we can deduce that types that want to be friends with Functor must be of kind * -> *.

8

INPUT AND OUTPUT

In this chapter, you're going to learn how to receive
input from the keyboard and print stuff to the screen.

But first, we'll cover the basics of input and output (I/O):

- What are I/O actions?
- How do I/O actions enable us to do I/O?
- When are I/O actions actually performed?

Dealing with I/O brings up the issue of constraints on how Haskell functions can work, so we'll look at how we get around that first.

Separating the Pure from the Impure

By now, you're used to the fact that Haskell is a purely functional language. Instead of giving the computer a series of steps to execute, you give it definitions of what certain things are. In addition, a function isn't allowed to have *side effects*. A function can give us back only some result based on the parameters we supplied to it. If a function is called two times with the same parameters, it must return the same result.

While this may seem a bit limiting at first, it's actually really cool. In an imperative language, you have no guarantee that a simple function that should just crunch some numbers won't burn down your house or kidnap your dog while crunching those numbers. For instance, when we were making a binary search tree in the previous chapter, we didn't insert an element into a tree by modifying the tree itself; instead, our function actually returned a *new* tree with the new element inserted into that.

The fact that functions cannot change state—like updating global variables, for example—is good, because it helps us reason about our programs. However, there's one problem with this: If a function can't change anything in the world, how is it supposed to tell us what it calculated? To do that, it must change the state of an output device (usually the state of the screen), which then emits photons that travel to our brain, which changes the state of our mind, man.

But don't despair, all is not lost. Haskell has a really clever system for dealing with functions that have side effects. It neatly separates the part of our program that is pure and the part of our program that is impure, which does all the dirty work like talking to the keyboard and the screen. With those two parts separated, we can still reason about our pure program and take advantage of all the things that purity offers—like laziness, robustness, and composability—while easily communicating with the outside world. You'll see this at work in this chapter.

Hello, World!

Until now, we've always loaded our functions into GHCi to test them. We've also explored the standard library functions in that way. Now we're finally going to write our first real Haskell program! Yay! And sure enough, we're going to do the good old Hello, world! schtick.

For starters, punch the following into your favorite text editor:

```
main = putStrLn "hello, world"
```

We just defined main, and in it we call a function called putStrLn with the parameter "hello, world". Save that file as *helloworld.hs*.

We're going to do something we've never done before: compile our program, so that we get an executable file that we can run! Open your terminal, navigate to the directory where *helloworld.hs* is located, and enter the following:

```
$ ghc --make helloworld
```

This invokes the GHC compiler and tells it to compile our program. It should report something like this:

```
[1 of 1] Compiling Main ( helloworld.hs, helloworld.o )
Linking helloworld ...
```

Now you can run your program by entering the following at the terminal:

```
$ ./helloworld
```

NOTE *If you're using Windows, instead of doing ./helloworld, just type in **helloworld.exe** to run your program.*

Our program prints out the following:

```
hello, world
```

And there you go—our first compiled program that prints something to the terminal. How extraordinarily boring!

Let's examine what we wrote. First, let's look at the type of the function putStrLn:

```
ghci> :t putStrLn
putStrLn :: String -> IO ()
ghci> :t putStrLn "hello, world"
putStrLn "hello, world" :: IO ()
```

We can read the type of putStrLn like this: putStrLn takes a string and returns an *I/O action* that has a result type of () (that is, the empty tuple, also known as *unit*).

An I/O action is something that, when performed, will carry out an action with a side effect (such as reading input or printing stuff to the screen or a file) and will also present some result. We say that an I/O action *yields* this result. Printing a string to the terminal doesn't really have any kind of meaningful return value, so a dummy value of () is used.

NOTE *The empty tuple is the value (), and it also has a type of ().*

So when will an I/O action be performed? Well, this is where main comes in. An I/O action will be performed when we give it a name of main and then run our program.

Gluing I/O Actions Together

Having your whole program be just one I/O action seems kind of limiting. That's why we can use do syntax to glue together several I/O actions into one. Take a look at the following example:

```
main = do
    putStrLn "Hello, what's your name?"
    name <- getLine
    putStrLn ("Hey " ++ name ++ ", you rock!")
```

Ah, interesting—new syntax! And this reads pretty much like an imperative program. If you compile and run it, it will behave just as you expect.

Notice that we said do and then we laid out a series of steps, as we would in an imperative program. Each of these steps is an I/O action. By putting them together with do syntax, we glued them into one I/O action. The action that we got has a type of IO (), as that's the type of the last I/O action inside. Because of that, main always has a type signature of main :: IO *something*, where *something* is some concrete type. We don't usually specify a type declaration for main.

How about that third line, which states name <- getLine? It looks like it reads a line from the input and stores it into a variable called name. Does it really? Well, let's examine the type of getLine.

```
ghci> :t getLine
getLine :: IO String
```

We see that getLine is an I/O action that yields a String. That makes sense, because it will wait for the user to input something at the terminal, and then that something will be represented as a string.

So what's up with name <- getLine then? You can read that piece of code like this: perform the I/O action getLine, and then bind its result value to name. getLine has a type of IO String, so name will have a type of String.

You can think of an I/O action as a box with little feet that will go out into the real world and do something there (like write some graffiti on a wall) and maybe bring back some data. Once it has fetched that data for you, the only way to open the box and get the data inside it is to use the <- construct. And if we're taking data out of an I/O action, we can take it out only when we're inside another I/O action. This is how Haskell manages to neatly separate the pure and impure parts of our code. getLine is impure, because its result value is not guaranteed to be the same when performed twice.

When we do `name <- getLine`, `name` is just a normal string, because it represents what's inside the box. For example, we can have a really complicated function that takes your name (a normal string) as a parameter and tells you your fortune based on your name, like this:

```
main = do
    putStrLn "Hello, what's your name?"
    name <- getLine
    putStrLn $ "Zis is your future: " ++ tellFortune name
```

The `tellFortune` function (or any of the functions it passes `name` to) does not need to know anything about I/O—it's just a normal `String -> String` function!

To see how normal values differ from I/O actions, consider the following line. Is it valid?

```
nameTag = "Hello, my name is " ++ getLine
```

If you said no, go eat a cookie. If you said yes, drink a bowl of molten lava. (Just kidding—don't!) This doesn't work because ++ requires both its parameters to be lists over the same type. The left parameter has a type of `String` (or `[Char]`, if you will), while `getLine` has a type of `IO String`. Remember that you can't concatenate a string and an I/O action. First, you need to get the result out of the I/O action to get a value of type `String`, and the only way to do that is to do something like `name <- getLine` inside some other I/O action.

If we want to deal with impure data, we must do it in an impure environment. The taint of impurity spreads around much like the undead scourge, and it's in our best interest to keep the I/O parts of our code as small as possible.

Every I/O action that is performed yields a result. That's why our previous example could also have been written like this:

```
main = do
    foo <- putStrLn "Hello, what's your name?"
    name <- getLine
    putStrLn ("Hey " ++ name ++ ", you rock!")
```

However, `foo` would just have a value of (), so doing that would be kind of moot. Notice that we didn't bind the last `putStrLn` to anything. That's because in a do block, the last action cannot be bound to a name as the first two were. You'll see exactly why that is so when we venture off into the world of monads, starting in Chapter 13. For now, the important point is that the do block automatically extracts the value from the last action and yields that as its own result.

Except for the last line, every line in a do block that doesn't bind can also be written with a bind. So `putStrLn "BLAH"` can be written as `_ <- putStrLn`

"BLAH". But that's useless, so we leave out the <- for I/O actions that don't yield an important result, like putStrLn.

What do you think will happen when we do something like the following?

```
myLine = getLine
```

Do you think it will read from the input and then bind the value of that to name? Well, it won't. All this does is give the getLine I/O action a different name called myLine. Remember that to get the value out of an I/O action, you must perform it inside another I/O action by binding it to a name with <-.

I/O actions will be performed when they are given a name of main or when they're inside a bigger I/O action that we composed with a do block. We can also use a do block to glue together a few I/O actions, and then we can use that I/O action in another do block, and so on. They will be performed if they eventually fall into main.

There's also one more case when I/O actions will be performed: when we type out an I/O action in GHCi and press ENTER.

```
ghci> putStrLn "HEEY"
HEEY
```

Even when we just punch in a number or call a function in GHCi and press ENTER, GHCi will apply show to the resulting value, and then it will print it to the terminal by using putStrLn.

Using let Inside I/O Actions

When using do syntax to glue together I/O actions, we can use let syntax to bind values to names. Whereas <- is used to perform I/O actions and bind their results to names, let is used when we just want to give names to normal values inside I/O actions. It's similar to the let syntax in list comprehensions.

Let's take a look at an I/O action that uses both <- and let to bind names.

```
import Data.Char

main = do
    putStrLn "What's your first name?"
    firstName <- getLine
    putStrLn "What's your last name?"
    lastName <- getLine
    let bigFirstName = map toUpper firstName
        bigLastName = map toUpper lastName
    putStrLn $ "hey " ++ bigFirstName ++ " "
                    ++ bigLastName
                    ++ ", how are you?"
```

See how the I/O actions in the do block are lined up? Also notice how the let is lined up with the I/O actions, and the names of the let are lined up with each other? That's good practice, because indentation is important in Haskell.

We wrote map toUpper firstName, which turns something like "John" into a much cooler string like "JOHN". We bound that uppercased string to a name and then used it in a string that we printed to the terminal.

You may be wondering when to use <- and when to use let bindings. <- is for performing I/O actions and binding their results to names. map toUpper firstName, however, isn't an I/O action—it's a pure expression in Haskell. So you can use <- when you want to bind the results of I/O actions to names, and you can use let bindings to bind pure expressions to names. Had we done something like let firstName = getLine, we would have just called the getLine I/O action a different name, and we would still need to run it through a <- to perform it and bind its result.

Putting It in Reverse

To get a better feel for doing I/O in Haskell, let's make a simple program that continuously reads a line and prints out the same line with the words reversed. The program's execution will stop when we input a blank line. This is the program:

```
main = do
    line <- getLine
    if null line
        then return ()
        else do
            putStrLn $ reverseWords line
            main

reverseWords :: String -> String
reverseWords = unwords . map reverse . words
```

To get a feel for what it does, save it as *reverse.hs*, and then compile and run it:

```
$ ghc --make reverse.hs
[1 of 1] Compiling Main             ( reverse.hs, reverse.o )
Linking reverse ...
$ ./reverse
clean up on aisle number nine
naelc pu no elsia rebmun enin
the goat of error shines a light upon your life
eht taog fo rorre senihs a thgil nopu ruoy efil
it was all a dream
ti saw lla a maerd
```

Our reverseWords function is just a normal function. It takes a string like "hey there man" and applies words to it to produce a list of words like ["hey","there","man"]. We map reverse over the list, getting ["yeh","ereht", "nam"], and then we put that back into one string by using unwords. The final result is "yeh ereht nam".

What about main? First, we get a line from the terminal by performing getLine and call that line line. Next we have a conditional expression. Remember that in Haskell, every if must have a corresponding else, because every expression must have some sort of value. Our if says that when a condition is true (in our case, the line that we entered is blank), we perform one I/O action; when it isn't true, the I/O action under the else is performed.

Because we need to have exactly one I/O action after the else, we use a do block to glue together two I/O actions into one. We could also write that part as follows:

```
else (do
    putStrLn $ reverseWords line
    main)
```

This makes it clearer that the do block can be viewed as one I/O action, but it's uglier.

Inside the do block, we apply reverseWords to the line that we got from getLine and then print that to the terminal. After that, we just perform main. It's performed recursively, and that's okay, because main is itself an I/O action. So in a sense, we go back to the start of the program.

If null line is True, the code after the then is executed: return (). You might have used a return keyword in other languages to return from a subroutine or function. But return in Haskell is nothing like the return in most other languages.

In Haskell (and in I/O actions specifically), return makes an I/O action out of a pure value. Returning to the box analogy for I/O actions, return takes a value and wraps it up in a box. The resulting I/O action doesn't actually do anything; it just yields that value as its result. So in an I/O context, return "haha" will have a type of IO String.

What's the point of just transforming a pure value into an I/O action that doesn't do anything? Well, we needed some I/O action to carry out in the case of an empty input line. That's why we made a bogus I/O action that doesn't do anything by writing return ().

Unlike in other languages, using return doesn't cause the I/O do block to end in execution. For instance, this program will quite happily continue all the way to the last line:

```
main = do
    return ()
    return "HAHAHA"
    line <- getLine
    return "BLAH BLAH BLAH"
```

```
return 4
putStrLn line
```

Again, all these uses of return do is make I/O actions that yield a result, which is then thrown away because it isn't bound to a name.

We can use return in combination with <- to bind stuff to names:

```
main = do
    a <- return "hell"
    b <- return "yeah!"
    putStrLn $ a ++ " " ++ b
```

So you see, return is sort of the opposite of <-. While return takes a value and wraps it up in a box, <- takes a box (and performs it) and takes the value out of it, binding it to a name. But doing this is kind of redundant, especially since you can use let in do blocks to bind to names, like so:

```
main = do
    let a = "hell"
        b = "yeah"
    putStrLn $ a ++ " " ++ b
```

When dealing with I/O do blocks, we mostly use return either because we need to create an I/O action that doesn't do anything or because we don't want the I/O action that's made up from a do block to have the result value of its last action. When we want it to have a different result value, we use return to make an I/O action that always yields our desired result, and we put it at the end.

Some Useful I/O Functions

Haskell comes with a bunch of useful functions and I/O actions. Let's take a look at some of them to see how they're used.

putStr

putStr is much like putStrLn, in that it takes a string as a parameter and returns an I/O action that will print that string to the terminal. However, putStr doesn't jump into a new line after printing out the string, whereas putStrLn does. For example, look at this code:

```
main = do
    putStr "Hey, "
    putStr "I'm "
    putStrLn "Andy!"
```

If we compile and run this, we get the following output:

```
Hey, I'm Andy!
```

putChar

The putChar function takes a character and returns an I/O action that will print it to the terminal:

```
main = do
    putChar 't'
    putChar 'e'
    putChar 'h'
```

putStr can be defined recursively with the help of putChar. The base case of putStr is the empty string, so if we're printing an empty string, we just return an I/O action that does nothing by using return (). If it's not empty, then we print the first character of the string by doing putChar and then print the rest of them recursively:

```
putStr :: String -> IO ()
putStr [] = return ()
putStr (x:xs) = do
    putChar x
    putStr xs
```

Notice how we can use recursion in I/O, just as we can use it in pure code. We define the base case and then think what the result actually is. In this case, it's an action that first outputs the first character and then outputs the rest of the string.

print

print takes a value of any type that's an instance of Show (meaning that we know how to represent it as a string), applies show to that value to "stringify" it, and then outputs that string to the terminal. Basically, it's just putStrLn . show. It first runs show on a value, and then feeds that to putStrLn, which returns an I/O action that will print out our value.

```
main = do
    print True
    print 2
    print "haha"
    print 3.2
    print [3,4,3]
```

Compiling this and running it, we get the following output:

```
True
2
"haha"
3.2
[3,4,3]
```

As you can see, it's a very handy function. Remember how we talked about how I/O actions are performed only when they fall into main or when we try to evaluate them at the GHCi prompt? When we type out a value (like 3 or [1,2,3]) and press ENTER, GHCi actually uses print on that value to display it on the terminal!

```
ghci> 3
3
ghci> print 3
3
ghci> map (++"!") ["hey","ho","woo"]
["hey!","ho!","woo!"]
ghci> print $ map (++"!") ["hey","ho","woo"]
["hey!","ho!","woo!"]
```

When we want to print out strings, we usually use putStrLn because we don't want the quotes around them. However, for printing out values of other types to the terminal, print is used the most often.

when

The when function is found in Control.Monad (to access it, use import Control.Monad). It's interesting because in a do block, it looks like a flow-control statement, but it's actually a normal function.

when takes a Bool and an I/O action, and if that Bool value is True, it returns the same I/O action that we supplied to it. However, if it's False, it returns the return () action, which doesn't do anything.

Here's a small program that asks for some input and prints it back to the terminal, but only if that input is SWORDFISH:

```
import Control.Monad

main = do
    input <- getLine
    when (input == "SWORDFISH") $ do
        putStrLn input
```

Without when, we would need to write the program like this:

```
main = do
    input <- getLine
    if (input == "SWORDFISH")
        then putStrLn input
        else return ()
```

As you can see, the when function is useful when we want to perform some I/O actions when a condition is met, but do nothing otherwise.

sequence

The sequence function takes a list of I/O actions and returns an I/O action that will perform those actions one after the other. The result that this I/O action yields will be a list of the results of all the I/O actions that were performed. For instance, we could do this:

```
main = do
    a <- getLine
    b <- getLine
    c <- getLine
    print [a,b,c]
```

Or we could do this:

```
main = do
    rs <- sequence [getLine, getLine, getLine]
    print rs
```

The results of both these versions are exactly the same. sequence [getLine, getLine, getLine] makes an I/O action that will perform getLine three times. If we bind that action to a name, the result is a list of all the results. So in this case, the result would be a list of three things that the user entered at the prompt.

A common pattern with sequence is when we map functions like print or putStrLn over lists. Executing map print [1,2,3,4] won't create an I/O action, but instead will create a list of I/O actions. Effectively, this is the same as writing this:

```
[print 1, print 2, print 3, print 4]
```

If we want to transform that list of I/O actions into an I/O action, we must sequence it:

```
ghci> sequence $ map print [1,2,3,4,5]
1
2
```

```
3
4
5
[(),(),(),(),()]
```

But what's with the [(),(),(),(),()] at the end of the output? Well, when we evaluate an I/O action in GHCi, that action is performed, and then its result is printed out, unless that result is (). That's why evaluating putStrLn "hehe" in GHCi just prints out hehe—putStrLn "hehe" yields (). But when we enter getLine in GHCi, the result of that I/O action is printed out, because getLine has a type of IO String.

mapM

Because mapping a function that returns an I/O action over a list and then sequencing it is so common, the utility functions mapM and mapM_ were introduced. mapM takes a function and a list, maps the function over the list, and then sequences it. mapM_ does the same thing, but it throws away the result later. We usually use mapM_ when we don't care what result our sequenced I/O actions have. Here's an example of mapM:

```
ghci> mapM print [1,2,3]
1
2
3
[(),(),()]
```

But we don't care about the list of three units at the end, so it's better to use this form:

```
ghci> mapM_ print [1,2,3]
1
2
3
```

forever

The forever function takes an I/O action and returns an I/O action that just repeats the I/O action it got forever. It's located in Control.Monad. The following little program will indefinitely ask the user for some input and spit it back in all uppercase characters:

```
import Control.Monad
import Data.Char

main = forever $ do
    putStr "Give me some input: "
```

```
l <- getLine
putStrLn $ map toUpper l
```

forM

forM (located in `Control.Monad`) is like `mapM`, but its parameters are switched around. The first parameter is the list, and the second is the function to map over that list, which is then sequenced. Why is that useful? Well, with some creative use of lambdas and do notation, we can do stuff like this:

```
import Control.Monad

main = do
    colors <- forM [1,2,3,4] (\a -> do
        putStrLn $ "Which color do you associate with the number "
                    ++ show a ++ "?"
        color <- getLine
        return color)
    putStrLn "The colors that you associate with 1, 2, 3 and 4 are: "
    mapM putStrLn colors
```

Here's what we get when we try this out:

```
Which color do you associate with the number 1?
white
Which color do you associate with the number 2?
blue
Which color do you associate with the number 3?
red
Which color do you associate with the number 4?
orange
The colors that you associate with 1, 2, 3 and 4 are:
white
blue
red
orange
```

The (`\a -> do ... `) lambda is a function that takes a number and returns an I/O action. Notice that we call `return color` in the inside do block. We do that so that the I/O action that the do block defines yields the string that represents our color of choice. We actually did not have to do that though, since `getLine` already yields our chosen color, and it's the last line in the do block. Doing `color <- getLine` and then `return color` is just unpacking the result from `getLine` and then repacking it—it's the same as just calling `getLine`.

The forM function (called with its two parameters) produces an I/O action, whose result we bind to colors. colors is just a normal list that holds strings. At the end, we print out all those colors by calling `mapM putStrLn colors`.

You can think of `forM` as saying, "Make an I/O action for every element in this list. What each I/O action will do can depend on the element that was used to make the action. Finally, perform those actions and bind their results to something." (Although we don't need to bind it; we could also just throw it away.)

We could have actually achieved the same result without `forM`, but using `forM` makes the code more readable. Normally, we use `forM` when we want to map and sequence some actions that we define on the spot using `do` notation.

I/O Action Review

Let's run through a quick review of the I/O basics. I/O actions are values much like any other value in Haskell. We can pass them as parameters to functions, and functions can return I/O actions as results.

What's special about I/O actions is that if they fall into the `main` function (or are the result in a GHCi line), they are performed. And that's when they get to write stuff on your screen or play "Yakety Sax" through your speakers. Each I/O action can also yield a result to tell you what it got from the real world.

9

MORE INPUT AND MORE OUTPUT

Now that you understand the concepts behind Haskell's I/O, we can start doing fun stuff with it. In this chapter, we'll interact with files, make random numbers, deal with command-line arguments, and more. Stay tuned!

Files and Streams

Armed with the knowledge about how I/O actions work, we can move on to reading and writing files with Haskell. But first, let's take a look at how we can use Haskell to easily process streams of data. A *stream* is a succession of pieces of data entering or exiting a program over time. For instance, when you're inputting characters into a program via the keyboard, those characters can be thought of as a stream.

Input Redirection

Many interactive programs get the user's input via the keyboard. However, it's often more convenient to get the input by feeding the contents of a text file to the program. To achieve this, we use *input redirection*.

Input redirection will come in handy with our Haskell programs, so let's take a look at how it works. To begin, create a text file that contains the following little haiku, and save it as *haiku.txt*:

```
I'm a lil' teapot
What's with that airplane food, huh?
It's so small, tasteless
```

Yeah, the haiku sucks—what of it? If anyone knows of any good haiku tutorials, let me know.

Now we'll write a little program that continuously gets a line from the input and then prints it back in all uppercase:

```
import Control.Monad
import Data.Char

main = forever $ do
    l <- getLine
    putStrLn $ map toUpper l
```

Save this program as *capslocker.hs* and compile it.

Instead of inputting lines via the keyboard, we'll have *haiku.txt* be the input by redirecting it into our program. To do that, we add a < character after our program name and then specify the file that we want to act as the input. Check it out:

```
$ ghc --make capslocker
[1 of 1] Compiling Main              ( capslocker.hs, capslocker.o )
Linking capslocker ...
$ ./capslocker < haiku.txt
I'M A LIL' TEAPOT
WHAT'S WITH THAT AIRPLANE FOOD, HUH?
IT'S SO SMALL, TASTELESS
capslocker <stdin>: hGetLine: end of file
```

What we've done is pretty much equivalent to running capslocker, typing our haiku at the terminal, and then issuing an end-of-file character (usually done by pressing CTRL-D). It's like running capslocker and saying, "Wait, don't read from the keyboard. Take the contents of this file instead!"

Getting Strings from Input Streams

Let's take a look at an I/O action that makes processing input streams easier by allowing us to treat them as normal strings: getContents. getContents reads everything from the standard input until it encounters an end-of-file character. Its type is getContents :: IO String. What's cool about getContents is that it does lazy I/O. This means that when we do foo <- getContents, getContents doesn't read all of the input at once, store it in memory, and then bind it to foo. No, getContents is lazy! It will say, "Yeah yeah, I'll read the input from the terminal later as we go along, when you really need it!"

In our *capslocker.hs* example, we used forever to read the input line by line and then print it back in uppercase. If we opt to use getContents, it takes care of the I/O details for us, such as when to read input and how much of that input to read. Because our program is about taking some input and transforming it into some output, we can make it shorter by using getContents:

```
import Data.Char

main = do
    contents <- getContents
    putStr $ map toUpper contents
```

We run the getContents I/O action and name the string it produces contents. Then we map toUpper over that string and print that result to the terminal. Keep in mind that because strings are basically lists, which are lazy, and getContents is I/O lazy; it won't try to read all of the content at once and store that into memory before printing out the caps-locked version. Rather, it will print out the caps-locked version as it reads, because it will read a line from the input only when it must.

Let's test it:

```
$ ./capslocker < haiku.txt
I'M A LIL' TEAPOT
WHAT'S WITH THAT AIRPLANE FOOD, HUH?
IT'S SO SMALL, TASTELESS
```

So, it works. What if we just run capslocker and try to type in the lines ourselves? (To exit the program, just press CTRL-D.)

```
$ ./capslocker
hey ho
HEY HO
lets go
LETS GO
```

Pretty nice! As you can see, it prints our caps-locked input line by line.

When the result of getContents is bound to contents, it's not represented in memory as a real string, but more like a promise that the string will be produced eventually. When we map toUpper over contents, that's also a promise to map that function over the eventual contents. Finally, when putStr happens, it says to the previous promise, "Hey, I need a caps-locked line!" It doesn't have any lines yet, so it says to contents, "How about getting a line from the terminal?" And that's when getContents actually reads from the terminal and gives a line to the code that asked it to produce something tangible. That code then maps toUpper over that line and gives it to putStr, which prints the line. And then putStr says, "Hey, I need the next line—come on!" This repeats until there's no more input, which is signified by an end-of-file character.

Now let's make a program that takes some input and prints out only those lines that are shorter than 10 characters:

```
main = do
    contents <- getContents
    putStr (shortLinesOnly contents)

shortLinesOnly :: String -> String
shortLinesOnly = unlines . filter (\line -> length line < 10) . lines
```

We've made the I/O part of our program as short as possible. Because our program is supposed to print something based on some input, we can implement it by reading the input contents, running a function on them, and then printing out what that function gives back.

The shortLinesOnly function takes a string, like "short\nloooooooong\nbort". In this example, that string has three lines: two of them are short, and the middle one is long. It applies the lines function to that string, which converts it to ["short", "loooooooong", "bort"]. That list of strings is then filtered so that only those lines that are shorter than 10 characters remain in the list, producing ["short", "bort"]. Finally, unlines joins that list into a single newline-delimited string, giving "short\nbort".

Let's give it a go. Save the following text as *shortlines.txt*.

```
i'm short
so am i
i am a loooooooooong line!!!
yeah i'm long so what hahahaha!!!!!!
short line
loooooooooooooooooooooooooooong
short
```

And now we'll compile our program, which we saved as *shortlinesonly.hs*:

```
$ ghc --make shortlinesonly
[1 of 1] Compiling Main             ( shortlinesonly.hs, shortlinesonly.o )
Linking shortlinesonly ...
```

To test it, we're going to redirect the contents of *shortlines.txt* into our program, as follows:

```
$ ./shortlinesonly < shortlines.txt
i'm short
so am i
short
```

You can see that only the short lines were printed to the terminal.

Transforming Input

The pattern of getting some string from the input, transforming it with a function, and outputting the result is so common that there is a function that makes that job even easier, called interact. interact takes a function of type String -> String as a parameter and returns an I/O action that will take some input, run that function on it, and then print out the function's result. Let's modify our program to use interact:

```
main = interact shortLinesOnly

shortLinesOnly :: String -> String
shortLinesOnly = unlines . filter (\line -> length line < 10) . lines
```

We can use this program either by redirecting a file into it or by running it and then giving it input from the keyboard, line by line. Its output is the same in both cases, but when we're doing input via the keyboard, the output is interspersed with what we typed in, just as when we manually typed in our input to our capslocker program.

Let's make a program that continuously reads a line and then outputs whether or not that line is a palindrome. We could just use getLine to read a line, tell the user if it's a palindrome, and then run main all over again. But it's simpler if we use interact. When using interact, think about what you need to do to transform some input into the desired output. In our case, we want to replace each line of the input with either "palindrome" or "not a palindrome".

```
respondPalindromes :: String -> String
respondPalindromes =
    unlines .
    map (\xs -> if isPal xs then "palindrome" else "not a palindrome") .
    lines

isPal :: String -> Bool
isPal xs = xs == reverse xs
```

This program is pretty straightforward. First, it turns a string like this:

```
"elephant\nABCBA\nwhatever"
```

into an array like this:

```
["elephant", "ABCBA", "whatever"]
```

Then it maps the lambda over it, giving the results:

```
["not a palindrome", "palindrome", "not a palindrome"]
```

Next, unlines joins that list into a single, newline-delimited string. Now we just make a main I/O action:

```
main = interact respondPalindromes
```

Let's test it:

```
$ ./palindromes
hehe
not a palindrome
ABCBA
palindrome
cookie
not a palindrome
```

Even though we created a program that transforms one big string of input into another, it acts as if we made a program that does it line by line. That's because Haskell is lazy, and it wants to print the first line of the result string, but it can't because it doesn't have the first line of the input yet. So as soon as we give it the first line of input, it prints the first line of the output. We get out of the program by issuing an end-of-line character.

We can also use this program by just redirecting a file into it. Create the following file and save it as *words.txt*.

```
dogaroo
radar
rotor
madam
```

This is what we get by redirecting it into our program:

```
$ ./palindrome < words.txt
not a palindrome
palindrome
palindrome
palindrome
```

Again, we get the same output as if we had run our program and put in the words ourselves at the standard input. We just don't see the input that our program gets because that input came from the file.

So now you see how lazy I/O works and how we can use it to our advantage. You can just think in terms of what the output is supposed to be for some given input and write a function to do that transformation. In lazy I/O, nothing is eaten from the input until it absolutely must be, because what we want to print right now depends on that input.

Reading and Writing Files

So far, we've worked with I/O by printing stuff to the terminal and reading from it. But what about reading and writing files? Well, in a way, we've already been doing that.

One way to think about reading from the terminal is that it's like reading from a (somewhat special) file. The same goes for writing to the terminal—it's kind of like writing to a file. We can call these two files *stdout* and *stdin*, meaning standard output and standard input, respectively. Writing to and reading from files is very much like writing to the standard output and reading from the standard input.

We'll start off with a really simple program that opens a file called *girlfriend.txt*, which contains a verse from Avril Lavigne's hit song "Girlfriend," and just prints out to the terminal. Here's *girlfriend.txt*:

```
Hey! Hey! You! You!
I don't like your girlfriend!
No way! No way!
I think you need a new one!
```

And here's our program:

```
import System.IO

main = do
    handle <- openFile "girlfriend.txt" ReadMode
    contents <- hGetContents handle
    putStr contents
    hClose handle
```

If we compile and run it, we get the expected result:

```
$ ./girlfriend
Hey! Hey! You! You!
I don't like your girlfriend!
No way! No way!
I think you need a new one!
```

Let's go over this line by line. The first line is just four exclamations, to get our attention. In the second line, Avril tells us that she doesn't like our current partner of the female persuasion. The third line serves to emphasize that disapproval, and the fourth line suggests we should go about finding a suitable replacement.

Let's also go over the program line by line. Our program is several I/O actions glued together with a do block. In the first line of the do block is a new function called openFile. It has the following type signature:

```
openFile :: FilePath -> IOMode -> IO Handle
```

openFile takes a file path and an IOMode and returns an I/O action that will open a file and yield the file's associated handle as its result. FilePath is just a type synonym for String, defined as follows:

```
type FilePath = String
```

IOMode is a type that's defined like this:

```
data IOMode = ReadMode | WriteMode | AppendMode | ReadWriteMode
```

Just like our type that represents the seven possible values for the days of the week, this type is an enumeration that represents what we want to do with our opened file. Notice that this type is IOMode and not IO Mode. IO Mode would be the type of I/O action that yields a value of some type Mode as its result. IOMode is just a simple enumeration.

Finally, openFile returns an I/O action that will open the specified file in the specified mode. If we bind that action's result to something, we get a Handle, which represents where our file is. We'll use that handle so we know which file to read from.

In the next line, we have a function called hGetContents. It takes a Handle, so it knows which file to get the contents from, and returns an IO String—an I/O action that holds contents of the file as its result. This function is pretty much like getContents. The only difference is that getContents will automatically read from the standard input (that is, from the terminal), whereas hGetContents takes a file handle that tells it which file to read from. In all other respects, they work the same.

Just like getContents, hGetContents won't attempt to read all the file at once and store it in memory but will read the content only as needed. This is really cool because we can treat contents as the whole content of the file, but it's not really loaded in memory. So if this were a really huge file, doing hGetContents wouldn't choke up our memory.

Note the difference between a handle and the actual contents of the file. A handle just points to our current position in the file. The contents are what's actually in the file. If you imagine your whole filesystem as a really big book, the handle is like a bookmark that shows where you're currently reading (or writing).

With putStr contents, we print the contents out to the standard output, and then we do hClose, which takes a handle and returns an I/O action that closes the file. You need to close the file yourself after opening it with openFile! Your program may terminate if you try to open a file whose handle hasn't been closed.

Using the withFile Function

Another way of working with the contents of a file as we just did is to use the withFile function, which has the following type signature:

```
withFile :: FilePath -> IOMode -> (Handle -> IO a) -> IO a
```

It takes a path to a file, an IOMode, and a function that takes a handle and returns some I/O action. Then it returns an I/O action that will open that file, do something with the file, and close it. Furthermore, if anything goes wrong while we're operating on our file, withFile makes sure that the file handle gets closed. This might sound a bit complicated, but it's really simple, especially if we use lambdas.

Here's our previous example rewritten to use `withFile`:

```
import System.IO

main = do
    withFile "girlfriend.txt" ReadMode (\handle -> do
        contents <- hGetContents handle
        putStr contents)
```

(`\handle -> ...`) is the function that takes a handle and returns an I/O action, and it's usually done like this, with a lambda. It needs to take a function that returns an I/O action, rather than just taking an I/O action to do and then closing the file, because the I/O action that we would pass to it wouldn't know on which file to operate. This way, `withFile` opens the file and then passes the handle to the function we gave it. It gets an I/O action back from that function and then makes an I/O action that's just like the original action, but it also makes sure that the file handle gets closed, even if something goes awry.

It's Bracket Time

Usually, if a piece of code calls `error` (such as when we try to apply `head` to an empty list) or if something goes very wrong when doing input and output, our program terminates, and we see some sort of error message. In such circumstances, we say that an *exception* gets raised. The `withFile` function makes sure that despite an exception being raised, the file handle is closed.

This sort of scenario comes up often. We acquire some resource (like a file handle), and we want to do something with it, but we also want to make sure that the resource gets released (for example, the file handle is closed). Just for such cases, the `Control.Exception` module offers the `bracket` function. It has the following type signature:

```
bracket :: IO a -> (a -> IO b) -> (a -> IO c) -> IO c
```

Its first parameter is an I/O action that acquires a resource, such as a file handle. Its second parameter is a function that releases that resource. This function gets called even if an exception has been raised. The third parameter is a function that also takes that resource and does something with it. The third parameter is where the main stuff happens, like reading from a file or writing to it.

Because bracket is all about acquiring a resource, doing something with it, and making sure it gets released, implementing withFile is really easy:

```
withFile :: FilePath -> IOMode -> (Handle -> IO a) -> IO a
withFile name mode f = bracket (openFile name mode)
    (\handle -> hClose handle)
    (\handle -> f handle)
```

The first parameter that we pass to bracket opens the file, and its result is a file handle. The second parameter takes that handle and closes it. bracket makes sure that this happens even if an exception is raised. Finally, the third parameter to bracket takes a handle and applies the function f to it, which takes a file handle and does stuff with that handle, like reading from or writing to the corresponding file.

Grab the Handles!

Just as hGetContents works like getContents but for a specific file, functions like hGetLine, hPutStr, hPutStrLn, hGetChar, and so on work just like their counterparts without the h but take only a handle as a parameter and operate on that specific file instead of on standard input or standard output. For example, putStrLn takes a string and returns an I/O action that will print out that string to the terminal and a newline after it. hPutStrLn takes a handle and a string and returns an I/O action that will write that string to the file associated with the handle and then put a newline after it. In the same vein, hGetLine takes a handle and returns an I/O action that reads a line from its file.

Loading files and then treating their contents as strings is so common that we have three nice little functions to make our work even easier: readFile, writeFile, and appendFile.

The readFile function has a type signature of readFile :: FilePath -> IO String. (Remember that FilePath is just a fancy name for String.) readFile takes a path to a file and returns an I/O action that will read that file (lazily, of course) and bind its contents to something as a string. It's usually more handy than calling openFile and then calling hGetContents with the resulting handle. Here's how we could have written our previous example with readFile:

```
import System.IO

main = do
    contents <- readFile "girlfriend.txt"
    putStr contents
```

Because we don't get a handle with which to identify our file, we can't close it manually, so Haskell does that for us when we use readFile.

The writeFile function has a type of writeFile :: FilePath -> String -> IO (). It takes a path to a file and a string to write to that file and returns an I/O action that will do the writing. If such a file already exists, it will be stomped down to zero length before being written to. Here's how to turn *girlfriend.txt* into a caps-locked version and write it to *girlfriendcaps.txt*:

```
import System.IO
import Data.Char

main = do
    contents <- readFile "girlfriend.txt"
    writeFile "girlfriendcaps.txt" (map toUpper contents)
```

The appendFile function has the same type signature as writeFile and acts almost the same way. The only difference is that appendFile doesn't truncate the file to zero length if it already exists. Instead, it appends stuff to the end of that file.

To-Do Lists

Let's put the appendFile function to use by making a program that adds a task to a text file that lists stuff that we have to do. We'll assume that the file is named *todo.txt* and that it contains one task per line. Our program will take a line from the standard input and add it to our to-do list:

```
import System.IO

main = do
    todoItem <- getLine
    appendFile "todo.txt" (todoItem ++ "\n")
```

Notice that we added the "\n" to the end of each line, because getLine doesn't give us a newline character at the end.

Save the file as *appendtodo.hs*, compile it, and then run it a few times and give it some to-do items.

```
$ ./appendtodo
Iron the dishes
$ ./appendtodo
Dust the dog
$ ./appendtodo
Take salad out of the oven
$ cat todo.txt
Iron the dishes
Dust the dog
Take salad out of the oven
```

cat is a program on Unix-type systems that can be used to print text files to the terminal. On Windows systems, you can use your favorite text editor to see what's inside todo.txt *at any given time.*

Deleting Items

We already made a program to add a new item to our to-do list in *todo.txt*. Now let's make a program to remove an item. We'll use a few new functions from System.Directory and one new function from System.IO, which will all be explained after the code listing.

```
import System.IO
import System.Directory
import Data.List

main = do
    contents <- readFile "todo.txt"
    let todoTasks = lines contents
        numberedTasks = zipWith (\n line -> show n ++ " - " ++ line)
                                [0..] todoTasks
    putStrLn "These are your TO-DO items:"
    mapM_ putStrLn numberedTasks
    putStrLn "Which one do you want to delete?"
    numberString <- getLine
    let number = read numberString
        newTodoItems = unlines $ delete (todoTasks !! number) todoTasks
    (tempName, tempHandle) <- openTempFile "." "temp"
    hPutStr tempHandle newTodoItems
    hClose tempHandle
    removeFile "todo.txt"
    renameFile tempName "todo.txt"
```

First, we read *todo.txt* and bind its contents to contents. Then we split the contents into a list of strings, with one line for each string. So todoTasks is now something like this:

```
["Iron the dishes", "Dust the dog", "Take salad out of the oven"]
```

We zip the numbers from 0 onward and that list with a function that takes a number (like 3) and a string (like "hey") and returns a new string (like "3 - hey"). Now numberedTasks looks like this:

```
["0 - Iron the dishes"
,"1 - Dust the dog"
,"2 - Take salad out of the oven"
]
```

We then use `mapM_ putStrLn numberedTasks` to print each task on a separate line, ask the user which one to delete, and wait for the user to enter a number. Let's say we want to delete number 1 (`Dust the dog`), so we punch in `1`. `numberString` is now `"1"`, and because we want a number rather than a string, we apply `read` to that to get `1` and use a `let` to bind that to `number`.

Remember the `delete` and `!!` functions from `Data.List`? `!!` returns an element from a list with some index. `delete` deletes the first occurrence of an element in a list and returns a new list without that occurrence. (`todoTasks !! number`) results in `"Dust the dog"`. We delete the first occurrence of `"Dust the dog"` from `todoTasks` and then join that into a single line with `unlines` and name that `newTodoItems`.

Then we use a function that we haven't met before, from `System.IO`: `openTempFile`. Its name is pretty self-explanatory. It takes a path to a temporary directory and a template name for a file and opens a temporary file. We used `"."` for the temporary directory, because `.` denotes the current directory on just about any operating system. We used `"temp"` as the template name for the temporary file, which means that the temporary file will be named *temp* plus some random characters. It returns an I/O action that makes the temporary file, and the result in that I/O action is a pair of values: the name of the temporary file and a handle. We could just open a normal file called *todo2.txt* or something like that, but it's better practice to use `openTempFile` so you know you're probably not overwriting anything.

Now that we have a temporary file opened, we write `newTodoItems` to it. The old file is unchanged, and the temporary file contains all the lines that the old one does, except the one we deleted.

After that, we close both the original and the temporary files, and remove the original one with `removeFile`, which takes a path to a file and deletes it. After deleting the old *todo.txt*, we use `renameFile` to rename the temporary file to *todo.txt*. `removeFile` and `renameFile` (which are both in `System.Directory`) take file paths, not handles, as their parameters.

Save this as *deletetodo.hs*, compile it, and try it:

```
$ ./deletetodo
These are your TO-DO items:
0 - Iron the dishes
1 - Dust the dog
2 - Take salad out of the oven
Which one do you want to delete?
1
```

Now let's see which items remain:

```
$ cat todo.txt
Iron the dishes
Take salad out of the oven
```

Ah, cool! Let's delete one more item:

```
$ ./deletetodo
These are your TO-DO items:
0 - Iron the dishes
1 - Take salad out of the oven
Which one do you want to delete?
0
```

And examining the file, we see that only one item remains:

```
$ cat todo.txt
Take salad out of the oven
```

So, everything is working. However, there's one thing that about this program that's kind of off. If something goes wrong after we open our temporary file, the program terminates, but the temporary file doesn't get cleaned up. Let's remedy that.

Cleaning Up

To make sure our temporary file is cleaned up in case of a problem, we're going to use the bracketOnError function from Control.Exception. It's very similar to bracket, but whereas the bracket will acquire a resource and then make sure that some cleanup always gets done after we've used it, bracketOnError performs the cleanup only if an exception has been raised. Here's the code:

```haskell
import System.IO
import System.Directory
import Data.List
import Control.Exception

main = do
    contents <- readFile "todo.txt"
    let todoTasks = lines contents
        numberedTasks = zipWith (\n line -> show n ++ " - " ++ line)
                               [0..] todoTasks
    putStrLn "These are your TO-DO items:"
    mapM_ putStrLn numberedTasks
    putStrLn "Which one do you want to delete?"
    numberString <- getLine
    let number = read numberString
        newTodoItems = unlines $ delete (todoTasks !! number) todoTasks
    bracketOnError (openTempFile "." "temp")
        (\(tempName, tempHandle) -> do
            hClose tempHandle
            removeFile tempName)
```

```
(\(tempName, tempHandle) -> do
    hPutStr tempHandle newTodoItems
    hClose tempHandle
    removeFile "todo.txt"
    renameFile tempName "todo.txt")
```

Instead of just using `openTempFile` normally, we use it with `bracketOnError`. Next, we write what we want to happen if an error occurs; that is, we want to close the temporary handle and remove the temporary file. Finally, we write what we want to do with the temporary file while things are going well, and these lines are the same as they were before. We write the new items, close the temporary handle, remove our current file, and rename the temporary file.

Command-Line Arguments

Dealing with command-line arguments is pretty much a necessity if you want to make a script or application that runs on a terminal. Luckily, Haskell's standard library has a nice way of getting command-line arguments for a program.

In the previous section, we made one program for adding an item to our to-do list and one program for removing an item. A problem with them is that we just hardcoded the name of our to-do file. We decided that the file will be named *todo.txt* and that users will never have a need for managing several to-do lists.

One solution is to always ask the users which file they want to use as their to-do list. We used that approach when we wanted to know which item to delete. It works, but it's not the ideal solution because it requires the users to run the program, wait for the program to ask them something, and then give the program some input. That's called an *interactive* program.

The difficult bit with interactive command-line programs is this: What if you want to automate the execution of that program, as with a script? It's harder to make a script that interacts with a program than a script that just calls one or more programs. That's why we sometimes want users to tell a program what they want when they run the program, instead of having the program ask the user once it's running. And what better way to have the users tell the program what they want it to do when they run it than via command-line arguments?

The `System.Environment` module has two cool I/O actions that are useful for getting command-line arguments: `getArgs` and `getProgName`. `getArgs` has a type of `getArgs :: IO [String]` and is an I/O action that will get the arguments that the program was run with and yield a list of those arguments.

getProgName has a type of getProgName :: IO String and is an I/O action that yields the program name. Here's a small program that demonstrates how these two work:

```
import System.Environment
import Data.List

main = do
   args <- getArgs
   progName <- getProgName
   putStrLn "The arguments are:"
   mapM putStrLn args
   putStrLn "The program name is:"
   putStrLn progName
```

First, we bind the command-line arguments to args and program name to progName. Next, we use putStrLn to print all the program's arguments and then the name of the program itself. Let's compile this as arg-test and try it out:

```
$ ./arg-test first second w00t "multi word arg"
The arguments are:
first
second
w00t
multi word arg
The program name is:
arg-test
```

More Fun with To-Do Lists

In the previous examples, we made one program for adding tasks and an entirely separate program for deleting them. Now we're going to join that into a single program, and whether it adds or deletes items will depend on the command-line arguments we pass to it. We'll also make it able to operate on different files, not just *todo.txt*.

We'll call our program todo, and it will be able to do three different things:

- View tasks
- Add tasks
- Delete tasks

To add a task to the *todo.txt* file, we enter it at the terminal:

```
$ ./todo add todo.txt "Find the magic sword of power"
```

To view the tasks, we enter the view command:

```
$ ./todo view todo.txt
```

To remove a task, we use its index:

```
$ ./todo remove todo.txt 2
```

A Multitasking Task List

We'll start by making a function that takes a command in the form of a string, like "add" or "view", and returns a function that takes a list of arguments and returns an I/O action that does what we want:

```
import System.Environment
import System.Directory
import System.IO
import Data.List
import Control.Exception

dispatch :: String -> [String] -> IO ()
dispatch "add" = add
dispatch "view" = view
dispatch "remove" = remove
```

We'll define main like this:

```
main = do
    (command:argList) <- getArgs
    dispatch command argList
```

First, we get the arguments and bind them to (command:argList). This means that the first argument will be bound to command, and the rest of the arguments will be bound to argList. In the next line of our main block, we apply the dispatch function to the command, which results in the add, view, or remove function. We then apply that function to argList.

Suppose we call our program like this:

```
$ ./todo add todo.txt "Find the magic sword of power"
```

command is "add", and argList is ["todo.txt", "Find the magic sword of power"]. That way, the second pattern match of the dispatch function will succeed, and it will return the add function. Finally, we apply that to argList, which results in an I/O action that adds the item to our to-do list.

Now let's implement the add, view, and remove functions, starting with add:

```
add :: [String] -> IO ()
add [fileName, todoItem] = appendFile fileName (todoItem ++ "\n")
```

We might call our program like so:

```
./todo add todo.txt "Find the magic sword of power"
```

The "add" will be bound to command in the first pattern match in the main block, whereas ["todo.txt", "Find the magic sword of power"] will be passed to the function that we get from the dispatch function. So, because we're not dealing with bad input right now, we just pattern match against a list with those two elements immediately and return an I/O action that appends that line to the end of the file, along with a newline character.

Next, let's implement the list-viewing functionality. If we want to view the items in a file, we do ./todo view todo.txt. So in the first pattern match, command will be "view", and argList will be ["todo.txt"]. Here's the function in full:

```haskell
view :: [String] -> IO ()
view [fileName] = do
    contents <- readFile fileName
    let todoTasks = lines contents
        numberedTasks = zipWith (\n line -> show n ++ " - " ++ line)
                        [0..] todoTasks
    putStr $ unlines numberedTasks
```

When we made our deletetodo program, which could only delete items from a to-do list, it had the ability to display the items in a to-do list, so this code is very similar to that part of the previous program.

Finally, we're going to implement remove. It's very similar to the program that only deleted the tasks, so if you don't understand how deleting an item here works, review "Deleting Items" on page 181. The main difference is that we're not hardcoding the filename as *todo.txt* but instead getting it as an argument. We're also getting the target task number as an argument, rather than prompting the user for it.

```haskell
remove :: [String] -> IO ()
remove [fileName, numberString] = do
    contents <- readFile fileName
    let todoTasks = lines contents
        numberedTasks = zipWith (\n line -> show n ++ " - " ++ line)
                        [0..] todoTasks
    putStrLn "These are your TO-DO items:"
    mapM_ putStrLn numberedTasks
    let number = read numberString
        newTodoItems = unlines $ delete (todoTasks !! number) todoTasks
    bracketOnError (openTempFile "." "temp")
        (\(tempName, tempHandle) -> do
            hClose tempHandle
            removeFile tempName)
```

```
            (\(tempName, tempHandle) -> do
                hPutStr tempHandle newTodoItems
                hClose tempHandle
                removeFile fileName
                renameFile tempName fileName)
```

We opened the file based on fileName and opened a temporary file, deleted the line with the index that the user wants to delete, wrote that to the temporary file, removed the original file, and renamed the temporary file back to fileName.

Here's the whole program in all its glory:

```haskell
import System.Environment
import System.Directory
import System.IO
import Data.List

dispatch :: String -> [String] -> IO ()
dispatch "add" = add
dispatch "view" = view
dispatch "remove" = remove

main = do
    (command:argList) <- getArgs
    dispatch command argList

add :: [String] -> IO ()
add [fileName, todoItem] = appendFile fileName (todoItem ++ "\n")

view :: [String] -> IO ()
view [fileName] = do
    contents <- readFile fileName
    let todoTasks = lines contents
        numberedTasks = zipWith (\n line -> show n ++ " - " ++ line)
                        [0..] todoTasks
    putStr $ unlines numberedTasks

remove :: [String] -> IO ()
remove [fileName, numberString] = do
    contents <- readFile fileName
    let todoTasks = lines contents
        numberedTasks = zipWith (\n line -> show n ++ " - " ++ line)
                            [0..] todoTasks
    putStrLn "These are your TO-DO items:"
    mapM_ putStrLn numberedTasks
    let number = read numberString
        newTodoItems = unlines $ delete (todoTasks !! number) todoTasks
```

```
bracketOnError (openTempFile "." "temp")
    (\(tempName, tempHandle) -> do
        hClose tempHandle
        removeFile tempName)
    (\(tempName, tempHandle) -> do
        hPutStr tempHandle newTodoItems
        hClose tempHandle
        removeFile "todo.txt"
        renameFile tempName "todo.txt")
```

To summarize our solution, we made a dispatch function that maps from commands to functions that take some command-line arguments in the form of a list and return an I/O action. We see what the command is, and based on that, we get the appropriate function from the dispatch function. We call that function with the rest of the command-line arguments to get back an I/O action that will do the appropriate thing, and then just perform that action. Using higher-order functions allows us to just tell the dispatch function to give us the appropriate function, and then tell that function to give us an I/O action for some command-line arguments.

Let's try our app!

```
$ ./todo view todo.txt
0 - Iron the dishes
1 - Dust the dog
2 - Take salad out of the oven

$ ./todo add todo.txt "Pick up children from dry cleaners"

$ ./todo view todo.txt
0 - Iron the dishes
1 - Dust the dog
2 - Take salad out of the oven
3 - Pick up children from dry cleaners

$ ./todo remove todo.txt 2

$ ./todo view todo.txt
0 - Iron the dishes
1 - Dust the dog
2 - Pick up children from dry cleaners :
```

Another cool thing about using the dispatch function is that it's easy to add functionality. Just add an extra pattern to dispatch and implement the corresponding function, and you're laughing! As an exercise, you can try implementing a bump function that will take a file and a task number and return an I/O action that bumps that task to the top of the to-do list.

Dealing with Bad Input

We could extend this program to make it fail a bit more gracefully in the case of bad input, instead of printing out an ugly error message from Haskell. We can start by adding a catchall pattern at the end the dispatch function and making it return a function that ignores the argument list and tells us that such a command doesn't exist:

```
dispatch :: String -> [String] -> IO ()
dispatch "add" = add
dispatch "view" = view
dispatch "remove" = remove
dispatch command = doesntExist command

doesntExist :: String -> [String] -> IO ()
doesntExist command _ =
    putStrLn $ "The " ++ command ++ " command doesn't exist"
```

We might also add catchall patterns to the add, view, and remove functions, so that the program tells users if they have supplied the wrong number of arguments to a given command. Here's an example:

```
add :: [String] -> IO ()
add [fileName, todoItem] = appendFile fileName (todoItem ++ "\n")
add _ = putStrLn "The add command takes exactly two arguments"
```

If add is applied to a list that doesn't have exactly two elements, the first pattern match will fail, but the second one will succeed, helpfully informing users of their erronous ways. We can add a catchall pattern like this to view and remove as well.

Note that we haven't covered all of the cases where our input is bad. For instance, suppose we run our program like this:

```
./todo
```

In this case, it will crash, because we use the (command:argList) pattern in our do block, but that doesn't consider the possibility that there are no arguments at all! We also don't check to see if the file we're operating on exists before trying to open it. Adding these precautions isn't hard, but it is a bit tedious, so making this program completely idiot-proof is left as an exercise to the reader.

Randomness

Many times while programming, you need to get some random data (well, *pseudo*-random data, since we all know that the only true source of randomness is a monkey on a unicycle with cheese in one hand and its butt in the other). For example, you may be making a game where a die needs to be thrown, or you need to generate some data to test your program. In this section, we'll take a look at how to make Haskell generate seemingly random data and why we need external input to generate values that are random enough.

Most programming languages have functions that give you back some random number. Each time you call that function, you retrieve a different random number. How about Haskell? Well, remember that Haskell is a purely functional language. That means it has referential transparency. And *that* means a function, if given the same parameters twice, must produce the same result twice. That's really cool, because it allows us to reason about programs, and it enables us to defer evaluation until we really need it. However, this makes it a bit tricky for getting random numbers.

Suppose we have a function like this:

```
randomNumber :: Int
randomNumber = 4
```

It's not very useful as a random number function, because it will always return 4. (Even though I can assure you that the 4 is completely random, because I used a die to determine it.)

How do other languages make seemingly random numbers? Well, they take some initial data, like the current time, and based on that, generate numbers that are seemingly random. In Haskell, we can generate random numbers by making a function that takes as its parameter some initial data, or randomness, and produces a random number. We use I/O to bring randomness into our program from outside.

Enter the System.Random module. It has all the functions that satisfy our need for randomness. Let's just dive into one of the functions it exports: random. Here is its type signature:

```
random :: (RandomGen g, Random a) => g -> (a, g)
```

Whoa! We have some new type classes in this type declaration! The RandomGen type class is for types that can act as sources of randomness. The Random type class is for types whose values can be random. We can generate random Boolean values by randomly producing either True or False. We can also generate numbers that are random. Can a function take on a random value? I don't think so! If we try to translate the type declaration of random to English, we get something like this: It takes a random generator (that's our source of randomness) and returns a random value and a new random generator. Why does it also return a new generator as well as a random value? Well, you'll see in a moment.

To use our random function, we need to get our hands on one of those random generators. The System.Random module exports a cool type, namely StdGen, which is an instance of the RandomGen type class. We can make a StdGen manually, or we can tell the system to give us one based on a multitude of (sort of) random stuff.

To manually make a random generator, use the mkStdGen function. It has a type of mkStdGen :: Int -> StdGen. It takes an integer, and based on that, gives us a random generator. Okay then, let's try using random and mkStdGen in tandem to get a (hardly) random number.

```
ghci> random (mkStdGen 100)
<interactive>:1:0:
    Ambiguous type variable `a' in the constraint:
      `Random a' arising from a use of `random' at <interactive>:1:0-20
    Probable fix: add a type signature that fixes these type variable(s)
```

What's this? Ah, right, the random function can return a value of any type that's part of the Random type class, so we need to inform Haskell which type we want. Also let's not forget that it returns a random value and a random generator in a pair.

```
ghci> random (mkStdGen 100) :: (Int, StdGen)
(-1352021624,651872571 1655838864)
```

Finally, a number that looks kind of random! The first component of the tuple is our number, and the second component is a textual representation of our new random generator. What happens if we call random with the same random generator again?

```
ghci> random (mkStdGen 100) :: (Int, StdGen)
(-1352021624,651872571 1655838864)
```

Of course, we get the same result for the same parameters. So let's try giving it a different random generator as a parameter:

```
ghci> random (mkStdGen 949494) :: (Int, StdGen)
(539963926,466647808 1655838864)
```

Great, a different number! We can use the type annotation to get different types back from that function.

```
ghci> random (mkStdGen 949488) :: (Float, StdGen)
(0.8938442,1597344447 1655838864)
```

```
ghci> random (mkStdGen 949488) :: (Bool, StdGen)
(False,1485632275 40692)
ghci> random (mkStdGen 949488) :: (Integer, StdGen)
(1691547873,1597344447 1655838864)
```

Tossing a Coin

Let's make a function that simulates tossing a coin three times. If random
didn't return a new generator along with a random value, we would need
to make this function take three random generators as a parameter and return coin tosses for each of them. But if one generator can make a random
value of type Int (which can take on a load of different values), it should be
able to make three coin tosses (which can have only eight different end results). So this is where random returning a new generator along with a value
comes in handy.

We'll represent a coin with a simple Bool: True is tails, and False is heads.

```
threeCoins :: StdGen -> (Bool, Bool, Bool)
threeCoins gen =
    let (firstCoin, newGen) = random gen
        (secondCoin, newGen') = random newGen
        (thirdCoin, newGen'') = random newGen'
    in  (firstCoin, secondCoin, thirdCoin)
```

We call random with the generator we got as a parameter to get a coin
and a new generator. Then we call it again, only this time with our new
generator, to get the second coin. We do the same for the third coin.
Had we called it with the same generator every time, all the coins would
have had the same value, so we would get only (False, False, False) or
(True, True, True) as a result.

```
ghci> threeCoins (mkStdGen 21)
(True,True,True)
ghci> threeCoins (mkStdGen 22)
(True,False,True)
ghci> threeCoins (mkStdGen 943)
(True,False,True)
ghci> threeCoins (mkStdGen 944)
(True,True,True)
```

Notice that we didn't need to call random gen :: (Bool, StdGen). Since
we already specified that we want Booleans in the type declaration of the
function, Haskell can infer that we want a Boolean value in this case.

More Random Functions

What if we want to flip more coins? For that, there's a function called `randoms`, which takes a generator and returns an infinite sequence of values based on that generator.

```
ghci> take 5 $ randoms (mkStdGen 11) :: [Int]
[-1807975507,545074951,-1015194702,-1622477312,-502893664]
ghci> take 5 $ randoms (mkStdGen 11) :: [Bool]
[True,True,True,True,False]
ghci> take 5 $ randoms (mkStdGen 11) :: [Float]
[7.904789e-2,0.62691015,0.26363158,0.12223756,0.38291094]
```

Why doesn't `randoms` return a new generator as well as a list? We could implement the `randoms` function very easily like this:

```
randoms' :: (RandomGen g, Random a) => g -> [a]
randoms' gen = let (value, newGen) = random gen in value:randoms' newGen
```

This is a recursive definition. We get a random value and a new generator from the current generator, and then make a list that has the value as its head and random numbers based on the new generator as its tail. Because we need to be able to potentially generate an infinite amount of numbers, we can't give the new random generator back.

We could make a function that generates a finite stream of numbers and a new generator like this:

```
finiteRandoms :: (RandomGen g, Random a) => Int -> g -> ([a], g)
finiteRandoms 0 gen = ([], gen)
finiteRandoms n gen =
    let (value, newGen) = random gen
        (restOfList, finalGen) = finiteRandoms (n-1) newGen
    in  (value:restOfList, finalGen)
```

Again, this is a recursive definition. We say that if we want zero numbers, we just return an empty list and the generator that was given to us. For any other number of random values, we first get one random number and a new generator. That will be the head. Then we say that the tail will be n - 1 numbers generated with the new generator. Then we return the head and the rest of the list joined and the final generator that we got from getting the n - 1 random numbers.

What if we want a random value in some sort of range? All the random integers so far were outrageously big or small. What if we want to throw a die? Well, we use `randomR` for that purpose. It has this type:

```
randomR :: (RandomGen g, Random a) :: (a, a) -> g -> (a, g)
```

This means that it's kind of like `random`, but it takes as its first parameter a pair of values that set the lower and upper bounds, and the final value produced will be within those bounds.

```
ghci> randomR (1,6) (mkStdGen 359353)
(6,1494289578 40692)
ghci> randomR (1,6) (mkStdGen 35935335)
(3,1250031057 40692)
```

There's also `randomRs`, which produces a stream of random values within our defined ranges. Check this out:

```
ghci> take 10 $ randomRs ('a','z') (mkStdGen 3) :: [Char]
"ndkxbvmomg"
```

It looks like a super secret password, doesn't it?

Randomness and I/O

You may be wondering what this section has to do with I/O. We haven't done anything concerning I/O so far. We've always made our random number generator manually by creating it with some arbitrary integer. The problem is that if we do that in our real programs, they will always return the same random numbers, which is no good for us. That's why `System.Random` offers the `getStdGen` I/O action, which has a type of `IO StdGen`. It asks the system for some initial data and uses it to jump-start the *global generator*. `getStdGen` fetches that global random generator when you bind it to something.

Here's a simple program that generates a random string:

```
import System.Random

main = do
    gen <- getStdGen
    putStrLn $ take 20 (randomRs ('a','z') gen)
```

Now let's test it:

```
$ ./random_string
pybphhzzhuepknbykxhe
$ ./random_string
eiqgcxykivpudlsvvjpg
$ ./random_string
nzdceoconysdgcyqjruo
$ ./random_string
bakzhnnuzrkgvesqplrx
```

But you need to be careful. Just performing getStdGen twice will ask the system for the same global generator twice. Suppose we do this:

```
import System.Random

main = do
    gen <- getStdGen
    putStrLn $ take 20 (randomRs ('a','z') gen)
    gen2 <- getStdGen
    putStr $ take 20 (randomRs ('a','z') gen2)
```

We will get the same string printed out twice!

The best way to get two different strings is to use the newStdGen action, which splits our current random generator into two generators. It updates the global random generator with one of them and yields the other as its result.

```
import System.Random

main = do
    gen <- getStdGen
    putStrLn $ take 20 (randomRs ('a','z') gen)
    gen' <- newStdGen
    putStr $ take 20 (randomRs ('a','z') gen')
```

Not only do we get a new random generator when we bind newStdGen to something, but the global one gets updated as well. This means that if we do getStdGen again and bind it to something, we'll get a generator that's not the same as gen.

Here's a little program that will make the user guess which number it's thinking of:

```
import System.Random
import Control.Monad(when)

main = do
    gen <- getStdGen
    askForNumber gen

askForNumber :: StdGen -> IO ()
askForNumber gen = do
    let (randNumber, newGen) = randomR (1,10) gen :: (Int, StdGen)
    putStrLn "Which number in the range from 1 to 10 am I thinking of? "
    numberString <- getLine
    when (not $ null numberString) $ do
        let number = read numberString
```

```
    if randNumber == number
        then putStrLn "You are correct!"
        else putStrLn $ "Sorry, it was " ++ show randNumber
    askForNumber newGen
```

We make a function askForNumber, which takes a random number generator and returns an I/O action that will prompt you for a number, and then tell you if you guessed it right.

In askForNumber, we first generate a random number and a new generator based on the generator that we got as a parameter and call them randNumber and newGen. (For this example, let's say that the number generated was 7.) Then we tell the user to guess which number we're thinking of. We perform getLine and bind its result to numberString. When the user enters 7, numberString becomes "7". Next, we use when to check if the string the user entered is an empty string. If it isn't, the action consisting of the do block that is passed to when is performed. We use read on numberString to convert it to a number, so number is now 7.

NOTE   *If the user enters some input that read can't parse (like "haha"), our program will crash with an ugly error message. If you don't want your program to crash on erronous input, use reads, which returns an empty list when it fails to read a string. When it succeeds, it returns a singleton list with a tuple that has your desired value as one component and a string with what it didn't consume as the other. Try it!*

We check if the number that we entered is equal to the one generated randomly and give the user the appropriate message. Then we perform askForNumber recursively, but this time with the new generator that we got. This gives us an I/O action that's just like the one we performed, except that it depends on a different generator.

main consists of just getting a random generator from the system and calling askForNumber with it to get the initial action.

Here's our program in action:

```
$ ./guess_the_number
Which number in the range from 1 to 10 am I thinking of?
4
Sorry, it was 3
Which number in the range from 1 to 10 am I thinking of?
10
You are correct!
```

```
Which number in the range from 1 to 10 am I thinking of?
2
Sorry, it was 4
Which number in the range from 1 to 10 am I thinking of?
5
Sorry, it was 10
Which number in the range from 1 to 10 am I thinking of?
```

Here's another way to make this same program:

```
import System.Random
import Control.Monad(when)

main = do
    gen <- getStdGen
    let (randNumber, _) = randomR (1,10) gen :: (Int, StdGen)
    putStrLn "Which number in the range from 1 to 10 am I thinking of? "
    numberString <- getLine
    when (not $ null numberString) $ do
        let number = read numberString
        if randNumber == number
            then putStrLn "You are correct!"
            else putStrLn $ "Sorry, it was " ++ show randNumber
        newStdGen
        main
```

It's very similar to the previous version, but instead of making a function that takes a generator and then calls itself recursively with the new updated generator, we do all the work in main. After telling the user whether he was correct in his guess, we update the global generator and then call main again. Both approaches are valid, but I like the first one more since it does less stuff in main and also provides a function I can reuse easily.

Bytestrings

Lists are certainly useful. So far, we've used them pretty much everywhere. There are a multitude of functions that operate on them, and Haskell's laziness allows us to exchange the for and while loops of other languages for filtering and mapping over lists. Since evaluation will happen only when it really needs to, things like infinite lists (and even infinite lists of infinite lists!) are no problem for us. That's why lists can also be used to represent streams, either when reading from the standard input or

when reading from files. We can just open a file and read it as a string, even though it will be accessed only when the need arises.

However, processing files as strings has one drawback: It tends to be slow. Lists are really lazy. Remember that a list like [1,2,3,4] is syntactic sugar for 1:2:3:4:[]. When the first element of the list is forcibly evaluated (say by printing it), the rest of the list 2:3:4:[] is still just a promise of a list, and so on. We call that promise a *thunk*.

A thunk is basically a deferred computation. Haskell achieves its laziness by using thunks and computing them only when it must, instead of computing everything up front. So you can think of lists as promises that the next element will be delivered once it really has to be, and along with it, the promise of the element after it. It doesn't take a big mental leap to conclude that processing a simple list of numbers as a series of thunks might not be the most efficient technique in the world.

That overhead doesn't bother us most of the time, but it turns out to be a liability when reading big files and manipulating them. That's why Haskell has *bytestrings*. Bytestrings are sort of like lists, only each element is one byte (or 8 bits) in size. The way they handle laziness is also different.

Strict and Lazy Bytestrings

Bytestrings come in two flavors: strict and lazy. Strict bytestrings reside in Data.ByteString, and they do away with the laziness completely. There are no thunks involved. A strict bytestring represents a series of bytes in an array. You can't have things like infinite strict bytestrings. If you evaluate the first byte of a strict bytestring, you must evaluate the whole thing.

The other variety of bytestrings resides in Data.ByteString.Lazy. They're lazy, but not quite as lazy as lists. Since there are as many thunks in a list as there are elements, they are kind of slow for some purposes. Lazy bytestrings take a different approach. They are stored in chunks (not to be confused with thunks!), and each chunk has a size of 64KB. So if you evaluate a byte in a lazy bytestring (by printing it, for example), the first 64KB will be evaluated. After that, it's just a promise for the rest of the chunks. Lazy bytestrings are kind of like lists of strict bytestrings, with a size of 64KB. When you process a file with lazy bytestrings, it will be read chunk by chunk. This is cool because it won't cause the memory usage to skyrocket, and the 64KB probably fits neatly into your CPU's L2 cache.

If you look through the documentation for Data.ByteString.Lazy, you will see that it has a lot of functions with the same names as the ones from Data.List, but the type signatures have ByteString instead of [a] and Word8 instead of a. These functions are similar to the ones that work on lists. Because the names are the same, we're going to do a qualified import in a script and then load that script into GHCi to play with bytestrings:

```
import qualified Data.ByteString.Lazy as B
import qualified Data.ByteString as S
```

B has lazy bytestring types and functions, whereas S has strict ones. We'll mostly be using the lazy versions.

The pack function has the type signature pack :: [Word8] -> ByteString. This means that it takes a list of bytes of type Word8 and returns a ByteString. You can think of it as taking a list, which is lazy, and making it less lazy, so that it's lazy only at 64KB intervals.

The Word8 type is like Int, but it represents an unsigned 8-bit number. This means that it has a much smaller range of only 0 to 255. And just like Int, it's in the Num type class. For instance, we know that the value 5 is polymorphic in that it can act like any numeric type, including Word8.

Here's how we pack lists of numbers into bytestrings:

```
ghci> B.pack [99,97,110]
Chunk "can" Empty
ghci> B.pack [98..120]
Chunk "bcdefghijklmnopqrstuvwx" Empty
```

We packed only a handful of values into a bytestring, so they fit inside one chunk. Empty is like [] for lists—they both represent an empty sequence.

As you can see, you don't need to specify that your numbers are of type Word8, because the type system can make numbers choose that type. If you try to use a big number like 336 as a Word8, it will just wrap around to 80.

When we need to examine a bytestring byte by byte, we need to unpack it. The unpack function is the inverse of pack. It takes a bytestring and turns it into a list of bytes. Here's an example:

```
ghci> let by = B.pack [98,111,114,116]
ghci> by
Chunk "bort" Empty
ghci> B.unpack by
[98,111,114,116]
```

You can also go back and forth between strict and lazy bytestrings. The toChunks function takes a lazy bytestring and converts it to a list of strict ones. The fromChunks function takes a list of strict bytestrings and converts it to a lazy bytestring:

```
ghci> B.fromChunks [S.pack [40,41,42], S.pack [43,44,45], S.pack [46,47,48]]
Chunk "()*" (Chunk "+,-" (Chunk "./0" Empty))
```

This is good if you have a lot of small strict bytestrings and you want to process them efficiently without joining them into one big strict bytestring in memory first.

The bytestring version of : is called cons. It takes a byte and a bytestring and puts the byte at the beginning.

```
ghci> B.cons 85 $ B.pack [80,81,82,84]
Chunk "U" (Chunk "PQRT" Empty)
```

The bytestring modules have a load of functions that are analogous to those in Data.List, including, but not limited to, head, tail, init, null, length, map, reverse, foldl, foldr, concat, takeWhile, filter, and so on. For a complete listing of bytestring functions, check out the documentation for the bytestring package at *http://hackage.haskell.org/package/bytestring/*.

The bytestring modules also have functions that have the same name and behave the same as some functions found in System.IO, but Strings are replaced with ByteStrings. For instance, the readFile function in System.IO has this type:

```
readFile :: FilePath -> IO String
```

The readFile function from the bytestring modules has the following type:

```
readFile :: FilePath -> IO ByteString
```

NOTE *If you're using strict bytestrings and you attempt to read a file, all of that file will be read into memory at once! With lazy bytestrings, the file will be read in neat chunks.*

Copying Files with Bytestrings

Let's make a program that takes two filenames as command-line arguments and copies the first file into the second file. Note that System.Directory already has a function called copyFile, but we're going to implement our own file-copying function and program anyway. Here's the code:

```
import System.Environment
import System.Directory
import System.IO
import Control.Exception
import qualified Data.ByteString.Lazy as B

main = do
    (fileName1:fileName2:_) <- getArgs
    copy fileName1 fileName2

copy source dest = do
    contents <- B.readFile source
    bracketOnError
        (openTempFile "." "temp")
        (\(tempName, tempHandle) -> do
            hClose tempHandle
            removeFile tempName)
        (\(tempName, tempHandle) -> do
```

```
B.hPutStr tempHandle contents
hClose tempHandle
renameFile tempName dest)
```

To begin, in `main`, we just get the command-line arguments and call our copy function, which is where the magic happens. One way to do this would be to just read from one file and write to another. But if something goes wrong (such as we don't have enough disk space to copy the file), we'll be left with a messed-up file. So we'll write to a temporary file first. Then if something goes wrong, we can just delete that file.

First, we use `B.readFile` to read the contents of our source file. Then we use `bracketOnError` to set up our error handling. We acquire the resource with `openTempFile "." "temp"`, which yields a tuple that consists of a temporary filename and a handle. Next, we say what we want to happen if an error occurs. If something goes wrong, we close the handle and remove the temporary file. Finally, we do the copying itself. We use `B.hPutStr` to write the contents to our temporary file. We close the temporary file and rename it to what we want it to be in the end.

Notice that we just used `B.readFile` and `B.hPutStr` instead of their regular variants. We didn't need to use special bytestring functions for opening, closing, and renaming files. We just need to use the bytestring functions when reading and writing.

Let's test it:

```
$ ./bytestringcopy bart.txt bort.txt
```

A program that doesn't use bytestrings could look just like this. The only difference is that we used `B.readFile` and `B.writeFile` instead of `readFile` and `writeFile`.

Many times, you can convert a program that uses normal strings to a program that uses bytestrings just by doing the necessary imports and then putting the qualified module names in front of some functions. Sometimes, you need to convert functions that you wrote to work on strings so that they work on bytestrings, but that's not hard.

Whenever you need better performance in a program that reads a lot of data into strings, give bytestrings a try. Chances are you'll get some good performance boosts with very little effort on your part. I usually write programs using normal strings and then convert them to use bytestrings if the performance is not satisfactory.

10

FUNCTIONALLY SOLVING PROBLEMS

In this chapter, we'll look at a couple of interesting problems, and we'll think about how to solve them as elegantly as possible using functional programming techniques. This will give you the opportunity to flex your newly acquired Haskell muscles and practice your coding skills.

Reverse Polish Notation Calculator

Usually, when we work with algebraic expressions in school, we write them in an infix manner. For instance, we write 10 - (4 + 3) ∗ 2. Addition (+), multiplication (∗), and subtraction (-) are infix operators, just like the infix functions in Haskell (+ `elem`, and so on). As humans, we can parse this form easily in our minds. The downside is that we need to use parentheses to denote precedence.

Another way to write algebraic expressions is to use *reverse polish notation*, or *RPN*. In RPN, the operator comes after the numbers, rather than being sandwiched between them. So, instead of writing 4 + 3, we write 4 3 +. But how do we write expressions that contain several operators? For example, how would we write an expression that adds 4 and 3 and then multiplies that by 10? It's simple: 4 3 + 10 *. Because 4 3 + is equivalent to 7, that whole expression is the same as 7 10 *.

Calculating RPN Expressions

To get a feel for how to calculate RPN expressions, think of a stack of numbers. We go over the expression from left to right. Every time a number is encountered, put it on top of the stack (*push* it onto the stack). When we encounter an operator, we take the two numbers that are on top of the stack (*pop* them), use the operator with those two, and then push the resulting number back onto the stack. When we reach the end of the expression, we should be left with a single number that represents the result (assuming the expression was well formed).

Let's see how we would calculate the RPN expression 10 4 3 + 2 * -:

1. We push 10 onto the stack, so the stack consists of 10.

2. The next item is 4, so we push it onto the stack as well. The stack is now 10, 4.

3. We do the same with 3, and the stack is now 10, 4, 3.

4. We encounter an operator: +. We pop the two top numbers from the stack (so now the stack is just 10), add those numbers together, and push that result to the stack. The stack is now 10, 7.

5. We push 2 to the stack, and the stack becomes 10, 7, 2.

6. We encounter another operator. We pop 7 and 2 off the stack, multiply them, and push that result to the stack. Multiplying 7 and 2 produces 14, so the stack is now 10, 14.

7. Finally, there's a -. We pop 10 and 14 from the stack, subtract 14 from 10, and push that back.

8. The number on the stack is now -4. Because there are no more numbers or operators in our expression, that's our result!

So, that's how to calculate an RPN expression by hand. Now let's think about how to make a Haskell function to do the same thing.

Writing an RPN Function

Our function will take a string that contains an RPN expression as its parameter (like "10 4 3 + 2 * -") and give us back that expression's result.

What would the type of that function be? We want it to take a string as a parameter and produce a number as its result. Let's say that we want the result to be a floating-point number of double precision, because we want to include division as well. So its type will probably be something like this:

```
solveRPN :: String -> Double
```

NOTE   *It really helps to first think what the type declaration of a function should be before dealing with the implementation. In Haskell, a function's type declaration tells you a whole lot about the function, due to the very strong type system.*

When implementing a solution to a problem in Haskell, it can be helpful to consider how you did it by hand. For our RPN expression calculation, we treated every number or operator that was separated by a space as a single item. So it might help us if we start by breaking a string like "10 4 3 + 2 * -" into a list of items, like this:

```
["10","4","3","+","2","*","-"].
```

Next up, what did we do with that list of items in our head? We went over it from left to right and kept a stack as we did that. Does that process remind you of anything? In "I Fold You So" on page 73, you saw that pretty much any function where you traverse a list element by element, and build up (*accumulate*) some result—whether it's a number, a list, a stack, or something else—can be implemented with a fold.

In this case, we're going to use a left fold, because we go over the list from left to right. The accumulator value will be our stack, so the result from the fold will also be a stack (though as we've seen, it will contain only one item).

One more thing to think about is how we will represent the stack. Let's use a list and keep the top of our stack at the head of the list. Adding to the head (beginning) of a list is much faster than adding to the end of it. So if we have a stack of, say, 10, 4, 3, we'll represent that as the list [3,4,10].

Now we have enough information to roughly sketch our function. It's going to take a string like "10 4 3 + 2 * -" and break it down into a list of items by using words. Next, we'll do a left fold over that list and end up with a stack that has a single item (in this example, [-4]). We take that single item out of the list, and that's our final result!

Here's a sketch of that function:

```
solveRPN :: String -> Double
solveRPN expression = head (foldl foldingFunction [] (words expression))
    where  foldingFunction stack item = ...
```

We take the expression and turn it into a list of items. Then we fold over that list of items with the folding function. Notice the [], which represents the starting accumulator. The accumulator is our stack, so [] represents an empty stack, which is what we start with. After getting the final stack with a single item, we apply head to that list to get the item out.

All that's left now is to implement a folding function that will take a stack, like [4,10], and an item, like "3", and return a new stack [3,4,10]. If the stack is [4,10] and the item is "*", then the function will need to return [40].

Before we write the folding function, let's turn our function into point-free style, because it has a lot of parentheses that are kind of freaking me out:

```
solveRPN :: String -> Double
solveRPN = head . foldl foldingFunction [] . words
    where  foldingFunction stack item = ...
```

That's much better.

The folding function will take a stack and an item and return a new stack. We'll use pattern matching to get the top items of a stack and to pattern match against operators like "*" and "-". Here it is with the folding function implemented:

```
solveRPN :: String -> Double
solveRPN = head . foldl foldingFunction [] . words
    where  foldingFunction (x:y:ys) "*" = (y * x):ys
           foldingFunction (x:y:ys) "+" = (y + x):ys
           foldingFunction (x:y:ys) "-" = (y - x):ys
           foldingFunction xs numberString = read numberString:xs
```

We laid this out as four patterns. The patterns will be tried from top to bottom. First, the folding function will see if the current item is "*". If it is, then it will take a list like [3,4,9,3] and name its first two elements x and y, respectively. So in this case, x would be 3, and y would be 4. ys would be [9,3]. It will return a list that's just like ys, but with x and y multiplied as its head. With this, we pop the two topmost numbers off the stack, multiply them, and push the result back onto the stack. If the item is not "*", the pattern matching will fall through, "+" will be checked, and so on.

If the item is none of the operators, we assume it's a string that represents a number. If it's a number, we just apply read to that string to get a number from it and return the previous stack but with that number pushed to the top.

For the list of items ["2","3","+"], our function will start folding from the left. The initial stack will be []. It will call the folding function with [] as the stack (accumulator) and "2" as the item. Because that item is not an operator, it will be read and then added to the beginning of [ ]. So the new stack is now [2]. The folding function will be called with [2] as the stack and "3" as the item, producing a new stack of [3,2]. Then it's called for the third time with [3,2] as the stack and "+" as the item. This causes these two numbers to be popped off the stack, added together, and pushed back. The final stack is [5], which is the number that we return.

Let's play around with our function:

```
ghci> solveRPN "10 4 3 + 2 * -"
-4.0
ghci> solveRPN "2 3.5 +"
5.5
ghci> solveRPN "90 34 12 33 55 66 + * - +"
-3947.0
ghci> solveRPN "90 34 12 33 55 66 + * - + -"
4037.0
ghci> solveRPN "90 3.8 -"
86.2
```

Cool, it works!

Adding More Operators

One nice thing about this solution is that it can be easily modified to support various other operators. They don't even need to be binary operators. For instance, we can make an operator "log" that just pops one number off the stack and pushes back its logarithm. We can also make operators that operate on several numbers, like "sum", which pops off all the numbers and pushes back their sum.

Let's modify our function to accept a few more operators.

```
solveRPN :: String -> Double
solveRPN = head . foldl foldingFunction [] . words
    where   foldingFunction (x:y:ys) "*" = (y * x):ys
            foldingFunction (x:y:ys) "+" = (y + x):ys
            foldingFunction (x:y:ys) "-" = (y - x):ys
            foldingFunction (x:y:ys) "/" = (y / x):ys
            foldingFunction (x:y:ys) "^" = (y ** x):ys
            foldingFunction (x:xs) "ln" = log x:xs
            foldingFunction xs "sum" = [sum xs]
            foldingFunction xs numberString = read numberString:xs
```

The / is division, of course, and ** is exponentiation. With the logarithm operator, we just pattern match against a single element and the rest of the stack, because we need only one element to perform its natural logarithm. With the sum operator, we return a stack that has only one element, which is the sum of the stack so far.

```
ghci> solveRPN "2.7 ln"
0.9932517730102834
ghci> solveRPN "10 10 10 10 sum 4 /"
10.0
ghci> solveRPN "10 10 10 10 10 sum 4 /"
12.5
ghci> solveRPN "10 2 ^"
100.0
```

I think that making a function that can calculate arbitrary floating-point RPN expressions and has the option to be easily extended in 10 lines is pretty awesome.

NOTE *This RPN calculation solution is not really fault tolerant. When given input that doesn't make sense, it might result in a runtime error. But don't worry, you'll learn how to make this function more robust in Chapter 14.*

Heathrow to London

Suppose that we're on a business trip. Our plane has just landed in England, and we rent a car. We have a meeting really soon, and we need to get from Heathrow Airport to London as fast as we can (but safely!).

There are two main roads going from Heathrow to London, and a number of regional roads cross them. It takes a fixed amount of time to travel from one crossroad to another. It's up to us to find the optimal path to take so that we get to our meeting in London on time. We start on the left side and can either cross to the other main road or go forward.

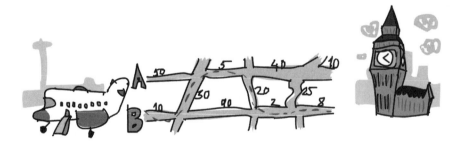

As you can see in the picture, the quickest path from Heathrow to London in this case is to start on main road B, cross over, go forward on A, cross over again, and then go forward twice on B. If we take this path, it takes us 75 minutes. Had we chosen any other path, it would take longer.

Our job is to make a program that takes input that represents a road system and prints out the quickest path across it. Here's what the input would look like for this case:

```
50
10
30
5
90
20
40
2
25
10
8
0
```

To mentally parse the input file, read it in threes and mentally split the road system into sections. Each section is composed of road A, road B, and a crossing road. To have it neatly fit into threes, we say that there's a last crossing section that takes 0 minutes to drive over. That's because we don't care where we arrive in London, as long as we're in London, mate!

Just as we did when considering the RPN calculator problem, we'll solve this problem in three steps:

1. Forget Haskell for a minute and think about how to solve the problem by hand. In the RPN calculator section, we first figured out that when calculating an expression by hand, we keep a sort of stack in our minds and then go over the expression one item at a time.

2. Think about how we're going to represent our data in Haskell. For our RPN calculator, we decided to use a list of strings to represent our expression.

3. Figure out how to operate on that data in Haskell so that we produce a solution. For the calculator, we used a left fold to walk over the list of strings, while keeping a stack to produce a solution.

Calculating the Quickest Path

So how do we figure out the quickest path from Heathrow to London by hand? Well, we can just look at the whole picture and try to guess what the quickest path is and hope our guess is correct. That solution works for very small inputs, but what if we have a road that has 10,000 sections? Yikes! We also won't be able to say for certain that our solution is the optimal one; we can just say that we're pretty sure. So, that's not a good solution.

Here's a simplified picture of our road system:

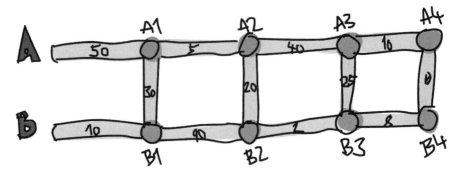

Can we figure out the quickest path to the first crossroads (the first dot on A, marked A1) on road A? That's pretty trivial. We just see if it's faster to go directly forward on A or to go forward on B and then cross over. Obviously, it's faster to go forward via B and then cross over, because that takes 40 minutes, whereas going directly via A takes 50 minutes. What about crossroads B1? We see that it's a lot faster to just go directly via B (incurring a cost of 10 minutes), because going via A and then crossing over would take us 80 minutes!

Now we know the quickest path to A1: Go via B and then cross over. We'll say that's path B, C with a cost of 40 minutes. We also know the quickest path to B1: Go directly via B. So that's a path consisting just of B for 10 minutes. Does this knowledge help us at all if we want to know the quickest path to the next crossroads on both main roads? Gee golly, it sure does!

Let's see what the quickest path to A2 would be. To get to A2, we'll either go directly to A2 from A1 or we'll go forward from B1 and then cross over (remember that we can only move forward or cross to the other side). And because we know the cost to A1 and B1, we can easily figure out the best path to A2. It takes us 40 minutes to get to A1 and then 5 minutes to get from A1 to A2, so that's path B, C, A, for a cost of 45. It takes us only 10 minutes to get to B1, but then it would take an additional 110 minutes to go to B2 and then cross over! So obviously, the quickest path to A2 is B, C, A. In the same way, the quickest way to B2 is to go forward from A1 and then cross over.

NOTE   *Maybe you're asking yourself, "But what about getting to A2 by first crossing over at B1 and then going forward?" Well, we already covered crossing from B1 to A1 when we were looking for the best way to A1, so we don't need to take that into account in the next step as well.*

Now that we have the best path to A2 and B2, we can repeat this until we reach the end. Once we have calculated the best paths for A4 and B4, the one that takes less time is the optimal path.

So in essence, for the second section, we just repeat the step we did at first, but we take into account the previous best paths on A and B. We could say that we also took into account the best paths on A and on B in the first step—they were both empty paths with a cost of 0 minutes.

In summary, to get the best path from Heathrow to London, we do this:

1. We see what the best path to the next crossroads on main road A is. The two options are going directly forward or starting at the opposite road, going forward and then crossing over. We remember the cost and the path.

2. We use the same method to find the best path to the next crossroads on main road B and remember that.

3. We see if the path to the next crossroads on A takes less time if we go from the previous A crossroads or if we go from the previous B crossroads and then cross over. We remember the quicker path. We do the same for the crossroads opposite of it.

4. We do this for every section until we reach the end.

5. Once we've reached the end, the quicker of the two paths that we have is our optimal path.

So, in essence, we keep one quickest path on the A road and one quickest path on the B road. When we reach the end, the quicker of those two is our path.

We now know how to figure out the quickest path by hand. If you had enough time, paper, and pencils, you could figure out the quickest path through a road system with any number of sections.

Representing the Road System in Haskell

How do we represent this road system with Haskell's data types?

Thinking back to our solution by hand, we checked the durations of three road parts at once: the road part on the A road, its opposite part on the B road, and part C, which touches those two parts and connects them. When we were looking for the quickest path to A1 and B1, we dealt with the durations of only the first three parts, which were 50, 10, and 30. We'll call that one section. So the road system that we use for this example can be easily represented as four sections:

- 50, 10, 30
- 5, 90, 20
- 40, 2, 25
- 10, 8, 0

It's always good to keep our data types as simple as possible (although not any simpler!). Here's the data type for our road system:

```
data Section = Section { getA :: Int, getB :: Int, getC :: Int }
    deriving (Show)

type RoadSystem = [Section]
```

This is as simple as it gets, and I have a feeling it will work perfectly for implementing our solution.

`Section` is a simple algebraic data type that holds three integers for the durations of its three road parts. We introduce a type synonym as well, saying that `RoadSystem` is a list of sections.

NOTE   *We could also use a triple of* (Int, Int, Int) *to represent a road section. Using tuples instead of making your own algebraic data types is good for some small, localized stuff, but it's usually better to make a new type for more complex representations. It gives the type system more information about what's what. We can use* (Int, Int, Int) *to represent a road section or a vector in 3D space, and we can operate on those two, but that allows us to mix them up. If we use* Section *and* Vector *data types, then we can't accidentally add a vector to a section of a road system.*

Our road system from Heathrow to London can now be represented like this:

```
heathrowToLondon :: RoadSystem
heathrowToLondon = [ Section 50 10 30
                   , Section 5 90 20
                   , Section 40 2 25
                   , Section 10 8 0
                   ]
```

All we need to do now is implement the solution in Haskell.

Writing the Optimal Path Function

What should the type declaration for a function that calculates the quickest path for any given road system be? It should take a road system as a parameter and return a path. We'll represent a path as a list as well.

Let's introduce a `Label` type that's just an enumeration of A, B, or C. We'll also make a type synonym called `Path`.

```
data Label = A | B | C deriving (Show)
type Path = [(Label, Int)]
```

Our function, which we'll call `optimalPath`, should have the following type:

```
optimalPath :: RoadSystem -> Path
```

If called with the road system `heathrowToLondon`, it should return the following path:

```
[(B,10),(C,30),(A,5),(C,20),(B,2),(B,8)]
```

We're going to need to walk over the list with the sections from left to right and keep the optimal path on A and optimal path on B as we go along.

We'll accumulate the best path as we walk over the list, left to right. What does that sound like? Ding, ding, ding! That's right, a *left fold*!

When doing the solution by hand, there was a step that we repeated over and over. It involved checking the optimal paths on A and B so far and the current section to produce the new optimal paths on A and B. For instance, at the beginning, the optimal paths were [] and [] for A and B, respectively. We examined the section Section 50 10 30 and concluded that the new optimal path to A1 was [(B,10),(C,30)] and the optimal path to B1 was [(B,10)]. If you look at this step as a function, it takes a pair of paths and a section and produces a new pair of paths. So its type is this:

```
roadStep :: (Path, Path) -> Section -> (Path, Path)
```

Let's implement this function, because it's bound to be useful:

```
roadStep :: (Path, Path) -> Section -> (Path, Path)
roadStep (pathA, pathB) (Section a b c) =
    let timeA = sum (map snd pathA)
        timeB = sum (map snd pathB)
        forwardTimeToA = timeA + a
        crossTimeToA = timeB + b + c
        forwardTimeToB = timeB + b
        crossTimeToB = timeA + a + c
        newPathToA = if forwardTimeToA <= crossTimeToA
                        then (A, a):pathA
                        else (C, c):(B, b):pathB
        newPathToB = if forwardTimeToB <= crossTimeToB
                        then (B, b):pathB
                        else (C, c):(A, a):pathA
    in  (newPathToA, newPathToB)
```

What's going on here? First, we calculate the optimal time on road A based on the best so far on A, and we do the same for B. We do sum (map snd pathA), so if pathA is something like [(A,100),(C,20)], timeA becomes 120.

forwardTimeToA is the time that it would take to get to the next crossroads on A if we went there directly from the previous crossroads on A. It equals the best time to our previous A plus the duration of the A part of the current section.

crossTimeToA is the time that it would take if we went to the next A by going forward from the previous B and then crossing over. It's the best time to the previous B so far plus the B duration of the section plus the C duration of the section.

We determine forwardTimeToB and crossTimeToB in the same manner.

Now that we know the best way to A and B, we just need to make the new paths to A and B based on that. If it's quicker to go to A by just going forward, we set newPathToA to be (A, a):pathA. Basically, we prepend the Label A and the section duration a to the optimal path on A so far. We say that the best path to the next A crossroads is the path to the previous A crossroads and then one section forward via A. Remember that A is just a label, whereas a has a type of Int.

Why do we prepend instead of doing pathA ++ [(A, a)]? Well, adding an element to the beginning of a list is much faster than adding it to the end. This means that the path will be the wrong way around once we fold over a list with this function, but it's easy to reverse the list later.

If it's quicker to get to the next A crossroads by going forward from road B and then crossing over, newPathToA is the old path to B that then goes forward and crosses to A. We do the same thing for newPathToB, except that everything is mirrored.

Finally, we return newPathToA and newPathToB in a pair.

Let's run this function on the first section of heathrowToLondon. Because it's the first section, the best paths on parameters A and B will be a pair of empty lists.

```
ghci> roadStep ([], []) (head heathrowToLondon)
([[(C,30),(B,10)],[(B,10)]])
```

Remember that the paths are reversed, so read them from right to left. From this, we can read that the best path to the next A is to start on B and then cross over to A. The best path to the next B is to just go directly forward from the starting point at B.

NOTE   *When we do timeA = sum (map snd pathA), we're calculating the time from the path on every step. We wouldn't need to do that if we implemented roadStep to take and return the best times on A and B, along with the paths themselves.*

Now that we have a function that takes a pair of paths and a section, and produces a new optimal path, we can easily do a left fold over a list of sections. roadStep is called with ([], []) and the first section, and returns a pair of optimal paths to that section. Then it's called with that pair of paths and the next section, and so on. When we've walked over all the sections, we're left with a pair of optimal paths, and the shorter of them is our answer. With this in mind, we can implement optimalPath:

```
optimalPath :: RoadSystem -> Path
optimalPath roadSystem =
    let (bestAPath, bestBPath) = foldl roadStep ([], []) roadSystem
    in  if sum (map snd bestAPath) <= sum (map snd bestBPath)
            then reverse bestAPath
            else reverse bestBPath
```

We left fold over `roadSystem` (remember that it's a list of sections) with the starting accumulator being a pair of empty paths. The result of that fold is a pair of paths, so we pattern match on the pair to get the paths themselves. Then we check which one of these was quicker and return it. Before returning it, we also reverse it, because the optimal paths so far were reversed due to us choosing prepending over appending.

Let's test this!

```
ghci> optimalPath heathrowToLondon
[(B,10),(C,30),(A,5),(C,20),(B,2),(B,8),(C,0)]
```

This is the result that we were supposed to get! It differs from our expected result a bit, because there's a step (C,0) at the end, which means that we cross over to the other road once we're in London. But because that crossing doesn't take any time, this is still the correct result.

Getting a Road System from the Input

We have the function that finds an optimal path, so now we just need to read a textual representation of a road system from the standard input, convert it into a type of `RoadSystem`, run that through our `optimalPath` function, and print the resulting path.

First, let's make a function that takes a list and splits it into groups of the same size. We'll call it `groupsOf`:

```
groupsOf :: Int -> [a] -> [[a]]
groupsOf 0 _ = undefined
groupsOf _ [] = []
groupsOf n xs = take n xs : groupsOf n (drop n xs)
```

For a parameter of [1..10], groupsOf 3 should result in the following:

```
[[1,2,3],[4,5,6],[7,8,9],[10]]
```

As you can see, it's a standard recursive function. Doing groupsOf 3 [1..10] equals the following:

```
[1,2,3] : groupsOf 3 [4,5,6,7,8,9,10]
```

When the recursion is done, we get our list in groups of three. And here's our main function, which reads from the standard input, makes a `RoadSystem` out of it, and prints out the shortest path:

```
import Data.List

main = do
    contents <- getContents
    let threes = groupsOf 3 (map read $ lines contents)
```

```
    roadSystem = map (\[a,b,c] -> Section a b c) threes
    path = optimalPath roadSystem
    pathString = concat $ map (show . fst) path
    pathTime = sum $ map snd path
putStrLn $ "The best path to take is: " ++ pathString
putStrLn $ "Time taken: " ++ show pathTime
```

First, we get all the contents from the standard input. Then we apply lines to our contents to convert something like "50\n10\n30\n ... to something cleaner, like ["50","10","30" .... We then map read over that to convert it to a list of numbers. We apply groupsOf 3 to it so that we turn it to a list of lists of length 3. We map the lambda (\[a,b,c] -> Section a b c) over that list of lists.

As you can see, the lambda just takes a list of length 3 and turns it into a section. So roadSystem is now our system of roads, and it even has the correct type: RoadSystem (or [Section]). We apply optimalPath to that, get the path and the total time in a nice textual representation, and print it out.

We save the following text in a file called *paths.txt*:

```
50
10
30
5
90
20
40
2
25
10
8
0
```

Then we feed it to our program like so:

```
$ runhaskell heathrow.hs < paths.txt
The best path to take is: BCACBBC
Time taken: 75
```

Works like a charm!

You can use your knowledge of the Data.Random module to generate a much longer system of roads, which you can then feed to the code we just wrote. If you get stack overflows, you can change foldl to foldl' and sum to foldl' (+) 0. Alternatively, try compiling it like this before running it:

```
$ ghc --make -O heathrow.hs
```

Including the O flag turns on optimizations that help prevent functions such as foldl and sum from causing stack overflows.

11

APPLICATIVE FUNCTORS

Haskell's combination of purity, higher-order functions, parameterized algebraic data types, and type classes makes implementing polymorphism much easier than in other languages. We don't need to think about types belonging to a big hierarchy. Instead, we consider what the types can act like and then connect them with the appropriate type classes. An Int can act like a lot of things—an equatable thing, an ordered thing, an enumerable thing, and so on.

Type classes are open, which means that we can define our own data type, think about what it can act like, and connect it with the type classes that define its behaviors. We can also introduce a new type class and then make already existing types instances of it. Because of that, and because Haskell's type system allows us to know a lot about a function just by its type declaration, we can define type classes that define very general and abstract behavior.

We've talked about type classes that define operations for seeing if two things are equal and comparing two things by some ordering. Those are very abstract and elegant behaviors, although we don't think of them as very special, since we've been dealing with them for most of our lives. Chapter 7 introduced functors, which are types whose values can be mapped over. That's an example of a useful and yet still pretty abstract property that type classes can describe. In this chapter, we'll take a closer look at functors, along with slightly stronger and more useful versions of functors called *applicative functors*.

Functors Redux

As you learned in Chapter 7, functors are things that can be mapped over, like lists, Maybes, and trees. In Haskell, they're described by the type class Functor, which has only one type class method: fmap. fmap has a type of fmap :: (a -> b) -> f a -> f b, which says, "Give me a function that takes an a and returns a b and a box with an a (or several of them) inside it, and I'll give you a box with a b (or several of them) inside it." It applies the function to the element inside the box.

We can also look at functor values as values with an added *context*. For instance, Maybe values have the extra context that they might have failed. With lists, the context is that the value can actually be several values at once or none. fmap applies a function to the value while preserving its context.

If we want to make a type constructor an instance of Functor, it must have a kind of * -> *, which means that it takes exactly one concrete type as a type parameter. For example, Maybe can be made an instance because it takes one type parameter to produce a concrete type, like Maybe Int or Maybe String. If a type constructor takes two parameters, like Either, we need to partially apply the type constructor until it takes only one type parameter. So we can't write instance Functor Either where, but we *can* write instance Functor (Either a) where. Then if we imagine that fmap is only for Either a, it would have this type declaration:

---

fmap :: (b -> c) -> Either a b -> Either a c

As you can see, the Either a part is fixed, because Either a takes only one type parameter.

I/O Actions As Functors

You've learned how a lot of types (well, type constructors really) are instances of Functor: [], and Maybe, Either a, as well as a Tree type that we created in Chapter 7. You saw how you can map functions over them for great good. Now, let's take a look at the IO instance.

If some value has a type of, say, IO String, that means it's an I/O action that will go out into the real world and get some string for us, which it will then yield as a result. We can use <- in do syntax to bind that result to a name. In Chapter 8, we talked about how I/O actions are like boxes with little feet that go out and fetch some value from the outside world for us. We can inspect what they fetched, but after inspecting, we need to wrap the value back in IO. Considering this box with feet analogy, you can see how IO acts like a functor.

Let's see how IO is an instance of Functor. When we fmap a function over an I/O action, we want to get back an I/O action that does the same thing but has our function applied over its result value. Here's the code:

```
instance Functor IO where
    fmap f action = do
        result <- action
        return (f result)
```

The result of mapping something over an I/O action will be an I/O action, so right off the bat, we use the do syntax to glue two actions and make a new one. In the implementation for fmap, we make a new I/O action that first performs the original I/O action and calls its result result. Then we do return (f result). Recall that return is a function that makes an I/O action that doesn't do anything but only yields something as its result.

The action that a do block produces will always yield the result value of its last action. That's why we use return to make an I/O action that doesn't really do anything; it just yields f result as the result of the new I/O action. Check out this piece of code:

```
main = do line <- getLine
          let line' = reverse line
          putStrLn $ "You said " ++ line' ++ " backwards!"
          putStrLn $ "Yes, you said " ++ line' ++ " backwards!"
```

The user is prompted for a line, which we give back, but reversed. Here's how to rewrite this by using fmap:

```
main = do line <- fmap reverse getLine
          putStrLn $ "You said " ++ line ++ " backwards!"
          putStrLn $ "Yes, you really said " ++ line ++ " backwards!"
```

Just as we can fmap reverse over Just "blah" to get Just "halb", we can fmap reverse over getLine. getLine is an I/O action that has a type of IO String, and mapping reverse over it gives us an I/O action that will go out into the real world and get a line and then apply reverse to its result. In the same way that we can apply a function to something that's inside a Maybe box, we can apply a function to what's inside an IO box, but it must go out into the real world to get something. Then when we bind it to a name using <-. The name will reflect the result that already has reverse applied to it.

The I/O action `fmap (++"!") getLine` behaves just like `getLine`, except that its result always has `"!"` appended to it!

If `fmap` were limited to `IO`, its type would be `fmap :: (a -> b) -> IO a -> IO b`. `fmap` takes a function and an I/O action and returns a new I/O action that's like the old one, except that the function is applied to its contained result.

If you ever find yourself binding the result of an I/O action to a name, only to apply a function to that and call that something else, consider using `fmap`. If you want to apply multiple functions to some data inside a functor, you can declare your own function at the top level, make a lambda function, or, ideally, use function composition:

```
import Data.Char
import Data.List

main = do line <- fmap (intersperse '-' . reverse . map toUpper) getLine
          putStrLn line
```

Here's what happens if we run this with the input `hello there`:

```
$ ./fmapping_io
hello there
E-R-E-H-T- -O-L-L-E-H
```

The `intersperse '-' . reverse . map toUpper` function takes a string, maps `toUpper` over it, applies `reverse` to that result, and then applies `intersperse '-'` to that result. It's a prettier way of writing the following:

```
(\xs -> intersperse '-' (reverse (map toUpper xs)))
```

Functions As Functors

Another instance of `Functor` that we've been dealing with all along is `(->) r`. But wait! What the heck does `(->) r` mean? The function type `r -> a` can be rewritten as `(->) r a`, much like we can write `2 + 3` as `(+) 2 3`. When we look at it as `(->) r a`, we can see `(->)` in a slightly different light. It's just a type constructor that takes two type parameters, like `Either`.

But remember that a type constructor must take exactly one type parameter so it can be made an instance of `Functor`. That's why we can't make `(->)` an instance of `Functor`; however, if we partially apply it to `(->) r`, it doesn't pose any problems. If the syntax allowed for type constructors to be partially applied with sections (like we can partially apply + by doing `(2+)`, which is the same as `(+) 2`), we could write `(->) r` as `(r ->)`.

How are functions functors? Let's take a look at the implementation, which lies in `Control.Monad.Instances`:

```
instance Functor ((->) r) where
    fmap f g = (\x -> f (g x))
```

First, let's think about fmap's type:

```
fmap :: (a -> b) -> f a -> f b
```

Next, let's mentally replace each f, which is the role that our functor instance plays, with (->) r. This will let us see how fmap should behave for this particular instance. Here's the result:

```
fmap :: (a -> b) -> ((->) r a) -> ((->) r b)
```

Now we can write the (->) r a and (->) r b types as infix r -> a and r -> b, as we normally do with functions:

```
fmap :: (a -> b) -> (r -> a) -> (r -> b)
```

Okay, mapping a function over a function must produce a function, just like mapping a function over a Maybe must produce a Maybe, and mapping a function over a list must produce a list. What does the preceding type tell us? We see that it takes a function from a to b and a function from r to a and returns a function from r to b. Does this remind you of anything? Yes, function composition! We pipe the output of r -> a into the input of a -> b to get a function r -> b, which is exactly what function composition is all about. Here's another way to write this instance:

```
instance Functor ((->) r) where
    fmap = (.)
```

This makes it clear that using fmap over functions is just function composition. In a script, import Control.Monad.Instances, since that's where the instance is defined, and then load the script and try playing with mapping over functions:

```
ghci> :t fmap (*3) (+100)
fmap (*3) (+100) :: (Num a) => a -> a
ghci> fmap (*3) (+100) 1
303
ghci> (*3) `fmap` (+100) $ 1
303
ghci> (*3) . (+100) $ 1
303
ghci> fmap (show . (*3)) (+100) 1
"303"
```

We can call fmap as an infix function so that the resemblance to . is clear. In the second input line, we're mapping (*3) over (+100), which results in a function that will take an input, apply (+100) to that, and then apply (*3) to that result. We then apply that function to 1.

Just like all functors, functions can be thought of as values with contexts. When we have a function like (+3), we can view the value as the eventual result of the function, and the context is that we need to apply the function to something to get to the result. Using fmap (*3) on (+100) will create another function that acts like (+100), but before producing a result, (*3) will be applied to that result.

The fact that fmap is function composition when used on functions isn't so terribly useful right now, but at least it's very interesting. It also bends our minds a bit and lets us see how things that act more like computations than boxes (IO and (->) r) can be functors. The function being mapped over a computation results in the same sort of computation, but the result of that computation is modified with the function.

Before we go on to the rules that fmap should follow, let's think about the type of fmap once more:

```
fmap :: (Functor f) => (a -> b) -> f a -> f b
```

The introduction of curried functions in Chapter 5 began by stating that all Haskell functions actually take one parameter. A function a -> b -> c takes just one parameter of type a and returns a function b -> c, which takes one parameter and returns c. That's why calling a function with too few parameters (partially applying it) gives us back a function that takes the number of parameters that we left out (if we're thinking about functions as taking several parameters again). So a -> b -> c can be written as a -> (b -> c), to make the currying more apparent.

In the same vein, if we write fmap :: (a -> b) -> (f a -> f b), we can think of fmap not as a function that takes one function and a functor value and returns a functor value, but as a function that takes a function and returns a new function that's just like the old one, except that it takes a functor value as a parameter and returns a functor value as the result. It takes an a -> b function and returns a function f a -> f b. This is called *lifting* a function. Let's play around with that idea using GHCi's :t command:

```
ghci> :t fmap (*2)
fmap (*2) :: (Num a, Functor f) => f a -> f a
ghci> :t fmap (replicate 3)
fmap (replicate 3) :: (Functor f) => f a -> f [a]
```

The expression fmap (*2) is a function that takes a functor f over numbers and returns a functor over numbers. That functor can be a list, a Maybe, an Either String, or anything else. The expression fmap (replicate 3) will take a functor over any type and return a functor over a list of elements of that type. This is even more apparent if we partially apply, say, fmap (++"!") and then bind it to a name in GHCi.

You can think of fmap in two ways:

- As a function that takes a function and a functor value and then maps that function over the functor value
- As a function that takes a function and lifts that function so it operates on functor values

Both views are correct.

The type fmap (replicate 3) :: (Functor f) => f a -> f [a] means that the function will work on any functor. What it will do depends on the functor. If we use fmap (replicate 3) on a list, the list's implementation for fmap will be chosen, which is just map. If we use it on Maybe a, it will apply replicate 3 to the value inside the Just. If it's Nothing, it stays Nothing. Here are some examples:

```
ghci> fmap (replicate 3) [1,2,3,4]
[[1,1,1],[2,2,2],[3,3,3],[4,4,4]]
ghci> fmap (replicate 3) (Just 4)
Just [4,4,4]
ghci> fmap (replicate 3) (Right "blah")
Right ["blah","blah","blah"]
ghci> fmap (replicate 3) Nothing
Nothing
ghci> fmap (replicate 3) (Left "foo")
Left "foo"
```

Functor Laws

All functors are expected to exhibit certain kinds of properties and behaviors. They should reliably behave as things that can be mapped over. Calling fmap on a functor should just map a function over the functor—nothing more. This behavior is described in the *functor laws*. All instances of Functor should abide by these two laws. They aren't enforced by Haskell automatically, so you need to test them yourself when you make a functor. All the Functor instances in the standard library obey these laws.

Law 1

The first functor law states that if we map the id function over a functor value, the functor value that we get back should be the same as the original functor value. Written a bit more formally, it means that fmap id = id. So essentially, this says that if we do fmap id over a functor value, it should be the same as just applying id to the value. Remember that id is the identity function, which just returns its parameter unmodified. It can also be written as \x -> x. If we view the functor value as something that can be mapped over, the fmap id = id law seems kind of trivial or obvious.

Let's see if this law holds for a few values of functors.

```
ghci> fmap id (Just 3)
Just 3
ghci> id (Just 3)
Just 3
ghci> fmap id [1..5]
[1,2,3,4,5]
ghci> id [1..5]
[1,2,3,4,5]
ghci> fmap id []
[]
ghci> fmap id Nothing
Nothing
```

Looking at the implementation of fmap for Maybe, for example, we can figure out why the first functor law holds:

```
instance Functor Maybe where
    fmap f (Just x) = Just (f x)
    fmap f Nothing = Nothing
```

We imagine that id plays the role of the f parameter in the implementation. We see that if we fmap id over Just x, the result will be Just (id x), and because id just returns its parameter, we can deduce that Just (id x) equals Just x. So now we know that if we map id over a Maybe value with a Just value constructor, we get that same value back.

Seeing that mapping id over a Nothing value returns the same value is trivial. So from these two equations in the implementation for fmap, we find that the law fmap id = id holds.

Law 2

The second law says that composing two functions and then mapping the resulting function over a functor should be the same as first mapping one function over the functor and then mapping the other one. Formally written, that means fmap (f . g) = fmap f . fmap g. Or to write it in another way, for any functor value x, the following should hold: fmap (f . g) x = fmap f (fmap g x).

If we can show that some type obeys both functor laws, we can rely on it having the same fundamental behaviors as other functors when it comes to mapping. We can know that when we use

fmap on it, there won't be anything other than mapping going on behind the scenes and that it will act like a thing that can be mapped over—that is, a functor.

We figure out how the second law holds for some type by looking at the implementation of fmap for that type and then using the method that we used to check if Maybe obeys the first law. So, to check out how the second functor law holds for Maybe, if we use fmap (f . g) over Nothing, we get Nothing, because calling fmap with any function over Nothing returns Nothing. If we call fmap f (fmap g Nothing), we get Nothing, for the same reason.

Seeing how the second law holds for Maybe if it's a Nothing value is pretty easy. But how about if it's a Just value? Well, if we use fmap (f . g) (Just x), we see from the implementation that it's implemented as Just ((f . g) x), which is Just (f (g x)). If we use fmap f (fmap g (Just x)), we see from the implementation that fmap g (Just x) is Just (g x). Ergo, fmap f (fmap g (Just x)) equals fmap f (Just (g x)), and from the implementation, we see that this equals Just (f (g x)).

If you're a bit confused by this proof, don't worry. Be sure that you understand how function composition works. Many times, you can intuitively see how these laws hold because the types act like containers or functions. You can also just try them on a bunch of different values of a type and be able to say with some certainty that a type does indeed obey the laws.

Breaking the Law

Let's take a look at a pathological example of a type constructor being an instance of the Functor type class but not really being a functor, because it doesn't satisfy the laws. Let's say that we have the following type:

```
data CMaybe a = CNothing | CJust Int a deriving (Show)
```

The C here stands for counter. It's a data type that looks much like Maybe a, but the Just part holds two fields instead of one. The first field in the CJust value constructor will always have a type of Int, and it will be some sort of counter. The second field is of type a, which comes from the type parameter, and its type will depend on the concrete type that we choose for CMaybe a. Let's play with our new type:

```
ghci> CNothing
CNothing
ghci> CJust 0 "haha"
CJust 0 "haha"
ghci> :t CNothing
CNothing :: CMaybe a
ghci> :t CJust 0 "haha"
CJust 0 "haha" :: CMaybe [Char]
ghci> CJust 100 [1,2,3]
CJust 100 [1,2,3]
```

If we use the CNothing constructor, there are no fields. If we use the CJust constructor, the first field is an integer and the second field can be any type. Let's make this an instance of Functor so that each time we use fmap, the function is applied to the second field, whereas the first field is increased by 1.

```
instance Functor CMaybe where
    fmap f CNothing = CNothing
    fmap f (CJust counter x) = CJust (counter+1) (f x)
```

This is kind of like the instance implementation for Maybe, except that when we do fmap over a value that doesn't represent an empty box (a CJust value), we don't just apply the function to the contents; we also increase the counter by 1. Everything seems cool so far. We can even play with this a bit:

```
ghci> fmap (++"ha") (CJust 0 "ho")
CJust 1 "hoha"
ghci> fmap (++"he") (fmap (++"ha") (CJust 0 "ho"))
CJust 2 "hohahe"
ghci> fmap (++"blah") CNothing
CNothing
```

Does this obey the functor laws? In order to see that something doesn't obey a law, it's enough to find just one counterexample:

```
ghci> fmap id (CJust 0 "haha")
CJust 1 "haha"
ghci> id (CJust 0 "haha")
CJust 0 "haha"
```

As the first functor law states, if we map id over a functor value, it should be the same as just calling id with the same functor value. Our example demonstrates that this is not true for our CMaybe functor. Even though it's part of the Functor type class, it doesn't obey this functor law and is therefore not a functor.

Since CMaybe fails at being a functor even though it pretends to be one, using it as a functor might lead to some faulty code. When we use a functor, it shouldn't matter if we first compose a few functions and then map them over the functor value or we just map each function over a functor value in succession. But with CMaybe it matters, because it keeps track of how many times it has been mapped over. Not cool! If we want CMaybe to obey the functor laws, we need to make it so that the Int field stays the same when we use fmap.

At first, the functor laws might seem a bit confusing and unnecessary. But if we know that a type obeys both laws, we can make certain assumptions about how it will act. If a type obeys the functor laws, we know that calling fmap on a value of that type will only map the function over it—nothing more. This leads to code that is more abstract and extensible, because we can use laws to reason about behaviors that any functor should have and make functions that operate reliably on any functor.

The next time you make a type an instance of Functor, take a minute to make sure that it obeys the functor laws. You can go over the implementation line by line and see if the laws hold or try to find a counterexample. Once you've dealt with enough functors, you will begin to recognize the properties and behaviors that they have in common, and begin to intuitively see if a type obeys the functor laws.

Using Applicative Functors

In this section, we'll take a look at applicative functors, which are beefed-up functors.

So far, we have focused on mapping functions that take only one parameter over functors. But what happens when we map a function that takes two parameters over a functor? Let's take a look at a couple of concrete examples of this.

If we have Just 3 and we call fmap (*) (Just 3), what do we get? From the instance implementation of Maybe for Functor, we know that if it's a Just value, it will apply the function to the value inside the Just. Therefore, doing fmap (*) (Just 3) results in Just ((*) 3), which can also be written as Just (* 3) if we use sections. Interesting! We get a function wrapped in a Just!

Here are some more functions inside functor values:

```
ghci> :t fmap (++) (Just "hey")
fmap (++) (Just "hey") :: Maybe ([Char] -> [Char])
ghci> :t fmap compare (Just 'a')
fmap compare (Just 'a') :: Maybe (Char -> Ordering)
ghci> :t fmap compare "A LIST OF CHARS"
fmap compare "A LIST OF CHARS" :: [Char -> Ordering]
ghci> :t fmap (\x y z -> x + y / z) [3,4,5,6]
fmap (\x y z -> x + y / z) [3,4,5,6] :: (Fractional a) => [a -> a -> a]
```

If we map compare, which has a type of (Ord a) => a -> a -> Ordering, over a list of characters, we get a list of functions of type Char -> Ordering, because the function compare gets partially applied with the characters in the list. It's not a list of (Ord a) => a -> Ordering function, because the first a applied was a Char, and so the second a must decide to be of type Char.

We see how by mapping "multiparameter" functions over functor values, we get functor values that contain functions inside them. So now what can we do with them? For one, we can map functions that take these functions as parameters over them, because whatever is inside a functor value will be given to the function that we're mapping over it as a parameter:

```
ghci> let a = fmap (*) [1,2,3,4]
ghci> :t a
a :: [Integer -> Integer]
ghci> fmap (\f -> f 9) a
[9,18,27,36]
```

But what if we have a functor value of Just (3 *) and a functor value of Just 5, and we want to take out the function from Just (3 *) and map it over Just 5? With normal functors, we're out of luck, because they support only mapping normal functions over existing functors. Even when we mapped \f -> f 9 over a functor that contained functions, we were just mapping a normal function over it. But we can't map a function that's inside a functor value over another functor value with what fmap offers us. We could pattern match against the Just constructor to get the function out of it and then map it over Just 5, but we're looking for a more general and abstract approach that works across functors.

Say Hello to Applicative

Meet the Applicative type class, in the Control.Applicative module. It defines two functions: pure and <*>. It doesn't provide a default implementation for either of them, so we need to define them both if we want something to be an applicative functor. The class is defined like so:

```
class (Functor f) => Applicative f where
    pure :: a -> f a
    (<*>) :: f (a -> b) -> f a -> f b
```

This simple three-line class definition tells us a lot! The first line starts the definition of the Applicative class, and it also introduces a class constraint. The constraint says that if we want to make a type constructor part of the Applicative type class, it must be in Functor first. That's why if we know that a type constructor is part of the Applicative type class, it's also in Functor, so we can use fmap on it.

The first method it defines is called pure. Its type declaration is pure :: a -> f a. f plays the role of our applicative functor instance here. Because Haskell has a very good type system, and because all a function can do is take some parameters and return some value, we can tell a lot from a type declaration, and this is no exception.

pure should take a value of any type and return an applicative value with that value inside it. "Inside it" refers to our box analogy again, even though we've seen that it doesn't always stand up to scrutiny. But the a -> f a type declaration is still pretty descriptive. We take a value and we wrap it in an applicative value that has that value as the result inside it. A better way of thinking about pure would be to say that it takes a value and puts it in some sort of default (or pure) context—a minimal context that still yields that value.

The `<*>` function is really interesting. It has this type declaration:

```
f (a -> b) -> f a -> f b
```

Does this remind you of anything? It's like fmap :: (a -> b) -> f a -> f b. You can think of the `<*>` function as sort of a beefed-up fmap. Whereas fmap takes a function and a functor value and applies the function inside the functor value, `<*>` takes a functor value that has a function in it and another functor, and extracts that function from the first functor and then maps it over the second one.

Maybe the Applicative Functor

Let's take a look at the Applicative instance implementation for Maybe:

```
instance Applicative Maybe where
    pure = Just
    Nothing <*> _ = Nothing
    (Just f) <*> something = fmap f something
```

Again, from the class definition, we see that the f that plays the role of the applicative functor should take one concrete type as a parameter, so we write instance Applicative Maybe where instead of instance Applicative (Maybe a) where.

Next, we have pure. Remember that it's supposed to take something and wrap it in an applicative value. We wrote pure = Just, because value constructors like Just are normal functions. We could have also written pure x = Just x.

Finally, we have the definition for `<*>`. We can't extract a function out of a Nothing, because it has no function inside it. So we say that if we try to extract a function from a Nothing, the result is a Nothing.

In the class definition for Applicative, there's a Functor class constraint, which means that we can assume that both of the `<*>` function's parameters are functor values. If the first parameter is not a Nothing, but a Just with some function inside it, we say that we then want to map that function over the second parameter. This also takes care of the case where the second parameter is Nothing, because doing fmap with any function over a Nothing will return a Nothing. So for Maybe, `<*>` extracts the function from the left value if it's a Just and maps it over the right value. If any of the parameters is Nothing, Nothing is the result.

Now let's give this a whirl:

```
ghci> Just (+3) <*> Just 9
Just 12
```

```
ghci> pure (+3) <*> Just 10
Just 13
ghci> pure (+3) <*> Just 9
Just 12
ghci> Just (++"hahah") <*> Nothing
Nothing
ghci> Nothing <*> Just "woot"
Nothing
```

You see how doing pure (+3) and Just (+3) is the same in this case. Use pure if you're dealing with Maybe values in an applicative context (using them with <*>); otherwise, stick to Just.

The first four input lines demonstrate how the function is extracted and then mapped, but in this case, they could have been achieved by just mapping unwrapped functions over functors. The last line is interesting, because we try to extract a function from a Nothing and then map it over something, which results in Nothing.

With normal functors, when you map a function over a functor, you can't get the result out in any general way, even if the result is a partially applied function. Applicative functors, on the other hand, allow you to operate on several functors with a single function.

The Applicative Style

With the Applicative type class, we can chain the use of the <*> function, thus enabling us to seamlessly operate on several applicative values instead of just one. For instance, check this out:

```
ghci> pure (+) <*> Just 3 <*> Just 5
Just 8
ghci> pure (+) <*> Just 3 <*> Nothing
Nothing
ghci> pure (+) <*> Nothing <*> Just 5
Nothing
```

We wrapped the + function inside an applicative value and then used <*> to call it with two parameters, both applicative values.

Let's take a look at how this happens, step by step. <*> is left-associative, which means that this:

```
pure (+) <*> Just 3 <*> Just 5
```

is the same as this:

```
(pure (+) <*> Just 3) <*> Just 5
```

First, the + function is put in an applicative value—in this case, a `Maybe` value that contains the function. So we have `pure (+)`, which is `Just (+)`. Next, `Just (+) <*> Just 3` happens. The result of this is `Just (3+)`. This is because of partial application. Only applying the + function to 3 results in a function that takes one parameter and adds 3 to it. Finally, `Just (3+) <*> Just 5` is carried out, which results in a `Just 8`.

Isn't this awesome? Applicative functors and the applicative style of `pure f <*> x <*> y <*> ...` allow us to take a function that expects parameters that aren't applicative values and use that function to operate on several applicative values. The function can take as many parameters as we want, because it's always partially applied step by step between occurrences of `<*>`.

This becomes even more handy and apparent if we consider the fact that `pure f <*> x` equals `fmap f x`. This is one of the applicative laws. We'll take a closer look at the applicative laws later in the chapter, but let's think about how it applies here. `pure` puts a value in a default context. If we just put a function in a default context and then extract and apply it to a value inside another applicative functor, that's the same as just mapping that function over that applicative functor. Instead of writing `pure f <*> x <*> y <*> ...`, we can write `fmap f x <*> y <*> ...`. This is why `Control.Applicative` exports a function called `<$>`, which is just `fmap` as an infix operator. Here's how it's defined:

```
(<$>) :: (Functor f) => (a -> b) -> f a -> f b
f <$> x = fmap f x
```

NOTE   *Remember that type variables are independent of parameter names or other value names. The f in the function declaration here is a type variable with a class constraint saying that any type constructor that replaces f should be in the Functor type class. The f in the function body denotes a function that we map over x. The fact that we used f to represent both of those doesn't mean that they represent the same thing.*

By using `<$>`, the applicative style really shines, because now if we want to apply a function f between three applicative values, we can write `f <$> x <*> y <*> z`. If the parameters were normal values rather than applicative functors, we would write `f x y z`.

Let's take a closer look at how this works. Suppose we want to join the values `Just "johntra"` and `Just "volta"` into one `String` inside a `Maybe` functor. We can do this:

```
ghci> (++) <$> Just "johntra" <*> Just "volta"
Just "johntravolta"
```

Before we see how this happens, compare the preceding line with this:

```
ghci> (++) "johntra" "volta"
"johntravolta"
```

To use a normal function on applicative functors, just sprinkle some `<$>` and `<*>` about, and the function will operate on applicatives and return an applicative. How cool is that?

Back to our `(++) <$> Just "johntra" <*> Just "volta"`: First `(++)`, which has a type of `(++) :: [a] -> [a] -> [a]`, is mapped over `Just "johntra"`. This results in a value that's the same as `Just ("johntra"++)` and has a type of `Maybe ([Char] -> [Char])`. Notice how the first parameter of `(++)` got eaten up and how the as turned into `Char` values. And now `Just ("johntra"++) <*> Just "volta"` happens, which takes the function out of the `Just` and maps it over `Just "volta"`, resulting in `Just "johntravolta"`. Had either of the two values been `Nothing`, the result would have also been `Nothing`.

So far, we've used only `Maybe` in our examples, and you might be thinking that applicative functors are all about `Maybe`. There are loads of other instances of `Applicative`, so let's meet them!

Lists

Lists (actually the list type constructor, `[]`) are applicative functors. What a surprise! Here's how `[]` is an instance of `Applicative`:

```
instance Applicative [] where
    pure x = [x]
    fs <*> xs = [f x | f <- fs, x <- xs]
```

Remember that `pure` takes a value and puts it in a default context. In other words, it puts it in a minimal context that still yields that value. The minimal context for lists would be the empty list, but the empty list represents the lack of a value, so it can't hold in itself the value on which we used pure. That's why `pure` takes a value and puts it in a singleton list. Similarly, the minimal context for the `Maybe` applicative functor would be a `Nothing`, but it represents the lack of a value instead of a value, so `pure` is implemented as `Just` in the instance implementation for `Maybe`.

Here's `pure` in action:

```
ghci> pure "Hey" :: [String]
["Hey"]
ghci> pure "Hey" :: Maybe String
Just "Hey"
```

What about `<*>`? If the `<*>` function's type were limited to only lists, we would get `(<*>) :: [a -> b] -> [a] -> [b]`. It's implemented with a list comprehension. `<*>` must somehow extract the function out of its left parameter and then map it over the right parameter. But the left list can have zero functions, one function, or several functions inside it, and the right list can also hold several values. That's why we use a list comprehension to draw from both lists. We apply every possible function from the left list to every possible value from the right list. The resulting list has every possible combination of applying a function from the left list to a value in the right one.

We can use `<*>` with lists like this:

```
ghci> [(*0),(+100),(^2)] <*> [1,2,3]
[0,0,0,101,102,103,1,4,9]
```

The left list has three functions, and the right list has three values, so the resulting list will have nine elements. Every function in the left list is applied to every value in the right one. If we have a list of functions that take two parameters, we can apply those functions between two lists.

In the following example, we apply two function between two lists:

```
ghci> [(+),(*)] <*> [1,2] <*> [3,4]
[4,5,5,6,3,4,6,8]
```

`<*>` is left-associative, so `[(+),(*)] <*> [1,2]` happens first, resulting in a list that's the same as `[(1+),(2+),(1*),(2*)]`, because every function on the left gets applied to every value on the right. Then `[(1+),(2+),(1*),(2*)] <*> [3,4]` happens, which produces the final result.

Using the applicative style with lists is fun!

```
ghci> (++) <$> ["ha","heh","hmm"] <*> ["?","!","."]
["ha?","ha!","ha.","heh?","heh!","heh.","hmm?","hmm!","hmm."]
```

Again, we used a normal function that takes two strings between two lists of strings just by inserting the appropriate applicative operators.

You can view lists as nondeterministic computations. A value like 100 or `"what"` can be viewed as a deterministic computation that has only one result, whereas a list like [1,2,3] can be viewed as a computation that can't decide on which result it wants to have, so it presents us with all of the possible results. So when you write something like (+) `<$>` [1,2,3] `<*>` [4,5,6], you can think of it as adding together two nondeterministic computations with +, only to produce another nondeterministic computation that's even less sure about its result.

Using the applicative style on lists is often a good replacement for list comprehensions. In Chapter 1, we wanted to see all the possible products of [2,5,10] and [8,10,11], so we did this:

```
ghci> [ x*y | x <- [2,5,10], y <- [8,10,11]]
[16,20,22,40,50,55,80,100,110]
```

We're just drawing from two lists and applying a function between every combination of elements. This can be done in the applicative style as well:

```
ghci> (*) <$> [2,5,10] <*> [8,10,11]
[16,20,22,40,50,55,80,100,110]
```

This seems clearer to me, because it's easier to see that we're just calling * between two nondeterministic computations. If we wanted all possible products of those two lists that are more than 50, we would use the following:

```
ghci> filter (>50) $ (*) <$> [2,5,10] <*> [8,10,11]
[55,80,100,110]
```

It's easy to see how pure f <*> xs equals fmap f xs with lists. pure f is just [f], and [f] <*> xs will apply every function in the left list to every value in the right one, but there's just one function in the left list, so it's like mapping.

IO Is An Applicative Functor, Too

Another instance of Applicative that we've already encountered is IO. This is how the instance is implemented:

```
instance Applicative IO where
    pure = return
    a <*> b = do
        f <- a
        x <- b
        return (f x)
```

Since pure is all about putting a value in a minimal context that still holds the value as the result, it makes sense that pure is just return. return makes an I/O action that doesn't do anything. It just yields some value as its result, without performing any I/O operations like printing to the terminal or reading from a file.

If <*> were specialized for IO, it would have a type of (<*>) :: IO (a -> b) -> IO a -> IO b. In the case of IO, it takes the I/O action a, which yields a function, performs the function, and binds that function to f. Then it performs b and binds its result to x. Finally, it applies the function f to x and yields that as the result. We used do syntax to implement it here. (Remember that do syntax is about taking several I/O actions and gluing them into one.)

With Maybe and [], we could think of <*> as simply extracting a function from its left parameter and then applying it over the right one. With IO, extracting is still in the game, but now we also have a notion of *sequencing*, because we're taking two I/O actions and gluing them into one. We need to extract the function from the first I/O action, but to extract a result from an I/O action, it must be performed. Consider this:

```
myAction :: IO String
myAction = do
    a <- getLine
    b <- getLine
    return $ a ++ b
```

This is an I/O action that will prompt the user for two lines and yield as its result those two lines concatenated. We achieved it by gluing together two getLine I/O actions and a return, because we wanted our new glued I/O action to hold the result of a ++ b. Another way of writing this is to use the applicative style:

```
myAction :: IO String
myAction = (++) <$> getLine <*> getLine
```

This is the same thing we did earlier when we were making an I/O action that applied a function between the results of two other I/O actions. Remember that getLine is an I/O action with the type getLine :: IO String. When we use <*> between two applicative values, the result is an applicative value, so this all makes sense.

If we return to the box analogy, we can imagine getLine as a box that will go out into the real world and fetch us a string. Calling (++) <$> getLine <*> getLine makes a new, bigger box that sends those two boxes out to fetch lines from the terminal and then presents the concatenation of those two lines as its result.

The type of the expression (++) <$> getLine <*> getLine is IO String. This means that the expression is a completely normal I/O action like any other, which also yields a result value, just like other I/O actions. That's why we can do stuff like this:

```
main = do
    a <- (++) <$> getLine <*> getLine
    putStrLn $ "The two lines concatenated turn out to be: " ++ a
```

Functions As Applicatives

Another instance of Applicative is (->) r, or functions. We don't often use functions as applicatives, but the concept is still really interesting, so let's take a look at how the function instance is implemented.

```
instance Applicative ((->) r) where
    pure x = (\_ -> x)
    f <*> g = \x -> f x (g x)
```

When we wrap a value into an applicative value with pure, the result it yields must be that value. A minimal default context still yields that value as a result. That's why in the function instance implementation, pure takes a value and creates a function that ignores its parameter and always returns that value. The type for pure specialized for the (->) r instance is pure :: a -> (r -> a).

```
ghci> (pure 3) "blah"
3
```

Because of currying, function application is left-associative, so we can omit the parentheses.

```
ghci> pure 3 "blah"
3
```

The instance implementation for <*> is a bit cryptic, so let's just take a look at how to use functions as applicative functors in the applicative style:

```
ghci> :t (+) <$> (+3) <*> (*100)
(+) <$> (+3) <*> (*100) :: (Num a) => a -> a
ghci> (+) <$> (+3) <*> (*100) $ 5
508
```

Calling <*> with two applicative values results in an applicative value, so if we use it on two functions, we get back a function. So what goes on here? When we do (+) <$> (+3) <*> (*100), we're making a function that will use + on the results of (+3) and (*100) and return that. With (+) <$> (+3) <*> (*100) $ 5, (+3) and (*100) are first applied to 5, resulting in 8 and 500. Then + is called with 8 and 500, resulting in 508.

The following code is similar:

```
ghci> (\x y z -> [x,y,z]) <$> (+3) <*> (*2) <*> (/2) $ 5
[8.0,10.0,2.5]
```

We create a function that will call the function \x y z -> [x,y,z] with the eventual results from (+3), (*2) and (/2). The 5 is fed to each of the three functions, and then \x y z -> [x, y, z] is called with those results.

NOTE   *It's not very important that you get how the (->) r instance for Applicative works, so don't despair if you don't understand this all right now. Try playing with the applicative style and functions to get some insight into using functions as applicatives.*

Zip Lists

It turns out there are actually more ways for lists to be applicative functors. We've already covered one way: calling <*> with a list of functions and a list of values, which results in a list containing all the possible combinations of applying functions from the left list to the values in the right list.

For example, if we write [(+3),(*2)] <*> [1,2], (+3) will be applied to both 1 and 2, and (*2) will also be applied to both 1 and 2, resulting in a list that has four elements: [4,5,2,4]. However, [(+3),(*2)] <*> [1,2] could also work in such a way that the first function in the left list is applied to the first value in the right one, the second function is applied to the second value, and so on. That would result in a list with two values: [4,4]. You could look at it as [1 + 3, 2 * 2].

An instance of Applicative that we haven't encountered yet is ZipList, and it lives in Control.Applicative.

Because one type can't have two instances for the same type class, the ZipList a type was introduced, which has one constructor (ZipList) with just one field (a list). Here's the instance:

```
instance Applicative ZipList where
        pure x = ZipList (repeat x)
        ZipList fs <*> ZipList xs = ZipList (zipWith (\f x -> f x) fs xs)
```

<*> applies the first function to the first value, the second function to the second value, and so on. This is done with zipWith (\f x -> f x) fs xs. Because of how zipWith works, the resulting list will be as long as the shorter of the two lists.

pure is also interesting here. It takes a value and puts it in a list that just has that value repeating indefinitely. pure "haha" results in ZipList (["haha", "haha","haha".... This might be a bit confusing, since you've learned that pure should put a value in a minimal context that still yields that value. And you might be thinking that an infinite list of something is hardly minimal. But it makes sense with zip lists, because it must produce the value on every position. This also satisfies the law that pure f <*> xs should equal fmap f xs. If pure 3 just returned ZipList [3], pure (*2) <*> ZipList [1,5,10] would result in ZipList [2], because the resulting list of two zipped lists has the length of the shorter of the two. If we zip a finite list with an infinite list, the length of the resulting list will always be equal to the length of the finite list.

So how do zip lists work in an applicative style? Well, the ZipList a type doesn't have a Show instance, so we need to use the getZipList function to extract a raw list from a zip list:

```
ghci> getZipList $ (+) <$> ZipList [1,2,3] <*> ZipList [100,100,100]
[101,102,103]
ghci> getZipList $ (+) <$> ZipList [1,2,3] <*> ZipList [100,100..]
[101,102,103]
ghci> getZipList $ max <$> ZipList [1,2,3,4,5,3] <*> ZipList [5,3,1,2]
[5,3,3,4]
```

```
ghci> getZipList $ (,,) <$> ZipList "dog" <*> ZipList "cat" <*> ZipList "rat"
[('d','c','r'),('o','a','a'),('g','t','t')]
```

NOTE *The (,,) function is the same as \x y z -> (x,y,z). Also, the (,) function is the same as \x y -> (x,y).*

Aside from zipWith, the standard library has functions such as zipWith3 and zipWith4, all the way up to zipWith7. zipWith takes a function that takes two parameters and zips two lists with it. zipWith3 takes a function that takes three parameters and zips three lists with it, and so on. By using zip lists with an applicative style, we don't need to have a separate zip function for each number of lists that we want to zip together. We just use the applicative style to zip together an arbitrary amount of lists with a function, and that's pretty handy.

Applicative Laws

Like normal functors, applicative functors come with a few laws. The most important law is the one that pure f <*> x = fmap f x holds. As an exercise, you can prove this law for some of the applicative functors that we've met in this chapter. The following are the other applicative laws:

- pure id <*> v = v

- pure (.) <*> u <*> v <*> w = u <*> (v <*> w)

- pure f <*> pure x = pure (f x)

- u <*> pure y = pure ($ y) <*> u

We won't go over them in detail because that would take up a lot of pages and be kind of boring. If you're interested, you can take a closer look at them and see if they hold for some of the instances.

Useful Functions for Applicatives

Control.Applicative defines a function that's called liftA2, which has the following type:

```
liftA2 :: (Applicative f) => (a -> b -> c) -> f a -> f b -> f c
```

It's defined like this:

```
liftA2 :: (Applicative f) => (a -> b -> c) -> f a -> f b -> f c
liftA2 f a b = f <$> a <*> b
```

It just applies a function between two applicatives, hiding the applicative style that we've discussed. However, it clearly showcases why applicative functors are more powerful than ordinary functors.

With ordinary functors, we can just map functions over one functor value. With applicative functors, we can apply a function between several functor values. It's also interesting to look at this function's type as (a -> b -> c) -> (f a -> f b -> f c). When we look at it like this, we can say that liftA2 takes a normal binary function and promotes it to a function that operates on two applicatives.

Here's an interesting concept: We can take two applicative values and combine them into one applicative value that has inside it the results of those two applicative values in a list. For instance, we have Just 3 and Just 4. Let's assume that the second one contains a singleton list, because that's really easy to achieve:

```
ghci> fmap (\x -> [x]) (Just 4)
Just [4]
```

Okay, so let's say we have Just 3 and Just [4]. How do we get Just [3,4]? That's easy:

```
ghci> liftA2 (:) (Just 3) (Just [4])
Just [3,4]
ghci> (:) <$> Just 3 <*> Just [4]
Just [3,4]
```

Remember that : is a function that takes an element and a list and returns a new list with that element at the beginning. Now that we have Just [3,4], could we combine that with Just 2 to produce Just [2,3,4]? Yes, we could. It seems that we can combine any amount of applicative values into one applicative value that has a list of the results of those applicative values inside it.

Let's try implementing a function that takes a list of applicative values and returns an applicative value that has a list as its result value. We'll call it sequenceA.

```
sequenceA :: (Applicative f) => [f a] -> f [a]
sequenceA [] = pure []
sequenceA (x:xs) = (:) <$> x <*> sequenceA xs
```

Ah, recursion! First, we look at the type. It will transform a list of applicative values into an applicative value with a list. From that, we can lay some groundwork for a base case. If we want to turn an empty list into an applicative value with a list of results, we just put an empty list in a default context. Now comes the recursion. If we have a list with a head and a tail (remember that x is an applicative value and xs is a list of them), we call sequenceA on the tail, which results in an applicative value with a list inside. Then we just prepend the value inside the applicative x into that applicative with a list, and that's it!

Suppose we do this:

```
sequenceA [Just 1, Just 2]
```

By definition, that's equal to the following:

```
(:) <$> Just 1 <*> sequenceA [Just 2]
```

Breaking this down further, we get this:

```
(:) <$> Just 1 <*> ((:) <$> Just 2 <*> sequenceA [])
```

We know that sequenceA [] ends up as being Just [], so this expression is now as follows:

```
(:) <$> Just 1 <*> ((:) <$> Just 2 <*> Just [])
```

which is this:

```
(:) <$> Just 1 <*> Just [2]
```

This equals Just [1,2]!

Another way to implement sequenceA is with a fold. Remember that pretty much any function where we go over a list element by element and accumulate a result along the way can be implemented with a fold:

```
sequenceA :: (Applicative f) => [f a] -> f [a]
sequenceA = foldr (liftA2 (:)) (pure [])
```

We approach the list from the right and start off with an accumulator value of pure []. We put liftA2 (:) between the accumulator and the last element of the list, which results in an applicative that has a singleton in it. Then we call liftA2 (:) with the now last element and the current accumulator and so on, until we're left with just the accumulator, which holds a list of the results of all the applicatives.

Let's give our function a whirl on some applicatives:

```
ghci> sequenceA [Just 3, Just 2, Just 1]
Just [3,2,1]
ghci> sequenceA [Just 3, Nothing, Just 1]
Nothing
ghci> sequenceA [(+3),(+2),(+1)] 3
[6,5,4]
ghci> sequenceA [[1,2,3],[4,5,6]]
[[1,4],[1,5],[1,6],[2,4],[2,5],[2,6],[3,4],[3,5],[3,6]]
ghci> sequenceA [[1,2,3],[4,5,6],[3,4,4],[]]
[]
```

When used on Maybe values, sequenceA creates a Maybe value with all the results inside it as a list. If one of the values is Nothing, then the result is also a Nothing. This is cool when you have a list of Maybe values, and you're interested in the values only if none of them is a Nothing.

When used with functions, sequenceA takes a list of functions and returns a function that returns a list. In our example, we made a function that took a number as a parameter and applied it to each function in the list and then returned a list of results. sequenceA [(+3),(+2),(+1)] 3 will call (+3) with 3, (+2) with 3, and (+1) with 3, and present all those results as a list.

Doing (+) <$> (+3) <*> (*2) will create a function that takes a parameter, feeds it to both (+3) and (*2), and then calls + with those two results. In the same vein, it makes sense that sequenceA [(+3),(*2)] makes a function that takes a parameter and feeds it to all of the functions in the list. Instead of calling + with the results of the functions, a combination of : and pure [] is used to gather those results in a list, which is the result of that function.

Using sequenceA is useful when we have a list of functions and we want to feed the same input to all of them and then view the list of results. For instance, suppose that we have a number and we're wondering whether it satisfies all of the predicates in a list. Here's one way to do that:

```
ghci> map (\f -> f 7) [(>4),(<10),odd]
[True,True,True]
ghci> and $ map (\f -> f 7) [(>4),(<10),odd]
True
```

Remember that and takes a list of Booleans and returns True if they're all True. Another way to achieve the same thing is with sequenceA:

```
ghci> sequenceA [(>4),(<10),odd] 7
[True,True,True]
ghci> and $ sequenceA [(>4),(<10),odd] 7
True
```

sequenceA [(>4),(<10),odd] creates a function that will take a number and feed it to all of the predicates in [(>4),(<10),odd] and return a list of Booleans. It turns a list with the type (Num a) => [a -> Bool] into a function with the type (Num a) => a -> [Bool]. Pretty neat, huh?

Because lists are homogenous, all the functions in the list must be functions of the same type. You can't have a list like [ord, (+3)], because ord takes a character and returns a number, whereas (+3) takes a number and returns a number.

When used with [], sequenceA takes a list of lists and returns a list of lists. It actually creates lists that have all possible combinations of their elements. For illustration, here's the preceding example done with sequenceA and then done with a list comprehension:

```
ghci> sequenceA [[1,2,3],[4,5,6]]
[[1,4],[1,5],[1,6],[2,4],[2,5],[2,6],[3,4],[3,5],[3,6]]
```

```
ghci> [[x,y] | x <- [1,2,3], y <- [4,5,6]]
[[1,4],[1,5],[1,6],[2,4],[2,5],[2,6],[3,4],[3,5],[3,6]]
ghci> sequenceA [[1,2],[3,4]]
[[1,3],[1,4],[2,3],[2,4]]
ghci> [[x,y] | x <- [1,2], y <- [3,4]]
[[1,3],[1,4],[2,3],[2,4]]
ghci> sequenceA [[1,2],[3,4],[5,6]]
[[1,3,5],[1,3,6],[1,4,5],[1,4,6],[2,3,5],[2,3,6],[2,4,5],[2,4,6]]
ghci> [[x,y,z] | x <- [1,2], y <- [3,4], z <- [5,6]]
[[1,3,5],[1,3,6],[1,4,5],[1,4,6],[2,3,5],[2,3,6],[2,4,5],[2,4,6]]
```

(+) <$> [1,2] <*> [4,5,6] results in a nondeterministic computation
x + y, where x takes on every value from [1,2] and y takes on every value
from [4,5,6]. We represent that as a list that holds all of the possible results. Similarly, when we call sequenceA [[1,2],[3,4],[5,6]], the result is a
nondeterministic computation [x,y,z], where x takes on every value from
[1,2], y takes on every value from [3,4] and so on. To represent the result
of that nondeterministic computation, we use a list, where each element in
the list is one possible list. That's why the result is a list of lists.

When used with I/O actions, sequenceA is the same thing as sequence! It
takes a list of I/O actions and returns an I/O action that will perform each
of those actions and have as its result a list of the results of those I/O actions. That's because to turn an [IO a] value into an IO [a] value, to make
an I/O action that yields a list of results when performed, all those I/O actions must be sequenced so that they're then performed one after the other
when evaluation is forced. You can't get the result of an I/O action without
performing it.

Let's sequence three getLine I/O actions:

```
ghci> sequenceA [getLine, getLine, getLine]
heyh
ho
woo
["heyh","ho","woo"]
```

In conclusion, applicative functors aren't just interesting, they're also
useful. They allow us to combine different computations—such as I/O computations, nondeterministic computations, computations that might have
failed, and so on—by using the applicative style. Just by using <$> and <*>,
we can employ normal functions to uniformly operate on any number of applicative functors and take advantage of the semantics of each one.

12

MONOIDS

This chapter features another useful and fun type class: `Monoid`. This type class is for types whose values can be combined together with a binary operation. We'll cover exactly what monoids are and what their laws state. Then we'll take a look at some monoids in Haskell and how they can be of use.

First, let's take a look at the `newtype` keyword, because we'll be using it a lot when we delve into the wonderful world of monoids.

Wrapping an Existing Type into a New Type

So far, you've learned how to make your own algebraic data types by using the `data` keyword. You've also seen how to give existing types synonyms with the `type` keyword. In this section, we'll look at how to make new types out of existing data types by using the `newtype` keyword. We'll also talk about why we would want to do that in the first place.

In Chapter 11, you saw a couple of ways for the list type to be an applicative functor. One way is to have `<*>` take every function out of the list that is its

left parameter and apply that to every value in the list that is on the right, resulting in every possible combination of applying a function from the left list to a value in the right list:

```
ghci> [(+1),(*100),(*5)] <*> [1,2,3]
[2,3,4,100,200,300,5,10,15]
```

The second way is to take the first function on the left side of <*> and apply it to the first value on the right, then take the second function from the list on the left side and apply it to the second value on the right, and so on. Ultimately, it's kind of like zipping the two lists together.

But lists are already an instance of Applicative, so how do we also make lists an instance of Applicative in this second way? As you learned, the ZipList a type was introduced for this reason. This type has one value constructor, ZipList, which has just one field. We put the list that we're wrapping in that field. Then ZipList is made an instance of Applicative, so that when we want to use lists as applicatives in the zipping manner, we just wrap them with the ZipList constructor. Once we're finished, we unwrap them with getZipList:

```
ghci> getZipList $ ZipList [(+1),(*100),(*5)] <*> ZipList [1,2,3]
[2,200,15]
```

So, what does this have to do with this newtype keyword? Well, think about how we might write the data declaration for our ZipList a type. Here's one way:

```
data ZipList a = ZipList [a]
```

This is a type that has just one value constructor, and that value constructor has just one field that is a list of things. We might also want to use record syntax so that we automatically get a function that extracts a list from a ZipList:

```
data ZipList a = ZipList { getZipList :: [a] }
```

This looks fine and would actually work pretty well. We had two ways of making an existing type an instance of a type class, so we used the data keyword to just wrap that type into another type and made the other type an instance in the second way.

The newtype keyword in Haskell is made exactly for cases when we want to just take one type and wrap it in something to present it as another type. In the actual libraries, ZipList a is defined like this:

```
newtype ZipList a = ZipList { getZipList :: [a] }
```

Instead of the data keyword, the newtype keyword is used. Now why is that? Well for one, newtype is faster. If you use the data keyword to wrap a type, there's some overhead to all that wrapping and unwrapping when your program is running. But if you use newtype, Haskell knows that you're just using it to wrap an existing type into a new type (hence the name), because you want it to be the same internally but have a different type. With that in mind, Haskell can get rid of the wrapping and unwrapping once it resolves which value is of which type.

So why not just use newtype instead of data all the time? When you make a new type from an existing type by using the newtype keyword, you can have only one value constructor, and that value constructor can have only one field. But with data, you can make data types that have several value constructors, and each constructor can have zero or more fields:

```
data Profession = Fighter | Archer | Accountant

data Race = Human | Elf | Orc | Goblin

data PlayerCharacter = PlayerCharacter Race Profession
```

We can also use the deriving keyword with newtype just as we would with data. We can derive instances for Eq, Ord, Enum, Bounded, Show, and Read. If we derive the instance for a type class, the type that we're wrapping must already be in that type class. It makes sense, because newtype just wraps an existing type. So now if we do the following, we can print and equate values of our new type:

```
newtype CharList = CharList { getCharList :: [Char] } deriving (Eq, Show)
```

Let's give that a go:

```
ghci> CharList "this will be shown!"
CharList {getCharList = "this will be shown!"}
ghci> CharList "benny" == CharList "benny"
True
ghci> CharList "benny" == CharList "oisters"
False
```

In this particular newtype, the value constructor has the following type:

```
CharList :: [Char] -> CharList
```

It takes a [Char] value, such as "my sharona" and returns a CharList value. From the preceding examples where we used the CharList value constructor, we see that really is the case. Conversely, the getCharList function, which was generated for us because we used record syntax in our newtype, has this type:

```
getCharList :: CharList -> [Char]
```

It takes a CharList value and converts it to a [Char] value. You can think of this as wrapping and unwrapping, but you can also think of it as converting values from one type to the other.

Using newtype to Make Type Class Instances

Many times, we want to make our types instances of certain type classes, but the type parameters just don't match up for what we want to do. It's easy to make Maybe an instance of Functor, because the Functor type class is defined like this:

```
class Functor f where
    fmap :: (a -> b) -> f a -> f b
```

So we just start out with this:

```
instance Functor Maybe where
```

Then we implement fmap.

All the type parameters add up because Maybe takes the place of f in the definition of the Functor type class. Looking at fmap as if it worked on only Maybe, it ends up behaving like this:

```
fmap :: (a -> b) -> Maybe a -> Maybe b
```

Isn't that just peachy? Now what if we wanted to make the tuple an instance of Functor in such a way that when we fmap a function over a tuple, it is applied to the first component of the tuple? That way, doing fmap (+3) (1, 1) would result in (4, 1). It turns out that writing the instance for that is kind of hard. With Maybe, we just say instance Functor Maybe where because only type constructors that take exactly one parameter can be made an instance of Functor. But it seems like there's no way to do something like that with  (a, b) so that the type parameter a ends up being the one that changes when we use fmap. To get around this, we can newtype our tuple in such a way that the second type parameter represents the type of the first component in the tuple:

```
newtype Pair b a = Pair { getPair :: (a, b) }
```

And now we can make it an instance of Functor so that the function is mapped over the first component:

```
instance Functor (Pair c) where
    fmap f (Pair (x, y)) = Pair (f x, y)
```

As you can see, we can pattern match on types defined with newtype. We pattern match to get the underlying tuple, apply the function f to the first component in the tuple, and then use the Pair value constructor to convert the tuple back to our Pair b a. If we imagine what the type fmap would be if it worked only on our new pairs, it would look like this:

```
fmap :: (a -> b) -> Pair c a -> Pair c b
```

Again, we said instance Functor (Pair c) where, and so Pair c took the place of the f in the type class definition for Functor:

```
class Functor f where
    fmap :: (a -> b) -> f a -> f b
```

Now if we convert a tuple into a Pair b a, we can use fmap over it, and the function will be mapped over the first component:

```
ghci> getPair $ fmap (*100) (Pair (2, 3))
(200,3)
ghci> getPair $ fmap reverse (Pair ("london calling", 3))
("gnillac nodnol",3)
```

On newtype Laziness

The only thing that can be done with newtype is turning an existing type into a new type, so internally, Haskell can represent the values of types defined with newtype just like the original ones, while knowing that their types are now distinct. This means that not only is newtype usually faster than data, its pattern-matching mechanism is lazier. Let's take a look at what this means.

As you know, Haskell is lazy by default, which means that only when we try to actually print the results of our functions will any computation take place. Furthemore, only those computations that are necessary for our function to tell us the result will be carried out. The undefined value in Haskell represents an erroneous computation. If we try to evaluate it (that is, force Haskell to actually compute it) by printing it to the terminal, Haskell will throw a hissy fit (technically referred to as an exception):

```
ghci> undefined
*** Exception: Prelude.undefined
```

However, if we make a list that has some undefined values in it but request only the head of the list, which is not undefined, everything will go smoothly. This is because Haskell doesn't need to evaluate any other elements in a list if we want to see only the first element. Here's an example:

```
ghci> head [3,4,5,undefined,2,undefined]
3
```

Now consider the following type:

```
data CoolBool = CoolBool { getCoolBool :: Bool }
```

It's your run-of-the-mill algebraic data type that was defined with the data keyword. It has one value constructor, which has one field whose type is Bool. Let's make a function that pattern matches on a CoolBool and returns the value "hello", regardless of whether the Bool inside the CoolBool was True or False:

```
helloMe :: CoolBool -> String
helloMe (CoolBool _) = "hello"
```

Instead of applying this function to a normal CoolBool, let's throw it a curveball and apply it to undefined!

```
ghci> helloMe undefined
"*** Exception: Prelude.undefined
```

Yikes! An exception! Why did this exception happen? Types defined with the data keyword can have multiple value constructors (even though CoolBool has only one). So in order to see if the value given to our function conforms to the (CoolBool _) pattern, Haskell must evaluate the value just enough to see which value constructor was used when we made the value. And when we try to evaluate an undefined value, even a little, an exception is thrown.

Instead of using the data keyword for CoolBool, let's try using newtype:

```
newtype CoolBool = CoolBool { getCoolBool :: Bool }
```

We don't need to change our helloMe function, because the pattern-matching syntax is the same whether you use newtype or data to define your type. Let's do the same thing here and apply helloMe to an undefined value:

```
ghci> helloMe undefined
"hello"
```

It worked! Hmmm, why is that? Well, as you've learned, when you use newtype, Haskell can internally represent the values of the new type in the same way as the original values. It doesn't need to add another box around them; it just must be aware of the values being of different types. And because Haskell knows that types made with the newtype keyword can have only one constructor, it doesn't need to evaluate the value passed to the function to make sure that the value conforms to the (CoolBool _) pattern, because newtype types can have only one possible value constructor and one field!

This difference in behavior may seem trivial, but it's actually pretty important. It shows that even though types defined with data and newtype behave similarly from the programmer's point of view (because they both have value constructors and fields), they are actually two different mechanisms. Whereas data can be used to make your own types from scratch, newtype is just for making a completely new type out of an existing type. Pattern matching on newtype values isn't like taking something out of a box (as it is with data), but more about making a direct conversion from one type to another.

type vs. newtype vs. data

At this point, you may be a bit confused about the differences between type, data, and newtype, so let's review their uses.

The type keyword is for making type synonyms. We just give another name to an already existing type so that the type is easier to refer to. Say we did the following:

```
type IntList = [Int]
```

All this does is allow us to refer to the [Int] type as IntList. They can be used interchangeably. We don't get an IntList value constructor or anything like that. Because [Int] and IntList are only two ways to refer to the same type, it doesn't matter which name we use in our type annotations:

```
ghci> ([1,2,3] :: IntList) ++ ([1,2,3] :: [Int])
[1,2,3,1,2,3]
```

We use type synonyms when we want to make our type signatures more descriptive. We give types names that tell us something about their purpose in the context of the functions where they're being used. For instance, when we used an association list of type [(String, String)] to represent a phone book in Chapter 7, we gave it the type synonym of PhoneBook so that the type signatures of our functions were easier to read.

The newtype keyword is for taking existing types and wrapping them in new types, mostly so it's easier to make them instances of certain type classes. When we use newtype to wrap an existing type, the type that we get is separate from the original type. Suppose we make the following newtype:

```
newtype CharList = CharList { getCharList :: [Char] }
```

We can't use ++ to put together a CharList and a list of type [Char]. We can't even use ++ to put together two CharList lists, because ++ works only on lists, and the CharList type isn't a list, even though it could be said that CharList contains a list. We can, however, convert two CharLists to lists, ++ them, and then convert that back to a CharList.

When we use record syntax in our newtype declarations, we get functions for converting between the new type and the original type—namely the value constructor of our newtype and the function for extracting the value in its field. The new type also isn't automatically made an instance of the type classes that the original type belongs to, so we need to derive or manually write it.

In practice, you can think of newtype declarations as data declarations that can have only one constructor and one field. If you catch yourself writing such a data declaration, consider using newtype.

The data keyword is for making your own data types. You can go hog wild with them. They can have as many constructors and fields as you wish and can be used to implement any algebraic data type—everything from lists and Maybe-like types to trees.

In summary, use the keywords as follows:

- If you just want your type signatures to look cleaner and be more descriptive, you probably want type synonyms.

- If you want to take an existing type and wrap it in a new type in order to make it an instance of a type class, chances are you're looking for a newtype.

- If you want to make something completely new, odds are good that you're looking for the data keyword.

About Those Monoids

Type classes in Haskell are used to present an interface for types that have some behavior in common. We started out with simple type classes like Eq, which is for types whose values can be equated, and Ord, which is for things that can be put in an order. Then we moved on to more interesting type classes, like Functor and Applicative.

When we make a type, we think about which behaviors it supports (what it can act like) and then decide which type classes to make it an instance of based on the behavior we want. If it makes sense for values of our type to be equated, we make our type an instance of the Eq type class. If we see that our type is some kind of functor, we make it an instance of Functor, and so on.

Now consider the following: * is a function that takes two numbers and multiplies them. If we multiply some number with a 1, the result is always equal to that number. It doesn't matter if we do 1 * x or x * 1— the result is always x. Similarly, ++ is a function that takes two things and returns a third. But instead of multiplying numbers, it takes two lists and concatenates them. And much like *, it also has a certain value that doesn't change the other one when used with ++. That value is the empty list: [].

```
ghci> 4 * 1
4
ghci> 1 * 9
9
ghci> [1,2,3] ++ []
[1,2,3]
ghci> [] ++ [0.5, 2.5]
[0.5,2.5]
```

It seems that * together with 1 and ++ along with [] share some common properties:

- The function takes two parameters.
- The parameters and the returned value have the same type.
- There exists such a value that doesn't change other values when used with the binary function.

There's another thing that these two operations have in common that may not be as obvious as our previous observations: When we have three or more values and we want to use the binary function to reduce them to a single result, the order in which we apply the binary function to the values doesn't matter. For example, whether we use (3 * 4) * 5 or 3 * (4 * 5), the result is 60. The same goes for ++:

```
ghci> (3 * 2) * (8 * 5)
240
ghci> 3 * (2 * (8 * 5))
240
ghci> "la" ++ ("di" ++ "da")
"ladida"
ghci> ("la" ++ "di") ++ "da"
"ladida"
```

We call this property *associativity*. * is associative, and so is ++. However, -, for example, is not associative; the expressions (5 - 3) - 4 and 5 - (3 - 4) result in different numbers.

By being aware of these properties, we have chanced upon monoids!

The Monoid Type Class

A *monoid* is made up of an associative binary function and a value that acts as an identity with respect to that function. When something acts as an identity with respect to a function, it means that when called with that function and some other value, the result is always equal to that other value. 1 is the identity with respect to *, and [] is the identity with respect to ++. There are a lot of other monoids to be found in the world of Haskell, which is why the Monoid type class exists. It's for types that can act like monoids. Let's see how the type class is defined:

```
class Monoid m where
    mempty :: m
    mappend :: m -> m -> m
    mconcat :: [m] -> m
    mconcat = foldr mappend mempty
```

The Monoid type class is defined in Data.Monoid. Let's take some time to get properly acquainted with it.

First, we see that only concrete types can be made instances of Monoid, because the m in the type class definition doesn't take any type parameters. This is different from Functor and Applicative, which require their instances to be type constructors that take one parameter.

The first function is mempty. It's not really a function, since it doesn't take parameters. It's a polymorphic constant, kind of like minBound from Bounded. mempty represents the identity value for a particular monoid.

Next up, we have mappend, which, as you've probably guessed, is the binary function. It takes two values of the same type and returns another value of that same type. The decision to call it mappend was kind of unfortunate, because it implies that we're appending two things in some way. While ++ does take two lists and append one to the other, * doesn't really do any appending; it just multiplies two numbers together. When you meet other instances of Monoid, you'll see that most of them don't append values either. So avoid thinking in terms of appending and just think in terms of mappend being a binary function that takes two monoid values and returns a third.

The last function in this type class definition is mconcat. It takes a list of monoid values and reduces them to a single value by using mappend between the list's elements. It has a default implementation, which just takes mempty as a starting value and folds the list from the right with mappend. Because the default implementation is fine for most instances, we won't concern ourselves with mconcat too much. When making a type an instance of Monoid, it suffices to just implement mempty and mappend. Although for some instances, there might be a more efficient way to implement mconcat, the default implementation is just fine for most cases.

The Monoid Laws

Before moving on to specific instances of Monoid, let's take a brief look at the monoid laws.

You've learned that there must be a value that acts as the identity with respect to the binary function and that the binary function must be associative. It's possible to make instances of Monoid that don't follow these rules, but such instances are of no use to anyone because when using the Monoid type class, we rely on its instances acting like monoids. Otherwise, what's the point? That's why when making Monoid instances, we need to make sure they follow these laws:

- mempty `mappend` x = x
- x `mappend` mempty = x
- (x `mappend` y) `mappend` z = x `mappend` (y `mappend` z)

The first two laws state that mempty must act as the identity with respect to mappend, and the third says that mappend must be associative (the order in which we use mappend to reduce several monoid values into one doesn't matter). Haskell doesn't enforce these laws, so we need to be careful that our instances do indeed obey them.

Meet Some Monoids

Now that you know what monoids are about, let's look at some Haskell types that are monoids, what their Monoid instances look like, and their uses.

Lists Are Monoids

Yes, lists are monoids! As you've seen, the ++ function and the empty list [] form a monoid. The instance is very simple:

```
instance Monoid [a] where
    mempty = []
    mappend = (++)
```

Lists are an instance of the Monoid type class, regardless of the type of the elements they hold. Notice that we wrote instance Monoid [a] and not instance Monoid [], because Monoid requires a concrete type for an instance.

Giving this a test run, we encounter no surprises:

```
ghci> [1,2,3] `mappend` [4,5,6]
[1,2,3,4,5,6]
ghci> ("one" `mappend` "two") `mappend` "tree"
"onetwotree"
```

```
ghci> "one" `mappend` ("two" `mappend` "tree")
"onetwotree"
ghci> "one" `mappend` "two" `mappend` "tree"
"onetwotree"
ghci> "pang" `mappend` mempty
"pang"
ghci> mconcat [[1,2],[3,6],[9]]
[1,2,3,6,9]
ghci> mempty :: [a]
[]
```

Notice that in the last line, we wrote an explicit type annotation. If we just wrote mempty, GHCi wouldn't know which instance to use, so we needed to say we want the list instance. We were able to use the general type of [a] (as opposed to specifying [Int] or [String]) because the empty list can act as if it contains any type.

Because mconcat has a default implementation, we get it for free when we make something an instance of Monoid. In the case of the list, mconcat turns out to be just concat. It takes a list of lists and flattens it, because that's the equivalent of doing ++ between all the adjacent lists in a list.

The monoid laws do indeed hold for the list instance. When we have several lists and we mappend (or ++) them together, it doesn't matter which ones we do first, because they're just joined at the ends anyway. Also, the empty list acts as the identity, so all is well.

Notice that monoids don't require that a `mappend` b be equal to b `mappend` a. In the case of the list, they clearly aren't:

```
ghci> "one" `mappend` "two"
"onetwo"
ghci> "two" `mappend` "one"
"twoone"
```

And that's okay. The fact that for multiplication 3 * 5 and 5 * 3 are the same is just a property of multiplication, but it doesn't hold for all (and indeed, most) monoids.

Product and Sum

We already examined one way for numbers to be considered monoids: Just let the binary function be * and the identity value be 1. Another way for numbers to be monoids is to have the binary function be + and the identity value be 0:

```
ghci> 0 + 4
4
ghci> 5 + 0
5
ghci> (1 + 3) + 5
9
ghci> 1 + (3 + 5)
9
```

The monoid laws hold, because if you add 0 to any number, the result is that number. And addition is also associative, so we have no problems there.

With two equally valid ways for numbers to be monoids, which way do we choose? Well, we don't have to pick. Remember that when there are several ways for some type to be an instance of the same type class, we can wrap that type in a newtype and then make the new type an instance of the type class in a different way. We can have our cake and eat it too.

The Data.Monoid module exports two types for this: Product and Sum. Product is defined like this:

```
newtype Product a =  Product { getProduct :: a }
    deriving (Eq, Ord, Read, Show, Bounded)
```

It's simple—just a newtype wrapper with one type parameter along with some derived instances. Its instance for Monoid goes something like this:

```
instance Num a => Monoid (Product a) where
    mempty = Product 1
    Product x `mappend` Product y = Product (x * y)
```

mempty is just 1 wrapped in a Product constructor. mappend pattern matches on the Product constructor, multiplies the two numbers, and then wraps the resulting number. As you can see, there's a Num a class constraint. This means that Product a is an instance of Monoid for all a values that are already an instance of Num. To use Product a as a monoid, we need to do some newtype wrapping and unwrapping:

```
ghci> getProduct $ Product 3 `mappend` Product 9
27
ghci> getProduct $ Product 3 `mappend` mempty
3
ghci> getProduct $ Product 3 `mappend` Product 4 `mappend` Product 2
24
ghci> getProduct . mconcat . map Product $ [3,4,2]
24
```

Sum is defined along the same lines as Product, and the instance is similar as well. We use it in the same way:

```
ghci> getSum $ Sum 2 `mappend` Sum 9
11
ghci> getSum $ mempty `mappend` Sum 3
3
ghci> getSum . mconcat . map Sum $ [1,2,3]
6
```

Any and All

Another type that can act like a monoid in two distinct but equally valid ways is Bool. The first way is to have the function ||, which represents a logical OR, act as the binary function along with False as the identity value. With the logical OR, if any of the two parameters is True, it returns True; otherwise, it returns False. So if we use False as the identity value, OR will return False when used with False and True when used with True. The Any newtype constructor is an instance of Monoid in this fashion. It's defined like this:

```
newtype Any = Any { getAny :: Bool }
    deriving (Eq, Ord, Read, Show, Bounded)
```

Its instance looks like this:

```
instance Monoid Any where
        mempty = Any False
        Any x `mappend` Any y = Any (x || y)
```

It's called Any because x `mappend` y will be True if *any* one of those two is True. Even if three or more Any wrapped Bool values are mappended together, the result will hold True if any of them are True:

```
ghci> getAny $ Any True `mappend` Any False
True
ghci> getAny $ mempty `mappend` Any True
True
ghci> getAny . mconcat . map Any $ [False, False, False, True]
True
ghci> getAny $ mempty `mappend` mempty
False
```

The other way for Bool to be an instance of Monoid is to kind of do the opposite: Have && be the binary function and then make True the identity value. Logical AND will return True only if both of its parameters are True.

This is the newtype declaration:

```
newtype All = All { getAll :: Bool }
        deriving (Eq, Ord, Read, Show, Bounded)
```

And this is the instance:

```
instance Monoid All where
        mempty = All True
        All x `mappend` All y = All (x && y)
```

When we mappend values of the All type, the result will be True only if *all* the values used in the mappend operations are True:

```
ghci> getAll $ mempty `mappend` All True
True
ghci> getAll $ mempty `mappend` All False
False
ghci> getAll . mconcat . map All $ [True, True, True]
True
ghci> getAll . mconcat . map All $ [True, True, False]
False
```

Just as with multiplication and addition, we usually explicitly state the binary functions instead of wrapping them in newtypes and then using mappend and mempty. mconcat seems useful for Any and All, but usually it's easier to use the or and and functions. or takes lists of Bool values and returns True if any of them are True. and takes the same values and returns True if all of them are True.

The Ordering Monoid

Remember the Ordering type? It's used as the result when comparing things, and it can have three values: LT, EQ, and GT, which stand for less than, equal, and greater than, respectively.

```
ghci> 1 `compare` 2
LT
ghci> 2 `compare` 2
EQ
ghci> 3 `compare` 2
GT
```

With lists, numbers, and Boolean values, finding monoids was just a matter of looking at already existing commonly used functions and seeing if they exhibited some sort of monoid behavior. With Ordering, we need to look a bit harder to recognize a monoid. It turns out that the ordering Monoid instance is just as intuitive as the ones we've met so far, and it's also quite useful:

```
instance Monoid Ordering where
    mempty = EQ
    LT `mappend` _ = LT
    EQ `mappend` y = y
    GT `mappend` _ = GT
```

The instance is set up like this: When we mappend two Ordering values, the one on the left is kept, unless the value on the left is EQ. If the value on the left is EQ, the right one is the result. The identity is EQ. At first, this may seem kind of arbitrary, but it actually resembles the way we alphabetically compare words. We look at the first two letters, and if they differ, we can already decide which word would go first in a dictionary. However, if the first two letters are equal, then we move on to comparing the next pair of letters and repeat the process.

For instance, when we alphabetically compare the words *ox* and *on*, we see that the first letter of each word is equal and then move on to comparing the second letter. Since *x* is alphabetically greater than *n*, we know how the words compare. To gain some understanding of EQ being the identity, note that if we were to cram the same letter in the same position in both words, it wouldn't change their alphabetical ordering; for example, *oix* is still alphabetically greater than *oin*.

It's important to note that in the Monoid instance for Ordering, x `mappend` y doesn't equal y `mappend` x. Because the first parameter is kept unless it's EQ, LT `mappend` GT will result in LT, whereas GT `mappend` LT will result in GT:

```
ghci> LT `mappend` GT
LT
ghci> GT `mappend` LT
GT
ghci> mempty `mappend` LT
LT
ghci> mempty `mappend` GT
GT
```

Okay, so how is this monoid useful? Let's say we are writing a function that takes two strings, compares their lengths, and returns an Ordering. But if the strings are of the same length, instead of returning EQ right away, we want to compare them alphabetically.

Here's one way to write this:

```
lengthCompare :: String -> String -> Ordering
lengthCompare x y = let a = length x `compare` length y
                        b = x `compare` y
                    in  if a == EQ then b else a
```

We name the result of comparing the lengths a and the result of the alphabetical comparison b, and then if the lengths are equal, we return their alphabetical ordering.

But by employing our understanding of how Ordering is a monoid, we can rewrite this function in a much simpler manner:

```
import Data.Monoid

lengthCompare :: String -> String -> Ordering
lengthCompare x y = (length x `compare` length y) `mappend`
                    (x `compare` y)
```

Let's try this out:

```
ghci> lengthCompare "zen" "ants"
LT
ghci> lengthCompare "zen" "ant"
GT
```

Remember that when we use mappend, its left parameter is kept unless it's EQ; if it's EQ, the right one is kept. That's why we put the comparison that we consider to be the first, more important, criterion as the first parameter. Now suppose that we want to expand this function to also compare for the number of vowels and set this to be the second most important criterion for comparison. We modify it like this:

```
import Data.Monoid

lengthCompare :: String -> String -> Ordering
lengthCompare x y = (length x `compare` length y) `mappend`
                    (vowels x `compare` vowels y) `mappend`
                    (x `compare` y)
    where vowels = length . filter (`elem` "aeiou")
```

We made a helper function, which takes a string and tells us how many vowels it has by first filtering it for only letters that are in the string "aeiou" and then applying length to that.

```
ghci> lengthCompare "zen" "anna"
LT
```

```
ghci> lengthCompare "zen" "ana"
LT
ghci> lengthCompare "zen" "ann"
GT
```

In the first example, the lengths are found to be different, and so LT is returned, because the length of "zen" is less than the length of "anna". In the second example, the lengths are the same, but the second string has more vowels, so LT is returned again. In the third example, they both have the same length and the same number of vowels, so they're compared alphabetically, and "zen" wins.

The Ordering monoid is very useful because it allows us to easily compare things by many different criteria and put those criteria in an order themselves, ranging from the most important to the least important.

Maybe the Monoid

Let's take a look at the various ways that Maybe a can be made an instance of Monoid and how those instances are useful.

One way is to treat Maybe a as a monoid only if its type parameter a is a monoid as well and then implement mappend in such a way that it uses the mappend operation of the values that are wrapped with Just. We use Nothing as the identity, and so if one of the two values that we're mappending is Nothing, we keep the other value. Here's the instance declaration:

```
instance Monoid a => Monoid (Maybe a) where
    mempty = Nothing
    Nothing `mappend` m = m
    m `mappend` Nothing = m
    Just m1 `mappend` Just m2 = Just (m1 `mappend` m2)
```

Notice the class constraint. It says that Maybe a is an instance of Monoid only if a is an instance of Monoid. If we mappend something with a Nothing, the result is that something. If we mappend two Just values, the contents of the Justs are mappended and then wrapped back in a Just. We can do this because the class constraint ensures that the type of what's inside the Just is an instance of Monoid.

```
ghci> Nothing `mappend` Just "andy"
Just "andy"
ghci> Just LT `mappend` Nothing
Just LT
ghci> Just (Sum 3) `mappend` Just (Sum 4)
Just (Sum {getSum = 7})
```

This is useful when we're dealing with monoids as results of computations that may have failed. Because of this instance, we don't need to check if the computations have failed by seeing if they're a Nothing or Just value; we can just continue to treat them as normal monoids.

But what if the type of the contents of the Maybe is not an instance of Monoid? Notice that in the previous instance declaration, the only case where we must rely on the contents being monoids is when both parameters of mappend are Just values. When we don't know if the contents are monoids, we can't use mappend between them, so what are we to do? Well, one thing we can do is discard the second value and keep the first one. For this purpose, the First a type exists. Here's its definition:

```
newtype First a = First { getFirst :: Maybe a }
    deriving (Eq, Ord, Read, Show)
```

We take a Maybe a and wrap it with a newtype. The Monoid instance is as follows:

```
instance Monoid (First a) where
    mempty = First Nothing
    First (Just x) `mappend` _ = First (Just x)
    First Nothing `mappend` x = x
```

mempty is just a Nothing wrapped with the First newtype constructor. If mappend's first parameter is a Just value, we ignore the second one. If the first one is a Nothing, then we present the second parameter as a result, regardless of whether it's a Just or a Nothing:

```
ghci> getFirst $ First (Just 'a') `mappend` First (Just 'b')
Just 'a'
ghci> getFirst $ First Nothing `mappend` First (Just 'b')
Just 'b'
ghci> getFirst $ First (Just 'a') `mappend` First Nothing
Just 'a'
```

First is useful when we have a bunch of Maybe values and we just want to know if any of them is a Just. The mconcat function comes in handy:

```
ghci> getFirst . mconcat . map First $ [Nothing, Just 9, Just 10]
Just 9
```

If we want a monoid on Maybe a such that the second parameter is kept if both parameters of mappend are Just values, Data.Monoid provides the Last a type, which works like First a, but the last non-Nothing value is kept when mappending and using mconcat:

```
ghci> getLast . mconcat . map Last $ [Nothing, Just 9, Just 10]
Just 10
ghci> getLast $ Last (Just "one") `mappend` Last (Just "two")
Just "two"
```

Folding with Monoids

One of the more interesting ways to put monoids to work is to have them help us define folds over various data structures. So far, we've done folds over lists, but lists aren't the only data structure that can be folded over. We can define folds over almost any data structure. Trees especially lend themselves well to folding.

Because there are so many data structures that work nicely with folds, the Foldable type class was introduced. Much like Functor is for things that can be mapped over, Foldable is for things that can be folded up! It can be found in Data.Foldable, and because it exports functions whose names clash with the ones from the Prelude, it's best imported qualified (and served with basil):

```
import qualified Data.Foldable as F
```

To save ourselves precious keystrokes, we've imported it qualified as F.

So what are some of the functions that this type class defines? Well, among them are foldr, foldl, foldr1, and foldl1. Huh? We already know these functions. What's so new about this? Let's compare the types of Foldable's foldr and foldr from Prelude to see how they differ:

```
ghci> :t foldr
foldr :: (a -> b -> b) -> b -> [a] -> b
ghci> :t F.foldr
F.foldr :: (F.Foldable t) => (a -> b -> b) -> b -> t a -> b
```

Ah! So whereas foldr takes a list and folds it up, the foldr from Data.Foldable accepts any type that can be folded up, not just lists! As expected, both foldr functions do the same for lists:

```
ghci> foldr (*) 1 [1,2,3]
6
ghci> F.foldr (*) 1 [1,2,3]
6
```

Another data structure that supports folds is the Maybe we all know and love!

```
ghci> F.foldl (+) 2 (Just 9)
11
ghci> F.foldr (||) False (Just True)
True
```

But folding over a Maybe value isn't terribly interesting. It just acts like a list with one element if it's a Just value and like an empty list if it's Nothing. Let's examine a data structure that's a little more complex.

Remember the tree data structure from Chapter 7? We defined it like this:

```
data Tree a = EmptyTree | Node a (Tree a) (Tree a) deriving (Show)
```

You learned that a tree is either an empty tree that doesn't hold any values or it's a node that holds one value and also two other trees. After defining it, we made it an instance of Functor, and with that we gained the ability to fmap functions over it. Now we're going to make it an instance of Foldable so we get the ability to fold it up.

One way to make a type constructor an instance of Foldable is to just directly implement foldr for it. But another, often much easier way, is to implement the foldMap function, which is also a part of the Foldable type class. The foldMap function has the following type:

```
foldMap :: (Monoid m, Foldable t) => (a -> m) -> t a -> m
```

Its first parameter is a function that takes a value of the type that our foldable structure contains (denoted here with a) and returns a monoid value. Its second parameter is a foldable structure that contains values of type a. It maps that function over the foldable structure, thus producing a foldable structure that contains monoid values. Then, by doing mappend between those monoid values, it joins them all into a single monoid value. This function may sound kind of odd at the moment, but you'll see that it's very easy to implement. And implementing this function is all it takes for our type to be made an instance of Foldable! So if we just implement foldMap for some type, we get foldr and foldl on that type for free.

This is how we make Tree an instance of Foldable:

```
instance F.Foldable Tree where
    foldMap f EmptyTree = mempty
    foldMap f (Node x l r) = F.foldMap f l `mappend`
                             f x            `mappend`
                             F.foldMap f r
```

If we are provided with a function that takes an element of our tree and returns a monoid value, how do we reduce our whole tree down to one single monoid value? When we were using fmap over our tree, we applied the function that we were mapping to a node, and then we recursively mapped the function over the left subtree as well as the right one. Here, we're tasked with not only  mapping a function, but also with joining up the results into a single monoid value by using mappend. First, we consider the case of the empty tree—a sad, sad, lonely tree that has no values or subtrees. It doesn't hold any value that we can give to our monoid-making function, so we just say that if our tree is empty, the monoid value it becomes is mempty.

The case of a nonempty node is a bit more interesting. It contains two subtrees as well as a value. In this case, we recursively foldMap the same function f over the left and right subtrees. Remember that our foldMap results in a single monoid value. We also apply our function f to the value in the node. Now we have three monoid values (two from our subtrees and one from applying f to the value in the node), and we just need to bang them together into a single value. For this purpose, we use mappend, and naturally the left subtree comes first, then the node value, followed by the right subtree.

Notice that we didn't need to provide the function that takes a value and returns a monoid value. We receive that function as a parameter to foldMap, and all we need to decide is where to apply that function and how to join the resulting monoids from it.

Now that we have a Foldable instance for our tree type, we get foldr and foldl for free! Consider this tree:

```
testTree = Node 5
            (Node 3
                (Node 1 EmptyTree EmptyTree)
                (Node 6 EmptyTree EmptyTree)
            )
            (Node 9
                (Node 8 EmptyTree EmptyTree)
                (Node 10 EmptyTree EmptyTree)
            )
```

It has 5 at its root, and then its left node has 3 with 1 on the left and 6 on the right. The root's right node has a 9 and then 8 to its left and 10 on the far right side. With a Foldable instance, we can do all of the folds that we can do on lists:

```
ghci> F.foldl (+) 0 testTree
42
ghci> F.foldl (*) 1 testTree
64800
```

foldMap isn't useful only for making new instances of Foldable. It also comes in handy for reducing our structure to a single monoid value. For instance, if we want to know if any number in our tree is equal to 3, we can do this:

```
ghci> getAny $ F.foldMap (\x -> Any $ x == 3) testTree
True
```

Here, \x -> Any $ x == 3 is a function that takes a number and returns a monoid value: a Bool wrapped in Any. foldMap applies this function to every element in our tree and then reduces the resulting monoids into a single monoid with mappend. Suppose we do this:

```
ghci> getAny $ F.foldMap (\x -> Any $ x > 15) testTree
False
```

All of the nodes in our tree will hold the value Any False after having the function in the lambda applied to them. But to end up True, mappend for Any must have at least one True value as a parameter. That's why the final result is False, which makes sense because no value in our tree is greater than 15.

We can also easily turn our tree into a list by doing a foldMap with the \x -> [x] function. By first projecting that function onto our tree, each element becomes a singleton list. The mappend action that takes place between all those singleton lists results in a single list that holds all of the elements that are in our tree:

```
ghci> F.foldMap (\x -> [x]) testTree
[1,3,6,5,8,9,10]
```

What's cool is that all of these tricks aren't limited to trees. They work on any instance of Foldable!

13

A FISTFUL OF MONADS

When we first talked about functors in Chapter 7, you saw that they are a useful concept for values that can be mapped over. Then, in Chapter 11, we took that concept one step further with applicative functors, which allow us to view values of certain data types as values with contexts and use normal functions on those values while preserving the meaning of those contexts.

In this chapter, you'll learn about *monads*, which are just beefed-up applicative functors, much like applicative functors are beefed-up functors.

Upgrading Our Applicative Functors

When we started off with functors, you saw that it's possible to map functions over various data types using the Functor type class. The introduction to functors had us asking the question, "When we have a function of type a -> b and some data type f a, how do we map that function over the data type to end up with f b?" You saw how to map something over a Maybe a, a list [a], an IO a, and so on. You even saw how to map a function a -> b over other functions of type r -> a to get functions of type r -> b. To answer the question of how to map a function over some data type, all we needed to do was look at the type of fmap:

```
fmap :: (Functor f) => (a -> b) -> f a -> f b
```

And then we just needed to make it work for our data type by writing the appropriate Functor instance.

Then you saw a possible improvement of functors and had a few more questions. What if that function a -> b is already wrapped inside a functor value? Say we have Just (*3)—how do we apply that to Just 5? What if we don't want to apply it to Just 5, but to a Nothing instead? Or if we have [(*2),(+4)], how do we apply that to [1,2,3]? How could that even work? For this, the Applicative type class was introduced:

```
(<*>) :: (Applicative f) => f (a -> b) -> f a -> f b
```

You also saw that you can take a normal value and wrap it inside a data type. For instance, we can take a 1 and wrap it so that it becomes a Just 1. Or we can make it into a [1]. It could even become an I/O action that does nothing and just yields 1. The function that does this is called pure.

An applicative value can be seen as a value with an added context—a *fancy* value, to put it in technical terms. For instance, the character 'a' is just a normal character, whereas Just 'a' has some added context. Instead of a Char, we have a Maybe Char, which tells us that its value might be a character, but it could also be an absence of a character. The Applicative type class allows us to use normal functions on these values with context, and that context is preserved. Observe an example:

```
ghci> (*) <$> Just 2 <*> Just 8
Just 16
ghci> (++) <$> Just "klingon" <*> Nothing
Nothing
ghci> (-) <$> [3,4] <*> [1,2,3]
[2,1,0,3,2,1]
```

So now that we treat them as applicative values, Maybe a values represent computations that might have failed, [a] values represent computations that have several results (nondeterministic computations), IO a values represent values that have side effects, and so on.

Monads are a natural extension of applicative functors, and they provide a solution to the following problem: If we have a value with a context, m a, how do we apply to it a function that takes a normal a and returns a value with a context? In other words, how do we apply a function of type a -> m b to a value of type m a? Essentially, we want this function:

```
(>>=) :: (Monad m) => m a -> (a -> m b) -> m b
```

If we have a fancy value and a function that takes a normal value but returns a fancy value, how do we feed that fancy value into the function? This is the main concern when dealing with monads. We write m a instead of f a, because the m stands for Monad, but monads are just applicative functors that support >>=. The >>= function is called *bind*.

When we have a normal value a and a normal function a -> b, it's really easy to feed the value to the function—we just apply the function to the value normally, and that's it. But when we're dealing with values that come with certain contexts, it takes a bit of thinking to see how these fancy values are fed to functions and how to take into account their behavior. But you'll see that it's as easy as one, two, three.

Getting Your Feet Wet with Maybe

Now that you have a vague idea of what monads are about, let's make that idea a little more concrete. Much to no one's surprise, Maybe is a monad. Here, we'll explore it a bit more to see how it works in this role.

NOTE *Make sure you understand applicative functors at this point. (We discussed them in Chapter 11.) You should have a feel for how the various Applicative instances work and what kinds of computations they represent. To understand monads, you'll be taking your existing applicative functor knowledge and upgrading it.*

A value of type Maybe a represents a value of type a, but with the context of possible failure attached. A value of Just "dharma" means that the string "dharma" is there. A value of Nothing represents its absence, or if you look at the string as the result of a computation, it means that the computation has failed.

When we looked at Maybe as a functor, we saw that if we want to fmap a function over it, the function is mapped over what's inside if that's a Just value. Otherwise, the Nothing is kept, because there's nothing to map it over!

```
ghci> fmap (++"!") (Just "wisdom")
Just "wisdom!"
ghci> fmap (++"!") Nothing
Nothing
```

As an applicative functor, Maybe functions similarly. However, with applicative functors, the function itself is in a context, along with the value to which it's being applied. Maybe is an applicative functor in such a way that when we use <*> to apply a function inside a Maybe to a value that's inside a

Maybe, they both must be Just values for the result to be a Just value; otherwise, the result is Nothing. This makes sense. If you're missing either the function or the thing you're applying it to, you can't make something up out of thin air, so you need to propagate the failure.

```
ghci> Just (+3) <*> Just 3
Just 6
ghci> Nothing <*> Just "greed"
Nothing
ghci> Just ord <*> Nothing
Nothing
```

Using the applicative style to have normal functions act on Maybe values works in a similar way. All the values must be Just values; otherwise, it's all for Nothing!

```
ghci> max <$> Just 3 <*> Just 6
Just 6
ghci> max <$> Just 3 <*> Nothing
Nothing
```

And now, let's think about how we would use >>= with Maybe. >>= takes a monadic value and a function that takes a normal value. It returns a monadic value and manages to apply that function to the monadic value. How does it do that if the function takes a normal value? Well, it must take into account the context of that monadic value.

In this case, >>= would take a Maybe a value and a function of type a -> Maybe b, and somehow apply the function to the Maybe a. To figure out how it does that, we can use the understanding that we have from Maybe being an applicative functor. Let's say that we have a function \x -> Just (x+1). It takes a number, adds 1 to it, and wraps it in a Just:

```
ghci> (\x -> Just (x+1)) 1
Just 2
ghci> (\x -> Just (x+1)) 100
Just 101
```

If we feed it 1, it evaluates to Just 2. If we give it the number 100, the result is Just 101. It seems very straightforward. But how do we feed a Maybe value to this function? If we think about how Maybe acts as an applicative functor, answering this is pretty easy. We feed it a Just value, take what's inside the Just, and apply the function to it. If we give it a Nothing, then we're left with a function but Nothing to apply it to. In that case, let's just do what we did before and say that the result is Nothing.

Instead of calling it >>=, let's call it `applyMaybe` for now. It takes a `Maybe a` and a function that returns a `Maybe b`, and manages to apply that function to the `Maybe a`. Here it is in code:

```
applyMaybe :: Maybe a -> (a -> Maybe b) -> Maybe b
applyMaybe Nothing f  = Nothing
applyMaybe (Just x) f = f x
```

Now let's play with it. We'll use it as an infix function so that the `Maybe` value is on the left side and the function is on the right:

```
ghci> Just 3 `applyMaybe` \x -> Just (x+1)
Just 4
ghci> Just "smile" `applyMaybe` \x -> Just (x ++ " :)")
Just "smile :)"
ghci> Nothing `applyMaybe` \x -> Just (x+1)
Nothing
ghci> Nothing `applyMaybe` \x -> Just (x ++ " :)")
Nothing
```

In this example, when we used `applyMaybe` with a `Just` value and a function, the function was simply applied to the value inside the `Just`. When we tried to use it with a `Nothing`, the whole result was `Nothing`. What about if the function returns a `Nothing`? Let's see:

```
ghci> Nothing `applyMaybe` \x -> if x > 2 then Just x else Nothing
Nothing
ghci> Just 1 `applyMaybe` \x -> if x > 2 then Just x else Nothing
Nothing
```

The results are just what we expected. If the monadic value on the left is a `Nothing`, the whole thing is `Nothing`. And if the function on the right returns a `Nothing`, the result is `Nothing` again. This is similar to when we used `Maybe` as an applicative and we got a `Nothing` result if there was a `Nothing` somewhere in the mix.

It looks like we've figured out how to take a fancy value, feed it to a function that takes a normal value, and return a fancy one. We did this by keeping in mind that a `Maybe` value represents a computation that might have failed.

You might be asking yourself, "How is this useful?" It may seem like applicative functors are stronger than monads, since applicative functors allow us to take a normal function and make it operate on values with contexts. In this chapter, you'll see that monads, as an upgrade of applicative functors, can also do that. In fact, they can do some other cool stuff that applicative functors can't do.

We'll come back to `Maybe` in a minute, but first, let's check out the type class that belongs to monads.

The Monad Type Class

Just like functors have the Functor type class, and applicative functors have the Applicative type class, monads come with their own type class: Monad! (Wow, who would have thought?)

```
class Monad m where
    return :: a -> m a

    (>>=) :: m a -> (a -> m b) -> m b

    (>>) :: m a -> m b -> m b
    x >> y = x >>= \_ -> y

    fail :: String -> m a
    fail msg = error msg
```

The first line says class Monad m where. But wait, didn't I say that monads are just beefed-up applicative functors? Shouldn't there be a class constraint in there along the lines of class (Applicative m) = > Monad m where, so that a type must be an applicative functor before it can be made a monad? Well, there should, but when Haskell was made, it hadn't occurred to people that applicative functors were a good fit for Haskell. But rest assured, every monad is an applicative functor, even if the Monad class declaration doesn't say so.

The first function that the Monad type class defines is return. It's the same as pure from the Applicative type class. So, even though it has a different name, you're already acquainted with it. return's type is (Monad m) => a -> m a. It takes a value and puts it in a minimal default context that still holds that value. In other words, return takes something and wraps it in a monad. We already used return when handling I/O in Chapter 8. We used it to take a value and make a bogus I/O action that does nothing but yield that value. For Maybe, it takes a value and wraps it in a Just.

NOTE *Just a reminder: return is nothing like the return that's in most other languages. It doesn't end function execution. It just takes a normal value and puts it in a context.*

The next function is >>=, or bind. It's like function application, but instead of taking a normal value and feeding it to a normal function, it takes a monadic value (that is, a value with a context) and feeds it to a function that takes a normal value but returns a monadic value.

Next up, we have >>. We won't pay too much attention to it for now because it comes with a default implementation, and it's rarely implemented when making Monad instances. We'll take a closer look at it in "Banana on a Wire" on page 278.

The final function of the Monad type class is fail. We never use it explicitly in our code. Instead, it's used by Haskell to enable failure in a special syntactic construct for monads that you'll meet later. We don't need to concern ourselves with fail too much for now.

Now that you know what the Monad type class looks like, let's take a look at how Maybe is an instance of Monad!

```
instance Monad Maybe where
    return x = Just x
    Nothing >>= f = Nothing
    Just x >>= f  = f x
    fail _ = Nothing
```

return is the same as pure, so that one is a no-brainer. We do what we did in the Applicative type class and wrap it in a Just. The >>= function is the same as our applyMaybe. When feeding the Maybe a to our function, we keep in mind the context and return a Nothing if the value on the left is Nothing. Again, if there's no value, then there's no way to apply our function to it. If it's a Just, we take what's inside and apply f to it.

We can play around with Maybe as a monad:

```
ghci> return "WHAT" :: Maybe String
Just "WHAT"
ghci> Just 9 >>= \x -> return (x*10)
Just 90
ghci> Nothing >>= \x -> return (x*10)
Nothing
```

There's nothing new or exciting on the first line, since we already used pure with Maybe, and we know that return is just pure with a different name.

The next two lines showcase >>= a bit more. Notice how when we fed Just 9 to the function \x -> return (x*10), the x took on the value 9 inside the function. It seems as though we were able to extract the value from a Maybe without pattern matching. And we still didn't lose the context of our Maybe value, because when it's Nothing, the result of using >>= will be Nothing as well.

Walk the Line

Now that you know how to feed a `Maybe` a value to a function of type `a -> Maybe b` while taking into account the context of possible failure, let's see how we can use `>>=` repeatedly to handle computations of several `Maybe a` values.

Pierre has decided to take a break from his job at the fish farm and try tightrope walking. He is not that bad at it, but he does have one problem: Birds keep landing on his balancing pole! They come and take a short rest, chat with their avian friends, and then take off in search of breadcrumbs. This wouldn't bother him so much if the number of birds on the left side of the pole were always equal to the number of birds on the right side. But sometimes, all the birds decide that they like one side better. They throw him off balance, which results in an embarrassing tumble for Pierre (he is using a safety net).

Let's say that Pierre keeps his balance if the number of birds on the left side of the pole and on the right side of the pole is within three. So if there's one bird on the right side and four birds on the left side, he is okay. But if a fifth bird lands on the left side, he loses his balance and takes a dive.

We're going to simulate birds landing on and flying away from the pole and see if Pierre is still at it after a certain number of bird arrivals and departures. For instance, we want to see what happens to Pierre if first one bird arrives on the left side, then four birds occupy the right side, and then the bird that was on the left side decides to fly away.

Code, Code, Code

We can represent the pole with a simple pair of integers. The first component will signify the number of birds on the left side and the second component the number of birds on the right side:

```
type Birds = Int
type Pole = (Birds, Birds)
```

First, we made a type synonym for `Int`, called `Birds`, because we're using integers to represent how many birds there are. And then we made a type synonym (`Birds`, `Birds`) and called it `Pole` (not to be confused with a person of Polish descent).

Now, how about adding functions that take a number of birds and land them on one side of the pole or the other?

```
landLeft :: Birds -> Pole -> Pole
landLeft n (left, right) = (left + n, right)

landRight :: Birds -> Pole -> Pole
landRight n (left, right) = (left, right + n)
```

Let's try them out:

```
ghci> landLeft 2 (0, 0)
(2,0)
ghci> landRight 1 (1, 2)
(1,3)
ghci> landRight (-1) (1, 2)
(1,1)
```

To make birds fly away, we just had a negative number of birds land on one side. Because landing a bird on the Pole returns a Pole, we can chain applications of landLeft and landRight:

```
ghci> landLeft 2 (landRight 1 (landLeft 1 (0, 0)))
(3,1)
```

When we apply the function landLeft 1 to (0, 0) we get (1, 0). Then we land a bird on the right side, resulting in (1, 1). Finally, two birds land on the left side, resulting in (3, 1). We apply a function to something by first writing the function and then writing its parameter, but here it would be better if the pole went first and then the landing function. Suppose we make a function like this:

```
x -: f = f x
```

We can apply functions by first writing the parameter and then the function:

```
ghci> 100 -: (*3)
300
ghci> True -: not
False
ghci> (0, 0) -: landLeft 2
(2,0)
```

By using this form, we can repeatedly land birds on the pole in a more readable manner:

```
ghci> (0, 0) -: landLeft 1 -: landRight 1 -: landLeft 2
(3,1)
```

Pretty cool! This version is equivalent to the one before where we repeatedly landed birds on the pole, but it looks neater. Here, it's more obvious that we start off with (0, 0) and then land one bird on the left, then one on the right, and finally, two on the left.

I'll Fly Away

So far so good, but what happens if ten birds land on one side?

```
ghci> landLeft 10 (0, 3)
(10,3)
```

Ten birds on the left side and only three on the right? That's sure to send poor Pierre falling through the air! This is pretty obvious here, but what if we had a sequence of landings like this:

```
ghci> (0, 0) -: landLeft 1 -: landRight 4 -: landLeft (-1) -: landRight (-2)
(0,2)
```

It might seem as if everything is okay, but if you follow the steps here, you'll see that at one time there are four birds on the right side and no birds on the left! To fix this, we need to take another look at our landLeft and landRight functions.

We want the landLeft and landRight functions to be able to fail. We want them to return a new pole if the balance is okay but fail if the birds land in a lopsided manner. And what better way to add a context of failure to value than by using Maybe! Let's rework these functions:

```
landLeft :: Birds -> Pole -> Maybe Pole
landLeft n (left, right)
    | abs ((left + n) - right) < 4 = Just (left + n, right)
    | otherwise                    = Nothing

landRight :: Birds -> Pole -> Maybe Pole
landRight n (left, right)
    | abs (left - (right + n)) < 4 = Just (left, right + n)
    | otherwise                    = Nothing
```

Instead of returning a Pole, these functions now return a Maybe Pole. They still take the number of birds and the old pole as before, but then they check if landing that many birds on the pole would throw Pierre off balance. We use guards to check if the difference between the number of birds on the new pole is less than 4. If it is, we wrap the new pole in a Just and return that. If it isn't, we return a Nothing, indicating failure.

Let's give these babies a go:

```
ghci> landLeft 2 (0, 0)
Just (2,0)
ghci> landLeft 10 (0, 3)
Nothing
```

When we land birds without throwing Pierre off balance, we get a new pole wrapped in a Just. But when many more birds end up on one side of the pole, we get a Nothing. This is cool, but we seem to have lost the ability to repeatedly land birds on the pole. We can't do landLeft 1 (landRight 1 (0, 0)) anymore, because when we apply landRight 1 to (0, 0), we don't get a Pole, but a Maybe Pole. landLeft 1 takes a Pole, rather than a Maybe Pole.

We need a way of taking a Maybe Pole and feeding it to a function that takes a Pole and returns a Maybe Pole. Luckily, we have >>=, which does just that for Maybe. Let's give it a go:

```
ghci> landRight 1 (0, 0) >>= landLeft 2
Just (2,1)
```

Remember that landLeft 2 has a type of Pole -> Maybe Pole. We couldn't just feed it the Maybe Pole that is the result of landRight 1 (0, 0), so we use >>= to take that value with a context and give it to landLeft 2. >>= does indeed allow us to treat the Maybe value as a value with context. If we feed a Nothing into landLeft 2, the result is Nothing, and the failure is propagated:

```
ghci> Nothing >>= landLeft 2
Nothing
```

With this, we can now chain landings that may fail, because >>= allows us to feed a monadic value to a function that takes a normal one. Here's a sequence of bird landings:

```
ghci> return (0, 0) >>= landRight 2 >>= landLeft 2 >>= landRight 2
Just (2,4)
```

At the beginning, we used return to take a pole and wrap it in a Just. We could have just applied landRight 2 to (0, 0)—it would have been the same—but this way, we can be more consistent by using >>= for every function. Just (0, 0) is fed to landRight 2, resulting in Just (0, 2). This, in turn, gets fed to landLeft 2, resulting in Just (2, 2), and so on.

Remember the following example from before we introduced failure into Pierre's routine?

```
ghci> (0, 0) -: landLeft 1 -: landRight 4 -: landLeft (-1) -: landRight (-2)
(0,2)
```

It didn't simulate his interaction with birds very well. In the middle, his balance was off, but the result didn't reflect that. Let's fix that now by using monadic application (>>=) instead of normal application:

```
ghci> return (0, 0) >>= landLeft 1 >>= landRight 4 >>= landLeft (-1) >>= landRight (-2)
Nothing
```

The final result represents failure, which is what we expected. Let's see how this result was obtained:

1. return puts (0, 0) into a default context, making it a Just (0, 0).

2. Just (0, 0) >>= landLeft 1 happens. Since the Just (0, 0) is a Just value, landLeft 1 gets applied to (0, 0), resulting in a Just (1, 0), because the birds are still relatively balanced.

3. Just (1, 0) >>= landRight 4 takes place, and the result is Just (1, 4), as the balance of the birds is still intact, although just barely.

4. Just (1, 4) gets fed to landLeft (-1). This means that landLeft (-1) (1, 4) takes place. Now because of how landLeft works, this results in a Nothing, because the resulting pole is off balance.

5. Now that we have a Nothing, it gets fed to landRight (-2), but because it's a Nothing, the result is automatically Nothing, as we have nothing to apply landRight (-2) to.

We couldn't have achieved this by just using Maybe as an applicative. If you try it, you'll get stuck, because applicative functors don't allow for the applicative values to interact with each other very much. They can, at best, be used as parameters to a function by using the applicative style.

The applicative operators will fetch their results and feed them to the function in a manner appropriate for each applicative, and then put the final applicative value together, but there isn't that much interaction going on between them. Here, however, each step relies on the previous one's result. On every landing, the possible result from the previous one is examined and the pole is checked for balance. This determines whether the landing will succeed or fail.

Banana on a Wire

Now let's devise a function that ignores the current number of birds on the balancing pole and just makes Pierre slip and fall. We'll call it banana:

```
banana :: Pole -> Maybe Pole
banana _ = Nothing
```

We can chain this function together with our bird landings. It will always cause our walker to fall, because it ignores whatever is passed to it and always returns a failure.

```
ghci> return (0, 0) >>= landLeft 1 >>= banana >>= landRight 1
Nothing
```

The value Just (1, 0) gets fed to banana, but it produces a Nothing, which causes everything to result in a Nothing. How unfortunate!

Instead of making functions that ignore their input and just return a predetermined monadic value, we can use the >> function. Here's its default implementation:

```
(>>) :: (Monad m) => m a -> m b -> m b
m >> n = m >>= \_ -> n
```

Normally, passing some value to a function that ignores its parameter and always returns some predetermined value always results in that predetermined value. With monads, however, their context and meaning must be considered as well. Here's how >> acts with Maybe:

```
ghci> Nothing >> Just 3
Nothing
ghci> Just 3 >> Just 4
Just 4
ghci> Just 3 >> Nothing
Nothing
```

If we replace >> with >>= _ ->, it's easy to see what's happening.

We can replace our banana function in the chain with a >> and then a Nothing for guaranteed and obvious failure:

```
ghci> return (0, 0) >>= landLeft 1 >> Nothing >>= landRight 1
Nothing
```

What would this look like if we hadn't made the clever choice of treating Maybe values as values with a failure context and feeding them to functions? Here's how a series of bird landings would look:

```
routine :: Maybe Pole
routine = case landLeft 1 (0, 0) of
    Nothing -> Nothing
    Just pole1 -> case landRight 4 pole1 of
        Nothing -> Nothing
        Just pole2 -> case landLeft 2 pole2 of
            Nothing -> Nothing
            Just pole3 -> landLeft 1 pole3
```

We land a bird on the left, and then we examine the possibility of failure and the possibility of success. In the case of failure, we return a Nothing.

In the case of success, we land birds on the right and then do the same thing all over again. Converting this monstrosity into a neat chain of monadic applications with >>= is a classic example of how the Maybe monad saves a lot of time when you need to successively do computations that are based on computations that might have failed.

Notice how the Maybe implementation of >>= features exactly this logic of seeing if a value is Nothing and acting on that knowledge. If the value is Nothing, it returns a Nothing immediately. If the value is not Nothing, it goes forward with what's inside the Just.

In this section, we looked at how some functions work better when the values that they return support failure. By turning those values into Maybe values and replacing normal function application with >>=, we got a mechanism for handling failure pretty much for free. This is because >>= is supposed to preserve the context of the value to which it applies functions. In this case, the context was that our values were values with failure. So, when we applied functions to such values, the possibility of failure was always taken into account.

do Notation

Monads in Haskell are so useful that they got their own special syntax, called do notation. You already encountered do notation in Chapter 8, when we used it for gluing together several I/O actions into one. Well, as it turns out, do notation isn't just for IO but can be used for any monad. Its principle is still the same: gluing together monadic values in sequence.

Consider this familiar example of monadic application:

```
ghci> Just 3 >>= (\x -> Just (show x ++ "!"))
Just "3!"
```

Been there, done that. Feeding a monadic value to a function that returns one—no big deal. Notice how when we do this, x becomes 3 inside the lambda. Once we're inside that lambda, it's just a normal value rather than a monadic value. Now, what if we had another >>= inside that function? Check this out:

```
ghci> Just 3 >>= (\x -> Just "!" >>= (\y -> Just (show x ++ y)))
Just "3!"
```

Ah, a nested use of >>=! In the outermost lambda, we feed Just "!" to the lambda \y -> Just (show x ++ y). Inside this lambda, the y becomes "!". x is still 3, because we got it from the outer lambda. All this sort of reminds me of the following expression:

```
ghci> let x = 3; y = "!" in show x ++ y
"3!"
```

The main difference here is that the values in our >>= example are monadic. They are values with a failure context. We can replace any of them with a failure:

```
ghci> Nothing >>= (\x -> Just "!" >>= (\y -> Just (show x ++ y)))
Nothing
ghci> Just 3 >>= (\x -> Nothing >>= (\y -> Just (show x ++ y)))
Nothing
ghci> Just 3 >>= (\x -> Just "!" >>= (\y -> Nothing))
Nothing
```

In the first line, feeding a Nothing to a function naturally results in a Nothing. In the second line, we feed Just 3 to a function, and the x becomes 3. But then we feed a Nothing to the inner lambda, and the result of that is Nothing, which causes the outer lambda to produce Nothing as well. So this is sort of like assigning values to variables in let expressions, except that the values in question are monadic values.

To further illustrate this point, let's write this in a script and have each Maybe value take up its own line:

```
foo :: Maybe String
foo = Just 3   >>= (\x ->
      Just "!" >>= (\y ->
      Just (show x ++ y)))
```

To save us from writing all these annoying lambdas, Haskell gives us do notation. It allows us to write the previous piece of code like this:

```
foo :: Maybe String
foo = do
    x <- Just 3
    y <- Just "!"
    Just (show x ++ y)
```

 It would seem as though we've gained the ability to temporarily extract things from Maybe values without needing to check if the Maybe values are Just values or Nothing values at every step. How cool! If any of the values that we try to extract from are Nothing, the whole do expression will result in a Nothing. We're yanking out their (possibly existing) values and letting >>= worry about the context that comes with those values.

do expressions are just different syntax for chaining monadic values.

Do As I Do

In a do expression, every line that isn't a let line is a monadic value. To inspect its result, we use <-. If we have a Maybe String and we bind it to a variable with <-, that variable will be a String, just as when we used >>= to feed monadic values to lambdas.

The last monadic value in a do expression—like Just (show x ++ y) here—can't be used with <- to bind its result, because that wouldn't make sense if we translated the do expression back to a chain of >>= applications. Rather, its result is the result of the whole glued-up monadic value, taking into account the possible failure of any of the previous ones. For instance, examine the following line:

```
ghci> Just 9 >>= (\x -> Just (x > 8))
Just True
```

Because the left parameter of >>= is a Just value, the lambda is applied to 9, and the result is a Just True. We can rewrite this in do notation, as follows:

```
marySue :: Maybe Bool
marySue = do
    x <- Just 9
    Just (x > 8)
```

Comparing these two versions, it's easy to see why the result of the whole monadic value is the result of the last monadic value in the do expression with all the previous ones chained into it.

Pierre Returns

Our tightrope walker's routine can also be expressed with do notation. landLeft and landRight take a number of birds and a pole and produce a pole wrapped in a Just. The exception is when the tightrope walker slips, in which case a Nothing is produced. We used >>= to chain successive steps because each one relied on the previous one, and each one had an added context of possible failure. Here are two birds landing on the left side, then two birds landing on the right, and then one bird landing on the left:

```
routine :: Maybe Pole
routine = do
    start <- return (0, 0)
    first <- landLeft 2 start
    second <- landRight 2 first
    landLeft 1 second
```

Let's see if he succeeds:

```
ghci> routine
Just (3,2)
```

He does!

When we were doing these routines by explicitly writing >>=, we usually said something like return (0, 0) >>= landLeft 2, because landLeft 2 is a function that returns a Maybe value. However, with do expressions, each line must feature a monadic value. So we explicitly pass the previous Pole to the landLeft and landRight functions. If we examined the variables to which we bound our Maybe values, start would be (0, 0), first would be (2, 0) and so on.

Because do expressions are written line by line, they may look like imperative code to some people. But they're just sequential, as each value in each line relies on the result of the previous ones, along with their contexts (in this case, whether they succeeded or failed).

Again, let's take a look at what this piece of code would look like if we hadn't used the monadic aspects of Maybe:

```
routine :: Maybe Pole
routine =
    case Just (0, 0) of
        Nothing -> Nothing
        Just start -> case landLeft 2 start of
            Nothing -> Nothing
            Just first -> case landRight 2 first of
                Nothing -> Nothing
                Just second -> landLeft 1 second
```

See how in the case of success, the tuple inside Just (0, 0) becomes start, the result of landLeft 2 start becomes first, and so on?

If we want to throw Pierre a banana peel in do notation, we can do the following:

```
routine :: Maybe Pole
routine = do
    start <- return (0, 0)
    first <- landLeft 2 start
    Nothing
    second <- landRight 2 first
    landLeft 1 second
```

When we write a line in do notation without binding the monadic value with <-, it's just like putting >> after the monadic value whose result we want to ignore. We sequence the monadic value but we ignore its result, because we don't care what it is. Plus, it's prettier than writing its equivalent form of _ <- Nothing.

When to use do notation and when to explicitly use >>= is up to you. I think this example lends itself to explicitly writing >>=, because each step relies specifically on the result of the previous one. With do notation, we need to specifically write on which pole the birds are landing, but every time we just use the pole that was the result of the previous landing. But still, it gave us some insight into do notation.

Pattern Matching and Failure

In do notation, when we bind monadic values to names, we can utilize pattern matching, just as in let expressions and function parameters. Here's an example of pattern matching in a do expression:

```
justH :: Maybe Char
justH = do
    (x:xs) <- Just "hello"
    return x
```

We use pattern matching to get the first character of the string "hello", and then we present it as the result. So justH evaluates to Just 'h'.

What if this pattern matching were to fail? When matching on a pattern in a function fails, the next pattern is matched. If the matching falls through all the patterns for a given function, an error is thrown, and the program crashes. On the other hand, failed pattern matching in let expressions results in an error being produced immediately, because the mechanism of falling through patterns isn't present in let expressions.

When pattern matching fails in a do expression, the fail function (part of the Monad type class) enables it to result in a failure in the context of the current monad, instead of making the program crash. Here's its default implementation:

```
fail :: (Monad m) => String -> m a
fail msg = error msg
```

So, by default, it does make the program crash. But monads that incorporate a context of possible failure (like Maybe) usually implement it on their own. For Maybe, it's implemented like so:

```
fail _ = Nothing
```

It ignores the error message and makes a Nothing. So when pattern matching fails in a Maybe value that's written in do notation, the whole value results in a Nothing. This is preferable to having your program crash. Here's a do expression with a pattern match that's bound to fail:

```
wopwop :: Maybe Char
wopwop = do
```

```
    (x:xs) <- Just ""
    return x
```

The pattern matching fails, so the effect is the same as if the whole line with the pattern were replaced with a `Nothing`. Let's try this out:

```
ghci> wopwop
Nothing
```

The failed pattern matching has caused a failure within the context of our monad instead of causing a program-wide failure, which is pretty neat.

The List Monad

So far, you've seen how `Maybe` values can be viewed as values with a failure context, and how we can incorporate failure handling into our code by using `>>=` to feed them to functions. In this section, we're going to take a look at how to use the monadic aspects of lists to bring nondeterminism into our code in a clear and readable manner.

In Chapter 11, we talked about how lists represent nondeterministic values when they're used as applicatives. A value like 5 is deterministic—it has only one result, and we know exactly what it is. On the other hand, a value like [3,8,9] contains several results, so we can view it as one value that is actually many values at the same time. Using lists as applicative functors showcases this nondeterminism nicely.

```
ghci> (*) <$> [1,2,3] <*> [10,100,1000]
[10,100,1000,20,200,2000,30,300,3000]
```

All the possible combinations of multiplying elements from the left list with elements from the right list are included in the resulting list. When dealing with nondeterminism, there are many choices that we can make, so we just try all of them. This means the result is a nondeterministic value as well, but it has many more results.

This context of nondeterminism translates to monads very nicely. Here's what the `Monad` instance for lists looks like:

```
instance Monad [] where
    return x = [x]
    xs >>= f = concat (map f xs)
    fail _ = []
```

As you know, return does the same thing as pure, and you're already familiar with return for lists. return takes a value and puts it in a minimal default context that still yields that value. In other words, return makes a list that has only that one value as its result. This is useful when we want to just wrap a normal value into a list so that it can interact with nondeterministic values.

>>= is about taking a value with a context (a monadic value) and feeding it to a function that takes a normal value and returns one that has context. If that function just produced a normal value instead of one with a context, >>= wouldn't be so useful—after one use, the context would be lost.

Let's try feeding a nondeterministic value to a function:

```
ghci> [3,4,5] >>= \x -> [x,-x]
[3,-3,4,-4,5,-5]
```

When we used >>= with Maybe, the monadic value was fed into the function while taking care of possible failures. Here, it takes care of nondeterminism for us.

[3,4,5] is a nondeterministic value, and we feed it into a function that returns a nondeterministic value as well. The result is also nondeterministic, and it features all the possible results of taking elements from the list [3,4,5] and passing them to the function \x -> [x,-x]. This function takes a number and produces two results: one negated and one that's unchanged. So when we use >>= to feed this list to the function, every number is negated and also kept unchanged. The x from the lambda takes on every value from the list that's fed to it.

To see how this is achieved, we can just follow the implementation. First, we start with the list [3,4,5]. Then we map the lambda over it and get the following result:

```
[[3,-3],[4,-4],[5,-5]]
```

The lambda is applied to every element, and we get a list of lists. Finally, we just flatten the list, and voilà, we've applied a nondeterministic function to a nondeterministic value!

Nondeterminism also includes support for failure. The empty list [] is pretty much the equivalent of Nothing, because it signifies the absence of a result. That's why failing is just defined as the empty list. The error message gets thrown away. Let's play around with lists that fail:

```
ghci> [] >>= \x -> ["bad","mad","rad"]
[]
ghci> [1,2,3] >>= \x -> []
[]
```

In the first line, an empty list is fed into the lambda. Because the list has no elements, there are none to be passed to the function, so the result is an empty list. This is similar to feeding Nothing to a function. In the second line, each element is passed to the function, but the element is ignored and the function just returns an empty list. Because the function fails for every element that goes in it, the result is a failure.

Just as with Maybe values, we can chain several lists with >>=, propagating the nondeterminism:

```
ghci> [1,2] >>= \n -> ['a','b'] >>= \ch -> return (n, ch)
[(1,'a'),(1,'b'),(2,'a'),(2,'b')]
```

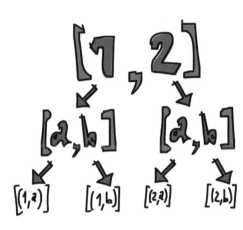

The numbers from the list [1,2] are bound to n, and the characters from the list ['a','b'] are bound to ch. Then we do return (n, ch) (or [(n, ch)]), which means taking a pair of (n, ch) and putting it in a default minimal context. In this case, it's making the smallest possible list that still presents (n, ch) as the result and features as little non-determinism as possible. Its effect on the context is minimal. We're saying, "For every element in [1,2], go over every element in ['a','b'] and produce a tuple of one element from each list."

Generally speaking, because return takes a value and wraps it in a minimal context, it doesn't have any extra effect (like failing in Maybe or resulting in more nondeterminism for lists), but it does present something as its result.

When you have nondeterministic values interacting, you can view their computation as a tree where every possible result in a list represents a separate branch. Here's the previous expression rewritten in do notation:

```
listOfTuples :: [(Int, Char)]
listOfTuples = do
    n <- [1,2]
    ch <- ['a','b']
    return (n, ch)
```

This makes it a bit more obvious that n takes on every value from [1,2] and ch takes on every value from ['a','b']. Just as with Maybe, we're extracting the elements from the monadic values and treating them like normal values, and >>= takes care of the context for us. The context in this case is nondeterminism.

do Notation and List Comprehensions

Using lists with do notation might remind you of something you've seen before. For instance, check out the following piece of code:

```ghci
ghci> [ (n, ch) | n <- [1,2], ch <- ['a','b'] ]
[(1,'a'),(1,'b'),(2,'a'),(2,'b')]
```

Yes, list comprehensions! In our do notation example, n became every result from [1,2]. For every such result, ch was assigned a result from ['a','b'], and then the final line put (n, ch) into a default context (a singleton list) to present it as the result without introducing any additional nondeterminism. In this list comprehension, the same thing happened, but we didn't need to write return at the end to present (n, ch) as the result, because the output part of a list comprehension did that for us.

In fact, list comprehensions are just syntactic sugar for using lists as monads. In the end, list comprehensions and lists in do notation translate to using >>= to do computations that feature nondeterminism.

MonadPlus and the guard Function

List comprehensions allow us to filter our output. For instance, we can filter a list of numbers to search only for numbers whose digits contain a 7:

```ghci
ghci> [ x | x <- [1..50], '7' `elem` show x ]
[7,17,27,37,47]
```

We apply show to x to turn our number into a string, and then we check if the character '7' is part of that string.

To see how filtering in list comprehensions translates to the list monad, we need to check out the guard function and the MonadPlus type class.

The MonadPlus type class is for monads that can also act as monoids. Here is its definition:

```
class Monad m => MonadPlus m where
    mzero :: m a
    mplus :: m a -> m a -> m a
```

mzero is synonymous with mempty from the Monoid type class, and mplus corresponds to mappend. Because lists are monoids as well as monads, they can be made an instance of this type class:

```
instance MonadPlus [] where
    mzero = []
    mplus = (++)
```

For lists, mzero represents a nondeterministic computation that has no results at all—a failed computation. mplus joins two nondeterministic values into one. The guard function is defined like this:

```
guard :: (MonadPlus m) => Bool -> m ()
guard True = return ()
guard False = mzero
```

guard takes a Boolean value. If that value is True, guard takes a () and puts it in a minimal default context that still succeeds. If the Boolean value is False, guard makes a failed monadic value. Here it is in action:

```
ghci> guard (5 > 2) :: Maybe ()
Just ()
ghci> guard (1 > 2) :: Maybe ()
Nothing
ghci> guard (5 > 2) :: [()]
[()]
ghci> guard (1 > 2) :: [()]
[]
```

This looks interesting, but how is it useful? In the list monad, we use it to filter out nondeterministic computations:

```
ghci> [1..50] >>= (\x -> guard ('7' `elem` show x) >> return x)
[7,17,27,37,47]
```

The result here is the same as the result of our previous list comprehension. How does guard achieve this? Let's first see how guard functions in conjunction with >>:

```
ghci> guard (5 > 2) >> return "cool" :: [String]
["cool"]
ghci> guard (1 > 2) >> return "cool" :: [String]
[]
```

If guard succeeds, the result contained within it is an empty tuple. So then we use >> to ignore that empty tuple and present something else as the result. However, if guard fails, then so will the return later on, because feeding an empty list to a function with >>= always results in an empty list. guard basically says, "If this Boolean is False, then produce a failure right here. Otherwise, make a successful value that has a dummy result of () inside it." All this does is to allow the computation to continue.

Here's the previous example rewritten in do notation:

```
sevensOnly :: [Int]
sevensOnly = do
    x <- [1..50]
    guard ('7' `elem` show x)
    return x
```

Had we forgotten to present x as the final result by using return, the resulting list would just be a list of empty tuples. Here's this again in the form of a list comprehension:

```
ghci> [ x | x <- [1..50], '7' `elem` show x ]
[7,17,27,37,47]
```

So filtering in list comprehensions is the same as using guard.

A Knight's Quest

Here's a problem that really lends itself to being solved with nondeterminism. Say we have a chessboard and only one knight piece on it. We want to find out if the knight can reach a certain position in three moves. We'll just use a pair of numbers to represent the knight's position on the chessboard. The first number will determine the column he is in, and the second number will determine the row.

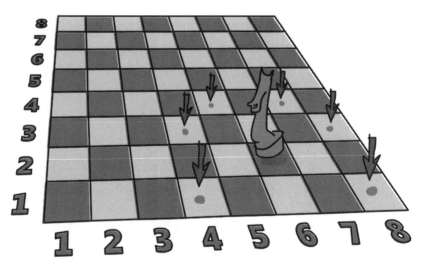

Let's make a type synonym for the knight's current position on the chessboard:

```
type KnightPos = (Int, Int)
```

Now suppose that the knight starts at (6, 2). Can he get to (6, 1) in exactly three moves? What's the best move to make next from his current position? I know—how about all of them! We have nondeterminism at our disposal, so instead of picking one move, let's pick all of them at once. Here is a function that takes the knight's position and returns all of his next moves:

```
moveKnight :: KnightPos -> [KnightPos]
moveKnight (c,r) = do
    (c', r') <- [(c+2,r-1),(c+2,r+1),(c-2,r-1),(c-2,r+1)
                ,(c+1,r-2),(c+1,r+2),(c-1,r-2),(c-1,r+2)
                ]
    guard (c' `elem` [1..8] && r' `elem` [1..8])
    return (c', r')
```

The knight can always take one step horizontally or vertically and two steps horizontally or vertically, but his movement must be both horizontal and vertical. (c', r') takes on every value from the list of movements and then guard makes sure that the new move, (c', r'), is still on the board. If it's not, it produces an empty list, which causes a failure and return (c', r') isn't carried out for that position.

This function can also be written without the use of lists as monads. Here is how to write it using filter:

```
moveKnight :: KnightPos -> [KnightPos]
moveKnight (c, r) = filter onBoard
    [(c+2,r-1),(c+2,r+1),(c-2,r-1),(c-2,r+1)
    ,(c+1,r-2),(c+1,r+2),(c-1,r-2),(c-1,r+2)
    ]
    where onBoard (c, r) = c `elem` [1..8] && r `elem` [1..8]
```

Both of these versions do the same thing, so pick the one that looks nicer to you. Let's give it a whirl:

```
ghci> moveKnight (6, 2)
[(8,1),(8,3),(4,1),(4,3),(7,4),(5,4)]
ghci> moveKnight (8, 1)
[(6,2),(7,3)]
```

Works like a charm! We take one position, and we just carry out all the possible moves at once, so to speak.

So now that we have a nondeterministic next position, we just use >>= to feed it to moveKnight. Here's a function that takes a position and returns all the positions that you can reach from it in three moves:

```
in3 :: KnightPos -> [KnightPos]
in3 start = do
    first <- moveKnight start
```

```
    second <- moveKnight first
    moveKnight second
```

If you pass it (6, 2), the resulting list is quite big. This is because if there are several ways to reach some position in three moves, the move crops up in the list several times.

Here's the preceding code without do notation:

```
in3 start = return start >>= moveKnight >>= moveKnight >>= moveKnight
```

Using >>= once gives us all possible moves from the start. When we use >>= the second time, for every possible first move, every possible next move is computed, and the same goes for the last move.

Putting a value in a default context by applying return to it and then feeding it to a function with >>= is the same as just normally applying the function to that value, but we did it here anyway for style.

Now, let's make a function that takes two positions and tells us if you can get from one to the other in exactly three steps:

```
canReachIn3 :: KnightPos -> KnightPos -> Bool
canReachIn3 start end = end `elem` in3 start
```

We generate all the possible positions in three steps, and then we see if the position we're looking for is among them. Here's how to check if we can get from (6, 2) to (6, 1) in three moves:

```
ghci> (6, 2) `canReachIn3` (6, 1)
True
```

Yes! How about from (6, 2) to (7, 3)?

```
ghci> (6, 2) `canReachIn3` (7, 3)
False
```

No! As an exercise, you can change this function so that when you can reach one position from the other, it tells you which moves to take. In Chapter 14, you'll see how to modify this function so that we also pass it the number of moves to take, instead of that number being hardcoded as it is now.

Monad Laws

Just like functors and applicative functors, monads come with a few laws that all monad instances must abide by. Just because something is made an instance of the Monad type class doesn't mean that it's actually a monad. For a type to truly be a monad, the monad laws must hold

for that type. These laws allow us to make reasonable assumptions about the type and its behavior.

Haskell allows any type to be an instance of any type class as long as the types check out. It can't check if the monad laws hold for a type though, so if we're making a new instance of the Monad type class, we need to be reasonably sure that all is well with the monad laws for that type. We can rely on the types that come with the standard library to satisfy the laws, but when we go about making our own monads, we need to manually check whether the laws hold. But don't worry, they're not complicated.

Left Identity

The first monad law states that if we take a value, put it in a default context with return, and then feed it to a function by using >>=, that's the same as just taking the value and applying the function to it. To put it formally, return x >>= f is the same damn thing as f x.

If you look at monadic values as values with a context, and return as taking a value and putting it in a default minimal context that still presents that value as the function's result, this law makes sense. If that context is really minimal, feeding this monadic value to a function shouldn't be much different than just applying the function to the normal value—and indeed, it isn't different at all.

For the Maybe monad, return is defined as Just. The Maybe monad is all about possible failure, and if we have a value that we want to put in such a context, treating it as a successful computation makes sense, because we know what the value is. Here are some examples of return usage with Maybe:

```
ghci> return 3 >>= (\x -> Just (x+100000))
Just 100003
ghci> (\x -> Just (x+100000)) 3
Just 100003
```

For the list monad, return puts something in a singleton list. The >>= implementation for lists goes over all the values in the list and applies the function to them. However, since there's only one value in a singleton list, it's the same as applying the function to that value:

```
ghci> return "WoM" >>= (\x -> [x,x,x])
["WoM","WoM","WoM"]
ghci> (\x -> [x,x,x]) "WoM"
["WoM","WoM","WoM"]
```

You've learned that for IO, using return makes an I/O action that has no side effects but just presents a value as its result. So it makes sense that this law holds for IO as well.

Right Identity

The second law states that if we have a monadic value and we use >>= to feed it to return, the result is our original monadic value. Formally, m >>= return is no different than just m.

This law might be a bit less obvious than the first one. Let's take a look at why it should hold. When we feed monadic values to functions by using >>=, those functions take normal values and return monadic ones. return is also one such function, if you consider its type.

return puts a value in a minimal context that still presents that value as its result. This means that, for instance, for Maybe, it doesn't introduce any failure; for lists, it doesn't introduce any extra nondeterminism.

Here's a test run for a few monads:

```
ghci> Just "move on up" >>= (\x -> return x)
Just "move on up"
ghci> [1,2,3,4] >>= (\x -> return x)
[1,2,3,4]
ghci> putStrLn "Wah!" >>= (\x -> return x)
Wah!
```

In this list example, the implementation for >>= is as follows:

```
xs >>= f = concat (map f xs)
```

So when we feed [1,2,3,4] to return, first return gets mapped over [1,2,3, 4], resulting in [[1],[2],[3],[4]]. Then this is concatenated, and we have our original list.

Left identity and right identity are basically laws that describe how return should behave. It's an important function for making normal values into monadic ones, and it wouldn't be good if the monadic value that it produced had any more than the minimal context needed.

Associativity

The final monad law says that when we have a chain of monadic function applications with >>=, it shouldn't matter how they're nested. Formally written, doing (m >>= f) >>= g is just like doing m >>= (\x -> f x >>= g).

Hmmm, now what's going on here? We have one monadic value, m, and two monadic functions, f and g. When we're using (m >>= f) >>= g, we're feeding m to f, which results in a monadic value. Then we feed that monadic value to g. In the expression m >>= (\x -> f x >>= g), we take a monadic value and we give it to a function that feeds the result of f x to g. It's not easy to see how those two are equal, so let's take a look at an example that makes this equality a bit clearer.

Remember when we had our tightrope walker, Pierre, walk a rope while birds landed on his balancing pole? To simulate birds landing on his balancing pole, we made a chain of several functions that might produce failure:

```
ghci> return (0, 0) >>= landRight 2 >>= landLeft 2 >>= landRight 2
Just (2,4)
```

We started with `Just (0, 0)` and then bound that value to the next monadic function, `landRight 2`. The result of that was another monadic value, which got bound to the next monadic function, and so on. If we were to explicitly parenthesize this, we would write the following:

```
ghci> ((return (0, 0) >>= landRight 2) >>= landLeft 2) >>= landRight 2
Just (2,4)
```

But we can also write the routine like this:

```
return (0, 0) >>= (\x ->
landRight 2 x >>= (\y ->
landLeft 2 y >>= (\z ->
landRight 2 z)))
```

`return (0, 0)` is the same as `Just (0, 0)`, and when we feed it to the lambda, the x becomes `(0, 0)`. `landRight` takes a number of birds and a pole (a tuple of numbers), and that's what it gets passed. This results in a `Just (0, 2)`, and when we feed this to the next lambda, y is `(0, 2)`. This goes on until the final bird landing produces a `Just (2, 4)`, which is indeed the result of the whole expression.

So it doesn't matter how you nest feeding values to monadic functions. What matters is their meaning. Let's consider another way to look at this law. Suppose we compose two functions named f and g:

```
(.) :: (b -> c) -> (a -> b) -> (a -> c)
f . g = (\x -> f (g x))
```

If the type of g is `a -> b` and the type of f is `b -> c`, we arrange them into a new function that has a type of `a -> c`, so that its parameter is passed between those functions. Now what if those two functions were monadic? What if the values they returned were monadic values? If we had a function of type `a -> m b`, we couldn't just pass its result to a function of type `b -> m c`, because that function accepts a normal b, not a monadic one. We could, however, use `>>=` to make that happen.

```
(<=<) :: (Monad m) => (b -> m c) -> (a -> m b) -> (a -> m c)
f <=< g = (\x -> g x >>= f)
```

So now we can compose two monadic functions:

```
ghci> let f x = [x,-x]
ghci> let g x = [x*3,x*2]
ghci> let h = f <=< g
ghci> h 3
[9,-9,6,-6]
```

Okay, that's cool. But what does that have to do with the associativity law? Well, when we look at the law as a law of compositions, it states that f <=< (g <=< h) should be the same as (f <=< g) <=< h. This is just another way of saying that for monads, the nesting of operations shouldn't matter.

If we translate the first two laws to use <=<, then the left identity law states that for every monadic function f, f <=< return is the same as writing just f. The right identity law says that return <=< f is also no different from f. This is similar to how if f is a normal function, (f . g) . h is the same as f . (g . h), f . id is always the same as f, and id . f is also just f.

In this chapter, we took a look at the basics of monads and learned how the Maybe monad and the list monad work. In the next chapter, we'll explore a whole bunch of other cool monads, and we'll also make our own.

14

FOR A FEW MONADS MORE

You've seen how monads can be used to take values
with contexts and apply them to functions, and how
using >>= or do notation allows you to focus on the
values themselves, while Haskell handles the context
for you.

You've met the Maybe monad and seen how it
adds a context of possible failure to values. You've
learned about the list monad and seen how it lets
us easily introduce nondeterminism into our programs. You've also learned how to work in the IO
monad, even before you knew what a monad was!

In this chapter, we'll cover a few other monads. You'll see how they can make your programs
clearer by letting you treat all sorts of values as
monadic ones. Further exploration of monads
will also solidify your intuition for recognizing and
working with monads.

The monads that we'll be exploring are all part
of the mtl package. (A Haskell *package* is a collection of modules.) The mtl package comes with the
Haskell Platform, so you probably already have
it. To check if you do, type `ghc-pkg list` from the

command line. This will show which Haskell packages you have installed, and one of them should be mtl, followed by a version number.

Writer? I Hardly Knew Her!

We've loaded our gun with the Maybe monad, the list monad, and the IO monad. Now let's put the Writer monad in the chamber and see what happens when we fire it!

Whereas the Maybe monad is for values with an added context of failure, and the list monad is for nondeterministic values, the Writer monad is for values that have another value attached that acts as a sort of log value. Writer allows us to do computations while making sure that all the log values are combined into one log value, which then is attached to the result.

For instance, we might want to equip our values with strings that explain what's going on, probably for debugging purposes. Consider a function that takes a number of bandits in a gang and tells us if that's a big gang. It's a very simple function:

```
isBigGang :: Int -> Bool
isBigGang x = x > 9
```

Now, what if instead of just giving us a True or False value, we want the function to also return a log string that says what it did? Well, we just make that string and return it alongside our Bool:

```
isBigGang :: Int -> (Bool, String)
isBigGang x = (x > 9, "Compared gang size to 9.")
```

So now, instead of just returning a Bool, we return a tuple, where the first component of the tuple is the actual value and the second component is the string that accompanies that value. There's some added context to our value now. Let's give this a go:

```
ghci> isBigGang 3
(False,"Compared gang size to 9.")
ghci> isBigGang 30
(True,"Compared gang size to 9.")
```

So far, so good. isBigGang takes a normal value and returns a value with a context. As you've just seen, feeding it a normal value is not a problem. Now what if we already have a value that has a log string attached to it, such as (3, "Smallish gang."), and we want to feed it to isBigGang? It seems like once again, we're faced with this question: If we have a function that takes a normal value and returns a value with a context, how do we take a value with a context and feed it to the function?

When we were exploring the Maybe monad in the previous chapter, we made a function applyMaybe. This function takes a Maybe a value and a function of type a -> Maybe b. We feed that Maybe a value into the function, even though the function takes a normal a instead of a Maybe a. It does this by minding the context that comes with Maybe a values, which is that they are values with possible failure. But inside the a -> Maybe b function, we can treat that value as just a normal value, because applyMaybe (which later becomes >>=) takes care of checking if it is a Nothing or a Just value.

In the same vein, let's make a function that takes a value with an attached log—that is, an (a, String) value—and a function of type a -> (b, String), and feeds that value into the function. We'll call it applyLog. But an (a, String) value doesn't carry with it a context of possible failure, but rather a context of an additional log value. So, applyLog will make sure that the log of the original value isn't lost, but is joined together with the log of the value that results from the function. Here's the implementation of applyLog:

```
applyLog :: (a, String) -> (a -> (b, String)) -> (b, String)
applyLog (x, log) f = let (y, newLog) = f x in (y, log ++ newLog)
```

When we have a value with a context that we want to feed to a function, we usually try to separate the actual value from the context, apply the function to the value, and then see whether the context is handled. In the Maybe monad, we checked if the value was a Just x, and if it was, we took that x and applied the function to it. In this case, it's very easy to find the actual value, because we're dealing with a pair where one component is the value and the other a log. So, first, we just take the value, which is x, and we apply the function f to it. We get a pair of (y, newLog), where y is the new result and newLog is the new log. But if we returned that as the result, the old log value wouldn't be included in the result, so we return a pair of (y, log ++ newLog). We use ++ to append the new log to the old one.

Here's applyLog in action:

```
ghci> (3, "Smallish gang.") `applyLog` isBigGang
(False,"Smallish gang.Compared gang size to 9.")
ghci> (30, "A freaking platoon.") `applyLog` isBigGang
(True,"A freaking platoon.Compared gang size to 9.")
```

The results are similar to before, except that now the number of people in the gang has its accompanying log, which is included in the result log.

Here are a few more examples of using applyLog:

```
ghci> ("Tobin", "Got outlaw name.") `applyLog` (\x -> (length x, "Applied length."))
(5,"Got outlaw name.Applied length.")
ghci> ("Bathcat", "Got outlaw name.") `applyLog` (\x -> (length x, "Applied length."))
(7,"Got outlaw name.Applied length.")
```

See how inside the lambda, x is just a normal string and not a tuple, and how applyLog takes care of appending the logs?

Monoids to the Rescue

Right now, applyLog takes values of type (a, String), but is there a reason that the log must be a String? It uses ++ to append the logs, so wouldn't this work on any kind of list, not just a list of characters? Sure, it would. We can change its type to this:

```
applyLog :: (a, [c]) -> (a -> (b, [c])) -> (b, [c])
```

Now the log is a list. The type of values contained in the list must be the same for the original list as well as for the list that the function returns. Otherwise, we wouldn't be able to use ++ to stick them together.

Would this work for bytestrings? There's no reason it shouldn't. However, the type we have now works only for lists. It seems as though we would need to make a separate applyLog for bytestrings. But wait! Both lists and bytestrings are monoids. As such, they are both instances of the Monoid type class, which means that they implement the mappend function. And for both lists and bytestrings, mappend is for appending. Watch it in action:

```
ghci> [1,2,3] `mappend` [4,5,6]
[1,2,3,4,5,6]
ghci> B.pack [99,104,105] `mappend` B.pack [104,117,97,104,117,97]
Chunk "chi" (Chunk "huahua" Empty)
```

Cool! Now our applyLog can work for any monoid. We need to change the type to reflect this, as well as the implementation, because we need to change ++ to mappend:

```
applyLog :: (Monoid m) => (a, m) -> (a -> (b, m)) -> (b, m)
applyLog (x, log) f = let (y, newLog) = f x in (y, log `mappend` newLog)
```

Because the accompanying value can now be any monoid value, we no longer need to think of the tuple as a value and a log; now we can think of it as a value with an accompanying monoid value. For instance, we can have a tuple that has an item name and an item price as the monoid value. We just use the Sum newtype to make sure that the prices are added as we operate with the items. Here's a function that adds drink to some cowboy food order:

```
import Data.Monoid

type Food = String
type Price = Sum Int

addDrink :: Food -> (Food, Price)
addDrink "beans" = ("milk", Sum 25)
addDrink "jerky" = ("whiskey", Sum 99)
addDrink _       = ("beer", Sum 30)
```

We use strings to represent foods and an Int in a Sum newtype wrapper to keep track of how many cents something costs. As a reminder, doing mappend with Sum results in the wrapped values being added together:

```
ghci> Sum 3 `mappend` Sum 9
Sum {getSum = 12}
```

The addDrink function is pretty simple. If we're eating beans, it returns "milk" along with Sum 25, so 25 cents wrapped in Sum. If we're eating jerky, we drink whiskey. And if we're eating anything else, we drink beer. Just normally applying this function to a food wouldn't be terribly interesting right now. But using applyLog to feed a food that comes with a price itself into this function is worth a look:

```
ghci> ("beans", Sum 10) `applyLog` addDrink
("milk",Sum {getSum = 35})
ghci> ("jerky", Sum 25) `applyLog` addDrink
("whiskey",Sum {getSum = 124})
ghci> ("dogmeat", Sum 5) `applyLog` addDrink
("beer",Sum {getSum = 35})
```

Milk costs 25 cents, but if we have it with beans that cost 10 cents, we'll end up paying 35 cents.

Now it's clear how the attached value doesn't always need to be a log. It can be any monoid value, and how two such values are combined depends on the monoid. When we were doing logs, they were appended, but now, the numbers are being added up.

Because the value that addDrink returns is a tuple of type (Food, Price), we can feed that result to addDrink again, so that it tells us what we should drink along with our meal and how much that will cost us. Let's give it a shot:

```
ghci> ("dogmeat", Sum 5) `applyLog` addDrink `applyLog` addDrink
("beer",Sum {getSum = 65})
```

Adding a drink to some dog meat results in a beer and an additional 30 cents, so ("beer", Sum 35). And if we use applyLog to feed that to addDrink, we get another beer, and the result is ("beer", Sum 65).

The Writer Type

Now that you've seen how a value with an attached monoid acts like a monadic value, let's examine the Monad instance for types of such values. The Control.Monad.Writer module exports the Writer w a type along with its Monad instance and some useful functions for dealing with values of this type.

To attach a monoid to a value, we just need to put them together in a tuple. The Writer w a type is just a newtype wrapper for this. Its definition is very simple:

```
newtype Writer w a = Writer { runWriter :: (a, w) }
```

It's wrapped in a newtype so that it can be made an instance of Monad and so that its type is separate from a normal tuple. The a type parameter represents the type of the value, and the w type parameter represents the type of the attached monoid value.

The Control.Monad.Writer module reserves the right to change the way it internally implements the Writer w a type, so it doesn't export the Writer value constructor. However, it does export the writer function, which does the same thing that the Writer constructor would do. Use it when you want to take a tuple and make a Writer value from it.

Because the Writer value constructor is not exported, you also can't pattern match against it. Instead, you need to use the runWriter function, which takes a tuple that's wrapped in a Writer newtype and unwraps it, returning a simple tuple.

Its Monad instance is defined like so:

```
instance (Monoid w) => Monad (Writer w) where
    return x = Writer (x, mempty)
    (Writer (x, v)) >>= f = let (Writer (y, v')) = f x in Writer (y, v `mappend` v')
```

First, let's examine >>=. Its implementation is essentially the same as applyLog, only now that our tuple is wrapped in the Writer newtype, we need to unwrap it when pattern matching. We take the value x and apply the function f to it. This gives us a Writer w a value, and we use a let expression to pattern match on it. We present y as the new result and use mappend to combine the old monoid value with the new one. We pack that up with the result value in a tuple and then wrap that with the Writer constructor so that our result is a Writer value, instead of just an unwrapped tuple.

So, what about return? It must take a value and put it in a default minimal context that still presents that value as the result. What would such a context be for Writer values? If we want the accompanying monoid value to affect other monoid values as little as possible, it makes sense to use mempty.

mempty is used to present identity monoid values, such as "" and Sum 0 and empty bytestrings. Whenever we use mappend between mempty and some other monoid value, the result is that other monoid value. So, if we use return to make a Writer value and then use >>= to feed that value to a function, the resulting monoid value will be only what the function returns.

Let's use return on the number 3 a bunch of times, pairing it with a different monoid each time:

```
ghci> runWriter (return 3 :: Writer String Int)
(3,"")
ghci> runWriter (return 3 :: Writer (Sum Int) Int)
(3,Sum {getSum = 0})
ghci> runWriter (return 3 :: Writer (Product Int) Int)
(3,Product {getProduct = 1})
```

Because Writer doesn't have a Show instance, we used runWriter to convert our Writer values to normal tuples that can be shown. For String, the identity value is the empty string. With Sum, it's 0, because if we add 0 to something, that something stays the same. For Product, the identity is 1.

The Writer instance doesn't feature an implementation for fail, so if a pattern match fails in do notation, error is called.

Using do Notation with Writer

Now that we have a Monad instance, we're free to use do notation for Writer values. It's handy when we have several Writer values and want to do stuff with them. As with other monads, we can treat them as normal values, and the context gets taken care of for us. In this case, all the monoid values that come attached are mappended, and so are reflected in the final result.

Here's a simple example of using do notation with Writer to multiply two numbers:

```
import Control.Monad.Writer

logNumber :: Int -> Writer [String] Int
logNumber x = writer (x, ["Got number: " ++ show x])

multWithLog :: Writer [String] Int
multWithLog = do
    a <- logNumber 3
    b <- logNumber 5
    return (a*b)
```

`logNumber` takes a number and makes a Writer value out of it. Notice how we used the `writer` function to construct a Writer value, instead of directly using the Writer value constructor. For the monoid, we use a list of strings, and we equip the number with a singleton list that just says that we have that number. `multWithLog` is a Writer value that multiplies 3 and 5 and makes sure that their attached logs are included in the final log. We use return to present a*b as the result. Because return just takes something and puts it in a minimal context, we can be sure that it won't add anything to the log.

Here's what we see if we run this code:

```
ghci> runWriter multWithLog
(15,["Got number: 3","Got number: 5"])
```

Sometimes, we just want some monoid value to be included at some particular point. For this, the `tell` function is useful. It's part of the MonadWriter type class. In the case of Writer, it takes a monoid value, like ["This is going on"], and creates a Writer value that presents the dummy value () as its result, but has the desired monoid value attached. When we have a monadic value that has () as its result, we don't bind it to a variable.

Here's `multWithLog` with some extra reporting included:

```
multWithLog :: Writer [String] Int
multWithLog = do
    a <- logNumber 3
    b <- logNumber 5
    tell ["Gonna multiply these two"]
    return (a*b)
```

It's important that return (a*b) is the last line, because the result of the last line in a do expression is the result of the whole do expression. Had we put `tell` as the last line, the result of this do expression would be (). We would lose the result of the multiplication. However, the log would be the same. Here's this in action:

```
ghci> runWriter multWithLog
(15,["Got number: 3","Got number: 5","Gonna multiply these two"])
```

Adding Logging to Programs

Euclid's algorithm takes two numbers and computes their greatest common divisor—that is, the biggest number that still divides both of them. Haskell already features the gcd function, which does exactly this, but let's implement our own function and then equip it with logging capabilities. Here's the normal algorithm:

```
gcd' :: Int -> Int -> Int
gcd' a b
```

```
| b == 0     = a
| otherwise = gcd' b (a `mod` b)
```

The algorithm is very simple. First, it checks if the second number is 0. If it is, then the result is the first number. If it isn't, then the result is the greatest common divisor of the second number and the remainder of dividing the first number with the second one.

For instance, if we want to know what the greatest common divisor of 8 and 3 is, we just follow this algorithm. Because 3 isn't 0, we need to find the greatest common divisor of 3 and 2 (if we divide 8 by 3, the remainder is 2). Next, we find the greatest common divisor of 3 and 2. 2 still isn't 0, so now we have have 2 and 1. The second number isn't 0, so we run the algorithm again for 1 and 0, as dividing 2 by 1 gives us a remainder of 0. And finally, because the second number is now 0, the final result is 1. Let's see if our code agrees:

```
ghci> gcd' 8 3
1
```

It does. Very good! Now, we want to equip our result with a context, and the context will be a monoid value that acts as a log. As before, we'll use a list of strings as our monoid. So, this should be the type of our new gcd' function:

```
gcd' :: Int -> Int -> Writer [String] Int
```

All that's left now is to equip our function with log values. Here is the code:

```
import Control.Monad.Writer

gcd' :: Int -> Int -> Writer [String] Int
gcd' a b
    | b == 0 = do
        tell ["Finished with " ++ show a]
        return a
    | otherwise = do
        tell [show a ++ " mod " ++ show b ++ " = " ++ show (a `mod` b)]
        gcd' b (a `mod` b)
```

This function takes two normal Int values and returns a Writer [String] Int—that is, an Int that has a log context. In the case where b is 0, instead of just giving a as the result, we use a do expression to put together a Writer value as a result. First, we use tell to report that we're finished, and then we use return to present a as the result of the do expression. Instead of this do expression, we could have also written this:

```
writer (a, ["Finished with " ++ show a])
```

However, I think the do expression is easier to read.

Next, we have the case when b isn't 0. In this case, we log that we're using mod to figure out the remainder of dividing a and b. Then the second line of the do expression just recursively calls gcd'. Remember that gcd' now ultimately returns a Writer value, so it's perfectly valid that gcd' b (a `mod` b) is a line in a do expression.

Let's try out our new gcd'. Its result is a Writer [String] Int value, and if we unwrap that from its newtype, we get a tuple. The first part of the tuple is the result. Let's see if it's okay:

```
ghci> fst $ runWriter (gcd' 8 3)
1
```

Good! Now what about the log? Because the log is a list of strings, let's use mapM_ putStrLn to print those strings on the screen:

```
ghci> mapM_ putStrLn $ snd $ runWriter (gcd' 8 3)
8 mod 3 = 2
3 mod 2 = 1
2 mod 1 = 0
Finished with 1
```

I think it's awesome how we were able to change our ordinary algorithm to one that reports what it does as it goes along. And we did this just by changing normal values to monadic values. We let the implementation of >>= for Writer take care of the logs for us.

You can add a logging mechanism to pretty much any function. You just replace normal values with Writer values where you want and change normal function application to >>= (or do expressions if it increases readability).

Inefficient List Construction

When using the Writer monad, you need to be careful which monoid to use, because using lists can sometimes turn out to be very slow. Lists use ++ for mappend, and using ++ to add something to the end of a list is slow if that list is really long.

In our gcd' function, the logging is fast because the list appending ends up looking like this:

```
a ++ (b ++ (c ++ (d ++ (e ++ f))))
```

A list is a data structure that's constructed from left to right. This is efficient, because we first fully construct the left part of a list and only then add a longer list on the right. But if we're not careful, using the Writer monad can produce list appending that looks like this:

```
(((( a ++ b) ++ c) ++ d) ++ e) ++ f
```

This associates to the left instead of to the right. It's inefficient because every time it wants to add the right part to the left part, it must construct the left part all the way from the beginning!

The following function works like gcd', but it logs stuff in reverse. First, it produces the log for the rest of the procedure, and then it adds the current step to the end of the log.

```
import Control.Monad.Writer

gcdReverse :: Int -> Int -> Writer [String] Int
gcdReverse a b
    | b == 0 = do
        tell ["Finished with " ++ show a]
        return a
    | otherwise = do
        result <- gcdReverse b (a `mod` b)
        tell [show a ++ " mod " ++ show b ++ " = " ++ show (a `mod` b)]
        return result
```

It does the recursion first and binds its resulting value to result. Then it adds the current step to the log, but the current step goes at the end of the log that was produced by the recursion. At the end, it presents the result of the recursion as the final result. Here it is in action:

```
ghci> mapM_ putStrLn $ snd $ runWriter (gcdReverse 8 3)
Finished with 1
2 mod 1 = 0
3 mod 2 = 1
8 mod 3 = 2
```

This function is inefficient because it ends up associating the use of ++ to the left instead of to the right.

Because lists can sometimes be inefficient when repeatedly appended in this manner, it's best to use a data structure that always supports efficient appending. One such data structure is the difference list.

Using Difference Lists

While similar to a normal list, a *difference list* is actually a function that takes a list and prepends another list to it. For example, the difference list equivalent of a list like [1,2,3] is the function \xs -> [1,2,3] ++ xs. A normal empty list is [], whereas an empty difference list is the function \xs -> [] ++ xs.

Difference lists support efficient appending. When we append two normal lists with ++, the code must walk all the way to the end of the list on the left of ++, and then stick the other one there. But what if we take the difference list approach and represent our lists as functions?

Appending two difference lists can be done like so:

```
f `append` g = \xs -> f (g xs)
```

Remember that f and g are functions that take lists and prepend something to them. For instance, if f is the function ("dog"++) (just another way of writing \xs -> "dog" ++ xs) and g is the function ("meat"++), then f `append` g makes a new function that's equivalent to the following:

```
\xs -> "dog" ++ ("meat" ++ xs)
```

We've appended two difference lists just by making a new function that first applies one difference list to some list and then to the other.

Let's make a newtype wrapper for difference lists so that we can easily give them monoid instances:

```
newtype DiffList a = DiffList { getDiffList :: [a] -> [a] }
```

The type that we wrap is [a] -> [a], because a difference list is just a function that takes a list and returns another list. Converting normal lists to difference lists and vice versa is easy:

```
toDiffList :: [a] -> DiffList a
toDiffList xs = DiffList (xs++)

fromDiffList :: DiffList a -> [a]
fromDiffList (DiffList f) = f []
```

To make a normal list into a difference list, we just do what we did before and make it a function that prepends it to another list. Because a difference list is a function that prepends something to another list, if we just want that something, we apply the function to an empty list!

Here's the Monoid instance:

```
instance Monoid (DiffList a) where
    mempty = DiffList (\xs -> [] ++ xs)
    (DiffList f) `mappend` (DiffList g) = DiffList (\xs -> f (g xs))
```

Notice how for difference lists, mempty is just the id function, and mappend is actually just function composition. Let's see if this works:

```
ghci> fromDiffList (toDiffList [1,2,3,4] `mappend` toDiffList [1,2,3])
[1,2,3,4,1,2,3]
```

Tip-top! Now we can increase the efficiency of our gcdReverse function by making it use difference lists instead of normal lists:

```
import Control.Monad.Writer

gcdReverse :: Int -> Int -> Writer (DiffList String) Int
gcdReverse a b
    | b == 0 = do
        tell (toDiffList ["Finished with " ++ show a])
        return a
    | otherwise = do
        result <- gcdReverse b (a `mod` b)
        tell (toDiffList [show a ++ " mod " ++ show b ++ " = " ++ show (a `mod` b)])
        return result
```

We just needed to change the type of the monoid from [String] to DiffList String and then when using tell, convert our normal lists into difference lists with toDiffList. Let's see if the log gets assembled properly:

```
ghci> mapM_ putStrLn . fromDiffList . snd . runWriter $ gcdReverse 110 34
Finished with 2
8 mod 2 = 0
34 mod 8 = 2
110 mod 34 = 8
```

We do gcdReverse 110 34, then use runWriter to unwrap it from the newtype, then apply snd to that to just get the log, then apply fromDiffList to convert it to a normal list, and, finally, print its entries to the screen.

Comparing Performance

To get a feel for just how much difference lists may improve your performance, consider the following function. It just counts down from some number to zero but produces its log in reverse, like gcdReverse, so that the numbers in the log will actually be counted up.

```
finalCountDown :: Int -> Writer (DiffList String) ()
finalCountDown 0 = do
    tell (toDiffList ["0"])
finalCountDown x = do
    finalCountDown (x-1)
    tell (toDiffList [show x])
```

If we give it 0, it just logs that value. For any other number, it first counts down its predecessor to 0, and then appends that number to the log. So, if we apply finalCountDown to 100, the string "100" will come last in the log.

If you load this function in GHCi and apply it to a big number, like 500000, you'll see that it quickly starts counting from 0 onward:

```
ghci> mapM_ putStrLn . fromDiffList . snd . runWriter $ finalCountDown 500000
0
1
2
...
```

However, if you change it to use normal lists instead of difference lists, like so:

```
finalCountDown :: Int -> Writer [String] ()
finalCountDown 0 = do
    tell ["0"]
finalCountDown x = do
    finalCountDown (x-1)
    tell [show x]
```

and then tell GHCi to start counting:

```
ghci> mapM_ putStrLn . snd . runWriter $ finalCountDown 500000
```

you'll see that the counting is really slow.

Of course, this is not the proper and scientific way to test the speed of your programs. However, we were able to see that, in this case, using difference lists starts producing results immediately, whereas normal lists take forever.

Oh, by the way, the song "Final Countdown" by Europe is now stuck in your head. Enjoy!

Reader? Ugh, Not This Joke Again

In Chapter 11, you saw that the function type (->) r is an instance of Functor. Mapping a function f over a function g will make a function that takes the same thing as g, applies g to it, and then applies f to that result. So basically, we're making a new function  that's like g, but before returning its result, f is applied to that result as well. Here's an example:

```
ghci> let f = (*5)
ghci> let g = (+3)
ghci> (fmap f g) 8
55
```

You've also seen that functions are applicative functors. They allow us to operate on the eventual results of functions as if we already had their results. Here's an example:

```
ghci> let f = (+) <$> (*2) <*> (+10)
ghci> f 3
19
```

The expression (+) <$> (*2) <*> (+10) makes a function that takes a number, gives that number to (*2) and (+10), and then adds together the results. For instance, if we apply this function to 3, it applies both (*2) and (+10) to 3, giving 6 and 13. Then it calls (+) with 6 and 13, and the result is 19.

Functions As Monads

Not only is the function type (->) r a functor and an applicative functor, but it's also a monad. Just like other monadic values that you've met so far, a function can also be considered a value with a context. The context for functions is that that value is not present yet and that we need to apply that function to something in order to get its result.

Because you're already acquainted with how functions work as functors and applicative functors, let's dive right in and see what their Monad instance looks like. It's located in Control.Monad.Instances, and it goes a little something like this:

```
instance Monad ((->) r) where
    return x = \_ -> x
    h >>= f = \w -> f (h w) w
```

You've seen how pure is implemented for functions, and return is pretty much the same thing as pure. It takes a value and puts it in a minimal context that always has that value as its result. And the only way to make a function that always has a certain value as its result is to make it completely ignore its parameter.

The implementation for >>= may seem a bit cryptic, but it's really not all that complicated. When we use >>= to feed a monadic value to a function, the result is always a monadic value. So, in this case, when we feed a function to another function, the result is a function as well. That's why the result starts off as a lambda.

All of the implementations of >>= so far somehow isolated the result from the monadic value and then applied the function f to that result. The same thing happens here. To get the result from a function, we need to apply it to something, which is why we use (h w) here, and then we apply f to that. f returns a monadic value, which is a function in our case, so we apply it to w as well.

The Reader Monad

If you don't get how >>= works at this point, don't worry. After a few examples, you'll see that this is a really simple monad. Here's a do expression that utilizes it:

```
import Control.Monad.Instances

addStuff :: Int -> Int
addStuff = do
    a <- (*2)
    b <- (+10)
    return (a+b)
```

This is the same thing as the applicative expression that we wrote earlier, but now it relies on functions being monads. A do expression always results in a monadic value, and this one is no different. The result of this monadic value is a function. It takes a number, then (*2) is applied to that number, and the result becomes a. (+10) is applied to the same number that (*2) was applied to, and the result becomes b. return, as in other monads, doesn't have any effect but to make a monadic value that presents some result. This presents a+b as the result of this function. If we test it, we get the same result as before:

```
ghci> addStuff 3
19
```

Both (*2) and (+10) are applied to the number 3 in this case. return (a+b) does as well, but it ignores that value and always presents a+b as the result. For this reason, the function monad is also called the *reader monad*. All the functions read from a common source. To make this even clearer, we can rewrite addStuff like so:

```
addStuff :: Int -> Int
addStuff x = let
    a = (*2) x
    b = (+10) x
    in a+b
```

You see that the reader monad allows us to treat functions as values with a context. We can act as if we already know what the functions will return. It does this by gluing functions together into one function and then giving that function's parameter to all of the functions that compose it. So, if we have a lot of functions that are all just missing one parameter, and they will eventually be applied to the same thing, we can use the reader monad to sort of extract their future results, and the >>= implementation will make sure that it all works out.

Tasteful Stateful Computations

Haskell is a pure language, and because of that, our programs are made of functions that can't change any global state or variables; they can only do some computations and return the results. This restriction actually makes it easier to think about our programs, as it frees us from worrying what every variable's value is at some point in time.

However, some problems are inherently stateful, in that they rely on some state that changes over time. While this isn't a problem for Haskell, these computations can be a bit tedious to model. That's why Haskell features the State monad, which makes dealing with stateful problems a breeze, while still keeping everything nice and pure.

When we were looking at random numbers back in Chapter 9, we dealt with functions that took a random generator as a parameter and returned a random number and a new random generator. If we wanted to generate several random numbers, we always needed to use the random generator that a previous function returned along with its result. For example, to create a function that takes a StdGen and tosses a coin three times based on that generator, we did this:

```
threeCoins :: StdGen -> (Bool, Bool, Bool)
threeCoins gen =
    let (firstCoin, newGen) = random gen
        (secondCoin, newGen') = random newGen
        (thirdCoin, newGen'') = random newGen'
    in  (firstCoin, secondCoin, thirdCoin)
```

This function takes a generator gen, and then random gen returns a Bool value along with a new generator. To throw the second coin, we use the new generator, and so on.

In most other languages, we wouldn't need to return a new generator along with a random number. We could just modify the existing one! But since Haskell is pure, we can't do that, so we need to take some state, make a result from it and a new state, and then use that new state to generate new results.

You would think that to avoid manually dealing with stateful computations in this way, we would need to give up the purity of Haskell. Well, we don't have to, since there's a special little monad called the State monad that handles all this state business for us, without impacting any of the purity that makes Haskell programming so cool.

Stateful Computations

To help demonstrate stateful computations, let's go ahead and give them a type. We'll say that a stateful computation is a function that takes some state and returns a value along with some new state. That function has the following type:

```
s -> (a, s)
```

s is the type of the state, and a is the result of the stateful computations.

NOTE   *Assignment in most other languages could be thought of as a stateful computation. For instance, when we do x = 5 in an imperative language, it will usually assign the value 5 to the variable x, and it will also have the value 5 as an expression. If you look at that functionally, it's like a function that takes a state (that is, all the variables that have been assigned previously) and returns a result (in this case, 5) and a new state, which would be all the previous variable mappings plus the newly assigned variable.*

This stateful computation—a function that takes a state and returns a result and a new state—can be thought of as a value with a context as well. The actual value is the result, whereas the context is that we must provide some initial state to actually get that result, and that apart from getting a result, we also get a new state.

Stacks and Stones

Say we want to model a stack. A *stack* is a data structure that contains a bunch of elements and supports exactly two operations:

- *Pushing* an element to the stack, which adds an element onto the top of the stack
- *Popping* an element off the stack, which removes the topmost element from the stack

We'll use a list to represent our stack, with the head of the list acting as the top of the stack. To help us with our task, we'll make two functions:

- pop will take a stack, pop one item, and return that item as the result. It will also return a new stack, without the popped item.
- push will take an item and a stack and then push that item onto the stack. It will return () as its result, along with a new stack.

Here are the functions in use:

```
type Stack = [Int]

pop :: Stack -> (Int, Stack)
pop (x:xs) = (x, xs)
```

```
push :: Int -> Stack -> ((), Stack)
push a xs = ((), a:xs)
```

We used () as the result when pushing to the stack because pushing
an item onto the stack doesn't have any important result value—its main
job is to change the stack. If we apply only the first parameter of push, we
get a stateful computation. pop is already a stateful computation because of
its type.

Let's write a small piece of code to simulate a stack using these functions. We'll take a stack, push 3 to it, and then pop two items, just for kicks.
Here it is:

```
stackManip :: Stack -> (Int, Stack)
stackManip stack = let
    ((), newStack1) = push 3 stack
    (a , newStack2) = pop newStack1
    in pop newStack2
```

We take a stack, and then we do push 3 stack, which results in a tuple.
The first part of the tuple is a (), and the second is a new stack, which we call
newStack1. Then we pop a number from newStack1, which results in a number
a (which is the 3) that we pushed and a new stack, which we call newStack2.
Then we pop a number off newStack2, and we get a number that's b and a
newStack3. We return a tuple with that number and that stack. Let's try it out:

```
ghci> stackManip [5,8,2,1]
(5,[8,2,1])
```

The result is 5, and the new stack is [8,2,1]. Notice how stackManip is itself a stateful computation. We've taken a bunch of stateful computations
and sort of glued them together. Hmm, sounds familiar.

The preceding code for stackManip is kind of tedious, since we're manually giving the state to every stateful computation and storing it and then
giving it to the next one. Wouldn't it be cooler if, instead of giving the stack
manually to each function, we could write something like the following?

```
stackManip = do
    push 3
    a <- pop
    pop
```

Well, using the State monad will allow us to do exactly that. With it, we
will be able to take stateful computations like these and use them without
needing to manage the state manually.

The State Monad

The Control.Monad.State module provides a newtype that wraps stateful computations. Here's its definition:

```
newtype State s a = State { runState :: s -> (a, s) }
```

A State s a is a stateful computation that manipulates a state of type s and has a result of type a.

Much like Control.Monad.Writer, Control.Monad.State doesn't export its value constructor. If you want to take a stateful computation and wrap it in the State newtype, use the state function, which does the same thing that the State constructor would do.

Now that you've seen what stateful computations are about and how they can even be thought of as values with contexts, let's check out their Monad instance:

```
instance Monad (State s) where
    return x = State $ \s -> (x, s)
    (State h) >>= f = State $ \s -> let (a, newState) = h s
                                        (State g) = f a
                                    in  g newState
```

Our aim with return is to take a value and make a stateful computation that always has that value as its result. That's why we just make a lambda \s -> (x, s). We always present x as the result of the stateful computation, and the state is kept unchanged, because return must put a value in a minimal context. So return will make a stateful computation that presents a certain value as the result and keeps the state unchanged.

What about >>=? Well, the result of feeding a stateful computation to a function with >>= must be a stateful computation, right? So, we start off with the State newtype wrapper, and then we type out a lambda. This lambda will be our new stateful computation. But what goes on in it? Well, we need to somehow extract the result value from the first stateful computation. Because we're in a stateful computation right now, we can give the stateful computation h our current state s, which results in a pair of the result and a new state: (a, newState).

So far, every time we implemented >>=, once we had extracted just the result from the monadic value, we applied the function f to it to get the new monadic value. In Writer, after doing that and getting the new monadic value, we still need to make sure that the context is taken care of by mappending the old monoid value with the new one. Here, we do f a, and we get a new stateful computation g. Now that we have a new stateful computation and a new state (which goes by the name of newState), we just apply that stateful computation g to the newState. The result is a tuple of the final result and final state!

So, with >>=, we kind of glue two stateful computations together. The second computation is hidden inside a function that takes the previous computation's result. Because pop and push are already stateful computations, it's easy to wrap them into a State wrapper:

```
import Control.Monad.State

pop :: State Stack Int
pop = state $ \(x:xs) -> (x, xs)

push :: Int -> State Stack ()
push a = state $ \xs -> ((), a:xs)
```

Notice how we used the state function to wrap a function into the State newtype instead of using the State value constructor directly.

pop is already a stateful computation, and push takes an Int and returns a stateful computation. Now we can rewrite our previous example of pushing 3 onto the stack and then popping two numbers off, like this:

```
import Control.Monad.State

stackManip :: State Stack Int
stackManip = do
    push 3
    a <- pop
    pop
```

See how we've glued a push and two pops into one stateful computation? When we unwrap it from its newtype wrapper, we get a function to which we can provide some initial state:

```
ghci> runState stackManip [5,8,2,1]
(5,[8,2,1])
```

We didn't need to bind the second pop to a, because we didn't use that a at all. So, we could have written it like this:

```
stackManip :: State Stack Int
stackManip = do
    push 3
    pop
    pop
```

Pretty cool. But what if we want to do something a little more complicated? Let's say we want to pop one number off the stack, and if that number is 5, we'll just push it back on the stack and stop. But if the number *isn't* 5, we'll push 3 and 8 back on instead. Here's the code:

```
stackStuff :: State Stack ()
stackStuff = do
    a <- pop
    if a == 5
        then push 5
        else do
            push 3
            push 8
```

This is quite straightforward. Let's run it with an initial stack:

```
ghci> runState stackStuff [9,0,2,1,0]
((),[8,3,0,2,1,0])
```

Remember that do expressions result in monadic values, and with the State monad, a single do expression is also a stateful function. Because stackManip and stackStuff are ordinary stateful computations, we can glue them together to produce further stateful computations:

```
moreStack :: State Stack ()
moreStack = do
    a <- stackManip
    if a == 100
        then stackStuff
        else return ()
```

If the result of stackManip on the current stack is 100, we run stackStuff; otherwise, we do nothing. return () just keeps the state as it is and does nothing.

Getting and Setting State

The Control.Monad.State module provides a type class called MonadState, which features two pretty useful functions: get and put. For State, the get function is implemented like this:

```
get = state $ \s -> (s, s)
```

It just takes the current state and presents it as the result.

The put function takes some state and makes a stateful function that replaces the current state with it:

```
put newState = state $ \s -> ((), newState)
```

So, with these, we can see what the current stack is or we can replace it with a whole other stack, like so:

```
stackyStack :: State Stack ()
stackyStack = do
    stackNow <- get
    if stackNow == [1,2,3]
        then put [8,3,1]
        else put [9,2,1]
```

We can also use get and put to implement pop and push. Here's pop:

```
pop :: State Stack Int
pop = do
    (x:xs) <- get
    put xs
    return x
```

We use get to get the whole stack, and then we use put to make everything but the top element the new state. Then we use return to present x as the result.

Here's push implemented with get and put:

```
push :: Int -> State Stack ()
push x = do
    xs <- get
    put (x:xs)
```

We just use get to get the current stack and use put to make the set the new state as our stack, with the element x on top.

It's worth examining what the type of >>= would be if it worked only for State values:

```
(>>=) :: State s a -> (a -> State s b) -> State s b
```

See how the type of the state s stays the same, but the type of the result can change from a to b? This means that we can glue together several stateful computations whose results are of different types, but the type of the state must stay the same. Now why is that? Well, for instance, for Maybe, >>= has this type:

```
(>>=) :: Maybe a -> (a -> Maybe b) -> Maybe b
```

It makes sense that the monad itself, Maybe, doesn't change. It wouldn't make sense to use >>= between two different monads. Well, for the State monad, the monad is actually State s, so if that s were different, we would be using >>= between two different monads.

Randomness and the State Monad

At the beginning of this section, we talked about how generating random numbers can sometimes be awkward. Every random function takes a generator and returns a random number along with a new generator, which must then be used instead of the old one if we want to generate another random number. The State monad makes dealing with this a lot easier.

The random function from System.Random has the following type:

```
random :: (RandomGen g, Random a) => g -> (a, g)
```

This means it takes a random generator and produces a random number along with a new generator. We can see that it's a stateful computation, so we can wrap it in the State newtype constructor by using the state function, and then use it as a monadic value so that passing the state is handled for us:

```
import System.Random
import Control.Monad.State

randomSt :: (RandomGen g, Random a) => State g a
randomSt = state random
```

So, now if we want to throw three coins (True is tails, and False is heads), we just do the following:

```
import System.Random
import Control.Monad.State

threeCoins :: State StdGen (Bool, Bool, Bool)
threeCoins = do
    a <- randomSt
    b <- randomSt
    c <- randomSt
    return (a, b, c)
```

threeCoins is now a stateful computation, and after taking an initial random generator, it passes that generator to the first randomSt, which produces a number and a new generator, which is passed to the next one, and so on. We use return (a, b, c) to present (a, b, c) as the result without changing the most recent generator.

Let's give this a go:

```
ghci> runState threeCoins (mkStdGen 33)
((True,False,True),680029187 2103410263)
```

Now doing things that require some state to be saved in between steps just became much less of a hassle!

Error Error on the Wall

You know by now that Maybe is used to add a context of possible failure to values. A value can be a Just something or a Nothing. However useful it may be, when we have a Nothing, all we know is that there was some sort of failure—there's no way to cram more information in there telling us what kind of failure it was.

The Either e a type also allows us to incorporate a context of possible failure into our values. It also lets us attach values to the failure, so they can describe what went wrong or provide other useful information regarding the failure. An Either e a value can either be a Right value, signifying the right answer and a success, or it can be a Left value, signifying failure. Here's an example:

```
ghci> :t Right 4
Right 4 :: (Num t) => Either a t
ghci> :t Left "out of cheese error"
Left "out of cheese error" :: Either [Char] b
```

This is pretty much just an enhanced Maybe, so it makes sense for it to be a monad. It can also be viewed as a value with an added context of possible failure, but now there's a value attached when there's an error as well.

Its Monad instance is similar to that of Maybe, and it can be found in Data.Either:

```
instance Monad (Either e) where
    return x = Right x
    Left l >>= _ = Left l
    Right r >>= k = k r
```

return, as always, takes a value and puts it in a default minimal context. It wraps our value in the Right constructor because we're using Right to represent a successful computation where a result is present. This is a lot like return for Maybe.

The >>= examines two possible cases: a Left and a Right. In the case of a Right, the function f is applied to the value inside it, similar to the case of a Just where the function is just applied to its contents. In the case of an error, the Left value is kept, along with its contents, which describe the failure.

Here are a few examples of usage:

```
ghci> Left "boom" >>= \x -> return (x+1)
Left "boom"
ghci> Left "boom " >>= \x -> Left "no way!"
Left "boom "
ghci> Right 100 >>= \x -> Left "no way!"
Left "no way!"
ghci> Right 3 >>= \x -> return (x + 100)
Right 103
```

When we use >>= to feed a Left value to a function, the function is ignored and an identical Left value is returned. When we feed a Right value to a function, the function is applied to what's on the inside.

Either is also an instance of the MonadError type class, which lives in Control.Monad.Error. This type class is for monads whose values can fail and provide some sort of data with their failure. It defines two functions for dealing with such values.

The first function is throwError, which takes some sort of error data and returns a value that fails with that data. In the case of Either, it just takes a value and wraps it in a Left constructor.

```
ghci> :m + Control.Monad.Error
ghci> throwError "warp core breach imminent!" :: Either String Ing
Left "warp core breach imminent!"
```

We had to use an explicit type declaration to tell ghci to give us an Either value because throwError can return a value of any type, as long as that type is an instance of MonadError.

The other function is catchError, which takes two parameters. The first one is a monadic value that can fail. The second one is a function that is evaluated if the given monadic value has failed. This function takes some error data and returns a new monadic value.

If the first parameter of catchError is a successful value, catchError simply returns that value. If it isn't, catchError feeds that value's error data to the supplied function, which can then either salvage the failure and return a successful value, or it can fail on its own. Here's a demonstration:

```
ghci> Right 100 `catchError` (\e -> throwError $ "Aborting! error: " ++ e)
Right 100
ghci> Left "Oops!" `catchError` (\e -> throwError $ "Aborting! Error: " ++ e)
Left "Aborting! Error: Oops!"
ghci> Right 1 `catchError` (\e -> return 999)
Right 1
ghci> Left "Oops!" `catchError` (\e -> return 999)
Right 999
```

NOTE   *In the previous chapter, we used the monadic aspects of* Maybe *to simulate birds land-ing on the balancing pole of a tightrope walker. As an exercise, you can rewrite that with the error monad so that when the tightrope walker slips and falls, you remember how many birds were on each side of the pole when he fell.*

Some Useful Monadic Functions

In this section, we're going to explore a few functions that operate on mo-nadic values or return monadic values as their results (or both!). Such func-tions are usually referred to as *monadic functions*. While some of them will be brand new, others will be monadic counterparts of functions that you al-ready know, like filter and foldl. Here, we'll look at liftM, join, filterM, and foldM.

liftM and Friends

When we started our journey to the top of Monad Mountain, we first looked at *functors*, which are for things that can be mapped over. Then we covered improved func-tors called *applicative functors*, which allow us to apply normal functions between several applicative values as well as to take a normal value and  put it in some default context. Finally, we introduced *monads* as improved applicative functors, which add the ability for these values with context to somehow be fed into normal functions.

So, every monad is an applicative functor, and every applicative func-tor is a functor. The Applicative type class has a class constraint such that our type must be an instance of Functor before we can make it an instance of Applicative. Monad should have the same constraint for Applicative, as every monad is an applicative functor, but it doesn't, because the Monad type class was introduced to Haskell long before Applicative.

But even though every monad is a functor, we don't need to rely on it having a Functor instance because of the liftM function. liftM takes a func-tion and a monadic value and maps the function over the monadic value. So it's pretty much the same thing as fmap! This is liftM's type:

```
liftM :: (Monad m) => (a -> b) -> m a -> m b
```

And this is the type of fmap:

```
fmap :: (Functor f) => (a -> b) -> f a -> f b
```

If the Functor and Monad instances for a type obey the functor and monad laws, these two amount to the same thing (and all the monads that we've met so far obey both). This is kind of like pure and return do the same thing, but one has an Applicative class constraint, whereas the other has a Monad constraint. Let's try out liftM:

```
ghci> liftM (*3) (Just 8)
Just 24
ghci> fmap (*3) (Just 8)
Just 24
ghci> runWriter $ liftM not $ Writer (True, "chickpeas")
(False,"chickpeas")
ghci> runWriter $ fmap not $ Writer (True, "chickpeas")
(False,"chickpeas")
ghci> runState (liftM (+100) pop) [1,2,3,4]
(101,[2,3,4])
ghci> runState (fmap (+100) pop) [1,2,3,4]
(101,[2,3,4])
```

You already know quite well how fmap works with Maybe values. And liftM does the same thing. For Writer values, the function is mapped over the first component of the tuple, which is the result. Running fmap or liftM over a stateful computation results in another stateful computation, but its eventual result is modified by the supplied function. Had we not mapped (+100) over pop before running it, it would have returned (1, [2,3,4]).

This is how liftM is implemented:

```
liftM :: (Monad m) => (a -> b) -> m a -> m b
liftM f m = m >>= (\x -> return (f x))
```

Or with do notation:

```
liftM :: (Monad m) => (a -> b) -> m a -> m b
liftM f m = do
    x <- m
    return (f x)
```

We feed the monadic value m into the function, and then we apply the function f to its result before putting it back into a default context. Because of the monad laws, this is guaranteed not to change the context; it changes only the result that the monadic value presents.

You see that liftM is implemented without referencing the Functor type class at all. This means that we can implement fmap (or liftM—whatever you want to call it) just by using the goodies that monads offer us. Because of this, we can conclude that monads are at least as strong as functors.

The `Applicative` type class allows us to apply functions between values with contexts as if they were normal values, like this:

```
ghci> (+) <$> Just 3 <*> Just 5
Just 8
ghci> (+) <$> Just 3 <*> Nothing
Nothing
```

Using this applicative style makes things pretty easy. `<$>` is just `fmap`, and `<*>` is a function from the `Applicative` type class that has the following type:

```
(<*>) :: (Applicative f) => f (a -> b) -> f a -> f b
```

So it's kind of like `fmap`, but the function itself is in a context. We need to somehow extract it from the context and map it over the `f a` value, and then reassemble the context. Because all functions are curried in Haskell by default, we can use the combination of `<$>` and `<*>` to apply functions that take several parameters between applicative values.

Anyway, it turns out that just like `fmap`, `<*>` can also be implemented by using only what the `Monad` type class gives us. The `ap` function is basically `<*>`, but with a `Monad` constraint instead of an `Applicative` one. Here's its definition:

```
ap :: (Monad m) => m (a -> b) -> m a -> m b
ap mf m = do
    f <- mf
    x <- m
    return (f x)
```

`mf` is a monadic value whose result is a function. Because the function as well as the value is in a context, we get the function from the context and call it `f`, then get the value and call that `x`, and, finally, apply the function to the value and present that as a result. Here's a quick demonstration:

```
ghci> Just (+3) <*> Just 4
Just 7
ghci> Just (+3) `ap` Just 4
Just 7
ghci> [(+1),(+2),(+3)] <*> [10,11]
[11,12,12,13,13,14]
ghci> [(+1),(+2),(+3)] `ap` [10,11]
[11,12,12,13,13,14]
```

Now we can see that monads are at least as strong as applicatives as well, because we can use the functions from `Monad` to implement the ones for `Applicative`. In fact, many times, when a type is found to be a monad, people first write up a `Monad` instance, and then make an `Applicative` instance by just saying that pure is return and <*> is ap. Similarly, if you already have a Monad instance for something, you can give it a Functor instance just by saying that fmap is liftM.

liftA2 is a convenience function for applying a function between two applicative values. It's defined like so:

```
liftA2 :: (Applicative f) => (a -> b -> c) -> f a -> f b -> f c
liftA2 f x y = f <$> x <*> y
```

The liftM2 function does the same thing, but with a Monad constraint. There are also liftM3, liftM4, and liftM5 functions.

You saw how monads are at least as strong as applicatives and functors and how even though all monads are functors and applicative functors, they don't necessarily have Functor and Applicative instances. We examined the monadic equivalents of the functions that functors and applicative functors use.

The join Function

Here's some food for thought: If the result of one monadic value is another monadic value (one monadic value is nested inside the other), can you flatten them to just a single, normal monadic value? For instance, if we have Just (Just 9), can we make that into Just 9? It turns out that any nested monadic value can be flattened and that this is actually a property unique to monads. For this, we have the join function. Its type is this:

```
join :: (Monad m) => m (m a) -> m a
```

So, join takes a monadic value within a monadic value and gives us just a monadic value—it flattens it, in other words. Here it is with some Maybe values:

```
ghci> join (Just (Just 9))
Just 9
ghci> join (Just Nothing)
Nothing
ghci> join Nothing
Nothing
```

The first line has a successful computation as a result of a successful computation, so they are both just joined into one big successful computation. The second line features a Nothing as a result of a Just value. Whenever we were dealing with Maybe values before and we wanted to combine several of them into one—be it with <*> or >>=—they all needed to be Just values for the result to be a Just value. If there was any failure along the way, the result was a failure, and the same thing happens here. In the third line, we try to flatten what is from the onset a failure, so the result is a failure as well.

Flattening lists is pretty intuitive:

```
ghci> join [[1,2,3],[4,5,6]]
[1,2,3,4,5,6]
```

As you can see, for lists, join is just concat. To flatten a Writer value whose result is a Writer value itself, we need to mappend the monoid value:

```
ghci> runWriter $ join (Writer (Writer (1, "aaa"), "bbb"))
(1,"bbbaaa")
```

The outer monoid value "bbb" comes first, and then "aaa" is appended to it. Intuitively speaking, when you want to examine the result of a Writer value, you need to write its monoid value to the log first, and only then can you look at what it has inside.

Flattening Either values is very similar to flattening Maybe values:

```
ghci> join (Right (Right 9)) :: Either String Int
Right 9
ghci> join (Right (Left "error")) :: Either String Int
Left "error"
ghci> join (Left "error") :: Either String Int
Left "error"
```

If we apply join to a stateful computation whose result is a stateful computation, the result is a stateful computation that first runs the outer stateful computation and then the resulting one. Watch it at work:

```
ghci> runState (join (state $ \s -> (push 10, 1:2:s))) [0,0,0]
((),[10,1,2,0,0,0])
```

The lambda here takes a state, puts 2 and 1 onto the stack, and presents push 10 as its result. So, when this whole thing is flattened with join and then run, it first puts 2 and 1 onto the stack, and then push 10 is carried out, pushing a 10 onto the top.

The implementation for join is as follows:

```
join :: (Monad m) => m (m a) -> m a
join mm = do
    m <- mm
    m
```

Because the result of mm is a monadic value, we get that result and then just put it on a line of its own because it's a monadic value. The trick here is that when we call m <- mm, the context of the monad that we are in is taken care of. That's why, for instance, Maybe values result in Just values only if the outer and inner values are both Just values. Here's what this would look like if the mm value were set in advance to Just (Just 8):

```
joinedMaybes :: Maybe Int
joinedMaybes = do
    m <- Just (Just 8)
    m
```

Perhaps the most interesting thing about join is that for every monad, feeding a monadic value to a function with >>= is the same thing as just mapping that function over the value and then using join to flatten the resulting nested monadic value! In other words, m >>= f is always the same thing as join (fmap f m). It makes sense when you think about it.

With >>=, we're always thinking about how to feed a monadic value to a function that takes a normal value but returns a monadic value. If we just map that function over the monadic value, we have a monadic value inside a monadic value. For instance, say we have Just 9 and the function \x -> Just (x+1). If we map this function over Just 9, we're left with Just (Just 10).

The fact that m >>= f always equals join (fmap f m) is very useful if we're making our own Monad instance for some type. This is because it's often easier to figure out how we would flatten a nested monadic value than to figure out how to implement >>=.

Another interesting thing is that join cannot be implemented by just using the functions that functors and applicatives provide. This leads us to conclude that not only are monads as strong as functors and applicatives, but they are in fact stronger, because we can do more stuff with them than we can with just functors and applicatives.

filterM

The filter function is pretty much the bread of Haskell programming (map being the butter). It takes a predicate and a list to filter and then returns a new list where only the elements that satisfy the predicate are kept. Its type is this:

```
filter :: (a -> Bool) -> [a] -> [a]
```

The predicate takes an element of the list and returns a `Bool` value. Now, what if the `Bool` value that it returned was actually a monadic value? What if it came with a context? For instance, what if every `True` or `False` value that the predicate produced also had an accompanying monoid value, like `["Accepted the number 5"]` or `["3 is too small"]`? If that were the case, we would expect the resulting list to also come with a log of all the log values that were produced along the way. So, if the `Bool` that the predicate returned came with a context, we would expect the final resulting list to have some context attached as well. Otherwise, the context that each `Bool` came with would be lost.

The `filterM` function from `Control.Monad` does just what we want! Its type is this:

```
filterM :: (Monad m) => (a -> m Bool) -> [a] -> m [a]
```

The predicate returns a monadic value whose result is a `Bool`, but because it's a monadic value, its context can be anything from a possible failure to nondeterminism and more! To ensure that the context is reflected in the final result, the result is also a monadic value.

Let's take a list and keep only those values that are smaller than 4. To start, we'll just use the regular `filter` function:

```
ghci> filter (\x -> x < 4) [9,1,5,2,10,3]
[1,2,3]
```

That's pretty easy. Now, let's make a predicate that, aside from presenting a `True` or `False` result, also provides a log of what it did. Of course, we'll be using the `Writer` monad for this:

```
keepSmall :: Int -> Writer [String] Bool
keepSmall x
    | x < 4 = do
        tell ["Keeping " ++ show x]
        return True
    | otherwise = do
        tell [show x ++ " is too large, throwing it away"]
        return False
```

Instead of just returning a `Bool`, this function returns a `Writer [String] Bool`. It's a monadic predicate. Sounds fancy, doesn't it? If the number is smaller than 4, we report that we're keeping it, and then return `True`.

Now, let's give it to `filterM` along with a list. Because the predicate returns a `Writer` value, the resulting list will also be a `Writer` value.

```
ghci> fst $ runWriter $ filterM keepSmall [9,1,5,2,10,3]
[1,2,3]
```

Examining the result of the resulting Writer value, we see that everything is in order. Now, let's print the log and see what we have:

```
ghci> mapM_ putStrLn $ snd $ runWriter $ filterM keepSmall [9,1,5,2,10,3]
9 is too large, throwing it away
Keeping 1
5 is too large, throwing it away
Keeping 2
10 is too large, throwing it away
Keeping 3
```

So, just by providing a monadic predicate to filterM, we were able to filter a list while taking advantage of the monadic context that we used.

A very cool Haskell trick is using filterM to get the powerset of a list (if we think of them as sets for now). The *powerset* of some set is a set of all subsets of that set. So if we have a set like [1,2,3], its powerset includes the following sets:

```
[1,2,3]
[1,2]
[1,3]
[1]
[2,3]
[2]
[3]
[]
```

In other words, getting a powerset is like getting all the combinations of keeping and throwing out elements from a set. For example, [2,3] is the original set with the number 1 excluded, [1,2] is the original set with 3 excluded, and so on.

To make a function that returns a powerset of some list, we're going to rely on nondeterminism. We take the list [1,2,3] and then look at the first element, which is 1, and we ask ourselves, "Should we keep it or drop it?" Well, we would like to do both actually. So, we are going to filter a list, and we'll use a predicate that nondeterministically both keeps and drops every element from the list. Here's our powerset function:

```
powerset :: [a] -> [[a]]
powerset xs = filterM (\x -> [True, False]) xs
```

Wait, that's it? Yup. We choose to drop and keep every element, regardless of what that element is. We have a nondeterministic predicate, so the resulting list will also be a nondeterministic value and will thus be a list of lists. Let's give this a go:

```
ghci> powerset [1,2,3]
[[1,2,3],[1,2],[1,3],[1],[2,3],[2],[3],[]]
```

This takes a bit of thinking to wrap your head around. Just consider lists as nondeterministic values that don't know what to be, so they decide to be everything at once, and the concept is a bit easier to grasp.

foldM

The monadic counterpart to `foldl` is `foldM`. If you remember your folds from Chapter 5, you know that `foldl` takes a binary function, a starting accumulator, and a list to fold up and then folds it from the left into a single value by using the binary function. `foldM` does the same thing, except it takes a binary function that produces a monadic value and folds the list up with that. Unsurprisingly, the resulting value is also monadic. The type of `foldl` is this:

```
foldl :: (a -> b -> a) -> a -> [b] -> a
```

Whereas `foldM` has the following type:

```
foldM :: (Monad m) => (a -> b -> m a) -> a -> [b] -> m a
```

The value that the binary function returns is monadic, so the result of the whole fold is monadic as well. Let's sum a list of numbers with a fold:

```
ghci> foldl (\acc x -> acc + x) 0 [2,8,3,1]
14
```

The starting accumulator is 0, and then 2 is added to the accumulator, resulting in a new accumulator that has a value of 2. 8 is added to this accumulator, resulting in an accumulator of 10, and so on. When we reach the end, the final accumulator is the result.

Now, what if we wanted to sum a list of numbers but with the added condition that if any number in the list is greater than 9, the whole thing fails? It would make sense to use a binary function that checks if the current number is greater than 9. If it is, the function fails; if it isn't, the function continues on its merry way. Because of this added possibility of failure, let's make our binary function return a `Maybe` accumulator instead of a normal one. Here's the binary function:

```
binSmalls :: Int -> Int -> Maybe Int
binSmalls acc x
    | x > 9     = Nothing
    | otherwise = Just (acc + x)
```

Because our binary function is now a monadic function, we can't use it with the normal `foldl`; we must use `foldM`. Here goes:

```
ghci> foldM binSmalls 0 [2,8,3,1]
Just 14
```

```
ghci> foldM binSmalls 0 [2,11,3,1]
Nothing
```

Excellent! Because one number in the list was greater than 9, the whole thing resulted in a Nothing. Folding with a binary function that returns a Writer value is cool as well, because then you log whatever you want as your fold goes along its way.

Making a Safe RPN Calculator

When we were solving the problem of implementing an RPN calculator in Chapter 10, we noted that it worked fine as long as the input that it got made sense. But if something went wrong, it caused our whole program to crash. Now that we know how to make already existing code monadic, let's take our RPN calculator and add error handling to it by taking advantage of the Maybe monad.

We implemented our RPN calculator by taking a string like "1 3 + 2 *", breaking it up into words to get something like ["1","3","+","2","*"]. Then we folded over that list by starting out with an empty stack and using a binary folding function that adds numbers to the stack or manipulates numbers on the top of the stack to add them together and divide them and such.

This was the main body of our function:

```
import Data.List

solveRPN :: String -> Double
solveRPN = head . foldl foldingFunction [] . words
```

We made the expression into a list of strings, and folded over it with our folding function. Then, when we were left with just one item in the stack, we returned that item as the answer. This was the folding function:

```
foldingFunction :: [Double] -> String -> [Double]
foldingFunction (x:y:ys) "*" = (y * x):ys
foldingFunction (x:y:ys) "+" = (y + x):ys
foldingFunction (x:y:ys) "-" = (y - x):ys
foldingFunction xs numberString = read numberString:xs
```

The accumulator of the fold was a stack, which we represented with a list of Double values. As the folding function went over the RPN expression, if the current item was an operator, it took two items off the top of the stack, applied the operator between them, and then put the result back on the stack. If the current item was a string that represented a number, it converted that string into an actual number and returned a new stack that was like the old one, except with that number pushed to the top.

Let's first make our folding function capable of graceful failure. Its type is going to change from what it is now to this:

```
foldingFunction :: [Double] -> String -> Maybe [Double]
```

So, it will either return Just a new stack or it will fail with Nothing.

The reads function is like read, except that it returns a list with a single element in case of a successful read. If it fails to read something, it returns an empty list. Apart from returning the value that it read, it also returns the part of the string that it didn't consume. We're going to say that it always must consume the full input to work, and make it into a readMaybe function for convenience. Here it is:

```
readMaybe :: (Read a) => String -> Maybe a
readMaybe st = case reads st of [(x, "")] -> Just x
                                _ -> Nothing
```

Now let's test it:

```
ghci> readMaybe "1" :: Maybe Int
Just 1
ghci> readMaybe "GOTO HELL" :: Maybe Int
Nothing
```

Okay, it seems to work. So, let's make our folding function into a monadic function that can fail:

```
foldingFunction :: [Double] -> String -> Maybe [Double]
foldingFunction (x:y:ys) "*" = return ((y * x):ys)
foldingFunction (x:y:ys) "+" = return ((y + x):ys)
foldingFunction (x:y:ys) "-" = return ((y - x):ys)
foldingFunction xs numberString = liftM (:xs) (readMaybe numberString)
```

The first three cases are like the old ones, except the new stack is wrapped in a Just (we used return here to do this, but we could just as well have written Just). In the last case, we use readMaybe numberString, and then we map (:xs) over it. So, if the stack xs is [1.0,2.0], and readMaybe numberString results in a Just 3.0, the result is Just [3.0,1.0,2.0]. If readMaybe numberString results in a Nothing, the result is Nothing.

Let's try out the folding function by itself:

```
ghci> foldingFunction [3,2] "*"
Just [6.0]
```

```
ghci> foldingFunction [3,2] "-"
Just [-1.0]
ghci> foldingFunction [] "*"
Nothing
ghci> foldingFunction [] "1"
Just [1.0]
ghci> foldingFunction [] "1 wawawawa"
Nothing
```

It looks like it's working! And now it's time for the new and improved solveRPN. Here it is ladies and gents!

```
import Data.List

solveRPN :: String -> Maybe Double
solveRPN st = do
    [result] <- foldM foldingFunction [] (words st)
    return result
```

Just as in the previous version, we take the string and make it into a list of words. Then we do a fold, starting with the empty stack, but instead of doing a normal foldl, we do a foldM. The result of that foldM should be a Maybe value that contains a list (that's our final stack), and that list should have only one value. We use a do expression to get that value, and we call it result. In case the foldM returns a Nothing, the whole thing will be a Nothing, because that's how Maybe works. Also notice that we pattern match in the do expression, so if the list has more than one value or none at all, the pattern match fails, and a Nothing is produced. In the last line, we just call return result to present the result of the RPN calculation as the result of the final Maybe value.

Let's give it a shot:

```
ghci> solveRPN "1 2 * 4 +"
Just 6.0
ghci> solveRPN "1 2 * 4 + 5 *"
Just 30.0
ghci> solveRPN "1 2 * 4"
Nothing
ghci> solveRPN "1 8 wharglbllargh"
Nothing
```

The first failure happens because the final stack isn't a list with one element in it, so the pattern matching in the do expression fails. The second failure happens because readMaybe returns a Nothing.

Composing Monadic Functions

When we were talking about the monad laws in Chapter 13, you learned that the <=< function is just like composition, but instead of working for normal functions like a -> b, it works for monadic functions like a -> m b. Here is an example:

```
ghci> let f = (+1) . (*100)
ghci> f 4
401
ghci> let g = (\x -> return (x+1)) <=< (\x -> return (x*100))
ghci> Just 4 >>= g
Just 401
```

In this example, we first composed two normal functions, applied the resulting function to 4, and then composed two monadic functions and fed Just 4 to the resulting function with >>=.

If you have a bunch of functions in a list, you can compose them all into one big function just by using id as the starting accumulator and the . function as the binary function. Here's an example:

```
ghci> let f = foldr (.) id [(+1),(*100),(+1)]
ghci> f 1
201
```

The function f takes a number and then adds 1 to it, multiplies the result by 100, and then adds 1 to that.

We can compose monadic functions in the same way, but instead of normal composition, we use <=<, and instead of id, we use return. We don't need to use a foldM over a foldr or anything like that, because the <=< function makes sure that composition happens in a monadic fashion.

When you were introduced to the list monad in Chapter 13, we used it to figure out if a knight can go from one position on a chessboard to another in exactly three moves. We created a function called moveKnight, which takes the knight's position on the board and returns all the possible moves that he can make next. Then, to generate all the possible positions that he can have after taking three moves, we made the following function:

```
in3 start = return start >>= moveKnight >>= moveKnight >>= moveKnight
```

And to check if he can go from start to end in three moves, we did the following:

```
canReachIn3 :: KnightPos -> KnightPos -> Bool
canReachIn3 start end = end `elem` in3 start
```

Using monadic function composition, we can make a function like in3, except instead of generating all the positions that the knight can have after making three moves, we can do it for an arbitrary number of moves. If you look at in3, you'll see that we used our moveKnight three times, and each time, we used >>= to feed it all the possible previous positions. So now, let's make it more general. Here's how:

```
import Data.List

inMany :: Int -> KnightPos -> [KnightPos]
inMany x start = return start >>= foldr (<=<) return (replicate x moveKnight)
```

First, we use replicate to make a list that contains x copies of the function moveKnight. Then we monadically compose all those functions into one, which gives us a function that takes a starting position and nondeterministically moves the knight x times. Then we just make the starting position into a singleton list with return and feed it to the function.

Now, we can change our canReachIn3 function to be more general as well:

```
canReachIn :: Int -> KnightPos -> KnightPos -> Bool
canReachIn x start end = end `elem` inMany x start
```

Making Monads

In this section, we're going to look at an example of how a type gets made, identified as a monad, and then given the appropriate Monad instance. We don't usually set out to make a monad with the sole purpose of making a monad. Rather, we make a type whose purpose is to model an aspect of some problem, and then later on, if we see that the type represents a value with a context and can act like a monad, we give it a Monad instance.

As you've seen, lists are used to represent nondeterministic values. A list like [3,5,9] can be viewed as a single nondeterministic value that just can't decide what it's going to be. When we feed a list into a function with >>=, it just makes all the possible choices of taking an element from the list and applying the function to it and then presents those results in a list as well.

If we look at the list [3,5,9] as the numbers 3, 5, and 9 occurring at once, we might notice that there's no information regarding the probability that each of those numbers occurs. What if we wanted to model a nondeterministic value like [3,5,9], but we wanted to express that 3 has a 50 percent chance of happening and 5 and 9 both have a 25 percent chance of happening? Let's try to make this work!

Let's say that every item in the list comes with another value: a probability of it happening. It might make sense to present that value like this:

```
[(3,0.5),(5,0.25),(9,0.25)]
```

In mathemathics, probabilities aren't usually expressed in percentages, but rather in real numbers between a 0 and 1. A 0 means that there's no chance in hell for something to happen, and a 1 means that it's happening for sure. Floating-point numbers can get messy fast because they tend to lose precision, but Haskell offers a data type for rational numbers. It's called Rational, and it lives in Data.Ratio. To make a Rational, we write it as if it were a fraction. The numerator and the denominator are separated by a %. Here are a few examples:

```
ghci> 1%4
1 % 4
ghci> 1%2 + 1%2
1 % 1
ghci> 1%3 + 5%4
19 % 12
```

The first line is just one-quarter. In the second line, we add two halves to get a whole. In the third line, we add one-third with five-quarters and get nineteen-twelfths. So, let's throw out our floating points and use Rational for our probabilities:

```
ghci> [(3,1%2),(5,1%4),(9,1%4)]
[(3,1 % 2),(5,1 % 4),(9,1 % 4)]
```

Okay, so 3 has a one-out-of-two chance of happening, while 5 and 9 will happen one time out of four. Pretty neat.

We took lists and we added some extra context to them, so this represents values with contexts as well. Before we go any further, let's wrap this into a newtype, because something tells me we'll be making some instances.

```
import Data.Ratio

newtype Prob a = Prob { getProb :: [(a, Rational)] } deriving Show
```

Is this a functor? Well, the list is a functor, so this should probably be a functor, too, because we just added some stuff to the list. When we map a function over a list, we apply it to each element. Here, we'll apply it to each element as well, but we'll leave the probabilities as they are. Let's make an instance:

```
instance Functor Prob where
    fmap f (Prob xs) = Prob $ map (\(x, p) -> (f x, p)) xs
```

We unwrap it from the newtype with pattern matching, apply the function f to the values while keeping the probabilities as they are, and then wrap it back up. Let's see if it works:

```
ghci> fmap negate (Prob [(3,1%2),(5,1%4),(9,1%4)])
Prob {getProb = [(-3,1 % 2),(-5,1 % 4),(-9,1 % 4)]}
```

Note that the probabilities should always add up to 1. If those are all the things that can happen, it doesn't make sense for the sum of their probabilities to be anything other than 1. A coin that lands tails 75 percent of the time and heads 50 percent of the time seems like it could work only in some other strange universe.

Now the big question: Is this a monad? Given how the list is a monad, this looks like it should be a monad as well. First, let's think about return. How does it work for lists? It takes a value and puts it in a singleton list. What about here? Well, since it's supposed to be a default minimal context, it should also make a singleton list. What about the probability? Well, return x is supposed to make a monadic value that always presents x as its result, so it doesn't make sense for the probability to be 0. If it always must present this value as its result, the probability should be 1!

What about >>=? Seems kind of tricky, so let's make use of the fact that m >>= f always equals join (fmap f m) for monads and think about how we would flatten a probability list of probability lists. As an example, let's consider this list where there's a 25 percent chance that exactly one of 'a' or 'b' will happen. Both 'a' and 'b' are equally likely to occur. Also, there's a 75 percent chance that exactly one of 'c' or 'd' will happen. 'c' and 'd' are also equally likely to happen. Here's a picture of a probability list that models this scenario:

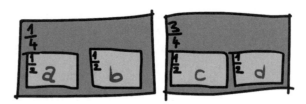

What are the chances for each of these letters to occur? If we were to draw this as just four boxes, each with a probability, what would those probabilites be? To find out, all we need to do is multiply each probability with all of the probabilities that it contains. 'a' would occur one time out of eight, as would 'b', because if we multiply one-half by one-quarter, we get one-eighth.

'c' would happen three times out of eight, because three-quarters multiplied by one-half is three-eighths. 'd' would also happen three times out of eight. If we sum all the probabilities, they still add up to one.

Here's this situation expressed as a probability list:

```
thisSituation :: Prob (Prob Char)
thisSituation = Prob
    [(Prob [('a',1%2),('b',1%2)], 1%4)
    ,(Prob [('c',1%2),('d',1%2)], 3%4)
    ]
```

Notice that its type is `Prob (Prob Char)`. So now that we've figured out how to flatten a nested probability list, all we need to do is write the code for this. Then we can write `>>=` simply as `join (fmap f m)`, and we have ourselves a monad! So here's `flatten`, which we'll use because the name `join` is already taken:

```
flatten :: Prob (Prob a) -> Prob a
flatten (Prob xs) = Prob $ concat $ map multAll xs
    where multAll (Prob innerxs, p) = map (\(x, r) -> (x, p*r)) innerxs
```

The function `multAll` takes a tuple of a probability list and a probability `p` that comes with it and then multiplies every inner probability with `p`, returning a list of pairs of items and probabilities. We map `multAll` over each pair in our nested probability list, and then we just flatten the resulting nested list.

Now we have all that we need. We can write a `Monad` instance!

```
instance Monad Prob where
    return x = Prob [(x,1%1)]
    m >>= f = flatten (fmap f m)
    fail _ = Prob []
```

Because we already did all the hard work, the instance is very simple. We also defined the `fail` function, which is the same as it is for lists, so if there's a pattern-match failure in a `do` expression, a failure occurs within the context of a probability list.

It's also important to check if the monad laws hold for the monad that we just made:

1. The first law says that `return x >>= f` should be equal to `f x`. A rigorous proof would be rather tedious, but we can see that if we put a value in a default context with `return`, then `fmap` a function over that, and then flatten the resulting probability list, every probability that results from the function would be multiplied

by the 1%1 probability that we made with return, so it wouldn't affect the context.

2. The second law states that m >>= return is no different than m. For our example, the reasoning for m >>= return being equal to just m is similar to that for the first law.

3. The third law states that f <=< (g <=< h) should be the same as (f <=< g) <=< h. This one is true as well, because it holds for the list monad that forms the basis of the probability monad and because multiplication is associative. 1%2 * (1%3 * 1%5) is equal to (1%2 * 1%3) * 1%5.

Now that we have a monad, what can we do with it? Well, it can help us do calculations with probabilities. We can treat probabilistic events as values with contexts, and the probability monad will make sure that those probabilities are reflected in the probabilities of the final result.

Say we have two normal coins and one loaded coin that lands tails an astounding nine times out of ten and heads only one time out of ten. If we throw all the coins at once, what are the odds of all of them landing tails? First, let's make probability values for a normal coin flip and for a loaded one:

```
data Coin = Heads | Tails deriving (Show, Eq)

coin :: Prob Coin
coin = Prob [(Heads,1%2),(Tails,1%2)]

loadedCoin :: Prob Coin
loadedCoin = Prob [(Heads,1%10),(Tails,9%10)]
```

And finally, the coin-throwing action:

```
import Data.List (all)

flipThree :: Prob Bool
flipThree = do
    a <- coin
    b <- coin
    c <- loadedCoin
    return (all (==Tails) [a,b,c])
```

Giving it a go, we see that the odds of all three landing tails are not that good, despite cheating with our loaded coin:

```
ghci> getProb flipThree
[(False,1 % 40),(False,9 % 40),(False,1 % 40),(False,9 % 40),
 (False,1 % 40),(False,9 % 40),(False,1 % 40),(True,9 % 40)]
```

All three of them will land tails 9 times out of 40, which is less than 25 percent. We see that our monad doesn't know how to join all of the `False` outcomes where all coins don't land tails into one outcome. That's not a big problem, since writing a function to put all the same outcomes into one outcome is pretty easy (and left as an exercise to you, the reader).

In this section, we went from having a question (what if lists also carried information about probability?) to making a type, recognizing a monad, and finally making an instance and doing something with it. I think that's quite fetching! By now, you should have a pretty good grasp of monads and what they're about.

15

ZIPPERS

While Haskell's purity comes with a whole bunch of benefits, it makes us tackle some problems differently than we would in impure languages.

Because of referential transparency, one value is as good as another in Haskell if it represents the same thing. So, if we have a tree full of fives (high fives, maybe?), and we want to change one of them into a six, we must have some way of knowing exactly which five in our tree we want to change. We need to know where it is in our tree. In impure languages, we could just note where the five is located in memory and change that. But in Haskell, one five is as good as another, so we can't discriminate based on their location in memory.

We also can't really *change* anything. When we say that we "change a tree," we actually mean that we take a tree and return a new one that's similar to the original, but slightly different.

One thing we can do is remember a path from the root of the tree to the element that we want to change. We could say, "Take this tree, go left, go right and then left

again, and change the element that's there." While this works, it can be inefficient. If we want to later change an element that's near the element that we previously changed, we need to walk all the way from the root of the tree to our element again!

In this chapter, you'll see how to take some data structure and equip it with something called a *zipper* to focus on a part of the data structure in a way that makes changing its elements easy and walking around it efficient. Nice!

Taking a Walk

As you learned in biology class, there are many different kinds of trees, so let's pick a seed that we will use to plant ours. Here it is:

```
data Tree a = Empty | Node a (Tree a) (Tree a) deriving (Show)
```

Our tree is either empty or it's a node that has an element and two subtrees. Here's a fine example of such a tree, which I give to you, the reader, for free!

```
freeTree :: Tree Char
freeTree =
    Node 'P'
        (Node 'O'
            (Node 'L'
                (Node 'N' Empty Empty)
                (Node 'T' Empty Empty)
            )
            (Node 'Y'
                (Node 'S' Empty Empty)
                (Node 'A' Empty Empty)
            )
        )
        (Node 'L'
            (Node 'W'
                (Node 'C' Empty Empty)
                (Node 'R' Empty Empty)
            )
            (Node 'A'
                (Node 'A' Empty Empty)
                (Node 'C' Empty Empty)
            )
        )
```

And here's this tree represented graphically:

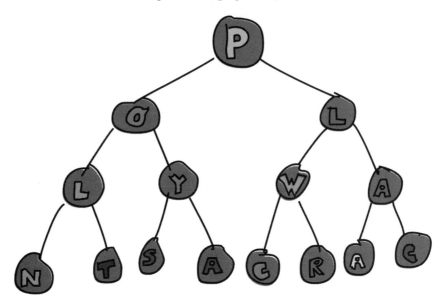

Notice that W in the tree there? Say we want to change it into a P. How would we go about doing that? Well, one way would be to pattern match on our tree until we find the element, by first going right and then left. Here's the code for this:

```
changeToP :: Tree Char -> Tree Char
changeToP (Node x l (Node y (Node _ m n) r)) = Node x l (Node y (Node 'P' m n) r)
```

Yuck! Not only is this rather ugly, it's also kind of confusing. What is actually happening here? Well, we pattern match on our tree and name its root element x (that becomes the 'P' in the root) and its left subtree l. Instead of giving a name to its right subtree, we further pattern match on it. We continue this pattern matching until we reach the subtree whose root is our 'W'. Once we've made the match, we rebuild the tree, but with the subtree that contained the 'W' at its root now having a 'P'.

Is there a better way of doing this? How about if we make our function take a tree along with a list of directions. The directions will be either L or R, representing left or right, respectively, and we'll change the element that we arrive at by following the supplied directions. Check it out:

```
data Direction = L | R deriving (Show)
type Directions = [Direction]

changeToP :: Directions -> Tree Char -> Tree Char
changeToP (L:ds) (Node x l r) = Node x (changeToP ds l) r
changeToP (R:ds) (Node x l r) = Node x l (changeToP ds r)
changeToP [] (Node _ l r) = Node 'P' l r
```

If the first element in the list of directions is L, we construct a new tree that's like the old tree, but its left subtree has an element changed to 'P'. When we recursively call changeToP, we give it only the tail of the list of directions, because we already took a left. We do the same thing in the case of an R. If the list of directions is empty, that means that we're at our destination, so we return a tree that's like the one supplied, except that it has 'P' as its root element.

To avoid printing out the whole tree, let's make a function that takes a list of directions and tells us the element at the destination:

```
elemAt :: Directions -> Tree a -> a
elemAt (L:ds) (Node _ l _) = elemAt ds l
elemAt (R:ds) (Node _ _ r) = elemAt ds r
elemAt [] (Node x _ _) = x
```

This function is actually quite similar to changeToP. The difference is that instead of remembering stuff along the way and reconstructing the tree, it ignores everything except its destination. Here, we change the 'W' to a 'P' and see if the change in our new tree sticks:

```
ghci> let newTree = changeToP [R,L] freeTree
ghci> elemAt [R,L] newTree
'P'
```

This seems to work. In these functions, the list of directions acts as a sort of *focus*, because it pinpoints one exact subtree of our tree. A direction list of [R] focuses on the subtree that's to the right of the root, for example. An empty direction list focuses on the main tree itself.

While this technique may seem cool, it can be rather inefficient, especially if we want to repeatedly change elements. Say we have a really huge tree and a long direction list that points to some element all the way at the bottom of the tree. We use the direction list to take a walk along the tree and change an element at the bottom. If we want to change another element that's close to the element that we just changed, we need to start from the root of the tree and walk all the way to the bottom again. What a drag!

In the next section, we'll find a better way of focusing on a subtree—one that allows us to efficiently switch focus to subtrees that are nearby.

A Trail of Breadcrumbs

For focusing on a subtree, we want something better than just a list of directions that we always follow from the root of our tree. Would it help if we started at the root of the tree and moved either left or right one step at a time, leaving "breadcrumbs" along the way? Using this approach, when we go left, we remember

that we went left, and when we go right, we remember that we went right. Let's try it.

To represent our breadcrumbs, we'll also use a list of direction values (L and R values), but instead of calling it Directions, we'll call it Breadcrumbs, because our directions will now be reversed as we leave them while going down our tree.

```
type Breadcrumbs = [Direction]
```

Here's a function that takes a tree and some breadcrumbs and moves to the left subtree while adding L to the head of the list that represents our breadcrumbs:

```
goLeft :: (Tree a, Breadcrumbs) -> (Tree a, Breadcrumbs)
goLeft (Node _ l _, bs) = (l, L:bs)
```

We ignore the element at the root and the right subtree, and just return the left subtree along with the old breadcrumbs with L as the head.

Here's a function to go right:

```
goRight :: (Tree a, Breadcrumbs) -> (Tree a, Breadcrumbs)
goRight (Node _ _ r, bs) = (r, R:bs)
```

It works the same way as the one to go left.

Let's use these functions to take our freeTree and go right and then left.

```
ghci> goLeft (goRight (freeTree, []))
(Node 'W' (Node 'C' Empty Empty) (Node 'R' Empty Empty),[L,R])
```

Now we have a tree that has 'W' in its root, 'C' in the root of its left subtree, and 'R' in the root of its right subtree. The breadcrumbs are [L,R], because we first went right and then went left.

To make walking along our tree clearer, we can use the -: function from Chapter 13 that we defined like so:

```
x -: f = f x
```

This allows us to apply functions to values by first writing the value, then a -:, and then the function. So, instead of goRight (freeTree, []), we can write (freeTree, []) -: goRight. Using this form, we can rewrite the preceding example so that it's more apparent that we're going right and then left:

```
ghci> (freeTree, []) -: goRight -: goLeft
(Node 'W' (Node 'C' Empty Empty) (Node 'R' Empty Empty),[L,R])
```

Going Back Up

What if we want to go back up in our tree? From our breadcrumbs, we know that the current tree is the left subtree of its parent and that its parent is the right subtree of its own parent, and that's all we know. The breadcrumbs don't tell us enough about the parent of the current subtree for us to be able to go up in the tree. It would seem that apart from the direction that we took, a single breadcrumb should also contain all the other data we need to go back up. In this case, that's the element in the parent tree along with its right subtree.

In general, a single breadcrumb should contain all the data needed to reconstruct the parent node. So, it should have the information from all the paths that we didn't take, and it should also know the direction that we did take. However, it must not contain the subtree on which we're currently focusing. That's because we already have that subtree in the first component of the tuple. If we also had it in the breadcrumb, we would have duplicate information.

We don't want duplicate information because if we were to change some elements in the subtree that we're focusing on, the existing information in the breadcrumbs would be inconsistent with the changes that we made. The duplicate information becomes outdated as soon as we change something in our focus. It can also hog a lot of memory if our tree contains a lot of elements.

Let's modify our breadcrumbs so that they also contain information about everything that we previously ignored when moving left and right. Instead of `Direction`, we'll make a new data type:

```
data Crumb a = LeftCrumb a (Tree a) | RightCrumb a (Tree a) deriving (Show)
```

Now, instead of just `L`, we have a `LeftCrumb`, which also contains the element in the node that we moved from and the right tree that we didn't visit. Instead of `R`, we have `RightCrumb`, which contains the element in the node that we moved from and the left tree that we didn't visit.

These breadcrumbs now contain all the data needed to re-create the tree that we walked through. So, instead of just being normal breadcrumbs, they're more like floppy disks that we leave as we go along, because they contain a lot more information than just the direction that we took.

In essence, every breadcrumb is now like a tree node with a hole in it. When we move deeper into a tree, the breadcrumb carries all the information that the node that we moved away from carried, *except* the subtree on which we chose to focus. It also needs to note where the hole is. In the case of a `LeftCrumb`, we know that we moved left, so the missing subtree is the left one.

Let's also change our `Breadcrumbs` type synonym to reflect this:

```
type Breadcrumbs a = [Crumb a]
```

Next up, we need to modify the goLeft and goRight functions to store information about the paths that we didn't take in our breadcrumbs, instead of ignoring that information as they did before. Here's goLeft:

```
goLeft :: (Tree a, Breadcrumbs a) -> (Tree a, Breadcrumbs a)
goLeft (Node x l r, bs) = (l, LeftCrumb x r:bs)
```

You can see that it's very similar to our previous goLeft, but instead of just adding an L to the head of our list of breadcrumbs, we add a LeftCrumb to signify that we went left. We also equip our LeftCrumb with the element in the node that we moved from (that's the x) and the right subtree that we chose not to visit.

Note that this function assumes that the current tree that's under focus isn't Empty. An empty tree doesn't have any subtrees, so if we try to go left from an empty tree, an error will occur. This is because the pattern match on Node won't succeed, and there's no pattern that takes care of Empty.

goRight is similar:

```
goRight :: (Tree a, Breadcrumbs a) -> (Tree a, Breadcrumbs a)
goRight (Node x l r, bs) = (r, RightCrumb x l:bs)
```

We were previously able to go left and right. What we have now is the ability to actually go back up by remembering stuff about the parent nodes and the paths that we didn't visit. Here's the goUp function:

```
goUp :: (Tree a, Breadcrumbs a) -> (Tree a, Breadcrumbs a)
goUp (t, LeftCrumb x r:bs) = (Node x t r, bs)
goUp (t, RightCrumb x l:bs) = (Node x l t, bs)
```

We're focusing on the tree t, and we check the latest Crumb. If it's a LeftCrumb, we construct a new tree using our tree t as the left subtree and using the information about the right subtree and element that we didn't visit to fill out the rest of the Node. Because we "moved back" and picked up the last breadcrumb, then used it to recreate the parent tree, the new list doesn't contain that breadcrumb.

Note that this function causes an error if we're already at the top of a tree and we want to move up. Later on, we'll use the Maybe monad to represent possible failure when moving focus.

With a pair of Tree a and Breadcrumbs a, we have all the information we need to rebuild the whole tree, and we also have a focus on a subtree. This scheme enables us to easily move up, left, and right.

A pair that contains a focused part of a data structure and its surroundings is called a *zipper*, because moving our focus up and down the data structure resembles the operation of a zipper on a pair of pants. So, it's cool to make a type synonym as such:

```
type Zipper a = (Tree a, Breadcrumbs a)
```

I would prefer naming the type synonym Focus, because that makes it clearer that we're focusing on a part of a data structure. But since the name Zipper is more widely used to describe such a setup, we'll stick with it.

Manipulating Trees Under Focus

Now that we can move up and down, let's make a function that modifies the element in the root of the subtree on which the zipper is focusing:

```
modify :: (a -> a) -> Zipper a -> Zipper a
modify f (Node x l r, bs) = (Node (f x) l r, bs)
modify f (Empty, bs) = (Empty, bs)
```

If we're focusing on a node, we modify its root element with the function f. If we're focusing on an empty tree, we leave it as is. Now we can start off with a tree, move to anywhere we want, and modify an element, all while keeping focus on that element so that we can easily move further up or down. Here's an example:

```
ghci> let newFocus = modify (\_ -> 'P') (goRight (goLeft (freeTree, [])))
```

We go left, then right, and then modify the root element by replacing it with a 'P'. This reads even better if we use -::

```
ghci> let newFocus = (freeTree, []) -: goLeft -: goRight -: modify (\_ -> 'P')
```

We can then move up if we want and replace an element with a mysterious 'X':

```
ghci> let newFocus2 = modify (\_ -> 'X') (goUp newFocus)
```

Or we can write it with -::

```
ghci> let newFocus2 = newFocus -: goUp -: modify (\_ -> 'X')
```

Moving up is easy because the breadcrumbs that we leave form the part of the data structure that we're not focusing on, but it's inverted, sort of like turning a sock inside out. That's why when we want to move up, we don't need to start from the root and make our way down. We just take the top of our inverted tree, thereby uninverting a part of it and adding it to our focus.

Each node has two subtrees, even if those subtrees are empty. So, if we're focusing on an empty subtree, one thing we can do is to replace it with a nonempty subtree, thus attaching a tree to a leaf node. The code for this is simple:

```
attach :: Tree a -> Zipper a -> Zipper a
attach t (_, bs) = (t, bs)
```

We take a tree and a zipper, and return a new zipper that has its focus replaced with the supplied tree. Not only can we extend trees this way by replacing empty subtrees with new trees, but we can also replace existing subtrees. Let's attach a tree to the far left of our freeTree:

```
ghci> let farLeft = (freeTree, []) -: goLeft -: goLeft -: goLeft -: goLeft
ghci> let newFocus = farLeft -: attach (Node 'Z' Empty Empty)
```

newFocus is now focused on the tree that we just attached, and the rest of the tree lies inverted in the breadcrumbs. If we were to use goUp to walk all the way to the top of the tree, it would be the same tree as freeTree, but with an additional 'Z' on its far left.

Going Straight to the Top, Where the Air Is Fresh and Clean!

Making a function that walks all the way to the top of the tree, regardless of what we're focusing on, is really easy. Here it is:

```
topMost :: Zipper a -> Zipper a
topMost (t, []) = (t, [])
topMost z = topMost (goUp z)
```

If our trail of beefed-up breadcrumbs is empty, that means we're already at the root of our tree, so we just return the current focus. Otherwise, we go up to get the focus of the parent node, and then recursively apply topMost to that.

So, now we can walk around our tree, going left, right, and up, applying modify and attach as we travel. Then, when we're finished with our modifications, we use topMost to focus on the root of our tree and see the changes that we've made in proper perspective.

Focusing on Lists

Zippers can be used with pretty much any data structure, so it's no surprise that they work with sublists of lists. After all, lists are pretty much like trees, except where a node in a tree has an element (or not) and several subtrees, a node in a list has an element and only a single sublist. When we implemented our own lists in Chapter 7, we defined our data type like so:

```
data List a = Empty | Cons a (List a) deriving (Show, Read, Eq, Ord)
```

Compare this with the definition of our binary tree, and it's easy to see how lists can be viewed as trees where each node has only one subtree.

A list like [1,2,3] can be written as 1:2:3:[]. It consists of the head of the list, which is 1, and then the list's tail, which is 2:3:[]. 2:3:[] also has a head, which is 2, and a tail, which is 3:[]. With 3:[], the 3 is the head, and the tail is the empty list [].

Let's make a zipper for lists. To change the focus on sublists of a list, we move either forward or back (whereas with trees, we move up, left, or right). The focused part will be a sublist, and along with that, we'll leave breadcrumbs as we move forward.

Now, what would a single breadcrumb for a list consist of? When we were dealing with binary trees, the breadcrumb needed to hold the element in the root of the parent node along with all the subtrees that we didn't choose. It also had to remember if we went left or right. So, it needed to have all the information that a node has, except for the subtree on which we chose to focus.

Lists are simpler than trees. We don't need to remember if we went left or right, because there's only one way to go deeper into a list. Because there's only one sublist to each node, we don't need to remember the paths that we didn't take either. It seems that all we must remember is the previous element. If we have a list like [3,4,5] and we know that the previous element was 2, we can go back by just putting that element at the head of our list, getting [2,3,4,5].

Because a single breadcrumb here is just the element, we don't really need to put it inside a data type, as we did when we made the Crumb data type for tree zippers.

```
type ListZipper a = ([a], [a])
```

The first list represents the list that we're focusing on, and the second list is the list of breadcrumbs. Let's make functions that go forward and backward in lists:

```
goForward :: ListZipper a -> ListZipper a
goForward (x:xs, bs) = (xs, x:bs)

goBack :: ListZipper a -> ListZipper a
goBack (xs, b:bs) = (b:xs, bs)
```

When we're going forward, we focus on the tail of the current list and leave the head element as a breadcrumb. When we're moving backward, we take the latest breadcrumb and put it at the beginning of the list. Here are these two functions in action:

```
ghci> let xs = [1,2,3,4]
ghci> goForward (xs, [])
([2,3,4],[1])
ghci> goForward ([2,3,4], [1])
([3,4],[2,1])
ghci> goForward ([3,4], [2,1])
([4],[3,2,1])
ghci> goBack ([4], [3,2,1])
([3,4],[2,1])
```

You can see that the breadcrumbs in the case of lists are nothing more than a reversed part of your list. The element that we move away from always goes into the head of the breadcrumbs. Then it's easy to move back by just taking that element from the head of the breadcrumbs and making it the head of our focus. This also makes it easier to see why we call this a *zipper*—it really looks like the slider of a zipper moving up and down.

If you were making a text editor, you could use a list of strings to represent the lines of text that are currently opened, and you could then use a zipper so that you know on which line the cursor is currently focused. Using a zipper would also make it easier to insert new lines anywhere in the text or delete existing ones.

A Very Simple Filesystem

To demonstrate how zippers work, let's use trees to represent a very simple filesystem. Then we can make a zipper for that filesystem, which will allow us to move between folders, just as we do when jumping around a real filesystem.

The average hierarchical filesystem is mostly made up of files and folders. *Files* are units of data and have names. *Folders* are used to organize those files and can contain files or other folders. For our simple example, let's say that an item in a filesystem is either one of these:

- A file, which comes with a name and some data
- A folder, which has a name and contains other items that are either files or folders themselves

Here's a data type for this and some type synonyms, so we know what's what:

```
type Name = String
type Data = String
data FSItem = File Name Data | Folder Name [FSItem] deriving (Show)
```

A file comes with two strings, which represent its name and the data it holds. A folder comes with a string that is its name and a list of items. If that list is empty, then we have an empty folder.

Here's a folder with some files and subfolders (actually what my disk contains right now):

```
myDisk :: FSItem
myDisk =
    Folder "root"
        [ File "goat_yelling_like_man.wmv" "baaaaaa"
        , File "pope_time.avi" "god bless"
        , Folder "pics"
            [ File "ape_throwing_up.jpg" "bleargh"
            , File "watermelon_smash.gif" "smash!!"
            , File "skull_man(scary).bmp" "Yikes!"
            ]
        , File "dijon_poupon.doc" "best mustard"
        , Folder "programs"
            [ File "fartwizard.exe" "10gotofart"
            , File "owl_bandit.dmg" "mov eax, h00t"
            , File "not_a_virus.exe" "really not a virus"
            , Folder "source code"
                [ File "best_hs_prog.hs" "main = print (fix error)"
                , File "random.hs" "main = print 4"
                ]
            ]
        ]
```

Making a Zipper for Our Filesystem

Now that we have a filesystem, all we need is
a zipper so we can zip and zoom around it,
and add, modify, and remove files and folders. As with binary trees and lists, our breadcrumbs will contain information about all
the stuff that we chose not to visit. A single
breadcrumb should store everything except
the subtree on which we're currently focusing. It should also note where the hole is, so
that once we move back up, we can plug our
previous focus into the hole.

In this case, a breadcrumb should be
like a folder, only it should be missing the
folder that we currently chose. "Why not
like a file?" you ask? Well, because once we're focusing on a file, we can't
move deeper into the filesystem, so it doesn't make sense to leave a breadcrumb that says that we came from a file. A file is sort of like an empty tree.

If we're focusing on the folder "root", and we then focus on the file
"dijon_poupon.doc", what should the breadcrumb that we leave look like?
Well, it should contain the name of its parent folder along with the items
that come before and after the file on which we're focusing. So, all we need
is a Name and two lists of items. By keeping separate lists for the items that
come before the item that we're focusing on and for the items that come after it, we know exactly where to place it once we move back up. That way, we
know the location of the hole.

Here's our breadcrumb type for the filesystem:

```
data FSCrumb = FSCrumb Name [FSItem] [FSItem] deriving (Show)
```

And here's a type synonym for our zipper:

```
type FSZipper = (FSItem, [FSCrumb])
```

Going back up in the hierarchy is very simple. We just take the latest
breadcrumb and assemble a new focus from the current focus and breadcrumb, like so:

```
fsUp :: FSZipper -> FSZipper
fsUp (item, FSCrumb name ls rs:bs) = (Folder name (ls ++ [item] ++ rs), bs)
```

Because our breadcrumb knew the parent folder's name, as well as
the items that came before our focused item in the folder (that's ls) and the
items that came after (that's rs), moving up was easy.

How about going deeper into the filesystem? If we're in the "root" and we want to focus on "dijon_poupon.doc", the breadcrumb that we leave will include the name "root", along with the items that precede "dijon_poupon.doc" and the ones that come after it. Here's a function that, given a name, focuses on a file or folder that's located in the current focused folder:

```
import Data.List (break)

fsTo :: Name -> FSZipper -> FSZipper
fsTo name (Folder folderName items, bs) =
    let (ls, item:rs) = break (nameIs name) items
    in  (item, FSCrumb folderName ls rs:bs)

nameIs :: Name -> FSItem -> Bool
nameIs name (Folder folderName _) = name == folderName
nameIs name (File fileName _) = name == fileName
```

fsTo takes a Name and an FSZipper and returns a new FSZipper that focuses on the file with the given name. That file must be in the current focused folder. This function doesn't search all over the place—it just looks in the current folder.

First, we use break to break the list of items in a folder into those that precede the file that we're searching for and those that come after it. break takes a predicate and a list and returns a pair of lists. The first list in the pair holds items for which the predicate returns False. Then, once the predicate returns True for an item, it places that item and the rest of the list in the second item of the pair. We made an auxiliary function called nameIs, which takes a name and a filesystem item and returns True if the names match.

Now ls is a list that contains the items that precede the item that we're searching for, item is that very item, and rs is the list of items that come after it in its folder. Now that we have these, we just present the item that we got from break as the focus and build a breadcrumb that has all the data it needs.

Note that if the name we're looking for isn't in the folder, the pattern item:rs will try to match on an empty list, and we'll get an error. And if our current focus is a file, rather than a folder, we get an error as well, and the program crashes.

So, we can move up and down our filesystem. Let's start at the root and walk to the file "skull_man(scary).bmp":

```
ghci> let newFocus = (myDisk, []) -: fsTo "pics" -: fsTo "skull_man(scary).bmp"
```

`newFocus` is now a zipper that's focused on the "skull_man(scary).bmp" file. Let's get the first component of the zipper (the focus itself) and see if that's really true:

```
ghci> fst newFocus
File "skull_man(scary).bmp" "Yikes!"
```

Let's move up and focus on its neighboring file "watermelon_smash.gif":

```
ghci> let newFocus2 = newFocus -: fsUp -: fsTo "watermelon_smash.gif"
ghci> fst newFocus2
File "watermelon_smash.gif" "smash!!"
```

Manipulating a Filesystem

Now that we can navigate our filesystem, manipulating it is easy. Here's a function that renames the currently focused file or folder:

```
fsRename :: Name -> FSZipper -> FSZipper
fsRename newName (Folder name items, bs) = (Folder newName items, bs)
fsRename newName (File name dat, bs) = (File newName dat, bs)
```

Let's rename our "pics" folder to "cspi":

```
ghci> let newFocus = (myDisk, []) -: fsTo "pics" -: fsRename "cspi" -: fsUp
```

We descended to the "pics" folder, renamed it, and then moved back up.

How about a function that makes a new item in the current folder? Behold:

```
fsNewFile :: FSItem -> FSZipper -> FSZipper
fsNewFile item (Folder folderName items, bs) =
    (Folder folderName (item:items), bs)
```

Easy as pie. Note that this would crash if we tried to add an item but were focusing on a file instead of a folder.

Let's add a file to our "pics" folder, and then move back up to the root:

```
ghci> let newFocus =
    (myDisk, []) -: fsTo "pics" -: fsNewFile (File "heh.jpg" "lol") -: fsUp
```

What's really cool about all this is that when we modify our filesystem, our changes are not actually made in place, but instead, the function returns a whole new filesystem. That way, we have access to our old filesystem (in this case, `myDisk`), as well as the new one (the first component of `newFocus`).

By using zippers, we get versioning for free. We can always refer to older versions of data structures, even after we've changed them. This isn't unique to zippers, but it is a property of Haskell, because its data structures are immutable. With zippers, however, we get the ability to easily and efficiently walk around our data structures, so the persistence of Haskell's data structures really begins to shine.

Watch Your Step

So far, while walking through our data structures—whether they were binary trees, lists, or filesystems—we didn't really care if we took a step too far and fell off. For instance, our goLeft function takes a zipper of a binary tree and moves the focus to its left subtree:

```
goLeft :: Zipper a -> Zipper a
goLeft (Node x l r, bs) = (l, LeftCrumb x r:bs)
```

But what if the tree we're stepping off from is an empty tree? What if it's not a Node, but an Empty? In this case, we would get a runtime error, because the pattern match would fail, and we have not made a pattern to handle an empty tree, which doesn't have any subtrees.

So far, we just assumed that we would never try to focus on the left subtree of an empty tree, as its left subtree doesn't exist. But going to the left subtree of an empty tree doesn't make much sense, and so far we've just conveniently ignored this.

Or what if we are already at the root of some tree and don't have any breadcrumbs but still try to move up? The same thing would happen. It seems that when using zippers, any step could be our last (cue ominous music). In other words, any move can result in a success, but it can also result in a failure. Does that remind you of something? Of course: monads! More specifically, the Maybe monad, which adds a context of possible failure to normal values.

Let's use the Maybe monad to add a context of possible failure to our movements. We're going to take the functions that work on our binary tree zipper and make them into monadic functions.

First, let's take care of possible failure in goLeft and goRight. So far, the failure of functions that could fail was always reflected in their result, and this example is no different.

Here are goLeft and goRight with an added possibility of failure:

```
goLeft :: Zipper a -> Maybe (Zipper a)
goLeft (Node x l r, bs) = Just (l, LeftCrumb x r:bs)
goLeft (Empty, _) = Nothing

goRight :: Zipper a -> Maybe (Zipper a)
goRight (Node x l r, bs) = Just (r, RightCrumb x l:bs)
goRight (Empty, _) = Nothing
```

Now, if we try to take a step to the left of an empty tree, we get a Nothing!

```
ghci> goLeft (Empty, [])
Nothing
ghci> goLeft (Node 'A' Empty Empty, [])
Just (Empty,[LeftCrumb 'A' Empty])
```

Looks good! How about going up? The problem before happened if we tried to go up but we didn't have any more breadcrumbs, which meant that we were already at the root of the tree. This is the goUp function that throws an error if we don't keep within the bounds of our tree:

```
goUp :: Zipper a -> Zipper a
goUp (t, LeftCrumb x r:bs) = (Node x t r, bs)
goUp (t, RightCrumb x l:bs) = (Node x l t, bs)
```

Let's modify it to fail gracefully:

```
goUp :: Zipper a -> Maybe (Zipper a)
goUp (t, LeftCrumb x r:bs) = Just (Node x t r, bs)
goUp (t, RightCrumb x l:bs) = Just (Node x l t, bs)
goUp (_, []) = Nothing
```

If we have breadcrumbs, everything is okay, and we return a successful new focus. If we don't have breadcrumbs, we return a failure.

Before, these functions took zippers and returned zippers, which meant that we could chain them like this to walk around:

```
gchi> let newFocus = (freeTree, []) -: goLeft -: goRight
```

But now, instead of returning Zipper a, they return Maybe (Zipper a), and chaining functions like this won't work. We had a similar problem when we were dealing with our tightrope walker in Chapter 13. He also walked one step at a time, and each of his steps could result in failure, because a bunch of birds could land on one side of his balancing pole and make him fall.

Now the joke is on us, because we're the ones doing the walking, and we're traversing a labyrinth of our own devising. Luckily, we can learn from the tightrope walker and just do what he did: replace normal function application with >>=. This takes a value with a context (in our case, the Maybe (Zipper a), which has a context of possible failure) and feeds it into a function, while making sure that the context is handled. So just like our tightrope walker, we're going to trade in all our -: operators for >>= operators. Then we will be able to chain our functions again! Watch how it works:

```
ghci> let coolTree = Node 1 Empty (Node 3 Empty Empty)
ghci> return (coolTree, []) >>= goRight
Just (Node 3 Empty Empty,[RightCrumb 1 Empty])
ghci> return (coolTree, []) >>= goRight >>= goRight
Just (Empty,[RightCrumb 3 Empty,RightCrumb 1 Empty])
ghci> return (coolTree, []) >>= goRight >>= goRight >>= goRight
Nothing
```

We used return to put a zipper in a Just, and then used >>= to feed that to our goRight function. First, we made a tree that has on its left an empty subtree and on its right a node that has two empty subtrees. When we try to go right once, the result is a success, because the operation makes sense. Going right twice is okay, too. We end up with the focus on an empty subtree. But going right three times doesn't make sense—we can't go to the right of an empty subtree. This is why the result is a Nothing.

Now we've equipped our trees with a safety net that will catch us should we fall off. (Wow, I nailed that metaphor.)

NOTE *Our filesystem also has a lot of cases where an operation could fail, such as trying to focus on a file or folder that doesn't exist. As an exercise, you can equip our filesystem with functions that fail gracefully by using the Maybe monad.*

Thanks for Reading!

Or just flipping to the last page! I hope you found this book useful and fun. I have strived to give you good insight into the Haskell language and its idioms. While there's always something new to learn in Haskell, you should now be able to code cool stuff, as well as read and understand other people's code. So hurry up and get coding! See you on the other side!

INDEX

Symbols & Numbers

&& (double ampersand)
  as Boolean operator conjunction, 2
  using with folds and lists, 78–79

' (apostrophe)
  using with functions, 7
  using with types, 149–150

* (asterisk)
  as multiplication function, 3
  using with kinds, 150

** (exponentiation), using with RPN functions, 207–208

\ (backslash), declaring lambdas with, 71

` (backticks) using with functions, 4–5

: (colon)
  as cons operator
    bytestring version of, 200
    using with applicatives, 238–239
    using with lists, 8–9
  using with infix constructors, 134

:: (double colon)
  using in record syntax, 116
  using with type annotations, 30, 118
  using with types, 24

:k command, identifying kinds with, 150–151

$ (function application operator), 80–81, 83

/ (division), using with RPN functions, 207–208

/= (not-equal-to) operator, 3, 28

= (equal) sign
  using with data keyword, 109
  using with data types, 122
  using with functions, 5

== (double equal sign), 3
  using with Eq type class, 28
  using with type instances, 139–140

!! (double exlamation point)
  in Data.List module, 182
  using with lists, 9

> (greater-than) operator, using with lists, 9–10

>> function, replacing, 279

>>= (bind) function
  in A Knight's Quest, 292
  nested use of, 280
  using with functions as monads, 311
  using with monads, 269–270, 272, 274–280, 283–284, 286
  using with Reader monad, 312
  using with State monad, 316–317
  using with Writer type, 302

-> (arrow)
  in type signature, 60–61
  using with functions, 25
  using with lambdas, 71

-> r as functor and monad, 311

< (less-than) operator, using with lists, 9–10

<*> function
  calling with applicative values, 236
  left-associative, 233
  specializing for IO, 234
  using with applicative style, 232
  using with liftM function, 325
  using with zip lists, 237

<= operator, using with lists, 9–10

<$>, using with applicative style, 231–232

<-, using with I/O actions and functors, 219

- (minus) operator, using with sections, 62

() (parentheses)
  minimizing use of, 81, 83
  placement with functions, 7
  using with operations, 2, 5
  using with sections, 62

(,,) function, using with zip lists, 238

The fonts used in *Learn You a Haskell for Great Good!* are New Baskerville, Futura, The Sans Mono Condensed, and Dogma. The book was typeset with LaTeX 2_ε package nostarch by Boris Veytsman *(2008/06/06 v1.3 Typesetting books for No Starch Press)*.

This book was printed and bound by Edwards Brothers Malloy in Ann Arbor, Michigan. The paper is 60# Husky Opaque, which is certified by the Sustainable Forestry Initiative (SFI).

The book uses a RepKover binding, in which the pages are bound together with a cold-set, flexible glue and the first and last pages of the resulting book block are attached to the cover with glue. The cover is not actually glued to the book's spine, and when open, the book lies flat and the spine doesn't crack.

The Electronic Frontier Foundation (EFF) is the leading organization defending civil liberties in the digital world. We defend free speech on the Internet, fight illegal surveillance, promote the rights of innovators to develop new digital technologies, and work to ensure that the rights and freedoms we enjoy are enhanced — rather than eroded — as our use of technology grows.

EFF.ORG

ELECTRONIC FRONTIER FOUNDATION

Protecting Rights and Promoting Freedom on the Electronic Frontier

UPDATES

Visit *http://www.nostarch.com/lyah.htm* for updates, errata, and other information.